COMMUNITY-BASED CORRECTIONS

PROBATION, PAROLE, AND INTERMEDIATE SANCTIONS

THIRD EDITION

THIRD EDITION

COMMUNITY-BASED CORRECTIONS

PROBATION, PAROLE, AND INTERMEDIATE SANCTIONS

PAUL F. CROMWELL

UNIVERSITY OF MIAMI

GEORGE G. KILLINGER

EMERITUS, SAM HOUSTON STATE UNIVERSITY

WEST PUBLISHING COMPANY

Minneapolis/St. Paul   New York   Los Angeles   San Francisco

WEST'S COMMITMENT TO THE ENVIRONMENT

In 1906, West Publishing Company began recycling materials left over from the production of books. This began a tradition of efficient and responsible use of resources. Today, up to 95 percent of our legal books and 70 percent of our college texts are printed on recycled, acid-free stock. West also recycles nearly 22 million pounds of scrap paper annually—the equivalent of 181,717 trees. Since the 1960s, West has devised ways to capture and recycle waste inks, solvents, oils, and vapors created in the printing process. We also recycle plastics of all kinds, wood, glass, corrugated cardboard, and batteries, and have eliminated the use of styrofoam book packaging. We at West are proud of the longevity and the scope of our commitment to our environment.

Production, Prepress, Printing and Binding by West Publishing Company.

TEXT IS PRINTED ON 10% POST CONSUMER RECYCLED PAPER   PRINTED WITH SOY INK

ARTWORK	Rolin Graphic Communication
COPYEDITOR	Carole Reagle
COMPOSITION	Carlisle Communications, Ltd.
TEXT DESIGN	K. M. Weber
COVER IMAGE	Ken Akiva Segan *The Prisoner* (Mixed Media), 40″ × 28″ West Art and The Law 1980. © 1980 West Publishing Corporation, Eagan, Minnesota.

PHOTO CREDITS ARE FOUND FOLLOWING THE INDEX.

Production, prepress, printing, and binding by West Publishing Company.

Printed in the United States of America

01 00 99 98 97 96 95 94   8 7 6 5 4 3 2 1 0

Library of Congress Cataloging-in-Publication Data

Cromwell, Paul F.
    Community-based corrections : probation, parole and intermediate
sanctions / Paul F. Cromwell, George Killinger, Charls Walker. — 3d
ed.
        p.   cm.
    Rev. ed. of: Probation and parole in the criminal justice system.
    Includes indexes
    ISBN 0-314-02570-7
    1. Probation—United States. 2. Parole—United States.
3. Alternatives to imprisonment—United States.   I. Killinger,
George Glenn, 1908–   . II. Walker, Charls C. (Charls Edward),
1923–   .   III. Probation and parole in the criminal justice system.
    IV. Title.
KF9750.P77   1994
345.73′077—dc20
    [347.30577]
                                              93-21289
                                                CIP

To my parents, Paul and Thelma Cromwell, for their support,
encouragement, love, and their wisdom. I could not have
wished for more.
P.C.

To Grace,
for her untiring support.

G.G.K.

This edition is dedicated to the memory of
George G. Killinger
who passed away as this book went to press.

Contents

7 Revocation of Probation 155

PART II
Parole 190

8 The History and Concept of Parole 191

9 Parole in Transition 205

10 The Parole Board and Parole Selection 219

11 Parole Conditions and Revocation 247

PART III
Intermediate Sanctions 266

12 Intermediate Sanctions: Between Probation and Prison 267

PART IV
Collateral Issues in Probation, Parole, and Community Corrections 310

13 Direct and Collateral Consequences of Conviction 313

14 Pardon and Restoration of Rights 333

15 The Effectiveness of Probation and Parole 349

Preface

By 1990 THE NUMBER of adults under some form of correctional supervision in the United States had reached an all-time high of 4.3 million, representing one out of every 43 adults in the country. More than 2.7 million of these persons were being supervised by probation, parole, and other community-based correctional programs. Clearly, most offenders serve their sentences in the community, and even those who are incarcerated eventually return to the community, often on parole. This book examines these community-based methods of corrections.

Our goal in writing *Community-Based Corrections: Probation, Parole, and Intermediate Sanctions* has been to provide the student with comprehensive, up-to-date, objective knowledge of the procedures, practices, and personnel that constitute probation, parole, and other community-based sanctions. We have sought to present community-based correctional programs in their historical, philosophical, social, and legal context and to integrate theory and practice to the greatest extent possible. We bring to this effort our years of experience as criminal justice professionals and academicians. Author Cromwell has served as a probation officer at both the state and federal level, chief probation officer in a large metropolitan area, a commissioner and chairman of the Texas Board of Pardons and Paroles, and as a college teacher. Author Killinger has served as the director of education for the United States Bureau of Prisons, chairman of the Army Clemency and Parole Board, chairman of the United States Board of Parole, chairman of the Texas Board of Pardons and Parole, and as a college teacher. We believe that our dual perspective as academics and practitioners helps us to integrate theory and practice and to provide a balanced treatment of community-based corrections.

Because we want this book to be as practical as possible, we have provided many examples of community-based programs, laws, and procedures from state and federal jurisdictions across the nation. We wrestled with the problem of using examples and laws from as many states as possible in order to make the materials relevant to a broad audience. However, the states' systems vary widely in their programs, laws, and sophistication. We decided we would not do the student justice if we included laws and examples from only the large, populous states, and we could not possibly incorporate examples and laws from every jurisdiction. We therefore decided to use the federal system, a model system, as our primary point of reference. We have cited state laws and programs throughout the book nonetheless.

ORGANIZATION OF THE BOOK

Community-Based Corrections, Third Edition is divided into four parts. Part I examines **Probation.** Chapter 1 discusses the historical, social, and legal foundations of probation. Chapter 2 addresses sentencing and the decision to grant probation. Various forms of probation are discussed and analyzed. Chapter 3, "The Presentence Investigation Report," considers the purposes, contents, and legal issues of this important document. Examples of two types of presentence report are represented. Chapter 4 examines the terms and conditions of probation. Recent court decisions are discussed. Chapter 5 provides a review of the organization and administration of probation services. Chapter 6 is a comprehensive analysis of probation and parole supervision. Chapter 7 considers probation revocation. Important court decisions are presented.

Part II, **Parole,** begins with a history of the concept and practice of parole in Chapter 8. Chapter 9, "Parole in Transition," reviews the past and present controversies regarding the use of parole and analyzes the issues currently being debated. Chapter 10 examines the parole board and parole decision making. Chapter 11 provides an overview of parole conditions and of the issues involved in parole revocation.

Part III is a review and analysis of **Intermediate Sanctions.** Chapter 12 provides overviews of intensive supervision, boot camps, house arrest, electronic monitoring, restitution, community service, and fines. Supplementary readings provide more comprehensive examinations of the major intermediate sanctions.

Part IV, **Collateral Issues in Probation, Parole, and Community Corrections,** is unique for a textbook of probation, parole, and other community sanctions. As criminal justice practitioners for many years, we became painfully aware of the collateral, or secondary, consequences of conviction. Probationers and parolees often face indirect, unanticipated sanctions: the loss of civil and political rights following conviction. The rights lost include not only basic citizenship rights such as the right to participate in our democracy by voting, but more subtlely the losses of "good character," of occupational and professional licenses, of the right to be bonded, and so on. These losses frequently work against the offender's efforts to put his or her life in order and to obtain and maintain employment. In Chapter 13 we discuss the civil, political, and social rights lost by the convicted person. In Chapter 14 we examine the means by which the offender may regain some of these lost rights, taking a close look at pardons. We believe that the information presented in these two chapters can be of enormous benefit to probation and parole officers and the probationers and parolees under their supervision. Chapter 15 examines the effectiveness of probation and parole and evaluates these programs as to their future vaiability. We argue for increased utilization of intermediate sanctions as an alternative or adjunct to traditional community based programs such as probation and parole.

FEATURES AND LEARNING TOOLS

Community-Based Corrections makes extensive use of **Supplemental Readings.** Most chapters are followed by one or more readings that are reprints of journal articles on research in community corrections, digests of relevant court decisions, examples of documents encountered in the community-based corrections field, examples of documents encountered in the community-based corrections field, or significant articles from recent criminal justice literature. These readings broaden the book's scope and allow the student to consult important sources directly.

Each chapter begins with an **Outline** and a list of the **Key Terms** used in the chapter. Key terms are usually defined in the margins of the text and in the **Glossary** at the end of the book.

Each chapter is followed by **Discussion Questions** that will encourage students to think critically about the materials presented in the chapter. These questions could also serve as written exercises in many cases or as topics for essays or research papers.

Most chapters contain **Boxed Features** that amplify particular issues, events, and processes.

The book contains many **photographs, tables,** and **figures,** that will help students to visualize the phenomena and processes under discussion.

Acknowledgements

This book could not have been written without the generous assistance of many colleagues and corrections professionals. We are especially grateful for the legal research skills of Charls Walker and J. O. Chaudhuri, both of Tempe, Arizona. We are indebted to Dane Miller, editor of *Probation and Parole Law Reports,* and to Khehans–Miller Publications, Warrensburg, Missouri, for making their materials available to us and for granting us permission to reprint some of them.

We leaned heavily on various documents published by the Administrative Office of the U.S. Courts and the U.S. Probation Service and on materials from the *Federal Probation Quarterly.* We also drew on published materials from the Bureau of Justice Statistics and the National Institute of Justice. These materials were essential to our effort.

Chief United States Probation Officer Harvey K. Whitehill, Western District of Texas, a friend and colleague of many years, was a most valuable resource. He acted as sounding board, advisor, and source of day-to-day knowledge about the U.S. probation system. Another long-time colleague and friend, John Byrd, Chief United States Pretrial Services Officer, Western District of Texas, generously served us as a source of information and referral.

In any undertaking of this sort, the extant literature in the field is relied upon for guidance and reference. In this regard we have benefited from the work of Rolando del Carmen, Howard Abadinsky, Joan Petersilia, Marilyn McShane, Wesley Krause, Belinda McCarthy, Bernard McCarthy, Velmer Burton, Frances Cullen, Lawrence Travis III, Hazel Kerper, John Ortiz Smykla, Harry Allen, Chris Eskridge, Edward Latessa, Gennaro Vito, Louis Jankowski, William E. Amos, Daniel Glaser, Robert Carter, Leslie Wilkins, Eugene Czajkoski, Thomas Blomberg, Norval Morris, Michael Tonry, Carl Klockars, Todd Clear, George Cole, Doris Layton MacKenzie, Edward Rhine, William R. Smith, and Ronald Jackson.

Joan Gill, our editor at West Publishing Company, did a superb job of keeping us on track and on schedule and encouraging us when our energy and enthusiasm occasionally waned. Her assistant, Rebecca Stovall, was also a stalwart, supportive guide. Certainly, without them this book would still be an idea.

Throughout the project, from concept to completion, Jimmie Douglas Cromwell was her ever capable self, typing the manuscript, editing, correcting copy, and generally acting as our quality-control specialist. This book is as much the result of her effort as ours.

Finally, we express our special appreciation to our colleagues who reviewed drafts of the book. Their insightful comments and suggestions proved invaluable. In particular, we appreciate the work of Professors Thomas C. Tomlinson, Roger Jarjoura, Mary Parker, J. Steven Smith, John P. Harlan, Robert L. Marsh, James Gilbert, Robert Harvie, Cheryl Banachowski-Fuller, Pearl Jacobs, Robert D. Mann, and John R. McGee, Jr.

Paul F. Cromwell
George G. Killinger

About the Authors

PAUL F. CROMWELL, Ph.D., is Professor of Sociology and Director of the Criminology Program at the University of Miami in Coral Gables, Florida. He received his Ph.D. in criminology from Florida State University in 1986, after a career in criminal justice that included service as a United States Probation Officer, chief juvenile probation officer, and commissioner and chairman of the Texas Board of Pardons and Paroles. He has authored and coauthored numerous articles and books, including *Probation and Parole in the Criminal Justice System* (West, 1985), *Penology: The Evolution of Corrections in America* (West, 1978), *Corrections in the Community* (West, 1978), and *Breaking and Entering: An Ethnography of Burglary* (Sage, 1991).

GEORGE G. KILLINGER, Ph.D., is Professor Emeritus of Criminal Justice at Sam Houston State University in Huntsville, Texas. He received his Ph.D. in clinical psychology from the University of North Carolina at Chapel Hill. In a criminal justice career that spanned 50 years, he served as the director of education for the United States Bureau of Prisons, chairman of the Army Clemency and Parole Board, chairman of the United States Parole Board, and chairman of the Texas Board of Pardons and Paroles. He has been Distinguished Professor of Criminology at Florida State University and professor and founding dean of the School of Criminal Justice at Sam Houston State University. He has authored and coauthored numerous articles and books, including *Probation and Parole in the Criminal Justice System* (West, 1985), *Penology: The Evolution of Corrections in America* (West, 1978), and *Corrections in the Community* (West, 1978). He currently resides in Huntsville, Texas.

I

PROBATION

THE CONCEPT UNDERLYING A SEN-
TENCE to probation is simple.
Sentencing is in large part concerned
with avoiding future crimes by helping the defendant to live productively in the community that he or
she has offended. Probation proceeds on the theory that the best
way to pursue this goal is to orient
the criminal sanction toward the
community setting in those cases
where it is compatible with the other
objectives of sentencing. Other
things being equal, a given defendant is more likely to learn how to
live successfully in the general community if he is dealt with in that
community, rather than shipped off
to the artificial, atypical environment
of a correctional institution. Banishment from society, in a word, is not
the way to integrate someone into
society. Yet, imprisonment constitutes just such banishment—albeit a
temporary one in most cases.

This is of course not to say that
probation should be used in all cases,
or that it will produce better results.
There are many goals of sentencing,
some of which may require the imposition of a sentence to imprisonment in a given case. And, there are
defendants for whom forced removal
from the environment that may have
contributed to their offense can be
the best beginning to a constructive,
useful life.

By the same token, however, probation is a good bit more than the
"matter of grace" or "leniency" that
characterizes the philosophy of the
general public and many judges and
legislatures. Probation is an affirmative correctional tool, a tool that is
used not because it offers maximum
benefit to the defendant (though, of
course, this is an important side
product), but because it offers maximum benefit to the public that is
supposed to be served by the sentencing of criminals. The automatic
response of many in the criminal
justice system that imprisonment is
the best sentence for crime unless
particular reasons exist for "mitigating" the sentence is not a sound
starting point in framing criminal
sanctions. Quite the opposite ought
to be the case; the automatic response in sentencing situations
ought to be probation, unless particularly aggravating factors emerge
in the case at hand. At least, if such
aggravating factors cannot be ad-

vanced as the basis of a more repressive sentence, probation offers more hope than imprisonment that the defendant will not become part of the depressing cycle in which the gates of our prisons are more like revolving doors than barriers to crime.

It must be realized that this thesis cannot be practiced in a vacuum. Too often a sentencing judge is faced with the "Hobson's choice" of sentencing the defendant to an overcrowded prison that almost guarantees that he will emerge a more dangerous person or to an essentially unsupervised probation that is little more than a release without sanction, and without incentive to avoid committing a new offense. Such a state of affairs represents a failure of the legislative process in the highest order. The U.S. criminal justice system has failed more for this reason than for any other; not enough attention has been paid to providing adequate correctional choices to those who must operate the system. An effective correctional system places great reliance on adequately funded and staffed probation services. Within such a context, probation can lead to significant improvement in the preventive effects of the criminal law at much lower cost than the typical prison sentence. This has been proven in jurisdictions where it has been given a chance to work. We should not treat lightly an approach to crime control that offers the hope of better results at less cost. This, in a sentence, is the hope of probation.

SOURCE: American Bar Association Project on Minimum Standards and Goals *Probation*

HISTORY AND LEGAL FOUNDATIONS OF PROBATION

1

KEY TERMS

Amercement
Benefit of clergy
"Neck verse"
Sanctuary
Abjuration
Judicial reprieve
Security for good behavior
Filing
Bail
Motion to quash
Commonwealth v. Chase
Recognizance
Suspended sentence
Suspension of imposition of
  sentence
Suspension of execution of
  sentence
Killits case
Peter Oxenbridge Thacher
Matthew Davenport Hill
John Augustus
Illinois Juvenile Court Act of
  1899

Amercement:

A monetary penalty imposed upon a person for some offense, he being *in mercy* for his conduct. It was imposed arbitrarily at the discretion of the court or the person's lord. *Black's Law Dictionary* distinguishes between amercements and fines in that fines are certain, are created by some statute, and can only be assessed by courts of record; amercements are arbitrarily imposed.

Benefit of clergy:

An exemption for members of the clergy that allowed them to avoid being subject to the jurisdiction of secular courts.

EARLY CRIMINAL LAW

Probation, as it is known and practiced today, evolved out of ancient precedents in England and the United States devised to avoid the mechanical application of the harsh penal codes of the day.[1] The early British criminal law was dominated by the objectives of retribution and punishment and it imposed rigid and severe penalties on offenders. The usual punishments were corporal—branding, flogging, mutilation, and execution. Capital punishment was common and it was inflicted upon children and animals as well as men and women. At the time of Henry VIII, for instance, more than 200 crimes were punishable by death, many of them relatively minor offenses against property.

Methods used to determine guilt—what today we would call *criminal procedure*—also put the accused in danger of life or limb. Trial might be by combat between the accused and the accuser, or a person's innocence might be determined by whether he or she sank when bound and thrown into a deep pond—the theory being that the pure water would reject wrongdoers. Thus, the choice was to drown as an innocent person or to survive the drowning only to be otherwise executed. Sometimes the offender could elect to be tried "by God," which involved undergoing some painful and frequently life-threatening ordeal, or "by country," a form of trial by jury for which the accused first had to pay an **amercement** to the king. The accepted premise was that the purpose of the criminal law was not to deter or rehabilitate, but to bring about justice for a past act deemed harmful to the society.

EARLY EFFORTS TO MITIGATE PUNISHMENT

In the early Middle Ages, there were efforts to mitigate the severity of punishment. Royal pardons, usually paid for by the accused, were sometimes granted. Judges could choose to interpret statutes narrowly or fail to apply them. Juries sometimes devalued stolen property so as to bring its value below that which required the imposition of capital punishment. Prosecutors dismissed charges or charged offenders with lesser offenses. Devices such as "benefit of clergy" and "judicial reprieve" benefited some defendants, while "sanctuary" and "abjuration" enabled some criminals to gain immunity from punishment. Courts began to release certain offenders on good behavior for a temporary period, which allowed them time to seek a pardon or commutation of sentence. Gradually, an "inherent" power of certain courts to suspend sentences was recognized, although the existence and limits on that power were almost at once the subject of controversy.

Benefit of clergy was a privilege originally given to ordained clerics, monks, and nuns accused of crimes. Benefit of clergy required representatives of the Church to be delivered to Church authorities for punishment, rather than secular courts. Although the ecclesiastical courts had the power to imprison for life, they seldom exacted such severe punishment. Thus the benefit of clergy served to mitigate the harsh (frequently capital) punishments prescribed by English law. Benefit of clergy was later extended to protect ordinary citizens. Judges used the benefit as a means of exercising discretion when the

Psalm 51: The "Neck Verse"

1. Have mercy upon me, O God, according to thy lovingkindness: according unto the multitude of thy tender mercies blot out my transgressions.

2. Wash me thoroughly from mine iniquity, and cleanse me from my sin.

3. For I acknowledge my transgressions: and my sin is ever before me.

4. Against thee, thee only, have I sinned, and done this evil in thy sight: that thou mightest be justified when thou speakest, and be clear when thou judgest.

5. Behold, I was shapen in iniquity; and in sin did my mother conceive me.

6. Behold, thou desirest truth in the inward parts: and in the hidden part thou shalt make me to know wisdom.

7. Purge me with hyssop, and I shall be clean: wash me, and I shall be whiter than snow.

8. Make me to hear joy and gladness; that the bones which thou has broken may rejoice.

9. Hide thy face from my sins, and blot out all mine iniquities.

10. Create in me a clean heart, O God; and renew a right spirit within me.

11. Cast me not away from thy presence; and take not thy holy spirit from me.

12. Restore unto me the joy of thy salvation; and uphold me with thy free spirit.

13. Then will I teach transgressors thy ways; and sinners shall be converted unto thee.

14. Deliver me from bloodguiltiness, O God, thou God of my salvation: and my tongue shall sing aloud of thy righteousness.

15. O Lord, open thou my lips; and my mouth shall shew forth thy praise.

16. For thou desirest not sacrifice; else would I give it: thou delightest not in burnt offering.

17. The sacrifices of God are a broken spirit: a broken and a contrite heart, O God, thou wilt not despise.

18. Do good in thy good pleasure unto Zion: build thou the walls of Jerusalem.

19. Then shalt thou be pleased with the sacrifices of righteousness, with burnt offering and whole burnt offering: then shall they offer bullocks upon thine altar.

prescribed punishment for a crime seemed too severe in particular cases. A person could qualify for benefit of clergy by demonstrating that he or she could read—a skill that only the clergy and some of the upper classes possessed. Over time the courts began to require these defendants to read in court the text of Psalm 51 as a test of their literacy. The psalm came to be known as the "**neck verse**," and common criminals soon memorized it and pretended to read it in court, using its protection to escape being hanged. The benefit was practiced in the United States for a brief period, but the procedure became so technical and legalistic that it was almost unworkable. It was finally abolished in 1827.

Sanctuary referred to a place (usually a church or vestry) the king's soldiers were not permitted to enter for the purpose of taking an accused into custody. Offenders were accorded sanctuary until negotiations with the accusers could be accomplished or arrangements could be made to smuggle the accused out of the country. Offenders who confessed their crimes while in sanctuary were allowed **abjuration**—to promise to leave England under pain of immediate punishment if they returned without the king's permission. One legal historian wrote, "For a man to take sanctuary, confess his crime, and abjure the realm was an everyday event. If the man who had taken sanctuary would neither confess to a crime nor submit to a trial, the state could do no more against him. It tried to teach the clergy that their duty was to starve him into submission, but the clergy resented this interference with holy things."[2]

Sanctuary:

In old English law, a consecrated place, such as a church or abbey, where offenders took refuge because they could not be arrested there.

Abjuration

An oath to forsake the realm forever taken by an accused person who claimed sanctuary.

A criminal is granted sanctuary.

Judicial reprieve:

Withdrawal of a sentence for an interval of time during which the offender was at liberty and imposition of other sanctions was postponed.

Judicial reprieve (from *reprendre,* "to take back") was another method by which judges who recognized that not all offenders are dangerous, evil persons avoided imposing the prescribed punishments for crimes. Judicial reprieve amounted to a withdrawal of the sentence for some interval of time—similar to what today is called *suspension of sentence.* During the period of judicial reprieve the offender was at liberty, and the imposition of other criminal sanctions was postponed. At the expiration of the specified time, the accused could apply to the Crown for a pardon.

Early American Law

Recognition of the doctrine of benefit of clergy was never widespread in the American colonies. Instead, distinct American practices developed, such as "security for good behavior" and a practice known in Massachusetts as *filing*.[3]

Security for good behavior:

A recognizance or bond given the court by a defendant before or after conviction conditioned on his being "on good behavior" or keeping the peace for a prescribed period.

Security for good behavior, also known as *good abearance,* was a fee paid to the state as collateral for a promise of good behavior. Much like the modern practice of bail, security for good behavior allowed the accused to go free in certain cases either before or after conviction. Under **filing,** the indictment was "laid on file" in cases where justice did not require an immediate sentence; however, the court could impose certain conditions on the defendant. The effect was that the case was laid at rest without either dismissal or final judgment, and without the necessity of asking for final continuances.

Filing:

A procedure under which an indictment was "laid on file," or held in abeyance, without either dismissal or final judgement in cases where justice did not require an immediate sentence.

Massachusetts judges also often granted a **motion to quash** after judgment, using any minor technicality or the slightest error in the proceedings to free the defendant in cases where they thought the statutory penalties inhumane. Some early forms of **bail** had the effect of suspending final action on a case, although the chief use of bail then as now was for the purpose of insuring appearance for trial. Since the sureties "went bail" and became responsible for the action of the defendant, they assumed supervision of the defendant, at least to the extent of keeping track of his or her whereabouts. The continuous availability of the defendant for further action by the court was one of the conditions of liberty.

All of these methods had the common objective of mitigating punishment by relieving selected offenders from the full effects of the legally prescribed penalties that substantial segments of the community, including many judges, viewed as excessive and inappropriate to their offenses. They were precursors to probation as it is known today. The procedures most closely related to modern probation, however, are recognizance and the suspended sentence.

RECOGNIZANCE AND SUSPENDED SENTENCE

As early as 1830 Massachusetts courts had begun to release some offenders through the use of innovative and possibly extralegal procedures instead of imposing the prescribed punishments. In the 1830 case of *Commonwealth v. Chase*,[4] often cited as example of the early use of release on **recognizance** (from *recognocere*, "to call to mind"), Judge Peter Oxenbridge Thacher found the defendant guilty on her plea, suspended the imposition of sentence, and ruled that the defendant was permitted, "upon her recognizance for her appearance in this court whenever she should be called for, to go at large."[5] Recognizance came to be used often in Massachusetts with young and minor offenders as a means of avoiding a final conviction in hope that they would avoid further criminal behavior. John Smykla asserts that the practice of recognizance has many distinctive parallels with present-day probation practices, including suspension of sentence, freedom to remain in the community, conditions for freedom, and the possibility of revocation of that freedom upon violation of the conditions.[6] Recognizance is used today to ensure a defendant's presence at court and is not a disposition in itself.

Suspended sentence is an order of court that is entered after a verdict, finding, or plea of guilty, which suspends or postpones the imposition or execution of sentence during the good behavior of the offender. Although suspension of sentence is, in a few jurisdictions, a form of disposition of the criminal offender that is separate from and in addition to probation,[7] we consider it here chiefly in its close historical and legal relationship to probation.

Where suspension of sentence exists independent of probation, it is distinguished from probation in that the offender is released without supervision. The only condition is the implicit, or sometimes explicit, imperative that the withholding or postponement of sentence will be revoked or terminated if the offender commits a new crime. As a disposition, suspension of sentence also differs from probation in that no term is specified. It is generally held, however, that the period of suspension of sentence is limited by the maximum period of commitment permitted by statute for the offense.

Two Kinds of Suspended Sentence

There are two kinds of suspended sentence—suspension of *imposition* of sentence and suspension of *execution* of sentence. In the case of **suspension of**

Recognizance:

Originally a device of preventive justice that obliged persons suspected of future misbehavior to stipulate with and give full assurance to the court and the public that the apprehended offense would not occur. Recognizance was later used with convicted or arraigned offenders with conditions of release set. Recognizance was usually entered into for a specified period.

Suspended sentence:

An order of the court after a verdict, finding, or plea of guilty that suspends or postpones the imposition or execution of sentence during a period of good behavior.

imposition of sentence, there may be a verdict or plea and a judgment, but no sentence is pronounced.

In the case of **suspension of execution of sentence,** the sentence is pronounced, but its execution is suspended; in other words, the defendant is not committed to a correctional institution or otherwise taken into custody. As we will see, the form of the suspension—whether of imposition or of execution of sentence—has different legal consequences and it directly impacts whether suspension of sentence is considered as a separate disposition of the offender, or as the basis for or equivalent to probation. The distinction is critical and may affect such later issues as:

- whether the offender has been "convicted",
- what civil rights he or she has forfeited,
- the term for which he or she may be committed upon resentence after revocation of the suspension,
- whether probation is a part of the criminal prosecution, and
- whether the probationer on revocation of probation is entitled to counsel under the holding in *Mempa v. Rhay*[8], or the right to counsel rules announced in *Morrissey v. Brewer*[9] and *Gagnon v. Scarpelli*.[10]

The Power to Suspend Sentence

Several variables must be considered when discussing the power to suspend sentence. For instance, it makes a difference whether:

- we are talking about the power to withhold or delay sentencing indefinitely, or for only a temporary period or a specific purpose.
- we are referring to a power inherent in the courts to suspend sentence, or to a power granted to the courts by a legislative act.
- we mean power to suspend imposition of sentence, power to suspend execution of sentence, or both.
- suspended sentence is a separate disposition or sentencing alternative, or connected with probation.
- probation depends upon the existence of the power to suspend sentence, or does not have the suspended sentence aspect; and
- probation is actually deemed to be a sentence.

It is generally conceded that at common law the English courts had the power to suspend sentence for a limited period or for a specified purpose. This power was used, for example, in judicial reprieve, where there was a temporary suspension of imposition or execution of sentence and in which the defendant—with neither the right of appeal nor the right to a new trial—could apply to the Crown for an absolute or conditional pardon.

Whether the common law recognized the inherent right of the courts to suspend sentence indefinitely is a matter of considerable dispute. Certain practices in both England and the American colonies support the view that such a right was recognized. Recognizance, used as early as 1830 in Massachusetts, permitted one Jerusha Chase, "upon her own recognizance for her appearance in this court whenever she was called for, to go at large."[11] Judicial reprieve was also cited as proof of the recognition of a court's inherent

> "The Killits Case"
> *Ex parte* United States,
> 242 U.S. 27 (1916)
>
> The defendant, John Killits, was convicted of embezzling nearly $5,000 from a bank in Toledo, Ohio. A first-offender with a good reputation in the community, Killits had made full restitution, and the bank did not wish to prosecute. The trial court suspended sentence indefinitely, and the prosecution appealed, alleging that the court did not have the power to suspend either the imposition or execution of sentence indefinitely.

right to suspend sentence indefinitely, particularly since in some cases the temporary suspension became indefinite when the court subsequently refused or failed to proceed within the case.

As far as the United States is concerned, the matter was resolved in 1916 in the so-called *Killetts* **case,** in which the Supreme Court held that the federal courts have no power to suspend indefinitely the imposition or execution of a sentence.[12]

The Court recognized that the temporary suspension of imposition or execution of sentence was frequently resorted to in both England and the colonies, since errors in the trial or miscarriage of justice could not be corrected by granting a new trial or by appeal under the existing system. Many of these temporary suspensions became indefinite because of a court's failure to proceed further in a criminal case. The Supreme Court pointed out, however, that

> * * * neither of these conditions serve to convert the mere exercise of a judicial discretion to temporarily suspend for the accomplishment of a purpose contemplated by law into the existence of an arbitrary judicial power to permanently refuse to enforce the law.[13]

The Court went on to hold that the practice was inconsistent with the Constitution, since

> "its exercise in the very nature of things amounts to a refusal by the judicial power to perform the duty resting on it, and, as a consequence thereof, to an interference with both the legislative and executive authority as fixed by the Constitution."[14]

Suspended Sentence and Probation

The Supreme Court indicated, somewhat inconsistently, that Congress had adequate power to authorize both temporary and indefinite suspension by statute. An earlier New York court had, indeed, upheld the power of a court to suspend sentences indefinitely where this right had been conferred upon the court by statute.[15] The aspect of *Killetts* that recognized the right of the legislative authority to grant the power of indefinite suspension to the courts was to make probation as now defined and practiced in the United States largely a creature of statute.

Consequence of the Killetts decision

When the Supreme Court decided that the federal courts, in the absence of permissive legislation by Congress, were without power to suspend sentence, some 2,000 convicted offenders previously released on unauthorized federal suspensions were pardoned by the President on the Court's recommendation.

The early controversy about the court's authority to suspend sentence has also resulted in differing ideas about the relationship between probation and suspended sentence. Depending upon the jurisdiction, four views are commonly held:

1. Probation may be granted on suspension of imposition of sentence.
2. Probation may be granted on suspension of imposition or of execution of sentence.
3. Suspended sentence is probation.
4. Probation does not have the suspended sentence aspect.

Supporting the fourth view, the *American Bar Association Standards relating to Probation* states that probation should not involve or require suspension of any other sentence.[16] The matter is also complicated by the problem of whether probation itself is or is not a sentence and by the varying definitions of "conviction." In 1984 the federal Sentencing Reform Act[17] abolished the authority of U.S. courts to suspend the imposition or execution of sentence in order to impose a term of probation. Instead, the act recognized probation as a sentence in itself.

Suspended Sentence as "Conviction"

There are two definitions of conviction. By the narrow definition, which follows popular usage, *conviction* denotes a plea, finding, or verdict of guilt. By the broad definition, it is a plea, finding, or verdict of guilty followed by a final judgment of conviction and sentence. Conviction in the narrow sense is followed by the imposition of criminal sanctions, but a determination of guilt is not accompanied by loss of civil rights and privileges. Conviction in the broad sense is followed by the imposition of criminal sanctions *and* loss of civil rights and privileges.

Whether there is a conviction if sentence is suspended often turns on the question of what is suspended. A conviction is more likely reached if the execution—rather than the imposition—of sentence has been suspended, although this is by no means always true.

EARLY PROBATION

The increasing awareness that prisons were not accomplishing their stated purpose of reforming the offender and that suspension of sentence without supervision was not a satisfactory alternative brought about the development of probation as we know it today. Although judges such as **Peter Oxenbridge Thacher** in Massachusetts introduced "probationlike" practices such as recognizance and suspension of sentence in the early nineteenth century, the credit for "founding" probation is reserved for John Augustus, a Boston bootmaker, and Matthew Davenport Hill, an English lawyer who held the judicial position of Recorder of Birmingham.

The development of probation in England has been traced to specialized practices for dealing with young offenders. Some judges adopted the practice of sentencing youthful offenders to a term of one day, on the condition that they return "to the care of their parents or master, to be by him more carefully watched and supervised in the future."[18] **Matthew Davenport Hill** had witnessed this practice as a young attorney and when he became the Recorder of Birmingham (a judicial post), he employed a similar practice when he perceived "that the individual was not wholly corrupt—when there was reasonable hope of reformation—and when there could be found persons to act as guardians kind enough to take charge of the young convict."[19] Under Hill's direction, police officers visited the guardians from time to time, "recording the progress of the offender and keeping a regular account."[20]

It was not until 1887 that a probation law was adopted in England that authorized the use of recognizance for first offenders. It did not provide for special conditions of probation or for supervision of those released.

It is generally agreed that the first true probation law was enacted in the United States in 1878. This legislation grew out of the work of **John Augustus,** the first person to apply the term *probation* to his new method. For this reason, he is regarded as the "Father of Probation," and probation is said to be of U.S. origin.[21] Augustus was a member of the Washington Total Abstinence Society, an organization devoted to the promotion of temperance.[22] In August 1841 this interest led him to bail out a "common drunkard" by permission of the Boston Police Court. Augustus later wrote of this first "probationer" in his journal, which appeared in 1852:

> He was ordered to appear for sentence in three weeks from that time. He signed the pledge and became a sober man; at the expiration of this period of probation, I accompanied him into the court room; his whole appearance was changed and no one, not even the scrutinizing officers, could have believed that he was the same person who less than a month before had stood trembling on the prisoner's stand.[23]

It is evident that he viewed probation as a selective process, although his first probationer was selected on his behavior, his manner of speech, and his protestation of a "firm resolve to quit liquor." In his journal Augustus wrote:

> Great care was observed, of course, to ascertain whether the prisoners were promising subjects for probation, and to this end it was necessary to take into consideration the previous character of the person, his age, and the influences by which he would in [the] future be likely to be surrounded.[24]

John Augustus continued his work in the Boston courts for eighteen years, during which he received some financial aid from other citizens of the community interested in the offender. His journal reports that of the first 1,100 probationers on whom he kept records, only one forfeited bond. As to reformation, he stated that if "only one-half of this number have become reformed, I have ample cause to be satisfied."[25]

As is true today, probation was not universally accepted. Augustus repeated over and over that "the object of the law is to reform criminals and to prevent crime, and not to punish maliciously or from a spirit of revenge," and he did not hesitate to castigate the police, the judges, and others who did not share his views.[26] As a result, a newspaper of the time described him as a "fellow who is called John Augustus," who "seems to have a great itching for notoriety, and dollars" and "hangs and loafs about the Police and Municipal Courts, almost every day, and takes more airs upon himself than all the judges and officers."[27] The newspaper continued:

> We know something about this Peter Funk Philanthropist, and peanut reformer, and unless he conducts himself henceforth with a great deal more propriety, we shall take it upon ourself to teach him decency.[28]

John Augustus and his immediate successors were not officials of the court and hence lacked official status, although Massachusetts had passed a law in 1689 that authorized an agent of the State Board of Charities to investigate cases of children tried before the criminal courts. In 1878, almost twenty years after the death of John Augustus, adult probation in Massachusetts was sanctified by statute. A law authorizing the mayor of Boston to appoint a paid probation officer to serve in the Boston criminal courts as a member of the police force was passed. For the first time, the probation officer was recognized as an official agent of the court. The statute included a provision that probation was to be available to "such persons as may reasonably be expected to be reformed without punishment." No other restrictions were inserted. Probation was thus made available in the city of Boston to men and women, felons and misdemeanants, and juveniles and adults, regardless of the nature of the offense or the amount or kind of punishment assessed.

Early Probation Legislation—State

Statewide probation was first enacted in Massachusetts in 1891 with a provision that appears in many modern statutes: that the probation officer should not be an active member of the regular police force. Although this early legislation provided for probation officers, it did not specifically give courts the power to grant probation. Missouri in 1897 and Vermont in 1898 remedied this omission, although the Missouri statute was labeled "an Act relating to the parole of prisoners" and used the words *probation* and *parole* interchangeably.

Several other states passed probation laws in the late nineteenth and early twentieth century. The statutes varied in their provisions. Illinois and Minnesota provided for juvenile probation only; Rhode Island placed restrictions on eligibility and excluded persons guilty of certain offenses. Some states provided for statewide probation, while others followed the example set by Vermont in adopting the county plan.[29]

Early Probation—Federal

As we have noted, the Supreme Court held in 1916 that the federal courts had no inherent power to suspend indefinitely the imposition or execution of a sentence.[30] The Court indicated, however, that the power to suspend sentence could be given to the courts by statute.[31] Between 1916 and 1925, several attempts were made to secure the passage of law authorizing federal judges to grant probation. In the closing days of the session in 1925, Congress enacted the National Probation Act, which authorized each federal district court, except in the District of Columbia, to appoint one salaried probation officer. In 1930, judges were empowered to appoint without reference to the civil service list, and the limitation of one officer to each district was removed. The attorney general was charged with the duty of coordinating the probation system, and probation officers were given certain duties with respect to parolees. The objectives of the probation law were stated by Chief Justice Taft as follows:

The great desideratum was the giving to young and new violators of law a chance to reform and to escape the contaminating influence of association with hardened or veteran criminals in the beginning of imprisonment. Probation is the attempted saving of a man who has taken one wrong step and whom the judge thinks to be a brand who can be plucked from the burning at the time of imposition of sentence.[32]

By virtue of the statute, the courts in the federal system had (until 1984) the power to suspend the imposition or execution of sentence. By 1925, probation was authorized by statutes in all forty-eight states, and it is now so authorized in all fifty states and in the federal system.

Early Probation—Juvenile

There is a tendency to think of juvenile probation only in connection with a juvenile court. Since the first juvenile court and apparently the use of the term *juvenile delinquency* were established in Illinois in 1899, some writers trace the development of juvenile probation from that date. In truth, however, as we have seen previously, some English courts put into practice many of the principles, characteristics, and procedures that today we equate with juvenile courts long before any separate tribunals for the handling of juveniles were established in the United States.

As early as 1630, a guidebook that sanctioned special treatment of juveniles was prepared for justices of the peace in England. One provision read:

And yet if an infant shall commit larceny, and shall be found guilty thereof before the Justice of the Peace, it shall not be amiss for them to respite the judgment and so hath it often beene [sic] done by the Judges.[33]

A report of criminal trials from the Old Bailey Sessions in London, 1686–93, contains an account of the trial of Chollis Searl, "a little youth, aged about twelve years," who was acquitted of picking pockets in a proceeding that would be familiar in today's juvenile courts.[34] One of the justices of the peace for the county of Warwick, writing between 1820 and 1827, proposed the appointment of legal guardians to children without supervision, to supply the place of their own relatives.

Between 1866 and 1871, a boy's "beadle," or "persuader," was employed as an unofficial probation officer by the Reformatory and Refuge Union in London. In 1881 an article on the "Massachusetts Method of Dealing with Juvenile Offenders," which advocated placing them on probation, was given wide publicity by the Howard Association of London.

Although the need for separate treatment of juveniles was recognized in the early nineteenth century in the United States, the development of special children's institutions proceeded more rapidly than did the development of special procedures and separate courts. Unfortunately, many of the special institutions came to be nothing more than children's prisons, and a system of contracting the labor of the children to private employers led to extremely harsh treatment and outright exploitation of children's labor. To protect children from this exploitation late in the nineteenth century the New York Children's Aid Society shipped wholesale lots of Manhattan street urchins to farmers out West; otherwise, they would have been committed to the House of Refuge. In 1890 the Children's Aid Society of Pennsylvania offered to place delinquents who would otherwise be sent to reform school in foster homes. Known as *placing out,* this practice was an early form of juvenile probation.[35] The system of apprenticeship was another early form of probation of children. It was used chiefly to detach poor children from their parents and attach them to masters who would teach them a trade.

THE FIRST JUVENILE COURT.   The **Illinois Juvenile Court Act of 1899** combined the Massachusetts and New York systems of probation with several New York laws to provide delinquents with special court sessions and separate detention facilities.[36] In an article that appeared in the *Harvard Law Review* in 1909, Julian W. Mack declared that juvenile court legislation

> . . . has assumed two aspects. In Great Britain and in New York, and in a few other jurisdictions, the protection [of children] is accomplished by suspending sentence and releasing the child under probation, or, in case of removal from the home, sending it to school instead of to a jail or penitentiary. But in Illinois, and following the lead of Illinois, in most jurisdictions, the form of proceeding is totally different. Proceedings are brought to have a guardian or representative of the state appointed to look after the child, to have the state intervene between the natural parent and child because the child needs it, as evidenced by some of its acts, and because the parent is either unwilling or unable to train the child properly.[37]

Mack continued with an analysis of the main principles of juvenile court legislation. The first principle was that child offenders should be kept separate from adult criminals and should receive a treatment differentiated to suit their special needs. That is, the courts should be agencies for the rescue as well as the punishment of children. The second principle was that parents of offenders must be made to feel more responsible for their children's wrongdoing. The third principle was that no matter what offense they have committed, placing children in the common jails is an unsuitable penalty. The fourth principle stated that removing children from their parents and sending them even to an industrial school should as far as possible be avoided, and

> . . . that when it is allowed to return home it should be under probation, subject to the guidance and friendly interest of the probation officer, the representative of the court. To raise the age of criminal responsibility from seven or ten to sixteen or eighteen without providing for an efficient system of probation, would indeed be disastrous. *Probation is, in fact, the keynote of juvenile court legislation.* [Emphasis added.][38]

Mack further related:

> Whenever juvenile courts have been established, a system of probation has been provided for, and even where as yet the juvenile court system has not been fully developed, some steps have been taken to substitute probation for imprisonment of the juvenile offender. What they need, more than anything else, is kindly assistance; and the aim of the court, appointing a probation officer for the child, is to have the child and the parents feel, not so much the power, as the friendly interest of the state; to show them that the object of the court is to help them to train the child right, and therefore the probation officers must be men and women fitted for these tasks.[39]

Summary

Probation grew out of efforts to mitigate the harsh punishments demanded by early English law. At the time of Henry VIII more than 200 offenses were punishable by death, many of them relatively minor offenses against property. Judges interpreted statutes narrowly or failed to apply them. Juries placed lower value on stolen property (to bring the value below that which required the imposition of the death penalty). Prosecutors dismissed charges or charged offenders with lesser offenses. Devices such as benefit of clergy, judicial reprieve, banishment, and sanctuary were utilized to reduce the otherwise unrelenting severity of the penal code.

In the American colonies, where English law prevailed, distinct American practices developed. *Filing, security for good behavior, recognizance,* and *suspension of imposition of sentence* were procedures by which American judges exercised their discretion to reduce the severity of punishment in cases where the circumstances of the crime or characteristics of the offender warranted leniency. These were the direct precursors of modern probation.

With the foundation laid by early judges in America and England, the later work of Matthew Davenport Hill, an English judge, and John Augustus, an American reformer, brought about the practice of probation as we know it today. The modern concept of probation depends on the power of the courts to suspend sentence. This power was the subject of much controversy in the early years of the use of probation. The issue was eventually settled by the United States Supreme Court in the so-called Killetts case in 1916. In this case the Court held that courts did not have an inherent power to suspend sentences indefinitely, but that power might be granted to the judiciary by the legislature. This aspect of the *Killetts* case—recognition of legislative authority to grant the power of indefinite suspension to the courts—was to make probation as now defined and practiced in the United States largely a creature of statute.

Although most writers trace the origins of juvenile probation to the creation of the first American juvenile court in Chicago in 1899, English courts had put into practice many of its principles, characteristics, and procedures long before. As early as 1630 a guidebook for the use of English justices of the peace recommended "respite of judgement" for crimes committed by "infants." Numerous accounts attest to procedures and practices of the seventeenth and eighteenth centuries that would be familiar to juvenile courts today. By 1899 the concept that crimes committed by children and those committed by adults should be dealt with differently, with special courts and special facilities for juveniles was formalized by the creation of the first juvenile court in Illinois.

Endnotes

1. *Probation and Related Measures* (United Nations, Department of Social Affairs, 1951).
2. Sol Rubin, Henry Weihofen, George Edwards, and Simon Rosenzweig, *The Law of Criminal Corrections* (St. Paul: West, 1963), p. 16, citing Stephen, *A History of the Criminal Law in England* (1883), pp. 491–492.

3. Commonwealth v. Chase, *Thacher's Criminal Cases,* 267 (1831), recorded in vol. eleven of the *Records of the Old Municipal Court of Boston,* p. 199.

4. *Id.*

5. *Id.*

6. John Ortiz Smykla, *Probation and Parole: Crime Control in the Community* (New York: Macmillan, 1984), pp. 64–65.

7. Sol Rubin advocated a greater use of suspended sentence without probation, arguing that this would provide an additional sentencing alternative of particular value in situations where apprehension and conviction have so thorough a corrective impact on the offender that supervision by probation is unnecessary. Sol Rubin, *The Law of Criminal Correction,* 2nd ed. (St. Paul: West, 1973), pp. 197–200.

8. Mempa v. Rhay, 389 U.S. 128, 88 S.Ct. 254, 19 L.Ed.2d 336 (1967).

9. Morrissey v. Brewer, 408 U.S. 471, 92 S.Ct. 2593, 33 L.Ed.2d 484 (1972).

10. Gagnon v. Scarpelli, 411 U.S. 778, 93 S.Ct. 1756, 36 L.Ed.2d 656 (1973).

11. Commonwealth v. Chase, *supra* note 3.

12. *Ex parte* United States, 242 U.S. 27, 37 S.Ct. 72, 61 L.Ed. 129 (1916).

13. *Id.*

14. *Id.*

15. People *ex rel.* Forsyth v. Court of Sessions, 141 N.Y. 288, 36 N.E. 386 (1894).

16. ABA, *Standards, Probation* § 1.1(b) reads: "In this report, the term 'probation' means a sentence not involving confinement which imposes conditions and retains authority in the sentencing court to modify the conditions of the sentence or to resentence the offender if he violates the conditions. *Such a sentence should not involve or require suspension of the imposition or the execution of any other sentence."* [Emphasis added.]

17. 18 U.S.C.A. § 3561.

18. Paul Tappan, *Crime, Justice, and Correction* (New York: McGraw-Hill, 1960), p. 542.

19. *Id.*

20. *Id.*

21. See John Augustus, *A Report of the Labors of John Augustus, for the Last Ten Years, in Aid of the Unfortunate* (Boston: Wright & Hasty, 1852); reprinted as *John Augustus, First Probation Officer* (New York: National Probation Association, 1939). See also Supplemental Reading, *infra,* "John Augustus: The First Probation Officer."

22. *John Augustus, First Probation Officer, supra* note 21.

23. *Id.*

24. *Id.* at 34.

25. *Id.* at 96.

26. *Id.* at 23.

27. *Id.* at 78–79.

28. *Id.*

29. *Attorney General's Survey, Digest,* vol. 1.

30. *Ex parte* United States, 242 U.S. 27, 37 S. Ct. 72, 61 L.Ed. 129 (1916).

31. *Id.*

32. United States v. Murray, 275 U.S. 347, 48 S.Ct. 146, 72 L.Ed. 309 (1928).

33. Frederic L. Faust and Paul J. Brantingham, *Juvenile Justice Philosophy* (St. Paul: West, 1974), p. 44.

34. *Id.* at 45.

35. *Id.* at 62.

36. *Id.* at 63.

37. Julian W. Mack, "The Juvenile Court," 23 *Harvard Law Review* 102 (1909), as quoted in Faust and Brantingham, *supra* note 33, at 159–69.

38. *Id.* at 162.

39. *Id.* at 163.

DISCUSSION QUESTIONS

1. How did the existence of extremely harsh penal laws in early England influence the evolution of probation?

2. Explain benefit of clergy. What was its original purpose, and how did it come to be used?

3. Why is Psalm 51 referred to as *the neck verse?*

4. What was judicial reprieve? How is it related to modern probation?

5. Explain the use of filing and security for good behavior in the American colonies.

6. What is the importance for probation of the ruling in *Commonwealth v. Chase?*

7. What are the two kinds of suspended sentence? Why is the distinction critical to an understanding of modern probation?

8. What is the "Killits" case? What was its impact on modern probation?

9. Distinguish between the narrow and broad definitions of *conviction.* What consequences arise from each?

10. Who were Matthew Davenport Hill and John Augustus? What did each contribute to modern criminal justice practices?

SUPPLEMENTAL READING

John Augustus: The First Probation Officer

The first probation law in the new world was passed in Massachusetts in 1878. This law, Chapter 198, Acts in 1878, authorized the mayor of Boston to appoint from the police force or from the city at large a person to attend the criminal courts in Suffolk County, to investigate the cases of those charged with or convicted of crimes, and to recommend to the courts the placing on probation of those who might be reformed without punishment. The act provided for the compensation of the first statutory probation officer from public funds.

It is important to remember that the act of 1878 did not create probation or initiate the probation movement. It created no new judicial power but provided only for the appointment and payment of a special officer in order that the courts might exercise more fully and broadly what had become a well-established, well-recognized, and approved usage. Defendants had been placed on probation in Boston as early as 1830. By judicial experiment and the use of volunteer probation officers, the probation movement came into being. The General Court, in enacting the act of 1878, reflected the public opinion in favor of placing defendants on probation which had been forming for nearly fifty years.

The probation movement as it developed before legislation is the story of devoted men and women of Massachusetts, many of them volunteers, who saw in probation an opportunity for the rehabilitation of men and women, of boys and girls. Of these, John Augustus made the first great contribution.

When on an August day in 1841 John Augustus appeared in the police court of Boston and the court bailed into his custody a poor inebriate who would otherwise have been committed to jail, probation was ready for its development. The courts were prepared, there was no lack of the human beings with whom probation is concerned, and John Augustus was imbued with the vision and the consecration necessary to make probation a really living movement.

Probation was not the "discovery" of John Augustus, [the idea was apparent in] the enlightened legal thought of Boston judges in the decade before him. But there could be no real development of probation until, in addition to the legal thought and practice which made it possible, there was a demonstration which would show its possibilities and value as a treatment process, which would gain the interest, understanding, and respect of the courts and of the public, and which would attract other workers to the field. Such a demonstration John Augustus, the bootmaker of Boston, made from 1841 until his death in 1859.

It was Augustus's practice to bail, after his conviction, an offender in whom there was hope of reformation. The man would be ordered to appear before the court at a stated time at the expiration of which Augustus would accompany him to the courtroom. If the judge was satisfied with Augustus's account of his stewardship, the offender, instead of being committed to the House of Correction, would be fined one cent and costs. The one cent and costs, which generally amounted to three to four dollars, Augustus paid.

Who was John Augustus? What was it that took him from boot factory to the police court in 1841? How did he do his work? Who financed it? How was he received by the personnel of the courts, by the press, and by the people of Boston? What were his accomplishments?

John Augustus was born in Burlington, Massachusetts (then part of Woburn), in 1785. About 1806, he moved to Lexington and carried on a shoe manufactory in part of his home. He apparently prospered, as he owned a large tract of land on both sides of Bedford Street. His old home, now renovated and restored at One Harrington Road and known as the Jonathan Harrington House, faces the Lexington Common.

Although John Augustus was in business in Boston as early as 1820, he continued to maintain his Lexington home and possibly his Lexington business until 1829, when the *Boston Directory* lists him as living in Boston on Chambers Street. It was in his shop at 5 Franklin Avenue near the police court, now only an alley, that Augustus received from 1841, according to his own account of his work, frequent calls from those who sought his help. His business there suffered, owing to the time he was required to spend away from it bailing people in the courts or attending to their needs elsewhere.

All of Augustus's residences from 1841 on are of particular interest, because as soon as he began his work in the courts, his home became a refuge for people he had bailed until more permanent plans could be made for them. From 1845 until his death in 1859, Augustus lived at 65 Chambers Street, in the West End of Boston. Nothing remains today of this old house.

There can be no doubt it was the Washingtonian temperance reform movement that led Augustus to the police court and later to the municipal court in Boston. It was the conviction of the Washingtonians that the drunkard could be saved through understanding, kindness, and moral suasion, rather than through commitment to prison.

The movement resulted in the formation of the Washington Total Abstinence Society in Boston on April 25, 1841. Its members pledged not only not to use intoxicating liquors themselves, but to reclaim and to restore to temperance those who were addicted to drunkenness.

The members were soon in the police court about the work to which they were pledged; and some of them were there before Augustus, as the first quarterly report of the society's auditor, published in July 1841, indicates:

> I take this opportunity, in the name, and in behalf of this Society, of tendering to the Justices and Clerks of the Police Court, my hearty thanks for their kindness in affording (as far as consistent with duty) every facility to our members in their attempts to rescue and bring back to the paths of temperance, the *poor, forsaken, heartbroken* Drunkard, who came under their cognizance. Many, very many, have been taken from this Court and restored to their families and friends, who do not appear in the Reports from the Houses of Correction and Industry. Thus it will be seen that a heavy expense has been saved to the city, and many a person has been brought back to usefulness, unknown to the public.

THE FIRST PROBATIONER

Let Augustus describe in his own words the moving story of his first probationer:

> In the month of August, 1841, I was in court one morning, when the door communicating with the lock-room was opened and an officer entered, followed by a ragged and wretched looking man, who took his seat upon the bench allotted to prisoners. I imagined from the man's appearance that his offence was that of yielding to his appetite for intoxicating drinks, and in a few moments I found that my suspicions were correct, for the clerk read the complaint, in which the man was charged with being a common drunkard. The case was clearly made out, but before sentence had been passed, I conversed with him a few moments, and found that he was not yet past all hope and reformation, although his appearance and his looks precluded a belief in the minds of others that he would ever become a *man* again. He told me that if he could be saved from the House of Correction, he never again would taste intoxicating liquors; there was such an earnestness in that tone, and a look expressive of firm resolve, that I determined to aid him; I bailed him, by permission of the Court. He was ordered to appear for sentence in three weeks from that time. He signed the pledge and became a sober man; at the expiration of this period of probation, I accompanied him into the court room; his whole appearance was changed and no one, not even the scrutinizing officers, could have believed that he was the same person who less than a month before, had stood trembling on the prisoner's stand. The Judge expressed himself much pleased with the account we gave of the man, and instead of the usual penalty—imprisonment in the House of Correction—he fined him *one cent and costs*, amounting in all to $3.76, which was immediately paid. The man continued industrious and sober, and without doubt has been, by this treatment, saved from a drunkard's grave.[1]

With this encouragement, Augustus continued to appear in court to receive on probation alcoholics who appeared likely prospects for reformation, to rehabilitate them, and then to return with them to court for a report on their progress. By January 1842 he had bailed seventeen other alcoholics.

---

[1] *John Augustus, First Probation Officer,* reprint of *Report of the Labors of John Augustus, for the Last Ten Years, in Aid of the Unfortunate* (Boston, Wright & Hasty, 1852), New York: (National Probation Association, 1939), p. 4.

His real consecration to this work occurred in August 1842, when he could say:

> I had labored about a year when it became evident that much, much good had been and might be performed, by laboring in the field in which I had commenced operations, and to promote this object, several kind and philanthropic individuals placed in my hands donations of various sums, which enabled me to accomplish a much greater amount of good than I could have done from my own limited means alone.

From this time on, Augustus's record is one of dedication to a cause, understood by some and misunderstood by others, to which he devoted the remainder of his life, much of his own financial resources, as well as the money contributed by Boston people. John Augustus set the general pattern to be followed by succeeding voluntary and official probation officers.

During the first year, Augustus bailed only men, but thereafter, year by year until 1859, his probationers were men and women, boys and girls whose offenses represented every bailable crime.

When in December 1851 John Augustus consulted his records preparatory to publishing an account of his labors in behalf of unfortunates during the preceding ten years, he found he had bailed in the police or municipal courts 1,102 persons, 674 males and 428 females. He had become bail for them to the amount of $19,464, and he had paid $2,417.65 for fines and costs.

Although this alone may be considered an impressive record, it is to be remembered that he continued such work in the courts for about seven and one-half years more; and in addition, he responded to calls for assistance from many in need of social services who were not court offenders. Up to 1858, we know that he had bailed 1,946 persons, 1,152 males and 794 women and girls.

Oppositions to Be Overcome

In the conduct of his work inside and outside the court, John Augustus faced opposition, misunderstanding, and even physical abuse. Charges were made that he was profiting financially from whose whom he bailed even though many of them were so poor they were unable to pay the fine and costs. Much of the opposition and misunderstanding he gradually overcame. Some if it remained, and Augustus expressed it in words that have been used in reference to probation from time to time up to this day:

> There is, however, much opposition to the plan of bailing on probation. Those who are opposed to this method tell us that it is rather an incentive to crime and, therefore, instead of proving salutary, it is detrimental to the interest of society, and so far from having a tendency to reform the person bailed, it rather presents inducements for them to continue a career of crime; the law is robbed of its terrors, and its punishments, and there is nothing, therefore, to deter them from repeating the offense with which they were previously charged.

To such thinking, Augustus replied:

> The premise upon which such reasoning is based is incorrect. Individuals and communities generally are but too prone to infer evil of a class, if they but occasionally observe it in individuals; if a person who has been bailed, or received the leniency of the court, proves false to his promises of amendment, people are ever ready to predict that all others will conduct in a similar manner; and this they persist in believing, although instances are very frequent, even three to one, where such persons have become good citizens, and regain their former station and relation in society. I shall leave the matter for others to discuss and decide, but I am content, feeling as I do, that by such humane means hundreds of the fallen have been raised even by my humble instrumentality.

Augustus varied his answers to his critics. To some he said that for each person bailed to him, a commitment to a house of correction was prevented. To those who understood social progress and justice only in terms of a dollar saved, he pointed out that the public was saved the greater expense of caring for the person in jail. When he was charged with cheating the jails of their rightful tenants, he replied that his form of treatment was more effective; that it saved the offender for his family and for society and did not disgrace him forever as a commitment would. How modern is the sound of some of these charges that Augustus had to answer!

It was the court officers—the clerk, the turnkeys, and the process servers—who were the first to oppose Augustus and who remained strongest in their opposition. Since their financial security was threatened in every case for which Augustus became bail, they lost no time or opportunity to show their displeasure over his work. For every person bailed by Augustus, the officer lost the fee of either seventy-five cents or sixty-two cents payable on the taking of the offender to jail; the clerk lost twenty-five cents, and the turnkey was out forty cents. But Augustus was not deterred.

Although the opposition of the court officers was discouraging, the judges and the press were friendly, and influential people in the community gave him both moral and financial support.

SECURING FUNDS

There is no evidence that Augustus was anything more than a man of limited means. To accomplish the work he felt called to do, more money was necessary than he could provide alone. Much of it had to come from others. It did not come, as was charged, from his probationers. In December 1851 Augustus wrote:

> . . . The first two years, 1841–42, I received nothing from any one except what I earned by my daily labor; in 1843, I received from various persons in aid of my work, seven hundred and fifty-eight dollars; in 1844–45–46, I received twelve hundred and thirteen dollars each year. I then gave up business at my shop, and for the last five years, my receipts have averaged, yearly, seventeen hundred and seventy-six dollars, all of which I have expended, and have not a dollar of this sum. The money which I have thus received came from kind friends to the cause in which I was engaged.

The busy life of the first career man in the field of probation came to a close on June 21, 1859. The morning after his death, the *Boston Herald* summed up the meaning of his life and work in these words:

DEATH OF A WELL-KNOWN CITIZEN

Mr. John Augustus died at his residence in Chambers Street, this city, last evening after a somewhat protracted and lingering illness, superinduced by old age and a general prostration of the system from overtaxation of its powers. The decreased was well know in this community in connection with his benevolent exertions in behalf of poor criminals, the latter years of his life being almost entirely spent in ameliorating their condition by becoming bondsman for their good behavior, and providing means and opportunities that would tend to a reformation. . . . Possessed of a living income from means accumulated in business pursuits, the deceased was in a position to carry out the dictates of a generous heart, and those who knew him best give him credit for sincerity of purpose, although there are many who saw nothing in his conduct toward criminals that was not the offspring of selfish motives. Undoubtedly, Mr. Augustus was the means of doing much good in his daily walks through our courts and penal institutions, and a charitable community will not be backward in revering his memory with this fact in remembrance.

SOURCE: Excerpted from a paper presented by John Moreland at the 35th Annual Conference of the National Probation Association, Boston, Mass., May 29, 1941.

Sentencing and the Decision to Grant Probation

2

KEY TERMS

Regular probation
Intensive supervision probation
Electronic monitoring
Deferred adjudication
Pretrial diversion
Sentencing
Sentence
Privilege theory
Model Penal Code
American Bar Association
  Standards
National Advisory Commission
  on Criminal Justice Standards
  and Goals
Presentence investigation report
Right of allocation
Presentence conference
Sentencing guidelines

INTRODUCTION

Since 1980 the U.S. prison population has increased by 150 percent, totaling 823,414 inmates by 1992.[1] State and federal prison populations grew 7 percent in 1991 alone, with 13 states recording increases of 10 percent or greater (see Table 2–1).[2] A 1985 report by the RAND Corporation revealed that a greater percentage of convicted felons are being imprisoned than ever before in our nation's history and that at the same time, budget limitations have made it impossible to build prisons fast enough to keep pace with the burgeoning influx of new inmates.[3] The RAND report concluded:

> The nation's prisons have become so critically overcrowded that the courts must now consider alternative sentences for an increasing number of convicted felons. Probation is the major—and in many cases, the only—alternative.[4]

In fact, the number of convicted offenders sentenced to probation grew nearly as fast as the number sentenced to prison: an increase of 126 percent between 1980 and 1989. By January 1990, more than 2.5 million adults were on probation in the United States (see Table 2–2).[5] Prison overcrowding virtually guarantees increases in the probation population.

WHAT IS PROBATION?

Although there are no authoritative classifications by law, probation may be generally classified in four categories:[6]

1. regular probation
2. intensive supervision probation
3. deferred adjudication probation
4. pretrial diversion probation

Regular Probation

Regular probation:

The release of a convicted offender by a court under court-imposed conditions for a specified period during which the imposition or execution of sentence is suspended.

Regular Probation can be defined as the release of a convicted offender under conditions imposed by the court for a specified period during which the court retains authority to modify the conditions of sentence or to resentence the offender if he or she violates the conditions. Regular probation is used in both misdemeanor and felony cases and is the type most often used, accounting for about 90 percent of all probation sentences.

Intensive Supervision Probation

Intensive supervision probation (ISP):

A form of probation for offenders who require more structure and surveillance than ordinary probationers but for whom incarceration may be too severe a sanction. ISP involves considerable restrictions on the offender's freedom of movement and limits many other aspects of his/her autonomy.

Intensive supervision probation (ISP) programs, for offenders who are too antisocial for the relative freedom afforded by regular probation yet not so seriously criminal to require incarceration, have sprung up around the country since 1980.[7] Intensive supervision probation, in some form, had been adopted in 40 states by 1990.[8] (See Table 2–3.) Although ISP was originally designed to enhance rehabilitation and/or to ensure public safety by affording greater contact between probation officers and probationers, the purposes of

TABLE 2-1

State and Federal Prisoners, 1990–1991

	TOTAL			SENTENCED TO MORE THAN 1 YEAR			
REGION AND JURISDICTION	1991	1990	Percent change, 1990–91	1991	1990	Percent change, 1990–91	Incarceration rate, 1991*
U.S. total	823,414	773,124	6.5%	789,261	739,142	6.8%	310
Federal	71,608	65,526	9.3	56,696	50,403	12.5	22
State	751,806	707,598	6.2	732,565	688,739	6.4	287
Northeast	131,813	123,392	6.8%	127,934	119,063	7.5%	248
Connecticut	10,977	10,500	4.5	8,585	7,771	10.5	262
Maine	1,621	1,523	6.4	1,600	1,480	8.1	127
Massachusetts	9,058	8,273	9.5	8,998	7,899	13.9	150
New Hampshire	1,533	1,342	14.2	1,533	1,342	14.2	132
New Jersey	23,483	21,128	11.1	23,483	21,128	11.1	300
New York	57,862	54,895	5.4	57,862	54,895	5.4	319
Pennsylvania	23,388	22,290	4.9	23,386	22,281	5.0	192
Rhode Island	2,772	2,392	15.9	1,749	1,586	10.3	172
Vermont	1,119	1,049	6.7	738	681	8.4	125
Midwest	155,469	145,793	6.6%	155,140	145,480	6.6%	254
Illinois	29,115	27,516	5.8	29,115	27,516	5.8	246
Indiana	13,008	12,736	2.1	12,876	12,615	2.1	226
Iowa	4,145	3,967	4.5	4,145	3,967	4.5	144
Kansas	5,903	5,777	2.2	5,903	5,777	2.2	230
Michigan	36,423	34,267	6.3	36,423	34,267	6.3	387
Minnesota	3,472	3,176	9.3	3,472	3,176	9.3	78
Missouri	15,411	14,943	3.1	15,411	14,943	3.1	294
Nebraska	2,506	2,403	4.3	2,389	2,286	4.5	146
North Dakota	492	483	1.9	441	435	1.4	68
Ohio	35,750	31,822	12.3	35,750	31,822	12.3	323
South Dakota	1,374	1,341	2.5	1,374	1,341	2.5	190
Wisconsin	7,870	7,362	6.9	7,841	7,335	6.9	158
South	301,265	284,029	6.1%	291,807	275,217	6.0%	332
Alabama	16,760	15,665	7.0	16,400	15,365	6.7	392
Arkansas	7,709	6,766	13.9	7,667	6,718	14.1	314
Delaware	3,721	3,471	7.2	2,406	2,241	7.4	342
District of Col.	10,251	9,947	3.1	6,893	6,798	1.4	1,168
Florida	46,533	44,387	4.8	46,531	44,380	4.8	346
Georgia	23,644	22,345	5.8	22,859	21,605	5.8	342
Kentucky	9,799	9,023	8.6	9,799	9,023	8.6	261
Louisiana	20,464	18,599	10.0	20,307	18,599	9.2	466
Maryland	19,291	17,848	8.1	17,824	16,734	6.5	366
Mississippi	9,070	8,375	8.3	8,848	8,084	9.5	335
North Carolina	18,899	18,411	2.7	18,288	17,764	2.9	270
Oklahoma	13,376	12,285	8.9	13,376	12,285	8.9	414
South Carolina	18,312	17,319	5.7	17,173	16,208	6.0	473
Tennessee	11,502	10,388	10.7	11,502	10,388	10.7	227
Texas	51,677	50,042	3.3	51,677	50,042	3.3	297
Virginia	18,755	17,593	6.6	18,755	17,418	7.7	297
West Virginia	1,502	1,565	–4.0	1,502	1,565	–4.0	82
West	163,259	154,384	5.7%	157,684	148,979	5.8%	290
Alaska	2,720	2,622	3.7	1,841	1,851	–.5	344
Arizona	15,415	14,261	8.1	14,843	13,781	7.7	398
California	101,808	97,309	4.6	98,515	94,122	4.7	320
Colorado	8,347	7,671	8.8	8,347	7,671	8.8	247
Hawaii	2,688	2,533	6.1	1,979	1,708	15.9	172
Idaho	2,211	1,961	12.7	2,211	1,961	12.7	212
Montana	1,478	1,425	3.7	1,478	1,425	3.7	182
Nevada	5,879	5,322	10.5	5,879	5,322	10.5	477
New Mexico	3,119	3,187	–2.1	3,016	3,067	–1.7	191
Oregon	6,760	6,492	4.1	6,760	6,492	4.1	229
Utah	2,624	2,496	5.1	2,605	2,474	5.3	149
Washington	9,156	7,995	14.5	9,156	7,995	14.5	183
Wyoming	1,054	1,110	–5.0	1,054	1,110	–5.0	225

SOURCE: "Prisoners in 1991," *Bureau of Justice Statistics Bulletin*, May 1992.

T A B L E 2–2

Adults on Probation, 1990

REGION AND JURISDICTION	PROBATION POPULATION, 1/1/90	NUMBER ON PROBATION ON 12/31/90 PER 100,000 ADULT RESIDENTS
U.S. total	2,521,525	1,443
Federal	59,106	31
State	2,462,419	1,411
Northeast	449,418	1,198
Connecticut	42,842	1,838
Maine	6,851	821
Massachusetts	88,529	1,554
New Hampshire	2,991	379
New Jersey	64,398	1,220
New York	136,686	1,058
Pennsylvania	89,491	1,071
Rhode Island	12,231	1,975
Vermont	5,399	1,408
Midwest	538,394	1,289
Illinois	93,944	1,128
Indiana	61,177	1,680
Iowa	13,722	675
Kansas	21,675	1,222
Michigan	122,459	1,952
Minnesota	58,648	1,849
Missouri	44,158	1,113
Nebraska	12,627	1,275
North Dakota	1,644	374
Ohio	78,299	1,036
South Dakota	2,757	635
Wisconsin	27,284	815
South	984,909	1,643
Alabama	25,519	928
Arkansas	15,552	924
Delaware	9,701	2,430
District of Columbia	10,132	1,988
Florida	192,731	2,093
Georgia	125,147	2,838
Kentucky	8,062	274
Louisiana	32,295	1,009
Maryland	84,456	2,291
Mississippi	7,333	450
North Carolina	72,325	1,550
Oklahoma	24,240	1,057
South Carolina	31,623	1,258
Tennessee	30,906	894
Texas	291,156	2,538
Virginia	19,085	455
West Virginia	4,646	375
West	489,698	1,385
Alaska	3,335	952
Arizona	27,340	1,133
California	284,437	1,389
Colorado	28,037	1,279
Hawaii	10,960	1,409
Idaho	4,025	627
Montana	3,459	702
Nevada	7,065	851
New Mexico	5,660	589
Oregon	31,878	1,777
Utah	5,524	532
Washington	74,918	2,353
Wyoming	3,060	937

SOURCE: Adapted from "Probation and Parole, 1990," *Bureau of Justice Statistics Bulletin*, November 1991.

TABLE 2-3

Estimated Number of Adults on Probation and Parole Under Intensive Supervision and Electronic Monitoring, 1990

REPORTING JURISDICTION	PROBATION		PAROLE	
	Intensive supervision	Electronic monitoring	Intensive supervision	Electronic monitoring
U.S. total	55,722	7,868	16,787	1,385
Federal	0	85	. . .	/
State	55,722	7,783	16,787	1,385
Alabama	705	91	5	144
Alaska	0	0	15	. . .
Arizona	2,232	127	. . .	116
Arkansas	0	0	66	. . .
California	/	/	7,207	40
Colorado	1,015	248	. . .	45
Connecticut	160	6	10	2
Delaware	951	93	100	10
District of Columbia	100	0	198	. . .
Florida	11,215	1,312	. . .	. . .
Georgia	2,820	0	422	. . .
Hawaii	22	6	70	11
Idaho	141	0	/	/
Illinois	660	/	49	41
Indiana	111	983	. . .	. . .
Iowa	/	/	269	60
Kentucky	506	0	883	. . .
Louisiana	50	6	/	/
Maine	95	10	. . .	. . .
Maryland	151	0	541	. . .
Massachusetts	0	0	34	. . .
Michigan	1,128	1,801	. . .	/
Mississippi	244	0	112	. . .
Missouri	460	96	. . .	38
Montana	35	19	8	. . .
Nebraska	45	45	37	1
Nevada	718	25	912	8
New Hampshire	25	10	41	1
New Jersey	572	263	373	49
New Mexico	270	135	54	27
New York	3,400	/	. . .	16
North Carolina	1,452	704	437	124
Ohio	2,341	358	. . .	. . .
Oregon	1,033	380	65	. . .
Pennsylvania	10,400	200	1,397	223
Rhode Island	0	0	. . .	23
South Carolina	1,824	0	426	. . .
South Dakota	50	0	64	. . .
Tennessee	735	280	. . .	. . .
Texas	7,124	463	2,110	306
Utah	140	0	199	38
Vermont	230	0	34	. . .
Virginia	327	0	426	6
Washington	1,996	50	. . .	. . .
Wisconsin	222	55	222	55
Wyoming	17	17	1	1

Note: Counts of persons under intensive supervision reported by some states include persons under electronic monitoring. Some jurisdictions were unable to provide separate counts of parole and probation populations under intensive supervision. The following states reported either not having persons under intensive supervision and electronic monitoring or not knowing their number: Kansas, Minnesota, North Dakota, and Oklahoma.

. . .No program.

/ Jurisdiction did not know.

SOURCE: "Probation and Parole, 1990," *Bureau of Justice Statistics Bulletin*, November 1990.

Electronic surveillance:

Electronic monitoring is a correctional technology that involves the wearing, by a probationer or parolee, of an electronic device that allows authorities to verify his or her wherabouts.

Deferred adjudication:

A form of probation which, after a plea of guilty or *nolo contendere,* defers further proceedings without an adjudication of guilt.

Pretrial diversion:

A form of probation imposed before a plea of guilt that can result in dismissal of the charges. Pretrial diversion is used primarily with offenders who need treatment or supervision and for whom criminal sanctions would be excessive.

Net-widening:

The tendency for social-control mechanisms to encompass a larger (or a different) population than originally planned.

newer programs include those of reducing costs and alleviating prison overcrowding. Intensive supervision programs are also seen as "socially cost-effective," in that they are less likely to contribute to the breakup of offenders' families than incarceration, they allow offenders to remain employed, and they lack the stigmatizing effects of prison. Although ISP programs vary from jurisdiction to jurisdiction, most require multiple weekly contacts with probation officers, random night and weekend visits, unscheduled drug testing, and strict enforcement of probation conditions. Many require community service restitution and some form of electronic surveillance.[9]

Probation officers who work with ISP clients generally have smaller caseloads than those with regular probation clients. Smaller caseloads allow for greater assistance to the probationer in his or her rehabilitation efforts and greater protection to the community through increased surveillance and control. One writer has observed that ISP is what most communities want all probation to be.[10] A more detailed discussion of intensive supervision appears in Chapter 12.

Deferred Adjudication

Most states and the federal system also provide for **deferred adjudication** under the general probation statutes. In this form of probation, the court, after a plea of guilty or *nolo contendere* (French "do not wish to contend"), defers further proceedings without entering an adjudication of guilt and places the defendant on probation, usually ordering some form of community service and/or restitution. Defendants who successfully complete the probation term have their charges dropped. Failure to comply with the terms of the deferred adjudication agreement may result in incarceration.

Pretrial Diversion

Pretrial diversion is another form of probation authorized by most state statutes and in the federal system. Criminal sanctions would be excessive for many persons who come to the attention of the criminal justice system because of their need for treatment or supervision.[11] Programs that provide these needed services without the stigma of criminal prosecution have proved quite attractive. Pretrial diversion is like deferred adjudication in that there is no finding of guilt. The difference is that probation is imposed *before* a plea of guilty in pretrial diversion, whereas deferred adjudication is imposed after a plea of guilty or *nolo contendere.*[12] Howard Abadinsky notes that pretrial diversion has been criticized based on research indicating that many persons who are diverted would not have been arrested or prosecuted in the first place were it not for the existence of a diversion program. Such **net-widening** increases the number of persons involved in the criminal justice system.[13]

THE DECISION TO GRANT PROBATION

Sentencing

Sentencing has long been considered the most difficult decision in the criminal justice process. **Sentencing** can be defined as the postconviction stage of the criminal process in which the defendant is brought before the court for the imposition of a sentence. A **sentence** is the formal judgment pronounced by a court or a judge after conviction that imposes some degree of punishment. Problems abound when the issue of fair, just sentencing is addressed. Sentencing demands making a choice from among a number of alternatives. Figure 2–1 shows the proportion of felony arrests that typically result in a sentence and the distribution of the sentences among the alternatives.

In many cases judges select sentences that involve a term of imprisonment or that sentence the offender to probation supervision. Probation may be supplemented with incarceration in some jurisdictions. In this chapter we examine the factors that go into decisions to grant probation. Sentencing decisions may be the most important decisions made in the criminal justice process. They are affected by the judge's sentencing philosophy, the types of

Sentencing:

The postconviction stage of the criminal process in which the defendant is brought before the court for the imposition of a sentence.

Sentence:

The formal judgment pronounced by a court or a judge after conviction that imposes some degree of punishment.

FIGURE 2–1

Typical Outcome of 100 Felony Arrests Brought by Police for Prosecution

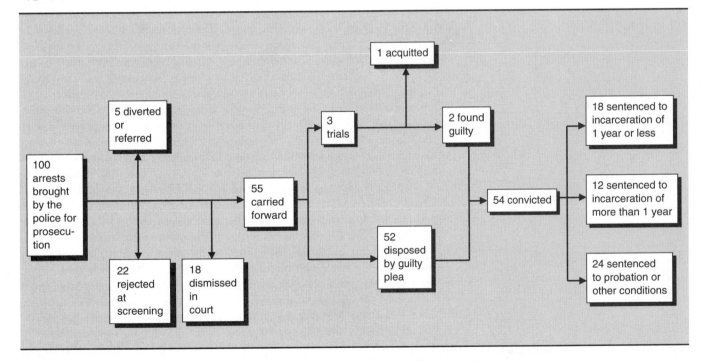

SOURCE: Bureau of Justice Statistics. *The Prosecution of Felony Arrests, 1986* (Washington, D.C.: USGPO, June 1989), cover page.

sentences available, plea bargaining between the defendant and the prosecutor, recommendations of probation officers, and many other factors. The Supplemental Reading at the end of the chapter provides an excellent discussion of sentencing philosophy and other factors that affect sentencing in general.

Factors that Affect the Probation Grant

The decision to grant probation to an individual offender must consider such factors as:

- the offender's eligibility for probation
- whether probation or incarceration is the preferred disposition
- the conditions of probation as fixed by statute
- the availability and quality of probation services
- the availability and quality of other sentencing dispositions
- the methods of developing sentencing information
- whether probation is appropriate for the offender

ELIGIBILITY FOR PROBATION. Courts have consistently held that probation is a *privilege,* not a right. The **privilege theory** considers probation a matter of grace and places the question of whether it should be granted in a particular instance entirely with the court. To phrase it differently, the decision to grant or withhold probation is a discretionary act of the trial court, and an offender has neither a constitutional nor statutory right to probation. Statutes provide for probation, however, and an eligible offender has the right to be *considered* for it. When the statute provides that a class of offenders is to be considered for probation, the defendant is entitled to fair treatment and is not to be made the victim of whim or caprice. Thus, it has been held that a judge was in error for considering probation only for defendants who pleaded guilty and for refusing to consider probation for a defendant who pleaded not guilty and stood trial. The court in the one case pointed out that there is nothing to bar the judge who entertains an application for probation from considering (among other things) whether the defendant pleaded guilty or stood trial, especially when the defendant has presented only a frivolous defense. The error occurred when the judge refused to consider as a class all defendants who had stood trial.[14] A judge who announced that he could "never grant probation to a drug pusher," committed a similar error.[15]

States sometimes legislate restrictions on the use of probation. Restrictions on eligibility tend to be of the nature of declaring ineligible defendants convicted of certain specified offenses (usually crimes of violence), those upon whom a term longer than a specified number of years is assessed, and those with a prior felony conviction. New York, for example, precludes probation for anyone with a prior felony conviction. Minnesota sentencing guidelines, on the other hand, direct judges to grant probation for persons convicted of larceny regardless of their prior convictions and requires judges who depart from the guidelines to justify the sentence. Generally, probation is more likely to be granted to first-time offenders who have committed less serious offenses. A survey of felony convictions in 1988 in the nation's 75 largest counties found that 37 percent of defendants with no prior felony convictions received probation, compared to 15 percent of repeat offenders.[16] However, some observers have noted that more and more serious felony offenders are being placed on probation due to plea bargaining and because of prison overcrowding.[17]

Federal statutes provide that probation may be used as an alternative to incarceration where the terms and conditions of probation can be fashioned so as to meet fully the statutory purposes of sentencing, including promoting respect for law, providing just punishment for the offense, achieving general deterrence, and protecting the public from further crime by the defendant.

PROBATION AS THE PREFERRED DISPOSITION. In jurisdictions where the ordinary and expected form of disposition of the offender is commitment to an institution, the problem is to meet criteria for *granting* probation. In jurisdictions where probation is deemed to be the preferred and expected disposition of the offender, the problem is to meet criteria for *denying* probation. With regard to adult offenders, the former type of sentencing statute is more frequently found. However, model statutes and standards for probation emphasize the latter type of statute and recommend that sentencing statutes provide that probation is preferable to incarceration, which should be ordered only when the welfare of the offender or the safety of society clearly demonstrates the need for withholding probation and sentencing imprisonment.[18] Statutes relating to juvenile probation have always tended to be of the second type. The objective in juvenile courts is to avoid institutionalizing the juvenile if possible. Thus, probation, suspension of judgment, or specialized placement are the most frequent court dispositions.

The criteria for probation are often stated in general terms. The California statute, for example, provides that "[i]f the court shall determine that there are circumstances in mitigation of punishment prescribed by law, or that the ends of justice would be subserved by granting probation to the defendant, the court shall have the power in its discretion to place the defendant on probation as hereinafter provided."[19]

New York follows its general statement with more specific criteria. Probation is allowed if the court is of the opinion that institutional confinement of the defendant is not necessary for the protection of the public; the defendant is in need of guidance, training, or other assistance, which, in the defendant's case, can be effectively administered through probation; and such disposition is not inconsistent with the ends of justice.[20]

The **Model Penal Code,** consistent with its position that the preferred sentence is either suspension of imposition of sentence or probation, requires an affirmative finding that imprisonment is necessary for protecting the public before imprisonment is allowed and lists detailed criteria that are to be accorded weight in favor of withholding sentence of imprisonment.[21]

The **American Bar Association Standards relating to Probation** also proceed from the premise that a sentence not involving total confinement is to be preferred in the absence of affirmative reasons to the contrary.[22] The *Standards* emphasize that probation decisions should not turn on generalizations about types of offenses or the existence of a prior criminal record, but

Model Penal Code:

A code developed (1950–62) by the American Law Institute as a simpler, more consistent statement of the law that states could use as a model, if they wished, whenever they undertook to revise or modernize their criminal codes.

American Bar Association Standards:

The ABA's *Minimum Standards for Criminal Justice,* which includes its were Standards relating to Probation, was developed after a thorough study of the U.S. criminal justice system. The resulting *Standards* made far-reaching recommendations for changes in all aspects of criminal justice.

should be rooted in the facts and circumstances of each case. The court should consider the nature and circumstances of the crime, the history and character of the offender, and available institutional and community resources. According to the *Standards,* probation should be the sentence *unless:*

1. The sentencing court finds that confinement is necessary to protect the public from further criminal activity by the offender.
2. The offender is in need of correctional treatment that can be most effectively provided if the offender is confined.
3. It would unduly deprecate the seriousness of the offense if a sentence of probation were imposed.

Whether the defendant pleads guilty, pleads not guilty, or intends to appeal is not relevant to the issue of whether probation is an appropriate sentence.[23]

The **National Advisory Commission on Criminal Justice Standards and Goals** proposed criteria for sentencing the nondangerous offender that give preference to probation over commitment.[24] The pattern is to list the permissible disposition on an ascending scale, from least serious to most serious disposition. The court would be required to impose the first of the alternatives that would reasonably protect the public safety. The record of the court must show affirmative justification for confinement.

CONDITIONS OF PROBATION FIXED BY STATUTE.   The conditions of probation as fixed by statute also must be considered in the probation-granting decision. If the presentence information about the defendant shows that he or she cannot meet the statutory conditions that must be imposed, then it is useless to grant probation.

An example that readily comes to mind is that of the chronic alcoholic whose past history indicates an inability to abstain from intoxicating beverages. Yet, the nature of the crime may require as a condition of probation complete abstinence from the use of alcohol. Such a situation imposes both legal and practical dilemmas on the court. Has the court the right to assume out-of-hand that this time the defendant "won't make it" simply because he or she has been unable to abstain on previous occasions? Conversely, can the court ignore the intractable nature of alcoholism, the lack of treatment facilities, and the discouraging statistics about "cures." In such a situation, the court's duty is probably to take all the factors into consideration, to assign such weight to each factor as in its best judgment the situation seems to require, and then to grant or withhold probation accordingly.

To avoid confronting the court with dilemmas of this sort, many authorities recommend that statutes refrain from making specific conditions for probation, leaving the matter open for the judge to exercise judgment based on the most up-to-date information that can be obtained by competent presentence investigations about the defendant and available treatment facilities and programs.

AVAILABILITY AND QUALITY OF PROBATION SERVICES.   The decision to grant probation is also affected by the availability and quality of community and probation services. A judge may consider it useless to grant probation if there are no organized probation services in the locality, if the

The **National Advisory Commission on Criminal Justice Standards and Goals** was appointed in 1971 by the administrator of the now-defunct Law Enforcement Assistance Administration (LEAP) to formulate national criminal justice standards and goals for crime reduction at state and local levels. In 1973 the Commission published its recommended guidelines covering all aspects of criminal justice practice.

probation department gives no supervision whatever to the misdemeanant placed on probation, or if the probation officers' caseloads are so large that meaningful and consistent supervision is not possible. On the other hand, efficient and effective probation services may be overused. At a time when the Miami juvenile probation department was widely acclaimed for its successes, parents became overeager to use its services. One officer was heard to remark ruefully, "The parents call us now if Junior refuses to take the garbage out in the morning."

The organizational structure of probation services and the training and ability of the probation officers are important determinants of the availability and quality of probation services.[25] In some states, probation is a part of the judicial branch of government, whereas in others it is part of the executive branch. Probation may be administered on a local or statewide basis and may or may not be combined with parole services. Juvenile and adult probation may be under a single administration, or they may be in separate departments. The trend seems to be toward the establishment of statewide probation departments in the executive branch of government.[26] This structure provides greater uniformity of services statewide and allows for standardization of services, training, and probation-officer qualifications. Until the mid 1970s probation services in Texas were administered entirely by county governments. This structure created a patchwork of service availability and quality. Some counties provided high-quality, well-funded probation services with qualified and trained officers. A much larger number of counties provided only minimal services, and their officers did not meet even the most basic level of education or training. More recently, however, the state's probation services have been standardized through the creation of a statewide agency with power to establish standards for education, training, and services and through a provision for state funding to assist local communities in improving and expanding their services. This organizational change has made probation services more uniformly available as a dispositional alternative.

Quality of probation service is also determined by the qualifications required of probation officers. These vary widely from place to place, even when minimum qualifications are set out in the probation statute. One state has very stringent qualification requirements and will certify only those persons who have successfully completed a baccalaureate degree at an accredited college or university and can document two years' full-time paid employment with juveniles or adults in responsible probation or correctional work or other appropriate social welfare work. For a long time this state had no minimum statutory qualifications for juvenile probation officers, except that they be persons of good character. The American Bar Association *Standards* suggest that a minimum qualification should be possession of a bachelor's degree supplemented by a year of graduate study in social work, corrections, counseling, law, criminology, psychology, sociology, or a related field (or by a year of full-time casework; counseling with community, correctional, or juvenile agencies; and dealing with offenders or disadvantaged persons). Further, a significant number of probation officers in a department should have a graduate degree in one of the subjects enumerated. These qualifications do not preclude the use of citizen or lay volunteers to assist qualified probation officers.[27]

Unfortunately, neither statutory requirements nor recommended qualification standards for probation officers assure that adequate probation services will be available to the sentencing court. In many areas, no probation department exists. Under such circumstances it is not uncommon for the judge to act as his own probation officer by setting up conditions and requiring that defendants report to the court at regular intervals. Police and prosecution officials are sometimes pressed into service as unofficial probation officers, although placing released persons in custody of police or prosecution officials is considered an unsound, unwise practice. The American Bar Association recommends that in no case should probation services be vested in an agency having prosecutorial functions.[28] In some cases, probation services are as "primitive" as they were in the days of John Augustus, when supervision over the conditionally released offender was by a concerned citizen, often a member of the clergy.

The use of probation varies widely throughout the country and even within a single state. This is so partially because of the unavailability of probation services, and also because of differing sentencing philosophies and differing degrees of community acceptance and involvement in probation.

A recent study of probation utilization showed that the southern states utilized probation to a greater extent than other areas.[29] The South reported 1,643 probationers per 100,000 adult residents. This ratio surpassed the West (1,385), the Midwest (1,298), and the Northeast (1,198). Georgia reported the highest individual rate of persons on probation (2,838). Texas, Delaware, Washington, Maryland, and Florida also had more than 2,000 persons on probation for every 100,000 adult males in the population. States that utilize probation less generously include New Hampshire (379), Iowa (675), North Dakota (374), Kentucky (274), and West Virginia (375). This suggests that among the factors that determine whether an offender will receive probation or a prison sentence is not only *what* he/she does but *where* he/she does it.

OTHER AVAILABLE SENTENCING DISPOSITIONS. Granting probation also depends upon the availability and quality of other sentencing dispositions. In the past decade state and federal statutes have provided a range of sentencing alternatives, including "boot camps," restitution, community service, monitored home confinement, and intensive supervision programs. These intermediate sanctions have gained approval in the courts and have become popular adjuncts to "regular" probation. Where such programs exist, probation is more widely utilized. Intermediate sanctions are discussed in greater detail in Chapter 12.

The court may also be influenced toward granting probation by its knowledge of overcrowding or deplorable conditions in the adult prison system or of lack of treatment in youth institutions, or by the fact that specialized facilities—such as those needed for sex offenders or narcotic addicts—are not available in the community or in state institutions. Juvenile dispositions are also influenced by the programs being offered in juvenile institutions and, even more, by the lack of juvenile probation services in some areas. The rate of commitment to state juvenile institutions is routinely higher from counties where commitment is the only viable dispositional alternative.

The American Bar Association *Standards relating to Sentencing Alternatives and Procedures* take a strong stand in favor of increasing the dispositional alternatives available to the sentencing judge. The *Standards* state:

> The sentencing court should be provided in all cases with a wide range of alternatives, with gradations of supervisory, supportive, and custodial facilities at its disposal so as to permit a sentence appropriate for each individual case.[30]

The necessity of statewide development of facilities to provide special treatment for certain types of offenders, particularly for the young, is also emphasized.[31]

Increased use of diversion strategies will tend to reduce the use of regular probation, but it may not reduce the need for probation services, since many diversion programs involve probation-type supervision of the offender. An increase in halfway houses, day-care centers, and specialized institutions for the care of alcohol and drug abusers provide the sentencing authority with additional dispositional alternatives, which may tend to reduce the use of probation. On the other hand, making probation the preferred disposition places new burdens on probation services. It is evident that the frequency with which probation and other sentencing dispositions are selected is changing as sentencing philosophy changes and other dispositional alternatives for the care and custody of offenders became available.

METHODS OF DEVELOPING SENTENCING INFORMATION.   The information required to enable a judge to impose an appropriate sentence is developed in a postconviction hearing, a presentence investigation, or in some states, a presentence conference. In the case of jury sentencing, the jury is furnished with information about the defendant's general reputation and character at a sentencing hearing.

If probation is one of the dispositions being considered, there is a particular need for accurate, complete information. Not all offenders can benefit from probation. Some offenders must be incarcerated, either for the public good or because they need specialized treatment that is not available with probation. In some cases, the nature and circumstances of the crime dictate incarceration of the offender, especially if the public's ideas of fairness and justice in the criminal process are to be upheld and vindicated. Granting probation thus demands an investigative process that will inform the sentencing authority of the circumstances of the offense and the nature of the offender.

Of the three methods of obtaining sentencing information, the one most closely identified with the granting of probation is the **presentence investigation report.** In fact, the origins of the presentence investigation can be traced to the use of probation as a disposition. (See Chapter 3, "The Presentence Investigation Report," for a detailed discussion.) In many states, the only time a presentence investigation is required by law is when the offender is to be placed on probation. In such cases the statutory authority and statutory requirements for the presentence investigation and report are contained in the probation statutes. In juvenile court, the judge is routinely furnished with a social history report (also termed *predispositional report*) prior to the dispositional hearing.

Presentence reports are seldom required or used in misdemeanor probation. In some instances, this is because no provision is made for misdemeanor probation. When a presentence report is prepared in a misdemeanor case, it is

Convicted offender exercising his right of allocution at the sentencing hearing.

shorter and more summary in nature. In practice, the judge who sentences for a misdemeanor relies on the police officer for information about the defendant's criminal history and the circumstances of the offense. The defendant is usually given a **right of allocution,** a common law privilege to speak to the question of sentencing. The defendant may also be given the right to submit a written memorandum that sets forth any information that may be pertinent to the question of sentence.

One or more **presentence conferences** may be held to resolve conflicts and discrepancies in sentencing information received by the court and to assist the court in its consideration of the sentence. The ABA *Standards relating to Sentencing Alternatives and Procedures* recommends a presentence conference and the development of a broad range of services and facilities from which the court can obtain more complete information about the defendant's mental, emotional, and physical condition.[32]. The National Advisory Commission *Standards* recommends a sentencing hearing and suggest that it is the duty of defense counsel to become familiar with sentencing alternatives that "most accurately meet the needs of [the] client and enhance his liberty."[33]

APPROPRIATENESS OF PROBATION. Probably the most important factor in the decision to grant probation is whether probation is an appropriate sentence for the particular offender. When probation is a statutory alternative, the decision to grant or deny it is seldom clear-cut. Individualized justice—that noble ideal of the criminal justice system—demands that the penalty fit the criminal as well as the crime. The needs of the offender, the protection of society, and the maintenance of social order must all be carefully weighed. This balancing of the best interests of both the offender and society is the crux of the probation decision process.

Such factors as the offender's age, criminal history, and potential for rehabilitation must be considered in probation decisions. The offender's history of substance abuse, potential for violence, community and family stability, and employment record also affect the judge's choice between prison and probation. Social and political attitudes in a community may affect the decision. The recommendations and advice of police, prosecutors, and victims can be significant considerations. Probation officer recommendations are frequently relied on. Seemingly extraneous factors such as overcrowded prison conditions may be considered. The defendant's attitude toward the offense and the existence or lack of remorse are often weighed in the decision. The judge's own biases, prejudices, and emotional responses toward the crime, the offender, and the victim(s) may affect the decision. In the final analysis, the decision is often subjective, and this has often led to sentencing disparity— markedly different sentences for individuals whose crimes and criminal history are similar.

Sentencing Guidelines

In recent years the advent of **sentencing guidelines** has introduced a completely new variable into the probation grant decision. Sentencing reformers have criticized current sentencing practices as abusive and as rooted in untenable assumptions. Although many different approaches have been suggested, none has yet satisfied the need to reduce or eliminate unjustifiable disparity in sentencing. Just what *does* constitute inequity or unjustified disparity in sentencing? The point is arguable, depending on one's philosophy. One writer has stated that

> "inequity exists when significant differences in sentencing occur which cannot be justified on the basis of the severity of the crime, the defendant's prior criminal history, or characterological considerations which have a demonstrable bearing upon the appropriate penalty or disposition."[34]

According to this, it is not uniformity in sentencing that should be the goal, but rather, a fair and rational approach to arriving at a sentence that allows for variability within a constantly applied framework.

Sentencing guidelines represent attempts to reduce sentencing disparity. Although guideline systems vary greatly from jurisdiction to jurisdiction, they generally establish an "appropriate" sentence based upon the severity of the offense and the offender's criminal history. In some jurisdictions—such as Michigan—use of the guidelines is voluntary—judges are not obligated to follow their recommendations. They merely provide the judge with information about the "usual" sentence for the offense and offender. Judges in some other jurisdictions—such as Minnesota, Pennsylvania, Washington, and the federal courts—have only limited discretion to sentence outside the ranges established by the guidelines. The federal sentencing guidelines, for example, state that if the minimum term of imprisonment specified by the guideline range in the Sentencing Table is more than six months, probation may not be granted. Minnesota's sentencing guidelines are shown in Figure 2–2.

The range and form of the prescribed sentence can vary significantly from state to state, as the cases of Minnesota and Pennsylvania demonstrate. In

Sentencing Guidelines:
Standardized instruments designed to provide clear and explicit direction to the court in determining the appropriate sentence. Guidelines typically consider offense severity and the offender's prior record. A matrix that relates these factors may be used.

FIGURE 2-2

Minnesota Guidelines Grid, Presumptive Sentence Lengths in Months

Severity Level of Conviction Offense		Criminal History Score						
		0	1	2	3	4	5	6 or more
Sale of a Simulated Controlled Substance	I	12*	12*	12*	13	15	17	19 *18–20*
Theft-Related Crimes ($2,500 or less) Check Forgery ($200–$2500)	II	12*	12*	13	15	17	19	21 *20–22*
Theft Crimes ($2,500 or less)	III	12*	13	15	17	19 *18–20*	22 *21–23*	25 *24–26*
Nonresidential Burglary Theft Crimes (over $2,500)	IV	12*	15	18	21	25 *24–26*	32 *30–34*	41 *37–45*
Residential Burglary Simple Robbery	V	18	23	27	30 *29–31*	38 *36–40*	46 *43–49*	54 *50–58*
Criminal Sexual Conduct 2nd Degree (a) & (b)	VI	21	26	30	34 *33–35*	44 *42–46*	54 *50–58*	65 *60–70*
Aggravated Robbery	VII	48 *44–52*	58 *54–62*	68 *64–72*	78 *74–82*	88 *84–92*	98 *94–102*	108 *104–112*
Criminal Sexual Conduct, 1st Degree Assault, 1st Degree	VIII	86 *81–91*	98 *93–103*	110 *105–115*	122 *117–127*	134 *129–139*	146 *141–151*	158 *153–163*
Murder, 3rd Degree Murder, 2nd Degree (felony murder)	IX	150 *144–156*	165 *159–171*	180 *174–186*	195 *189–201*	210 *204–216*	225 *219–231*	240 *234–246*
Murder, 2nd Degree (with intent)	X	306 *299–313*	326 *319–333*	346 *339–353*	366 *359–373*	386 *379–393*	406 *399–413*	426 *419–433*

▨ At the discretion of the judge, up to a year in jail and/or other nonjail sanctions can be imposed as conditions of probation.

▨ Presumptive commitment to state imprisonment.

First-degree murder is excluded from the guidelines by law and continues to have a mandatory life sentence. See section II.E, Mandatory Sentences, for policy regarding those sentences controlled by law.

*One year and one day.

Italicized numbers within the grid denote the range within which a judge may sentence without the sentence being deemed a departure.

Offenders with nonimprisonment felony sentences are subject to jail time according to law.

SOURCE: Minnesota Sentencing Guidelines Commission, *Report to the Legislature, 1990*, Figure 2.2.

Minnesota, probation is the recommended sentence for most property crimes when the offender's criminal history is not extensive. Pennsylvania guidelines, in contrast, generally specify nonconfinement only for misdemeanor offenses when mitigating circumstances are involved. For normal misdemeanor cases, minimum ranges of zero to six or zero to twelve months are specified, regardless of offenders' prior records. Furthermore, Minnesota sentencing guidelines provide judges with a relatively narrow sentence range for a given severity level of offense and a given criminal history score. From this range, one fixed term is chosen. Pennsylvania sentencing guidelines, however, are broad and they specify a minimum range, an aggravated minimum range, and a mitigated minimum range from which the judge chooses a minimum term (the maximum term being set by statute).

A sentencing commission in each jurisdiction monitors the use of the guidelines and departures from the recommended sentences by the judiciary. Written explanations are required from judges who depart from guidelines ranges. The Minnesota Sentencing Commission rules state that although the sentencing guidelines are "advisory" to the sentencing judge, departures from their established presumptive sentences should occur only when substantial, compelling circumstances exist. Pennsylvania sentencing guidelines stipulate that court failure to explain sentences deviating from the recommendations is grounds for vacating the sentence and resentencing the defendant. Furthermore, if the court does not consider the guidelines or it inaccurately or inappropriately applies them, an imposed sentence may be vacated upon appeal to a higher court by either the defense or the prosecution.

Summary

Since 1970 the number and rate of offenders sentenced to prison have increased alarmingly. As the nation's prisons have become critically overcrowded, courts have been forced to consider alternative sentences. Probation has emerged as a viable alternative. In fact, the number of persons sentenced to probation has expanded nearly as fast as the number sentenced to prison—increasing 126 percent between 1980 and 1990. Probation may generally be classified into four categories: regular probation, intensive supervision probation, deferred prosecution probation, and pretrial diversion probation. Each category of probation is regarded as appropriate for specific types of offenders. The decision to grant probation to an individual offender must consider many factors, one of the most critical being the jurisdiction's and/or the judge's philosophy of sentencing. Historically, sentencing has been influenced by philosophical justifications based on retribution, incapacitation, deterrence, rehabilitation and "just deserts." The extent to which probation is utilized in a jurisdiction is, at least, partially determined by these considerations. Other factors include the eligibility of the individual offender for probation as fixed by statute, whether probation or imprisonment is the preferred disposition, the conditions of probation as fixed by statute, the availability and quality of probation services, the availability and quality of other sentencing dispositions, the methods of developing sentencing information, and whether probation is appropriate for the particular offender. The use of sentencing guidelines is another variable recently introduced into the decision-making to reduce sentencing inequality and thus to ensure fairness.

ENDNOTES

1. Bureau of Justice Statistics, "Prisoners in 1991," *Bulletin,* May 1992. United States Department of Justice.

2. *Id.*

3. Joan Petersilia, Susan Turner, James Kahan, and Joyce Peterson, *Granting Felons Probation: Public Risks and Alternatives* (Santa Monica, Calif.: Rand Corporation, January 1985).

4. *Id.* at v.

5. Bureau of Justice Statistics, *supra* note 1, at 9.

6. Rolando del Carmen, Betsy Witt, Thomas Caywood, and Sally Layland, *Probation Law and Practice in Texas* (Criminal Justice Center, Sam Houston State University, 1989), pp. 29–35.

7. Petersilia et al., *supra,* at iv.

8. Bureau of Justice Statistics, "Probation and Parole, 1990," *Bulletin,* November 1990.

9. Joan Petersilia, *Expanding Options for Criminal Sentencing* (Santa Monica, Calif.: Rand Corporation, November 1987).

10. Alan Schuman, "The Cost of Correctional Services: Exploring a Poorly Charted Terrain," *Research in Corrections* 2, no. 1 (1989), pp. 27–34.

11. President's Commission on Law Enforcement and Administration of Justice, *The Challenge of Crime in a Free Society* (1967).

12. del Carmen et al., *supra* note 6, at 35.

13. Howard Abadinsky, *Probation and Parole: Theory and Practice,* 4th ed. (Englewood Cliffs, N.J.: Prentice Hall, 1991).

14. United States v. Wiley, 267 F.2d 453 (7th Cir.1959), *on remand* 184 F. Supp. 679 (N.D.Ill.E.D. 1960).

15. See also Burns v. United States, 287 U.S. 216, 53 S. Ct. 154, 77 L.Ed. 266 (1932).

16. Patrick A. Langan, and Mark Cunniff, "Recidivism of Felons on Probation, 1986–1989," *Bureau of Justice Statistics Special Report,* February 1992.

17. Richard W. Snarr, *Introduction to Corrections,* 2nd ed. (Dubuque, Ia.: Wm. C. Brown Publishers, 1992).

18. See Model Penal Code and American Bar Association, *Standards relating to Probation* (New York: American Bar Association, 1970).

19. Cal.Penal Code, § 1203 (West).

20. N.Y. Penal Law § 65.00-1 (McKinney).

21. Model Penal Code § 7.01—Criteria for Withholding Sentence of Imprisonment and for Placing Defendant on Probation.

22. ABA, *supra* note 18.

23. *Id.,* § 1.3.

24. National Advisory Commission, *Standards, Corrections,* Standard 5.2—Sentencing the Nondangerous Offender.

25. For a more detailed discussion of this subject, see Chapter 5, *infra,* Organization and Administration of Probation Services.

26. NACS, *supra* note 24, Standard 10.1—Organization of Probation.

27. ABA, *supra* note 18, § 6.5.

28. *Id.,* § 6.1(b).

29. Louis Jankowski, "Probation and Parole, 1990," *BJS Bulletin,* November 1991.

30. ABA, *Standards, Sentencing Alternatives and Procedures,* § 2.1(b).

31. *Id.,* § 2.6.

32. NACS, *supra* note 24, Standard 10.05—Probation and Release on Recognizance Programs.

33. NACS, *supra* note 24, Standard 5.18—Sentencing Hearing: Role of Counsel.

34. James D. Stanfiel, "Criminal Justice Decision Making: Discretion vs. Equity," *Federal Probation,* June 1983.

Discussion Questions

1. What has been the effect of prison overcrowding on the utilization of probation?

2. How do probation and deferred adjudication differ? How are they alike?

3. Discuss "net-widening". How does it relate to pretrial diversion programs?

4. Discuss the "right" versus the "privilege" theory of probation.

5. What should be the purpose of sentencing—rehabilitation, deterrence, incapacitation, or retribution?

6. Is it more important that sentences be consistent, or that they be individualized to the characteristics and needs of particular offenders?

7. What are sentencing guidelines? How might they affect the probation grant decision?

8. What are the two positions with regard to criteria for granting or withholding probation? Which position is more prevalent in practice? Which position is recommended by both the Model Penal Code and the American Bar Association? Explain your position on this issue.

9. What major factors determine the availability and quality of probation services? How might the existence of highly professional services result in "overuse" of the justice system?

10. In your opinion, should probation services be administered on a local or a statewide basis? Should they be provided by the executive or judicial branch of government? Ask a judge or probation administrator in your area for his or her opinion on this issue.

11. How might the availability and quality of other sentencing dispositions affect the probation grant decision? Give examples.

12. What are the three major methods by which a judge obtains sentencing information? Which do you believe is the most useful in establishing just and fair sentences? Why?

SUPPLEMENTAL READING

Sentencing

HISTORICAL BACKGROUND

Sentencing is the process by which judges impose punishment on persons convicted of crimes. The punishments imposed may range from probation without conditions to the death penalty and also include fines, community service, probation with conditions, and incarceration in jail or prison.

For most of the 20th century, all U.S. jurisdictions had "indeterminate" sentencing systems. Criminal statutes generally authorized judges to impose a sentence from within a wide range. Probation to 5 years was a common range; probation to 25 years was not unknown. The judge's decision was usually final; appellate courts seldom considered appeals from sentencing decisions.

For defendants sentenced to prison, the judge's sentence set the outer limits, but a parole board would decide when the offender was released. The judge might have imposed a "3-to-10-year sentence," but the parole boards often had authority to release after 1 year, or after the offender had served a designated fraction (often one third) of the sentence. Thus, whether the offender served 1 year in prison, or 3, or 5, was generally up to the parole board.

This system was called *indeterminate* because the prisoner's actual time in prison would not be known, or determined, until final release by the parole board. The system of indeterminate sentencing could be justified on a number of bases, but its primary theoretical rationale was that it permitted sentencing and parole release decisions to be individualized, often on the basis of the offender's rehabilitative progress or prospects.

Criminologists long accepted the view that an offender's criminal misbehavior could be analogized to a disease, which could be cured if properly treated in a proper institution. Cure became a major goal of both sentencing and incarceration; when released, the offender would enjoy a more satisfying, productive, and lawful life; he would not commit additional crimes,

and everyone's interests would be served. This medical model of disease and cure required that offenders be returned to the free world when professionals judged that they were "cured."

Treatment programs were seen as essential, and both vocational and psychological training programs were introduced into prisons. This rehabilitative outlook shaped even the vocabulary of criminal punishment. Prisons were often called "correctional" institutions; those for young adults were often called "reformatories." Indeterminate sentencing survived for so long because it could be many things to different people. For those not enamored of rehabilitation, its capacity for individualizing punishment meant that offenders seen as dangerous could be held for lengthy periods and thereby be *incapacitated*. For those concerned with *retribution,* indeterminate sentencing allowed sentences to be individualized on the basis of an assessment of each offender's unique circumstances and degree of moral guilt. Finally, the threat and possibilities of severe sentences could be seen as a *deterrent* to crime.

The discretions of judges and parole boards were exercised without legislative direction as to which sentencing goals were primary, or which factors should be considered in setting sentences or determining parole release. Different judges in the same courthouse could consider the same factor as either mitigating or aggravating the defendant's culpability. Thus, for example, while one judge might consider drug addiction as a mitigating factor that justified reducing the offender's sentence, another judge or parole board member might consider such information an indicator of future criminality, and a reason to increase the sentence.

RECENT CHANGES IN SENTENCING

By 1970, indeterminate sentencing had come under attack. Some critics claimed that the wide, unreviewable discretions of judges and parole boards resulted in discrimination against minorities and the poor. Some were concerned about unwarranted sentencing disparities. Because sentences could not be appealed, there was nothing a prisoner could do about a disparately severe sentence. A considerable body of research demonstrated the existence of unwarranted sentencing disparities, and many believed them to be inherent in indeterminate sentencing. In addition, highly publicized reviews of research on treatment programs concluded that their effectiveness could not be demonstrated; the resulting skepticism about rehabilitative programs undermined one of indeterminate sentencing's foundations.

None of these critiques of indeterminate sentencing was uncontroverted. Supporters of treatment programs argued that such programs could and do succeed, or that the evaluation research was flawed, or that programs failed because they were poorly managed, or underfunded, or targeted on the wrong categories of offenders. Judges, but not only judges, argued that sentencing disparities were not as great a problem as critics contended. First, because judges were able to consider all factors characterizing the offender, the offense, and the offender's prior criminal record, many judges argued that most sentences were soundly based and only appeared disparate. Second, because individual judges inevitably hold different opinions and values, and have different beliefs about the purpose of punishment, their sentences properly might reflect those differences.

The critics of indeterminate sentencing have successfully attacked it in many jurisdictions. Changes in sentencing laws have swept the country. Many new systems are "determinate" in that parole release has been eliminated and the duration of a prison sentence can be determined at the time of sentencing. States as different and dispersed as Maine and California, or Florida and Washington, have instituted major changes. These include the abolition of parole, the establishment of detailed statutory sentencing standards, and the establishment of various systems of "presumptive" sentencing. A number of jurisdictions have established new administrative agencies called *sentencing commissions* and delegated authority to them to develop guidelines for sentencing.

PAROLE REFORMS—ABOLITION AND GUIDELINES. The attacks upon indeterminate sentencing moved several

states to limit or eliminate the discretion of parole boards. A dozen states, including Pennsylvania, Connecticut, Maine, California, and Washington, have recently abolished their parole boards. While this has effectively eliminated the indeterminate aspect of sentencing, it has not necessarily affected the wide discretion held by judges. In the early 1970s, Maine eliminated the parole board but allowed judges to impose any sentence from within a very wide range authorized by law (e.g., probation to 15 years). The legislature provided no guidance as to the "appropriate" sentence within that range. At the other extreme, states like California abolished parole releases, but adopted detailed standards for judges' sentencing decisions. Some jurisdictions retained parole release but adopted parole guidelines. The Oregon parole board and the United States Parole Commission, among others, voluntarily adopted strict guidelines to standardize their release decisions. This reduced both the unpredictability of sentences and the *ad hoc* discretionary aspect of parole release that had bothered many critics.

SENTENCING COMMISSIONS. In several states, including Minnesota, Pennsylvania, and Washington, sentencing commissions have developed comprehensive "sentencing guidelines" which attempt to standardize sentences, primarily on the basis of the offender's crime and his past criminal record. Of course, even where the legislature delegates the task of setting sentencing guidelines to a commission, it retains the right to ratify or reject the commission's proposals. The details of the guidelines systems vary substantially, as have their impacts. In Minnesota, it appears that judges have generally followed the guidelines and that sentencing disparities have been reduced. In 1984, Congress established a federal sentencing commission to develop sentencing guidelines for the federal system.

PRESUMPTIVE SENTENCING. Some of the new determinate sentencing systems provide a range within which the judge should impose sentences in ordinary cases. Others, such as North Carolina, New Jersey, and California, have established a single presumptive sentence. In California the "presumptive" sentence for a number of crimes is 3 years, but a judge may sentence an offender for either 2 or 4 years and still remain within the range authorized by the statute. In an example from Minnesota the presumptive sentence is 49 months, but the judge may impose sentences between 45 and 53 months without leaving the range. In other states, however, that range may be much wider—20 to 50 years in Indiana for Class A felonies. If the range is too wide, one of the main reasons for removing indeterminacy—the effort to reduce disparities—may not have been achieved at all.

Not even the most restrictive of these schemes totally precludes the judge from imposing any sentence, so long as it is within the statutory minimum or maximum sentence. Even under sentencing guidelines, a judge may sentence outside the guidelines if a written statement of reasons is provided. Some states provide lists of aggravating and mitigating circumstances that may be considered in departing from the guideline sentence or range.

If the sentencing rules restrict discretion only for sentences of imprisonment but do not affect the judge's decision to imprison or not (the "in–out" decision), one purpose of the reform may be substantially frustrated. In California, for example, while the percentage of persons convicted of burglary who were sentenced to prison rose after new sentencing legislation was enacted, from 27 percent to 35 percent, nearly two thirds of persons convicted of burglary received no prison sentence, while one third received a prison term within relatively strict guidelines. In Minnesota, judges follow the in–out guideline in 91 to 94 percent of the cases, thereby establishing some consistency in these decisions. It could be argued that the decision of whether to imprison is more important, at least in terms of disparity, than the decision of how long to imprison.

VOLUNTARY GUIDELINES. Finally, many jurisdictions, such as Michigan and Denver, have experimented with "voluntary" sentencing guidelines, which provide judges with information on the "usual" sentence for the offense and the offender; the judge is not obligated to follow these guidelines. Voluntary guidelines have generally been developed by judges or by advisory committees appointed by the state's chief justice. Some judges favor voluntary guidelines, even though they believe judges should retain full discretion over each individual sentence.

ARGUMENTS AND COUNTERARGUMENTS

Recent changes in sentencing laws and practices have not gone unchallenged. Some, as noted above, question the premises for change and the critiques of indeterminate sentencing.

Other critics argue that retribution or "just deserts," the primary purpose of many modern sentencing laws, is philosophically unacceptable in the late 20th century, and that sentencing grids which substantially constrain judicial discretion are unfair because they forbid judges to consider mitigating factors and to act mercifully. Some also argue that the endorsement of retribution (albeit "equal" retribution) as a proper goal of sentencing has led to severely increased sentences, which these critics see as undesirable.

Another concern about the new sentencing laws is that the perceived rigidity of the statutes or guidelines enhances the discretion of the prosecutor, particularly during plea bargain negotiations. Judicial discretion at least is exercised in the open, while prosecutorial discretion is generally exercised behind closed doors.

There is another concern: If determinate sentencing systems retain "good time" (time off for good behavior) to reduce sentences, prison guards and other prison personnel may effectively become sentencers. Minnesota and most other states that have adopted determinate sentencing still provide for substantial good time; California recently enlarged the amount of good time a prisoner can earn off his determinate sentence and has therefore enlarged the discretionary power of prison officials to affect the actual duration of confinement.

Yet another criticism of sentencing reform is that it has contributed to recent increases in prison crowding, first, by causing the sentencing to prison of many offenders who previously would have received probation, and second, by removing the "safety valve" of early release on parole in the event of overcrowding. This problem was avoided in Minnesota, where the legislature specifically instructed the sentencing commission to take prison capacity into account when it developed the guidelines. Minnesota has entrusted to the commission the job of realigning the guidelines to avoid overcrowding if it arises. A similar provision is contained in newly enacted federal legislation. The provision should be emulated by any state considering changes in the sentencing system unless, of course, the state's citizens are willing to bear the financial burden of building more prisons.

The controversy over indeterminate and determinate sentencing reflects deeper arguments over the purposes of the criminal law. For the past century, those who argued for uncertainty and indeterminacy sought to use the criminal sentence as a means of crime control. They sought to frighten the potential offender, to rehabilitate the "treatable" offender, and to incapacitate the incorrigible in order to reduce victimization in society. Recent sentencing changes, while partly based on empirical disillusionment with these goals, also draw upon the retributive notion of a fair, certain, and equal punishment for all those who inflict the same harm upon society. The dispute over the purposes of criminal sanctions has persisted for centuries, and the recent changes are unlikely to resolve that dispute.

SOURCE: Richard Singer, *Crime File Study Guide* (Washington, D.C.: United States Department of Justice, National Institute of Justice, n.d.). This Supplemental Reading was prepared by Professor Richard Singer of Yeshiva University to accompany the National Institute of Justice's *Crime File* video "Sentencing."

THE PRESENTENCE
INVESTIGATION REPORT

3

Presentence investigation report:

A report prepared from the presentence investigation and provided to the court before sentencing that serves a number of purposes.

Presentence investigation (PSI):

An investigation undertaken by a probation officer at the request of the court for the purpose of obtaining information about the defendant that may assist the court in arriving at a rational, fair sentence.

Offender-based presentence investigation report:

A presentence investigation report that seeks to understand the offender and the circumstances of the offense and to evaluate the offender's potential as a law-abiding, productive citizen.

The **presentence investigation (PSI) report** has long been the major source of information on which courts base their sentence and is one of the major contributions of probation to the administration of criminal justice. This is especially true in indeterminate-sentencing jurisdictions, where judges have considerable discretion in imposing sentence. The original function of presentence investigation reports was to assist the court in resolving the issue of whether to grant probation. Over the years, however, many other uses for the report's information have been found. The total use to which presentence reports are now put encompasses the entire range of correctional programs.

PURPOSES OF THE PRESENTENCE REPORT

The primary purpose of the presentence report is to provide the sentencing court with timely, relevant, and accurate data on which to base a rational sentencing decision. The PSI also assists correctional institutions in their classification of inmates, institutional programming, and release planning. Paroling authorities use the PSI to obtain information that is pertinent to considerations of parole. Probation and parole officers use it in their supervision efforts. The PSI may also serve as a source of information for research.[1]

CONTENTS OF THE PRESENTENCE REPORT

What are the essentials of a good presentence report? The philosophy guiding the preparation of presentence reports may be characterized as either primarily offender-based or primarily offense-based.

Offender-Based PSI

Traditionally, **offender-based presentence investigation reports** have been used. Probation officers have been guided in their **presentence investigations** by a philosophy that attempts to understand the causes of an offender's antisocial behavior and to evaluate the offender's potential for change. One of the earliest references to the investigation states that its purpose is

> to learn the character and ability of the person under consideration, the influences that surround him, and those that may be brought to bear in the event of probation.[2]

Another writer asserted,

> What the investigation seeks is a full understanding of the offender from the point of view of his possible *reintegration* into society as a self-sufficient and permanently useful member.[3]

Another source states that a satisfactory PSI is one that

> describes a defendant's character and personality, evaluates his or her problems and needs, helps the reader understand the world in which the defendant lives, reveals the nature of his or her relationships with people, and discloses those factors which underline the defendant's specific offense and conduct in general. It suggests alternatives for sentencing and the supervision process.[4]

Contents of an Offender-Based Presentence Report

1. Offense
Official version
Defendant's version
Codefendant information
Statement of witnesses, complainants, and victims

2. Prior Record
Juvenile adjudications
Adult arrests
Adult convictions
3. Personal and Family Data
Defendant
Parents and siblings
Marital
Education
Employment
Health
 Physical
 Mental and emotional

Military service
Financial condition
 Assets
 Liabilities
4. Evaluative Summary
Alternative plans
 Sentencing data
5. Recommendation

These statements make little or no reference to the nature of the offense. They are wholly centered on the offender.

There are several excellent models on which a traditional (offender-based) presentence report might be based. We believe that the PSI prepared by U.S. Probation Officers for the federal courts in the pre-guidelines era (before 1984) was and is a model for jurisdictions with an offender-based sentencing philosophy. The format of a comprehensive offender-based presentence report[5] is shown in a box above this discussion.

Offense-Based PSI

In *determinate-sentencing* jurisdictions—those in which the statutes specify a similar sentence for every offender convicted of a particular offense—the emphasis is on an **offense-based PSI,** which is very different from the traditional document. Here also, certain information about the offender is considered relevant (prior criminal record, employment history, family ties, health, and drug use), but the dominant focus is on the offense. The sentencing court is concerned with the offender's culpability in the offense, whether anyone was injured, whether a firearm was used, the extent of loss to the victim(s), and other aspects of the offense. In jurisdictions where the court uses sentencing guidelines to determine appropriate sentences, the emphasis of the PSI is on applying the particular guidelines to the facts of the case.[6] In federal court, for example, the presentence report serves the major purpose of providing

> solid, well-researched, verifiable information that will aid the court in selecting the proper guideline range.[7]

The *Federal Sentencing Guidelines Handbook* advises,

> Among the only offender characteristics taken into consideration by the [federal sentencing] Guidelines are the defendant's criminal record and criminal livelihood, which will enhance the sentencing range, and the defendant's acceptance of responsibility for the crime, which will lower the range.[8]

Offense-based presentence investigation report:

A presentence investigation report that focuses primarily on the offense committed, the offender's culpability, and the offender's criminal history.

Contents of an Offense-Based Presentence Report

1. The Offense
Charge(s) and conviction(s)
Related cases
The offense conduct
Adjustment for obstruction of justice
Adjustment for acceptance of responsibility
Offense level computation

2. The Defendant's Criminal History
Juvenile adjudications
Criminal convictions
Criminal history computation
Other criminal conduct
Pending charges (include if pertinent)
3. Sentencing Options
Custody
Supervised released
Probation
4. Offender Characteristics
Family ties, family responsibilities, and community ties
Mental and emotional health

Physical condition, including drug dependence and alcohol abuse
Education and vocational skills
Employment record
4. Fines and Restitution
Statutory provisions
Guideline provisions for fines
Defendant's ability to pay
5. Factors that May Warrant Departure (from guidelines sentence)
6. The Impact of Plea Agreement (if pertinent)
7. Sentencing Recommendation

Although offender characteristics are not completely ignored, it is obvious that the crime, not the criminal, is the primary emphasis. Probation officers in some jurisdictions where sentencing guidelines are used no longer write presentence reports; they are responsible only for completing a guidelines worksheet and calculating the presumptive sentence.[9] This, of course, deprives other agencies of the criminal justice system of valuable information about the offender.

The current federal PSI is offense-based, with primary emphasis upon providing the court with the necessary information to accurately apply the sentencing guidelines. A box above this discussion shows the format of the offense-based presentence report used in federal court. It addresses all the significant issues of the sentencing guidelines.[10]

Therefore, what constitutes a good presentence report depends to some extent on whether the jurisdiction utilizes offender-based or offense-based sentencing. Certain criteria apply to all types of presentence reports, however; all presentence reports should be factual, germane, precise, and succinct. Certainly, a concise report, fully read, is more effective than a lengthy one that is not considered or used.[11] The effectiveness of a presentence report is directly related to the success with which the findings are communicated and the extent to which it is used. The report's length and content should be appropriate to the seriousness of the offense; the greater the consequences of a judgment, the more likely is the court or a subsequent decision-making body to need more information. Where an individual has committed a violent or potentially violent offense, consideration of release on probation, prison classification committee decisions, and parole release decisions will all require more knowledge of the individual than if the individual were a situational, nonviolent first-offender. Above all other considerations, the PSI report must be objective and completely accurate.

Several aspects of the new federal PSI report are worthy of comment. In the 1984 Criminal Fine Enforcement Act, Congress cited the need to determine

Victim Impact Statement

Mr. Ray Reed of Washington, D.C., was the victim in the instant offense in which the defendant hit him over the head and stole his wallet. The wallet contained $50, his driver's license, credit cards, and his car keys. The defendant also stole his car. The offense occurred at gunpoint outside Mr. Reed's apartment. Mr. Reed's 1982 Chrysler Le Baron was discovered by local police 4 weeks later in damaged condition in Charlotte, North Carolina.

Although Mr. Reed was covered by insurance, he was not compensated for the damage to his car by his insurance company, because his car was recovered and he did not have comprehensive coverage. Damages to his car included a broken windshield, two flat tires, and a smashed right front fender. Further, he had to travel to Charlotte, North Carolina, at his own expense, in order to pick up his car. Mr. Reed was also hospitalized for a slight concussion, and as a result, lost two weeks' work. Mr. Reed certified by receipts (with the exception of the cash) that his total loss, because of the defendant's offense, was as follows:

Hospital bill (deductible costs)	$100.00
Bus ticket to North Carolina	35.00
Gasoline (return trip)	18.50
Loss of two weeks' work at $6.70 per hr.	536.00
Two tires at $45 each	90.00
Windshield	150.00
Right front fender/paint job	200.00
Cost of new driver's license	20.00
Cash loss (unable to verify)	50.00
Replacement of wallet/keys	25.00
TOTAL	1,224.50

In addition to Mr. Reed's loss, the hospital bill paid by Immortal Insurance Co. was $450.00.

Mr. Reed also stated that he now suffers from anxiety attacks when he considers leaving his apartment at night. He would like to attend counseling for this problem but presently does not have the money for this expense. It would not be covered by his health insurance. An estimate of the cost of such counseling is $60 per session. Mr. Reed thought he might need as many as 10 counseling sessions to clear up this anxiety problem.

Mr. Reed has no savings, and even though he is employed, he is earning only $6.70 per hour and must support his wife and himself on this income. Thus, the probation officer's assessment of Mr. Reed's financial situation is that he is in dire need of being compensated for his financial losses and of receiving the money for 10 counseling sessions.

SOURCE: Administrative Offices of the United States Courts, *The Presentence Investigation Report*, Monograph no. 105, 1978, 21–22.

a defendant's ability to pay fines and restitution.[12] The federal presentence report and those of several states now includes an analysis of the defendant's financial status for the purpose of imposing fines, ordering restitution, and assessing probation fees. The federal presentence report also contains a **victim impact statement** in the "offense" section. The use of victim impact statements stems from renewed interest in victim rights in the 1980s. Restoring the victim's wholeness has become an integral part of the sentencing process. The victim impact statement is to include "information about the impact of the offense conduct on identifiable victims or the community."[13] It assesses the financial, social, psychological, and medical impact upon, and cost to, any individual victim. An example of a victim impact statement in a presentence report is given in a box above this discussion.

Victim impact statement:

Information in a presentence investigation report about the impact of the offense on identifiable victims or the community.

PREPARING THE PRESENTENCE REPORT

Preparing the PSI is one of the most critical and imposing duties of a probation officer. Many probation officers also consider it their most interesting task. It requires many important skills, including interviewing, investigating, and writing. The probation officer's responsibility is to search out the facts about the offense and the offender, verify the information received, and present it in an organized and objective format.[14]

The Initial Interview

The first task in preparing the PSI is to interview the newly convicted offender. This meeting usually occurs in the probation officer's office or, if the defendant has not been released on bail, in jail. In some cases the initial interview takes place at the defendant's home, which provides the officer the opportunity to observe the offender's home environment and thus adds an additional dimension to his/her understanding of the defendant. The initial interview, wherever conducted, is usually devoted to completing a "worksheet" that elicits information about the offender, his/her criminal history, education, employment, physical and emotional health, family, and other relevant data. The officer also uses this time to develop some initial "sense" of the offender's character, personality, needs, and problems.

Investigation and Verification

Following the initial interview, the probation officer begins the task of investigating and verifying information supplied by the offender and obtaining employment, military, education, and criminal history records from local, state, and federal agencies. Many of these records are protected by state and federal privacy laws, and obtaining them may require the defendant's written

Probation officer interviewing an offender and his spouse during a home visit for the purpose of preparing the Presentence Investigation Report.

permission. Friends, family, and employers are also excellent sources of information and they are frequently contacted to assist in developing a well-rounded, accurate depiction of the offender.

When obtaining information from any source—particularly from relatives, friends, acquaintances, and employers—the probation officer must be careful to distinguish between facts and conclusions. Much of the information given to the probation officer during the investigation will be opinions and conclusions that may have little basis in fact. As a general rule, the report should contain only information the probation officer knows to be accurate. In some cases, information may be presented that the officer has been unable to verify. When that is necessary, the information should be clearly denoted as "unconfirmed" or "unverified."

The Evaluative Summary

Writing the evaluative summary is perhaps the most difficult and painstaking task in preparing the presentence report—particularly in offender-based reports—as this has a significant bearing on the future course of the defendant's life. In writing the evaluative summary, probation officers call into play their analytical ability, diagnostic skills, and understandings of human behavior. They must bring into focus the kind of person that is before the court, the basic factors that brought the person into trouble, and the special assistance the defendant needs for resolving those difficulties.

LEGAL PROBLEMS CONCERNING THE PRESENTENCE REPORT

It is beyond the scope of this book to consider all of the legal questions surrounding the preparation and use of the presentence investigation report. Two problem areas will be discussed—when the presentence report should be made and whether the defendant is entitled to see the report.

When the PSI Should Be Prepared

The preferred practice is to conduct the presentence investigation and prepare the presentence report after adjudication of guilt. The American Bar Association's *Standards relating to Sentencing Alternatives and Procedures* gives four reasons the presentence investigation should not be undertaken until after a finding of guilt:

1. The investigation represents an invasion of the defendant's privacy if he or she is later acquitted. The defendant's friends, employers, and relatives must be questioned, and potentially embarrassing questions must be asked.
2. Certain information is sought from the defendant that can place him or her in an awkward position before the trial.
3. The material in the presentence report is not admissible at the trial on the question of guilt, and there is a chance that it may come to the attention of the court before guilt is determined.
4. It is economically unfeasible to compile a report that may never be used.

53

Exceptions to this rule are allowed when the defendant's attorney consents that the preparation of the report may begin before conviction and plea. This recognizes the fact that under certain circumstances, prompt preparation of the report is advantageous to the defendant.

Disclosure of the PSI

Disclosure:

The right of a defendant to read the presentence investigation report prior to sentencing.

Much more difficult than when the presentence report should be made is the question of whether the defendant should be permitted to see the presentence report—that is, be permitted **disclosure**—and have the opportunity to refute any statements contained therein. Compulsory disclosure has generally been opposed by judges and probation officers.[15] The main argument against allowing disclosure is that persons having knowledge about the offender may refuse to give information if they know that they can be called into court and subjected to cross-examination and that the defendant will know they have given information about him or her. The argument here is that disclosure of the presentence report to the defendant will dry up the sources of information. It is also contended that permitting the defendant to challenge the presentence report could interminably delay the proceedings. The fear is that the defendant will challenge everything in the report and transform the sentencing procedure into a new trial of facts. A third argument is that it could be harmful to the defendant to have some of the report's information—such as, for example, the evaluation of a psychiatrist or even of the probation officer who is to be the defendant's probation supervisor. It is further argued that after conviction, a case ceases to be an action at law and becomes a social problem. Those who adhere to this position maintain that there should be no compulsory disclosure of the presentence report. Some maintain that the report should be a completely private document; others would permit disclosure at the discretion of the trial judge.

The opposing view—advocating disclosure of the presentence report—is that in simple fairness, convicted persons should have access to the information on which their sentence is to be based so that they can correct inaccuracies and controvert falsehoods. It is pointed out that in jurisdictions where the accused has access to the reports, the sources of information have not dried up, nor have sentencing hearings turned into a prolonged adversarial proceedings. Supporters of this position argue that the defendants' attorneys cannot properly perform their constitutional duty to assure the accuracy of the information used in sentencing without having access to the information on which the judges are expected to act.

The United States Supreme Court has held that there is no denial of due process of law when a court considers a presentence investigation report without disclosing its contents to the defendant or giving the defendant an opportunity to rebut it.[16] However, in the case of *Kent v. United States,* which involved the certification of a juvenile for trial in an adult criminal court, a different decision was reached.[17] The court's waiver of jurisdiction was based on a social history report given to the judge, and access to the report was denied to the juvenile's attorney. The Supreme Court stated that the report should have been made available to the defense attorney.

A New Jersey decision went even further. In *State v. Kunz,*[18] the presentence report contained a statement that a stolen-vehicle ring—specializing in Cadillacs—was being operated by an individual "whose contact in New Jersey" was the defendant and that the defendant had been involved in several purchases of stolen automobiles in New Jersey. This information was given to the defense counsel, who claimed that the report was wholly false. The defense counsel was unable to obtain a copy of the report, however, and the defendant was not given the opportunity to controvert the charges. Upon appeal, the court remanded the defendant to the trial court for resentencing, stating that in all future sentencing proceedings, defendants would be entitled to disclosure of the presentence report with fair opportunity to be heard on any adverse matters relevant to the sentencing. The court provided that the presentence report may first be examined by the trial judge so that matters that will play no part in the sentencing process may be excluded. In this fashion, irrelevances can be eliminated, confidential sources can be protected, and disclosure to the defendant of diagnostic information that could harm his rehabilitation can be avoided. The court, however, warned that the report "thus edited and furnished to the defendant" must contain everything that will have any bearing on the sentencing.[19]

There is a trend toward a "middle position" on the question of disclosure of the presentence report. Although the entire report—which contains the names of informants—is not disclosed to the defendant, it may be shown to his or her attorney. Also, the defendant and his or her attorney may be informed as to the nature of any adverse information in the report and given the opportunity to controvert such information.

After an exhaustive consideration of the reasons for and against disclosure, the authors of the American Bar Association *Standards relating to Sentencing Alternatives and Procedures* took a position in favor of disclosure.[20] The Model Penal Code would require that the court advise the defendant or the defendant's counsel of the factual contents and the conclusions of any presentence investigation of psychiatric examination and afford fair opportunity, if the defendant so requests, to controvert them. The sources of confidential information need not, however, be disclosed.[21]

In 1975, the *Federal Rules of Criminal Procedure* regarding disclosure of the presentence report was amended. Rule 32(c)(3) requires that the report be disclosed to the defendant and his/her counsel and to the attorney for the government. This rule authorizes the court to exempt from disclosure:

1. diagnostic opinions, which, if disclosed might seriously disrupt a program of rehabilitation;
2. sources of information obtained upon a promise of confidentiality; and,
3. any other information which, if disclosed, might result in harm, physical or otherwise, to the defendant or other persons.

When withheld information is used in determining sentence, the court must provide the defendant and counsel with a summary of the withheld information and give the defendant or counsel the opportunity to comment on such information.

The federal rule as now promulgated represents an intermediate position between complete disclosure and complete secrecy. In those states practicing disclosure and in federal districts, the release of the presentence report has not resulted in the problems that have been anticipated by the opponents of the practice. Rather, it seems to have led the probation services to develop skills for analyzing the offense and the offender more objectively. With greater objectivity has come greater reliance on the reports by the courts and a resultant increase in the number of reports requested and persons granted probation.[22] These analytical rather than judgmental presentence reports are not only more useful to the courts, they are also more acceptable to the offender, for in them the offender may see that perhaps someone understands or at least attempts to understand his/her problems. This latter effect frequently results in a closer relationship between the offender and the probation officer. Further, disclosure is a requirement for fairness to the defendant. Thus, the presentence investigation report is an integral part of the correctional system and should be made available to the defendant or his or her counsel.

CRITICISMS OF THE PRESENTENCE REPORT

Some critics argue that judges place too much weight on the PSI in sentencing, which effectively shifts the sentencing decision from the court to the probation officer. Many studies have shown a high correlation between the PSI sentence recommendation and the actual sentence imposed by the court. A study by the American Justice Institute, for example, demonstrated that the probation officer's recommendation was adopted by the sentencing judge in 66 to 95 percent of the cases.[23] Among the factors that might explain this high correlation is that probation officers may make their recommendations in anticipation of what the judge desires. One of the authors of this book served as a U.S. Probation Officer for several years. He suggests that probation officers who work with judges for a period of time come to know the judges' biases and predispositions regarding offenses and offenders. They know, for example, that Judge X always sentences drug-sale defendants to the maximum allowable penalty and that Judge Y almost always grants probation to first-offenders. After awhile, the officers' recommendations come to reflect the inevitability of the situation. A federal judge once told this author, "Never give me a recommendation for probation in a drug case. I don't want to see it."

Other studies have suggested that prosecutors suggest a recommended sentence to the probation officer after making a plea agreement with the defendant.[24] Florida State University criminology professor Eugene Czajko-ski, himself a former U.S. Probation Officer, suggests that prosecuting attorneys often find a way to communicate the plea agreement to the probation officer, who responds with a conforming recommendation.[25] He writes:

> Like the judge's role, the probation officer's role in sentencing is diminishing. If it has become the judicial role of the judge to simply certify the plea bargaining process, then the probation officer's role is quasi-judicial in that he does the same thing. . . . [T]he probation officer does a perfunctory presentence report and aims his recommendation toward what he already knows will be the plea bargaining sentence.[26]

Other commentators suggest that judges vary widely in their reliance on the PSI report. Abraham Blumberg reports that some judges do not read the report at all, whereas others carefully select passages from the report to read aloud in court to justify their sentence.[27] Other judges discount the PSI because of the report's hearsay nature.[28] Howard Abadinsky points out that in many jurisdictions, the probation officer is overburdened with presentence investigations and

> "does not have the time to do an adequate investigation and prepare a (potentially) useful report. In courts where the judge usually pays little or no attention to the contents of the report, the PO will not be inclined to pursue the necessary information and prepare well-written reports."[29]

SUMMARY

The ultimate merit of probation as a correctional tool depends to a very great extent on the nature and quality of the presentence report. Probation is in essence a method of individualization and is predicated on the proper selection of offenders to be accorded this community-based correctional treatment. Although the primary purpose of a presentence investigation report is to examine and expose the factors that will mitigate for or against successful community adjustment in lieu of incarceration, use of the report should not be limited to the courts. It should also be made available to prison authorities for classification and treatment purposes and to the parole board to aid in the determination of parole grants and future aftercare needs of the offender.

ENDNOTES

1. The Administrative Office of the U.S. Courts first published *The Presentence Investigation Report* in 1965. Among the five functions of the report delineated in that year were terms such as *treatment programs,* changed to *institutional programs* in the 1978 version, and *to aid the probation officer in his rehabilitation effort . . .,* changed to *supervision efforts* in the 1978 version. [italics ours] This subtle change in wording reflects the movement of correctional philosophy from a treatment orientation to a justice orientation.

2. Bolster, "Adult Probation, Parole, and Suspended Sentence" *J.Crim.L.* 444 (1910).

3. Ferris, "The Case History in Probation Service," in Glueck, *Probation and Criminology* (1933).

4. *The Presentence Investigation Report,* monograph no. 103 (Administrative Office of the U.S. Courts, 1965).

5. These categories were excerpted from *The Presentence Investigation Report,* monograph no. 105 (Administrative Office of the U.S. Courts, 1978).

6. *Id.* at 6.

7. *Presentence Investigation Reports under the Sentencing Reform Act of 1984,* monograph no. 107 (Division of Probation, Administrative Office of the U.S. Courts, September 1987).

8. *Federal Sentencing Guidelines Handbook: Text, Analysis, Case Digests* (Shepard's/McGraw-Hill, 1990), p. 5.

9. Andrew E. Doom, Connie M. Roerich, and Thomas H. Zoey, "Sentencing Guidelines in Minnesota: The View from the Trenches," *Federal Probation* 52 (1988), 34–38.

10. *Presentence Investigation Reports under the Sentencing Reform Act of 1984, supra* note 7.

11. *Presentence Investigation Report, supra* note 5, at 6.

12. Howard Abadinsky, *Probation and Parole: Theory and Practice,* 4th ed. (Englewood Cliffs, N.J.: Prentice Hall, 1991), p. 97.

13. *Id.* at 21–22.

14. *Presentence Investigation Reports under the Sentencing Reform Act of 1984, supra* note 7, p. 6.

15. During the course of its study, the American Bar Association Advisory Committee obtained the views of circuit judges, district judges, and federal probation officers. The survey disclosed the following:

Circuit Judges
40 opposed compulsory disclosure,
7 were in favor of compulsory disclosure,
4 expressed no opinion;

District Judges
250 opposed compulsory disclosure,
18 were in favor of compulsory disclosure,
2 expressed no opinion;

Federal Probation Officers
340 opposed compulsory disclosure,
20 were in favor of compulsory disclosure,
8 expressed no opinion.

16. Williams v. Oklahoma, 358 U.S. 576, 79 S.Ct. 421, 3 L.Ed.2d 516 (1959); Williams v. New York, 337 U.S. 241, 69 Sup.Ct.1079, 93 L.Ed.1337 (1949). In *Williams v. New York,* the jury recommended life imprisonment. Their recommendation was not binding upon the court. After receipt of the presentence report which showed, according to the judge, that the defendant had confessed to 30 burglaries in the area where the murder occurred and that appellant possessed "a marked sexuality" and was a "menace to society," the court sentenced the defendant to death. The sentence of death was upheld upon appeal. The Supreme Court pointed out that strict evidentiary procedures "hedge" the guilt-finding process, but the sources of evidence for sentencing purposes have historically been much wider. "Undoubtedly the New York statutes [providing for presentence reports] emphasize a modern philosophy of penology that the punishment should fit the offender and not merely the crime."

17. * * * [The Juvenile Judge] * * * may not for purposes of a decision on waiver, receive and rely upon secret information, whether emanating from its staff or otherwise. * * * Kent v. United States, 383 U.S. 541, 86 S.Ct. 1045, 16 L.Ed.2d 84 (1966).

18. State v. Kunz, 55 N.J. 128, 259 A.2d 895 (1969).

19. *Id.*

20. ABA, *Standards relating to Sentencing Alternatives and Procedures,* §§ 4.3 and 4.4.

21. Model Penal Code, § 7.07(5).

22. From author interviews of probation officers and judges in courts practicing disclosure.

23. *Presentence Investigation Report Program* (Sacramento, Calif.: American Justice Institute, 1981).

24. Rodney Kingsnorth and Louis Rizzo, "Decision Making in the Criminal Court: Continuities and Discontinuities," *Criminology* 17, May 1979.

25. Eugene Czajkoski, "Exposing the Quasi-Judicial Role of the Probation Officer," *Federal Probation* 37, September 1973.

26. *Id.* at 120.
27. Abraham Blumberg, *Criminal Justice* (Chicago: Quadrangle Books, 1970).
28. Abadinsky, *supra* note 12, at 118.
29. *Id.* at 121.

DISCUSSION QUESTIONS

1. Discuss the importance of the presentence investigation report for the criminal justice system.
2. What is the primary purpose(s) of the PSI report? How might other agencies in the criminal justice system use it?
3. How has the introduction of sentencing guidelines affected the use and nature of the PSI report?
4. How do the PSI report prepared in a jurisdiction with offender-based sentencing and the PSI report prepared in an offense-based sentencing jurisdiction differ?
5. What is the purpose of the victim impact statement in a PSI report? What factors brought about the use of this victim impact statement?
6. What is the federal rule regarding disclosure of the PSI report? What are the arguments for and against disclosure? What is the middle-ground approach to disclosure?
7. What factor(s) might explain why probation officers' recommendations are so highly correlated with actual sentences imposed by judges?
8. Discuss some of the other criticisms of the PSI report. Do you believe these criticisms are valid? Why or why not?

SUPPLEMENTAL READINGS

An Offense-Based Presentence Report

IN UNITED STATES DISTRICT COURT
FOR THE NORTHERN DISTRICT OF OHIO

UNITED STATES OF AMERICA	)	
v.	)	Docket No. 93-00147-01
JANE GREEN	)	

Presentence Report

Prepared for	The Honorable John Smith Jones United States District Judge
Prepared by	Pridgen K. Jensen United States Probation Officer (216) 633-6226
Sentencing Date	September 26, 1993, at 9:00 A.M.
Offense	18 U.S.C. 656, Misapplication of Funds by Bank Employee, a class D felony
Release Status	$1,000 Personal Surety Bond (no presentence custodial credit)
Identifying Data	
Date of Birth: Social Security Number Address	February 2, 1971 881-22-4444 24 Apple Street Cleveland, Ohio 44114
Detainers	None
Codefendants	None

Assistant U.S. Attorney	*Defense Counsel*
Albert Henderson	Jerome Doe
U.S. Courthouse	113 Main Street
Cleveland, Ohio 44114	Cleveland, Ohio 44114
(216) 333-3333	(216) 444-4444

Date report prepared: September 2, 1993
Revised: September 12, 1993

PART A. THE OFFENSE

CHARGE(S) AND CONVICTION(S)

1. Jane Green, the defendant, was indicted by a Northern District of Ohio grand jury on June 15, 1993. The indictment alleged that on May 2, 1993, while she was employed by the Bank of Ohio in Cleveland, Ohio, the defendant misapplied bank funds, in violation of 18 U.S.C. 656. On July 25, 1993, Green pled guilty to the charge.

2. Since the offense took place after November 1, 1987, the Sentencing Reform Act of 1984 is applicable.

RELATED CASES

3. None.

THE OFFENSE CONDUCT

4. The defendant, Green began working at Bank of Ohio, 2100 Main Street, Cleveland, Ohio, in mid-January 1993. On April 30, 1993, she went to a local furniture store to purchase some bedroom furniture. The furniture she wanted to buy cost $5,000, and Green asked the salesman whether she could finance the purchase. The salesman advised Green that because she had not established a credit rating, she could finance only half of the purchase price and could pay the remainder of the purchase price, $2,500, by check. Green did not have sufficient funds in her checking account to cover a check in that amount, but thought she would have it as soon as she could contact her boyfriend, who was going to lend her the necessary funds. Believing that her boyfriend would give her the funds before her check to the furniture company could clear, Green wrote the company a check for $2,500. The check was presented for payment before she could make a deposit to cover it, and the bank, as a courtesy to an employee, paid it. When her boyfriend failed to advance her any funds to cover the overdraft, Green became desperate.

5. On May 2, 1993, Green devised a solution to her problem. On that day, Victor Garcia came to her teller's window and asked Green to deposit an $11,000 check to his savings account. Green deposited the money to her own checking account, instead.

6. On May 17, 1993, Garcia advised the bank that his account did not contain the $11,000 he had deposited on May 2. The bank immediately began an audit and soon discovered what Green had done. When the Audit Manager confronted Green with his discovery, Green admitted that she had placed Garcia's deposit in her account. She stated that when she diverted the check she was desperate, being fearful that she would lose her job for having overdrawn her checking account. Green asserts that she intended to return the money to Garcia's account but had not been able to obtain the $2,500 that she had spent when the auditor discovered the misapplication of the money. She had planned to replace the full $11,000 in one deposit entry to Mr. Garcia's account.

7. According to bank records, on June 3, 1993, Green paid the bank $8,500 of the funds she diverted. She still owes the bank the remaining $2,450. The bank has not filed a claim with its bonding company, which insured Green's fidelity, because Green has agreed to pay the $2,450 balance of the embezzlement.

ADJUSTMENT FOR OBSTRUCTION OF JUSTICE

8. The probation officer has no information suggesting that the defendant impeded or obstructed justice.

ADJUSTMENT FOR ACCEPTANCE OF RESPONSIBILITY

9. During the interview with the probation officer, Green was distraught and tearful regarding the offense, stating repeatedly that she is ashamed and embarrassed. When confronted by bank officials, Green readily

admitted that she committed the offense. Four days later, she made a $8,550 payment toward restitution. She is clearly remorseful.

OFFENSE-LEVEL COMPUTATION

10. Base Offense Level: The guideline for an 18. U.S.C. 656 offense is found in Section 2B1.1(a) of the Guidelines. The base offense level is 4.   4

11. Specific Offense Characteristics: Section 2B1.1(b) provides that if the value of the property taken is between $10,001 and $20,000, 5 levels are added. The instant offense entailed a loss of $11,000.   5

12. Adjustment for Role in the Offense: None   0

13. Victim-Related Adjustment: None   0

14. Adjustment for Obstruction of Justice: None   0

15. Adjustment for Acceptance of Responsibility: Based on the defendant's admission of guilt, her payment of restitution, and her remorse, pursuant to Section 3E1.1(a), two levels are subtracted.   –2

16. Total Offense Level: 7

PART B. THE DEFENDANT'S CRIMINAL HISTORY

JUVENILE ADJUDICATIONS

17. None.

CRIMINAL CONVICTIONS

18. None

CRIMINAL HISTORY COMPUTATION

19. The defendant has no criminal convictions. Therefore, she has zero criminal history and a criminal history category of 1.

OTHER CRIMINAL CONDUCT

20. None

PART C. SENTENCING OPTIONS

CUSTODY

21. Statutory Provisions: The maximum term of imprisonment is 5 years. 18 U.S.C. 656.

22. Guideline Provisions: Based on a total offense of 7 and a criminal history category of 1, the guideline imprisonment range is 1 to 7 months.

SUPERVISED RELEASE

23. Statutory Provisions: If a term of imprisonment is imposed, the court may impose a term of supervised release of not more than 3 years pursuant to 18 U.S.C. 3583(b)(2).

24. Guideline Provisions: If a sentence of imprisonment is imposed within the guideline range, a term of supervised release is not required but is optional. If more than 1 year of imprisonment is imposed on the basis of a departure, supervised release is required. According to Section 5D3.2, the term of supervised release for a class

D felony is at least 2 years but not more than 3 years. Pursuant to Section 5C2.1(c), the court could impose a sentence of imprisonment that includes a term of supervised release with a condition that substitutes community confinement for at least one half of the minimum term, but in no event less than 1 month.

PROBATION

25. Statutory Provisions: The defendant is eligible for probation by statute. Because the offense is a felony, 18 U.S.C. 3563(a)(2) requires that one of the following be imposed as a condition of probation: a fine, restitution, or community service. For a felony, the authorized term of probation is not less than 1 nor more than 5 years. 18 U.S.C. 3561(b)(1).

26. Guideline Provisions: The defendant is eligible for probation provided that the court impose a condition requiring intermittent confinement or community confinement for at least 1 month. Section 5B1.1(a)(2). Currently there are no facilities in the Cleveland area for intermittent confinement. However, there is currently bedspace available at the New Hope Halfway House at 500 Broadway Avenue in Cleveland. This facility appears to be a suitable facility if the defendant were ordered to serve a sentence of community confinement.

27. If the court were to impose probation, the term must be at least 1 year but no more than 5 years. Section 5B1.2(a)(1).

PART D. OFFENDER CHARACTERISTICS

FAMILY TIES, FAMILY RESPONSIBILITIES, AND COMMUNITY TIES

28. Jane Green was born on February 2, 1971, the fourth of seven children born to John and Anne Green. Green grew up in Fargo, North Dakota, and moved to Cleveland with her family at the age of 15, when her father obtained employment as a cook at a Cleveland hotel.

29. Green is single. She resides with her parents and younger siblings at 24 Apple Street, Cleveland. The defendant states that she has not told her parents about the criminal charges against her, as she is exceedingly embarrassed and feels that she cannot discuss the matter with them. Marcus Green, the defendant's older brother, verified background information about the defendant. He reported that prior to this offense, Green never posed any serious problems for the family.

MENTAL AND EMOTIONAL HEALTH

30. According to the defendant, she has never suffered from any mental or emotional problems that would require professional intervention. It was obvious to the probation officer during the interview with Ms. Green that she is extremely remorseful about her illegal activities and is emotionally upset with worry about the outcome of this case. Her brother confirmed that Green has no history of mental or emotional problems but recently has been very anxious about the instant case.

PHYSICAL CONDITION, INCLUDING DRUG DEPENDENCE AND ALCOHOL ABUSE

31. Jane Green reports that she is in good health and has never suffered from any serious illness or injuries. She states that she has never used illicit drugs and does not consume alcohol.

EDUCATION AND VOCATIONAL SKILLS

32. A transcript from Monroe High School of Cleveland indicates that Jane Green was graduated in June 1989 with a grade point average of 2.5. She attended the Bank Training Institute in Cleveland in 1992, completing a five-week training course. The probation officer verified this by examining Institute records. It was the training from this vocational school that qualified Green to be hired by Bank of Ohio.

EMPLOYMENT RECORD

33. At the present time, Green is employed as a receptionist at Video Reproductions, Incorporated, on Third Street in Cleveland. Her duties include answering telephones and processing invoices. Her supervisor, Howard Allen, verified that Green does not handle money. She has been employed at this company since July 5, 1993, and according to Allen, she has been a responsible employee. Allen is aware of the charges pending against Ms. Green.
34. On May 30, 1993, when Green was discharged from Bank of Ohio from the misapplication of the check, she had been working as a teller since January 20, 1993. From December 1990 until March 1992, Green was employed by Macy's Department Store in Cleveland as a sales clerk. She quit this job to attend the Bank Training Institute.

PART E. FINES AND RESTITUTION

STATUTORY PROVISIONS

35. The maximum fine is $250,000. 18 U.S.C. 3571(b).
36. A special assessment of $50 is mandatory. 18 U.S.C. 3013.
37. Restitution is owed to Bank of Ohio in the amount of $2,450 and is payable to the following address:

> Bank of Ohio Collections
> Security Division
> 133 Grape Avenue
> Cleveland, Ohio 44114
> Attention: Mr. Young

GUIDELINE PROVISIONS ABOUT FINES

38. The fine range for this offense is from $2,450 less any restitution ordered with a minimum of $500 (Section 5E4.2(c)(1)(B)) to $33,000 (Section 5E4.2(c)(2)(C)).
39. Subject to the defendant's ability to pay, the court shall impose an additional fine amount that is at least sufficient to pay the costs to the government of any imprisonment, probation, or supervised release. Section 5E4.2(1). The most recent advisory from the Administrative Office of the United States Courts, dated March 15, 1988, suggests that a monthly cost of $_____ be used for imprisonment and a monthly cost of $_____ for supervision.

DEFENDANT'S ABILITY TO PAY

40. Based on a financial statement submitted by Green, a review of her bank records, and a credit bureau check, the defendant's financial condition is as follows:

ASSETS		
Cash		
Cash on hand	$ 47	
Checking account	$ 130	
U.S. Savings Bond	$ 75	
UNENCUMBERED ASSETS		
Stereo system	$ 500	
EQUITY IN OTHER ASSETS		
1988 Toyota Corolla	$2,000	(equity based on Blue Book value)
TOTAL ASSETS	$2,752	
UNSECURED DEBTS		
Loan from brother	$ 300	
Attorney fees balance	$1,500	
TOTAL UNSECURED DEBT	$1,800	
NET WORTH	$ 952	
MONTHLY CASH FLOW		
Income		
Net salary	$ 752	
TOTAL INCOME	$ 752	
NECESSARY LIVING EXPENSES		
Room and board	$ 150	
Installment payment (car loan)	$ 242	
Gas & auto costs	$ 50	
Attorney fees	$ 100	
Clothing	$ 50	
TOTAL EXPENSES	$ 592	
NET MONTHLY CASH FLOW	$ 160	

41. Based on Green's financial profile, it appears that she has the ability to remit restitution if she makes monthly installments. However, her income is rather modest, and it does not appear that she could also pay a fine.

PART F. FACTORS THAT MAY WARRANT DEPARTURE

42. The probation officer has not identified any information that would warrant a departure from the guidelines.

Respectfully submitted,

BRAD ANTHONY
CHIEF PROBATION OFFICER

By _____
Pridgen K. Jensen
U.S. Probation Officer

Reviewed and Approved:

_____
MARK ADAMS
SUPERVISOR

ADDENDUM TO THE PRESENTENCE REPORT

The probation officer certifies that the presentence report, including any revision thereof, has been disclosed to the defendant, her attorney, and counsel for the Government, and that the content of the Addendum has been communicated to counsel. The Addendum fairly states any objections they have made.

OBJECTIONS
By the Government

The Government has no objections

By The Defendant

The defense attorney maintains that the defendant's youth, lack of a prior record, and her remorse are characteristics that should be considered for a departure from the guidelines. He will present argument at the sentencing hearing that community confinement is not necessary in this case and that the court should depart by a sentence of probation with restitution.

The probation officer does not believe that a departure is warranted. Remorse and lack of a prior record are factored into the guidelines. The Sentencing Commission policy statement on age (Section 5H1.1) suggests that youth is not a valid reason for departure.

CERTIFIED BY

BRAD ANTHONY
CHIEF PROBATION OFFICER

By_____
Pridgen K. Jensen
U.S. Probation Officer

Reviewed and Approved:

_____
MARK ADAMS
SUPERVISOR
Dated: September 12, 1993

SENTENCING RECOMMENDATION

United States v. Jane Green, Dkt. No. 93-00147-01,
U.S. District Court, District of Northern Ohio

CUSTODY

Statutory maximum	5 years
Guideline range	1 to 7 months
Recommendation	1 month community confinement

Justification

According to the Guidelines, the defendant is eligible for probation, provided that she serve at least one month of intermittent or community confinement. Green is a good candidate for probation, because she has no prior record, is willing to make restitution to the victim, and is gainfully employed. A prison sentence does not appear to be necessary in this case, since the defendant does not need to be incapacitated to deter her from further crime, and other sanctions will provide sufficient punishment.

FINE

Statutory maximum	$250,000
Guideline range	$2,450 (or $500 if restitution is ordered) to $33,000 plus cost of incarceration and/or supervision
Recommendation	$0

Justification

Restitution to the victim bank is recommended as a condition of probation. The defendant's modest income will necessitate that the restitution be paid in monthly installments. At this point, Green does not have the ability to pay both restitution and a fine.

PROBATION

Statutory term	Minimum of 1 year and a maximum of 5 years
Guideline term	Minimum of 1 year and a maximum of 5 years
Recommended term	4 years

Recommended Conditions

1. That the defendant not commit any crimes, Federal, state or local.
2. That the defendant abide by the standard conditions of probation recommended by the Sentencing Commission.
3. That the defendant be confined in a community treatment center or halfway house for 30 days, during which she will be allowed to maintain employment.
4. That the defendant pay restitution to Bank of Ohio in the amount of $2,450 in monthly installments of $55 per month.
5. That the defendant be prohibited from incurring new credit charges or opening additional lines of credit without the approval of the probation officer unless she is in compliance with the payment schedule.
6. That the defendant provide the probation officer with access to any requested financial information.
7. That if the defendant should hold a fiduciary position in her employment, she be required to inform her employer of the instant conviction.

Justification

A sentence of probation contingent upon 30 days' confinement in a halfway house and the payment of restitution will provide sufficient punishment for Green as well as a general deterrence to others. The guidelines require intermittent or community confinement as a condition of probation. Placement in a halfway house for the minimum sentence of 30 days is recommended so that Green can continue to work and pay restitution to the victim bank. Since she has a modest income and a substantial amount of restitution to pay, a four-year term of probation is recommended with the requirement that she pay no less than $55 per month toward restitution. Conditions of supervision requiring financial disclosure to the probation officer and a provision against incurring new credit debts are suggested in order to monitor the defendant's payments. Because the instant offense is a form of embezzlement, Green will be considered a third-party risk to an employer if she is to handle money. It is therefore suggested that while she is under supervision she be required to inform any employer of the instant conviction if she holds a fiduciary position.

SPECIAL ASSESSMENT $50

VOLUNTARY SURRENDER

If the court imposes a custodial sentence, Green appears to be a good candidate for a voluntary surrender.

Respectfully submitted,

BRAD ANTHONY
CHIEF PROBATION OFFICER

By _____
   Pridgen K. Jensen
   U.S. Probation Officer

Reviewed and Approved:

_____

MARK ADAMS
SUPERVISOR
DATE: September 12, 1993

SOURCE: *Presentence Investigation Reports under the Sentencing Reform Act of 1984,* monograph no. 107 (Administrative Office of the United States Courts, September 1987).

An Offender-Based Presentence Report

UNITED STATES DISTRICT COURT

PRESENTENCE REPORT

NAME (Last, First, Middle) Hasse, Herman P.					DICTATION DATE October 14, 1983

ADDRESS Hampden County House of Correction	LEGAL RESIDENCE 71 Lee Avenue Holyoke, Mass.	SCHEDULED SENT.DATE
		DOCKET NO. 83-00124-01
		CITIZENSHIP U.S.

AGE 28	RACE Caucasian	DATE OF BIRTH 11-15-54	PLACE OF BIRTH Boston, Mass.	SEX Male	EDUCATION 10th Grade
MARITAL STATUS Divorced			DEPENDENTS One. in custody of former wife		SOC.SEC.NO 987-65-4321
FBI NO. 999-888 H			U.S. MARSHALL NO.		OTHER IDENTIFYING NO.

OFFENSE
D/Mass.--Consp. & Dist. heroin, 21:USC. 841(a)(1) & 846

PENALTY
0-15 yrs. and/or $25,000 and SPT of at least 3 yrs. on each count

CUSTODIAL STATUS In custody in lieu of 100,000 surety bond since 8-15-83.	DATE OF ARREST

PLEA
Guilty to Mass. Ind, 9-29-83; will plead under Rule 20 to W/D Tx. Ind.

VERDICT

DETAINERS OR CHARGES PENDING
Rule 20, W/D Tx. Doc. # 83-00135-01. Violation of 21:USC, 952(a) & 960(a)(1) & 841(a)(1), same penalty.

OTHER DEFENDANTS
Nancy Rooney, in local custody in Mexico

ASSISTANT U.S. ATTORNEY David Crawford, Esq.	DEFENSE COUNSEL Philip Pratt. Esq. 981 Main Street Springfield, Mass. (413) 555-4321 (Retained)

DISPOSITION

SENTENCING JUDGE	DATE	PROBATION OFFICER

OFFENSE

OFFICIAL VERSION.   Herman Hesse is the subject of two separate indictments, one in the District of Massachusetts and one in the Western District of Texas. On August 20, 1983, the Massachusetts Grand Jury returned an indictment against Hesse and Nancy Rooney, charging that they conspired between May 28, 1983, and July 30, 1983, to distribute a quantity of heroin and that they distributed that heroin on June 23, 1983.

On August 26, 1983, a grand jury in El Paso, Texas, returned an indictment against Hesse and Rooney, charging that they imported 101.7 grams of heroin into the United States on or about July 30, 1983, and that they distributed that heroin on the same date at El Paso, Texas. Hesse appeared on September 29, 1983, and pleaded guilty to the Massachusetts indictment. He has indicated his intention to plead guilty to the Texas indictment under Rule 20.

This investigation began in May 1983, when the Drug Enforcement Agency received information that Hesse was looking for a buyer for a large quantity of heroin. On May 28, 1983, an undercover agent was introduced to Hesse at a bar in Springfield, and Hesse acknowledged that he was looking for a buyer for a kilo of heroin. He was initially reluctant to deal with a stranger, but after four meetings he offered to make the agent a partner if the agent agreed to purchase the heroin as soon as it came across the border into Texas. The agent accepted the offer but insisted on first receiving a sample of the heroin.

On June 23, 1983, the agent and Hesse met in Springfield and drove to a shopping mall where they met Hesse's girlfriend, Nancy Rooney. After receiving instructions from Hesse, Rooney went to her car and returned with a sample of 2.70 grams of heroin, which she gave to the agent. The latter paid Hesse $300. The substance was tested and found to contain 31.7 percent heroin.

On July 21, 1983, the agent informed Hesse that the sample was of acceptable quality. On July 24, Hesse instructed the agent to meet him on July 29 in El Paso, Texas. The agent flew to El Paso, where he met with Hesse and Nancy Rooney at the Yellow Rose Hotel. At 8:15 A.M. on July 30, Hesse and Rooney crossed the border into Juarez. They returned two hours later, and Hesse told the agent that he was able to obtain only a quarter kilogram of heroin. The agent expressed disappointment, but Hesse said that the heroin was of very high quality and could be cut many times. Hesse then sold the agent the first installment of 101.7 grams for $4,000. Tests determined that this substance contained 44.6 percent heroin. Hesse explained that Rooney and he would return to Mexico that afternoon to obtain the balance.

Hesse and Rooney crossed into Juarez and were arrested by Mexican police later in the day. Nancy Rooney had 147.3 grams of heroin in her possession. No heroin was found on Hesse, who was released after two days in custody. Rooney was held for trial. Hesse returned to Massachusetts, where he was arrested on August 15, 1983.

DEFENDANT'S VERSION.   "I was going to Mexico on a vacation, and Nancy decided to come with me. This guy she met in Springfield was pestering her to get him some heroin. I had seen him a couple of times in June. All of a sudden he shows up in El Paso and demands to know where the stuff is. She finally agreed to get him some and she asked me to come, in case anything happened. I was there, so I guess I'm guilty. All of a sudden I was arrested by the Mexican cops, but they let me go because they didn't have anything on me. Then, all of a sudden, I'm arrested up here. My lawyer says entrapment is hard to prove, so I guess I'm guilty. But I didn't say all those things the narc claims. I don't deserve to go to jail."

PRIOR RECORD

JUVENILE ADJUDICATIONS

11-05-68 Age 14	Using motor vehicle without authority	Springfield, Mass., Juvenile Court	1 year probation

Mr. Hesse was represented by counsel. He and two other juveniles stole a car and went on a "joy ride." Mr. Hesse made a good adjustment on probation during the initial months but became increasingly uncooperative thereafter.

10-28-69 Age 15	Breaking and entering	Holyoke District Ct.	Committed, Youth Service Board

Mr. Hesse was represented by counsel. He and another juvenile broke into a home in Holyoke. The Youth Service Board sent him to the Industrial School at Shirley, Massachusetts, where he remained until June 1964, when he was paroled. He was discharged one year later. His institutional performance was routine. He participated in a woodworking course and was placed on report on one occasion for fighting in the dining hall.

ADULT RECORD

12-23-74 Age 20	Shoplifting	Springfield P. D.	Dismissed, lack of prosecution

Hesse was arrested after he allegedly attempted to steal several jewelry items from a department store. The store manager declined to press charges.

5-11-75 Age 20	Receiving stolen property	Holyoke District Ct.	4 mos. County Jail ss; prob. 2 years

Mr. Hesse was represented by counsel. He was arrested after he sold a stolen television set to a pawn shop. The probation officer reports that he had little success with Mr. Hesse, who was constantly on the borderline of violation.

9-15-76 Age 21	Burglary and entering in the nighttime	Northampton District Ct.	6 mos. County Jail

Mr. Hesse was represented by counsel. He was apprehended at 2:15 A.M., inside a drugstore. He had activated a silent alarm when he entered the building. Jail officials recall that Mr. Hesse attempted to be reclusive while incarcerated. He voluntarily spent several months in segregation because of his fear of attack by other inmates.

6-27-82 Age 25	Larceny over $100 and forgery	Hampden Cty. Superior Ct.	2 yrs. prison ss; 18 mos. prob. w/ restitution

Mr. Hesse was represented by counsel. He withdrew $500 from a bank account, using a stolen passbook and forged withdrawal slips. He was identified through bank photographs. Mr. Hesse paid $310 in restitution, and the balance was remitted. He performed well under probation supervision.

PERSONAL AND FAMILY DATA

DEFENDANT. Herman Hesse was born on October 15, 1954, in Boston, Massachusetts. His parents, natives of Austria, came to the United States as displaced persons after World War II. The family has lived for the last fifteen years at their present residence in Holyoke. The defendant's early years were turbulent because of many violent arguments between his parents. Mrs. Hesse attributes these difficulties to her husband's excessive drinking. She summoned police assistance on several occasions, although no arrests were made. In 1961 Mrs. Hesse contracted tuberculosis. She was hospitalized for almost one year, and the father was unable to keep the family together. The defendant and his siblings were placed in the Western Massachusetts Home for Children, and the family was reunited when Mrs. Hesse recovered. The defendant remained with his family until he married at the age of twenty. He returned to the family home after his divorce three years later.

The defendant's parents picture their son as a well-intentioned individual whose difficulties with the law have been due to his unwise selection of associates. They are bitter toward codefendant Nancy Rooney, whom they believe was responsible for this offense. They view his previous juvenile and adult transgressions as minor matters that were treated with undue harshness by police and the courts. His parents describe the defendant as an intelligent and ambitious individual who values financial success above all else. They are proud of the fact that, in recent years, the defendant has acquired such material possessions as an expensive automobile and a boat. They also note that he has been especially generous with his younger brother and sister.

PARENTS AND SIBLINGS. The father, Henry Hesse, age 59, resides with his family and for the last seventeen years has been employed as a machine operator, earning a moderate salary. The home atmosphere improved considerably when Mr. Hesse stopped drinking approximately five years ago. The mother, Geraldine Ericksen Hesse, age 58, resides with her husband and is a housewife. Her health is poor due to respiratory ailments.

There are two siblings. Stanley Hesse, age 24, resides with his parents and is unemployed. Stanley believes that his brother is the victim of harassment by law-enforcement authorities. Audrey Hesse, age 19, resides with her parents and is a community college student.

MARITAL. Herman Hesse married Barbara Raymond in a civil ceremony in Hartford, Connecticut, on November 22, 1974. Both parties were twenty years old at the time, and she was pregnant. The couple had one child, Herman, Jr., who was born on April 29, 1975. Mrs. Hesse reports that the marriage was troubled from the start by financial problems, since the defendant was unemployed. He turned to illegal means of supporting the family, and his subsequent arrests caused even more strain on the couple's relationship. There were several brief separations during 1975 and 1976 and a longer separation when the defendant was sentenced to serve six months in September of 1976. When he was released, Mrs. Hesse found him a "different man" and that it was impossible to reconstitute their relationship. The Hampden County Probate Court granted a divorce on December 28, 1977, on grounds of incompatibility and awarded her custody of the child. The defendant was required to pay $20 a week child support. Mrs. Hesse is employed as a telephone operator. She reports that her ex-husband's support payments have been sporadic. He often goes for months without visiting the child or making any payments, but he will then arrive with lavish gifts for his son and lump-sum support payments. Mrs. Hesse says that her relationship with the defendant is now amicable, but they see each other infrequently.

Mr. Hesse asserts that he has no plans to marry again. He stated that Nancy Rooney was merely a friend.

EDUCATION. Mr. Hesse was educated in local public schools. He left junior high school in October 1969, when he was committed to the Youth Service Board. He returned to Baran High School in Holyoke in the fall of 1970 and dropped out of the eleventh grade in November 1971.

School officials describe Mr. Hesse as an intelligent individual who never worked up to his capabilities. His grades were generally C's and D's. Mr. Hesse left school because he was older than most of his classmates and wanted to get a job.

EMPLOYMENT. Between November 1982 and the time of his arrest, Mr. Hesse was unemployed and collected unemployment compensation of $72 a week. From August 1980 to November 1982, he was a forklift operator at the Smith Chemical Company in Northampton. He earned $4.10 an hour, but he was subject to frequent layoffs. Company officials described him as an uncooperative employee with a high degree of tardiness. He would not be considered for reemployment.

Between March 1978 and December 1979, Mr. Hesse worked in the warehouse of the United Rug Company in Easthampton, Massachusetts. He earned $2.75 an hour and he quit after a disagreement over hours. Between 1974 and 1977, Mr. Hesse was sporadically employed in the roofing business. This work paid well, but he seldom was able to get more than three or four months' work in any year.

After he left high school, Mr. Hesse worked on a delivery truck for Central Bakery, Inc., of Holyoke. He held this job between April 1972 and October 1974 and earned the minimum wage. He lost this job when the company went out of business.

Mr. Hesse said that he would like someday to open his own business. He had no clear ideas about the nature of this business, but stressed that he saw himself in a managerial capacity and would hire others to do the menial labor.

HEALTH

PHYSICAL. Mr. Hesse is in good physical condition. He denies having used drugs of any kind, and he specifically disclaims the use of heroin. Discussion with family members as well as with law enforcement sources revealed no information that would contradict Mr. Hesse's assertions in this respect. A physical examination and urinalysis test performed at the jail were negative for heroin use.

MENTAL AND EMOTIONAL. On two occasions Mr. Hesse was tested in public schools and received I.Q. scores of 102 and 113.

Mr. Hesse has been examined by mental health professional on two occasions. The first examination occurred shortly after Mr. Hesse was committed to the Youth Service Board in 1969. At that time a psychologist described him as "a person whose anxiety is stimulated by a frustrated need for affection," adding that "Herman has developed no healthy conscience. His response to social demands is not based on any close commitment to moral principles."

Mr. Hesse was examined once again as a result of this court's pretrial order. Dr. Robert Land administered a battery of psychological tests. Dr. Land wrote that the results suggested that Mr. Hesse "seems to be unusually fearful of being overpowered and destroyed. It is obvious that he has been unable to resolve childhood problems and continues to feel quite rejected. He tends to view threatening environmental forces as coming outside his control."

FINANCIAL CONDITION

ASSETS. Mr. Hesse lists two main assets. One is a 1982 Cadillac purchased in January of this year for $18,640. This automobile was confiscated by the Drug Enforcement Administration. The other asset is a 19-foot fiberglass speedboat with a 115-horsepower Mercury outboard engine worth approximately $6,000.

Mr. Hesse's parents displayed to the probation officer a savings account passbook with a present balance of $7,146.23. The account was in the names of Mr. Hesse and his mother, but the parents made it clear that the defendant had made the deposits. When questioned about this, Mr. Hesse asserted that the account in fact belonged to his mother and that his name was on it only as a matter of convenience. His mother subsequently contacted the probation officer and retracted her earlier statement. She said that she made a mistake and that the money in the account belonged to her.

LIABILITIES. The only debt Mr. Hesse lists is a loan from GMAC to finance the purchase of his 1982 Cadillac. The loan balance is presently $9,200, and Mr. Hesse plans to make no further payments until such time as his car is returned to him by the government.

EVALUATION

Although he attempts to shift responsibility to his codefendant, Mr. Hesse was the principal figure in the importation and sale of more than 100 grams of high-quality heroin. Were it not for the intervention of the Mexican authorities, he would have completed the sale of a quarter-kilogram to an undercover agent. Mr. Hesse is not a user of the drug. He apparently values financial success to the point that he made a calculated decision that heroin trafficking was profitable. His lack of concern about the moral aspects of his decision confirms the observation of mental health professionals that his personality lacks some of the constraints under which most people operate. For Mr. Hesse, participation in this offense, as well as in earlier offenses, was a logical means of satisfying his economic motives.

The members of Mr. Hesse's family are intensely loyal to him and they have an unrealistic view of his participation in criminal activities. They do not question the sources of his assets, which are surprisingly large for a person with his employment history. The family cannot be counted upon to exert the pressure that might convince Mr. Hesse to conform to law-abiding behavior. Mr. Hesse himself is unrealistic in his personal goals. Without much education or skill, he expects a high degree of financial compensation, but he has not thus far shown a willingness to work toward that goal. It is unlikely that Mr. Hesse will attempt conventional paths to economic success until he is convinced that illegal means are too hazardous.

ALTERNATIVE PLANS. Adult sentencing provisions apply in this case, and a special parole term of at least three years is required. Under any sentence imposed, Mr. Hesse will eventually come under the supervision of the probation office. An appropriate supervision plan would require immediate attention to Mr. Hesse's lack of marketable skills. The first step would be participation in a GED program, either in an institution or in the community. This would prepare him to accept more specialized training under the auspices of the Massachusetts Rehabilitation Commission. At least during the first six months of supervision, he would require maximum supervision with weekly reporting. The probation office suggests a requirement that he reside in Northrop House, where a highly structured environment is available. Northrop House has a contract with the Division of Legal Medicine and could provide Mr. Hesse with professional mental attention. Over the long term, the probation officer would pay particular attention to Mr. Hesse's financial dealings. He would also be encouraged to live independently of his family.

RECOMMENDATION

The probation office recommends commitment to the custody of the Attorney General and a mandatory special parole term of three years. This recommendation considers the quantity and quality of the heroin involved and the defendant's prior record.

The court may wish to consider imposing sentence under 18 U.S.C. 4205(b)(2) so that the Parole Commission can release him in the event that institutional conditions present a critical hazard to his mental health. The court might also consider recommending commitment to a minimum-security institution, where Mr. Hesse would feel less threatened.

Respectfully submitted,

Matilda Gormally
U.S. Probation Officer

INFORMATION EXCLUDED FROM THE PRESENTENCE REPORT AS POTENTIALLY EXEMPT FROM DISCLOSURE: RULE 32(c)(3)(A)

MARITAL. The defendant's ex-wife reported that when he was released from jail in early 1977 he showed no interest in resuming sexual relations with her. His behavior was also unusual in other respects, and he exhibited great tension and insomnia. Mrs. Hesse began to suspect that he had some experience in jail that had affected his sexual function. She questioned him about this on several occasions, and he responded with bitter denials. Mrs. Hesse became convinced that it was impossible to save the marriage and she filed for divorce. Mrs. Hesse was adamant that her husband not learn that she provided this information.

Officials of the Hampshire County Jail confirmed that Mr. Hesse was the victim of a homosexual assault in the jail. He refused to identify his attackers, but he asked to be moved to an isolated cell. This request was granted.

Officials of the Hampden County Jail, where Mr. Hesse is now lodged, report that he has displayed acute anxiety during his confinement. They are not aware of the reasons for this, but they note that Mr. Hesse has requested a transfer to the administrative segregation section. The jail has not complied with this request because of overcrowding.

MENTAL AND EMOTIONAL. The latest psychological report suggests that Mr. Hesse will continue to experience acute anxiety whenever he is placed in a situation that threatens recurrence of the homosexual assault. The psychologist believes that Mr. Hesse is not overtly homosexual, but that his sexual orientation is ambiguous. Since the attack, Mr. Hesse has reportedly experienced complete sexual dysfunction.

SUMMARY OF WITHHELD FACTUAL INFORMATION. If the court is of the view that the above information is excludable under Rule 32(c)(3)(A), and if the court intends to rely on that information in determining sentence, a summary of the withheld factual information is provided for disclosure to the defendant or his counsel:

> The court has received information about experiences of the defendant while previously incarcerated that caused him to have serious emotional problems. Subsequent psychological examination confirmed this existence.

SOURCE: Updated and adapted from *The Presentence Investigation Report*, monograph no. 105. (Administrative Office of the United States Courts, 1978).

CONDITIONS AND TERMS OF PROBATION

4

Probation conditions

The rules or terms under which a court releases an offender to community supervision. Conditions of release fall into two categories, standard and special. *Standard* conditions are imposed on all probationers in a jurisdiction. *Special* conditions are tailored to fit the particular needs of a individual offender.

American Probation and Parole Association (APPA)

The professional association for probation, parole, and community corrections workers. The APPA disseminates information about probation, parole, and community corrections to its members; provides technical assistance to community corrections agencies and governing bodies; conducts training; establishes and monitors professional standards; and provides a forum for a broad range of correctional issues and controversies.

CONDITIONS OF PROBATION

Probationers (and parolees) typically agree to abide by a set of rules or "conditions" of release. These **probation conditions** may be general rules that apply to all persons released under supervision, or they may be special conditions tailored to the needs of particular offenders. Ideally, the conditions are tailored to the special needs of the probationer. To accomplish this objective, probation statutes give the court considerable latitude in determining what conditions are to be imposed. The defendant is, of course, subject to the jurisdiction of the court during the period of probation.

Discretion to fix conditions of probation is derived from the court's powers to determine the nature and extent of the criminal penalties to be imposed on the defendant and to grant probation. Probation statutes state the power in general terms. One universal probation condition is that the person obey the law. The **American Probation and Parole Association (APPA)** recommends that this be the *only* condition imposed on persons sentenced to probation and that other conditions be tailored to the specific needs of each offender. The APPA suggests that conditions "be reasonably related to the avoidance of further criminal behavior and not unduly restrictive of the probationer's liberty or incompatible with his freedom of religion."

The federal probation statute (18 U.S.C. § 3563(a)) provides four *mandatory conditions* for all defendants convicted of a felony. They are that the defendant:

1. not commit another federal, state, or local crime;
2. abide by at least one condition; that is, a fine, restitution, or community service;
3. not possess illegal controlled substances; and
4. not possess a firearm.

Standard and Discretionary Conditions

Most jurisdictions routinely impose certain **standard conditions,** such as requirements that the probationer

■ work regularly and support his or her dependents,
■ not change residence or job without first notifying (or obtaining permission from) the probation officer,
■ not leave the jurisdiction without permission,
■ allow the probation officer to visit at any time,
■ not associate with persons who have criminal records, and
■ not enter into an agreement to act as an informer for any law enforcement agency without permission of the court.

Both federal and state statutes also provide for imposition of **special or discretionary conditions** of supervision. The federal statute requires that discretionary conditions imposed be weighed against (1) the nature and circumstances of the offense and the history and characteristics of the defendant and (2) the needs for the sentence most effectively to:

reflect the seriousness of the offense,

promote respect for law,

Survey of Probation Conditions

In a study of 79,000 probationers sentenced in 17 states in 1986, the Bureau of Justice Statistics found that 53 percent of all probationers had a special condition to satisfy, and 84 percent had a financial penalty to pay.

The most commonly imposed special conditions were for drug testing (31%), drug treatment (23%), and alcohol treatment (14%).

Types of financial penalties included victim restitution (29%), court costs (48%), and probation supervision fees (32%). The average financial penalty was $1,800, victim restitution $3,400; court costs, $560; and supervision fees, $680.

SOURCE: "Recidivism of Felons on Probation, 1986–89," *Bureau of Justice Statistics Special Report*, February 1992.

provide just punishment for the offense,

afford adequate deterrence for criminal conduct,

protect the public from further crimes of the defendant, and

provide the defendant with needed educational and vocational training, medical care, or other correctional treatment.

Special conditions may require the probationer to:

- pay a fine
- make restitution,
- do community service,
- participate in drug or alcohol treatment (and/or urine monitoring to assure abstinence),
- seek mental health treatment.

Statutes in some states recommend a range of probation conditions. Typically they require that the probationer:

1. commit no criminal offenses
2. not associate with persons who have criminal records
3. report to the probation officer as directed
4. permit the probation officer to visit him/her at home or elsewhere
5. work at suitable employment
6. remain within a specified place (city, county, state) unless given permission to leave by the probation officer
7. pay a fine, court costs, and/or restitution if ordered by the court
8. support his or her dependents
9. submit to testing for controlled substances

The court may impose all, some, or none of the conditions listed and it has the option to impose other conditions as it sees fit.[1] Some courts require the probationer to pay a fee toward the cost of his/her supervision, attend drug and/or alcohol treatment programs, attend literacy classes, reimburse the court for the cost of court-appointed counsel, and even serve a period of time in jail.

Purpose of Probation Conditions

The purpose of these conditions of probation are to assist the offender in living a law-abiding life. Some conditions have a *punitive* orientation; they

Standard Rules and Conditions of Probation, State of Florida

STATE OF FLORIDA
VS

FOR DADE COUNTY, FLORIDA

CRIMINAL DIVISION
CASE NO. _____

_____
DEFENDANT.

ORDER GRANTING PROBATION AND FIXING TERMS
THEREOF

IT APPEARING TO THE SATISFACTION OF THE COURT that you, the above-named defendant are not likely again to engage in a criminal course of conduct, and that the ends of justice and welfare of society do not require that you should presently suffer the penalty authorized by law,

IT IS THEREFORE ORDERED AND ADJUDGED that you are hereby placed on probation for a period of _____ years, beginning _____ under the supervision of the Florida Department of Offender Rehabilitation and its supervisors, such supervision to be subject to the provisions of the Laws of this State.

IT IS FURTHER ORDERED that you shall comply with the following conditions of probation:

(1) You will not change your residence or employment or leave the county of your residence without first procuring the consent of your Probation Supervisor.

(2) Not later than the fifth day of each month you will make a full and truthful report to your Probation Supervisor on the form provided for that purpose, unless otherwise directed by your Probation Supervisor.

(3) You will neither possess, carry or own any weapon or firearm without first procuring the consent of your Probation Supervisor.

(4) You will live and remain at liberty without violating any law. A conviction in a court of law shall not be necessary in order for such a violation to constitute a violation of your probation.

(5) You will not use intoxicants to excess; nor will you visit places where intoxicants, drugs or other dangerous substances are unlawfully sold, dispensed or used.

(6) You will work diligently at a lawful occupation and support any dependents to the best of your ability, as directed by your Probation Supervisor.

(7) You will promptly and truthfully answer all inquiries directed to you by the Court or the Probation Supervisor, and allow the Supervisor to visit in your home, at your employment site or elsewhere, and you will comply with all instructions he may give you.

(8) If at any time it becomes necessary to communicate with the Probation Supervisor for any purpose and he is not accessible, unless otherwise instructed, direct such communication to the Florida Department of Offender Rehabilitation, Tallahassee.

(9) You will make payments of ten dollars ($10.00) per month, as instructed by your Probation Supervisor, to the State of Florida, pursuant to 945.30 F.S. to cover part of the cost of your Supervision, while on Probation, unless any such payments are specifically waived according to law.

(10) You will comply with the special condition(s), if any, on the reverse side of this order.

YOU ARE HEREBY PLACED ON NOTICE THAT THE COURT may at any time rescind or modify any of the conditions of your probation, or may extend the period of probation as authorized by law, or may discharge you from further supervision; and that if you violate any of the conditions of your probation, you may be arrested and the Court may revoke your probation and impose any sentence which it might have imposed before placing you on probation.

IT IS FURTHER ORDERED that when you have reported to the Probation Supervisor and have been instructed as to the conditions of probation, unless otherwise specified on the reverse side of this order, you shall be released from custody if you are in custody and if you are at liberty on bond, the sureties thereon shall stand discharged from liability.

DONE AND ORDERED in open Court at Miami, Dade County, Florida,

this _____ day of _____, A.D., 19 _____

_____
JUDGE

I have read the above terms and conditions of my probation and understand them:

_____
PROBATIONER

I have (read) (interpreted) the above terms and conditions to the above named defendant:

_____
ATTORNEY/INTERPRETER

may require that the person serve time in jail or pay a fine, for example. Others, such as a requirement to attend a drug treatment program, are *therapeutic* in purpose. Regardless of the purpose of the probation condition, however, courts have consistently held that any conditions must be reasonably related to the offender's needs and the protection of society and not arbitrary, capricious, or beyond the ability of the offender to satisfy.[2]

DISCRETIONARY CONDITIONS

Jail

In some jurisdictions, the court may order a brief period of incarceration as a condition of probation. Known as **shock probation** or (*shock incarceration* or *split sentencing*), the practice is based on the premise that if offenders are given a taste of prison (the "shock"), they will be reluctant to violate the conditions of probation upon their release.[3] The federal probation statute states that the court may impose intermittent confinement as a condition of probation during the first year of probation.[4]

The practice of combining a jail sentence with probation—in effect, making a jail sentence a condition of probation—has been widely followed. Of the 583,000 felons convicted in state courts in 1986, 21 percent received probation combined with a period of prison or jail.[5] California imposes jail time with probation more than any other jurisdiction. In a recent sentencing survey, 85 percent of California probationers had a jail term with their probation.[6] In several states, nearly a third of those placed on probation are required to spend some time in confinement.[7]

The Model Penal Code permits a thirty-day period of imprisonment in connection with a probated term for a person convicted of a felony or misdemeanor.[8] The American Bar Association's *Standards relating to Sentencing Alternatives and Procedures* include among the range of sentencing alternatives "[c]ommitment to an institution for a short, fixed period followed by automatic release under supervision."[9] The commentary on this section recognizes widespread opposition to combining jail with probation. The National Advisory Commission recommended against the practice. The Commission argued that the goal of probation should be to maintain in the community all persons who, with support, can perform there acceptably and to select for some type of confinement only those who, on the basis of evidence, cannot complete probation successfully, even with optimal support. With this goal in mind, the Commission recommended that the practice of commitment to an institution for the initial period of probation should be discontinued, pointing out that it defeats the purpose of probation—which is the earliest possible reintegration of the offender into the community. Those who reject jail as a condition of probation assert that short-term commitment subjects the probationer to the destructive effects of institutionalization,

Inmates in a jail cell.

disrupts his or her life in the community, and stigmatizes him/her for having been in jail.[10]

Obviously, different jurisdictions and "experts" have arrived at different conclusions as to the effectiveness of shock probation. Probation "purists" see the practice as a negation of the basic meaning and objective of probation. Others believe that an initial period of incarceration makes the offender more receptive to probation supervision and significantly improves the person's chances of making successful community adjustment. In many cases, outcome may depend not so much on the method used as on the care with which offenders are selected when there is an option to include or not include incarceration as a condition of probation. Research on the efficacy of shock probation for reducing recidivism has been inconclusive. A more detailed discussion of this issue is found in Chapter 12.

Electronic Monitoring

Electronic monitoring is becoming increasingly popular as a condition of probation. It involves linking a monitor attached to the probationer's wrist or ankle to a home telephone, which, in turn, is linked to a computer at the probation agency. This gives the probation officer greatly enhanced surveillance ability. In most states electronic monitoring may be imposed by a judge as a discretionary condition, or may be specifically provided for by statute.

By 1991 nearly 8,000 probationers were under electronic monitoring. Although more than half of the states and the federal government were using electronic monitoring as a condition of probation, the states of Florida, Michigan, Indiana, and North Carolina accounted for about half of all electronic monitoring orders.[11] A more detailed discussion of electronic monitoring is found in Chapter 12.

Electronic monitoring

The use of small electronic transmitters attached to offenders' bodies to monitor their movement and thus enhance probation officers' surveillance capabilities.

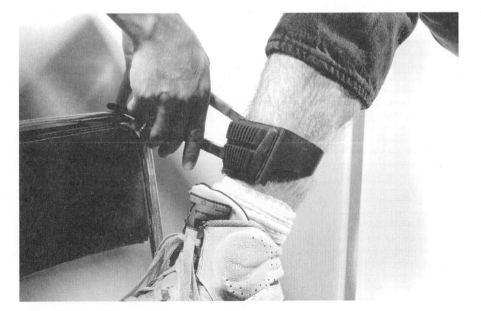

Electronic Monitoring device being attached to offender's ankle.

Fines

Fines

Monetary payments from offenders as punishment.

Fines require monetary payments from offenders as punishment. In fact, the *Federal Sentencing Guideline Handbook* specifically states, "The amount of the fine should always be sufficient that the fine, taken together with the other sanctions imposed, is punitive."[12] Both federal and state court judges frequently impose fines as a condition of probation. The use of fines has been criticized as causing a greater burden on the poor than on the wealthy, and many of the laws regarding fines are now being revised. Revisions are needed for ensuring equality in the imposition of fines, developing payment schedules, and restricting the use of incarceration to situations of refusal to pay.[13] One effort to make fines more equitable has been the experiment in New York and some other jurisdictions with the European system of "day fines." **Day fines** are keyed to the offender's daily wage, and the fine is assessed as some multiple of the daily wage, or "unit." For example, if an offender earns $100 per day and his fine is 5 units, he would be required to pay 5 times his daily wage, or $500. A day fine of 5 units imposed on an offender with an income of $1,000 a day would be $5,000.

Day Fines

Fines keyed to the offender's daily wage.

Failure to pay a fine imposed as a probation condition may result in revocation and incarceration. However, probation is seldom revoked for failure to pay fines alone. In the 1983 case of *Bearden v. Georgia,* the Supreme Court held that probation cannot be revoked solely because of an offender's inability to pay a fine or restitution.[14] The Court, however, differentiated between *indigency* (inability) and *unwillingness* (refusal) to pay. Refusal to pay court-ordered restitution or fines *may* result in revocation. Statutes in most states and the federal system provide for allowing a flexible payment schedule if the defendant is unable to pay the entire fine immediately, modifying the sentence to reduce the fine, and in some cases, remitting the fine and imposing an alternative sanction. A more detailed discussion of the use of fines as a condition of probation and as a sanction in itself is found in Chapter 12.

Restitution

Restitution

A condition of probation that requires offenders to compensate their victims for damages or monetary losses incurred as a result of their crimes.

Restitution is defined as "an equitable remedy under which a person is restored to his or her position prior to a loss or injury . . . compensation for the wrongful taking of property."[15] As a condition of probation, restitution requires offenders to compensate their victims for damages or loss of property. Restitution may take the form of direct monetary restitution to the victim or of "symbolic" restitution in the form of community service. In recent years restitution has become widely accepted and popular as a condition of probation, however it is not without potential for abuse. John Ortiz Smykla warns that:

> Restitution is not without its dangers. Because litigation has not contested its use, there is potential for abuse; the due process rights of probationers can be ignored in placing them in restitution programs, or they can be sentenced to prolonged periods of community service or to unfair amounts of restitution. For example, victims frequently exaggerate the amount of property damage inflicted upon them by offenders.[16]

Other critics allege that probationers may be required to pay so much that their dependents suffer. Further, some probation departments have so emphasized restitution that it has interfered with the work of the department. This has caused probation officers to complain that they have become collection agents.[17]

Generally, however, the practice is seen to have positive benefits for the probationer, the victim, and society as a whole. Douglas McDonald, in a National Institute of Justice report, wrote:

> Victim restitution . . . forces offenders to see firsthand the consequences of their deeds and thus may encourage the development of greater social responsibility and maturity.[18]

A 1992 Bureau of Justice Statistics study reported that in a sample of 79,000 probationers, 50 percent of all property offenders and 24 percent of all violent offenders were ordered restitution as a condition of probation. The average restitution ordered was $3,368. The study also reported that 60 percent of the offenders had completed their restitution by the time they completed their sentence.[19] Other studies have found that probationers receiving restitution orders have equal or lower recidivism rates than control groups receiving no restitution orders.[20]

Community Service

Many offenders coming through the criminal justice system have limited financial resources and cannot reasonably be expected to pay monetary restitution. Thus, **community service**—the performance of unpaid work for civic or nonprofit organizations—is becoming increasingly popular as an alternative means of restitution. In a study of 79,000 felons sentenced in 1986, Langdan and Cunniff (1992) reported that 14 percent had a special condition requiring community service.[21]

Federal courts have combined community service orders with probation in sentencing corporate defendants. Corporations have too often considered fines, even large ones, as merely a "cost of doing business,"[22] since the real costs of the fine are borne by the stockholders and consumers. Corporate probationary sentences requiring community service by company officers and employees are seen as an alternative. The federal probation system handbook, *Community Service: A Guide for Sentencing and Implementation* states:

> Corporations can be required to donate the effort of staff and other resources to projects that serve the public interest. The time of corporate executives or personnel should be the primary contribution to a community service project. . . .[23]

Restitution and community service orders are discussed in more detail in Chapter 12.

Community Service

A special condition of probation that requires offenders to perform unpaid work for civic or nonprofit organizations. Community service may be regarded as a substitute for financial compensation to victims or as symbolic restitution.

ILLEGAL CONDITIONS

Although the trial court has broad discretion in imposing the terms and conditions of probation, its powers are not boundless. Conditions imposed

Probationers performing community service.

must be *reasonable* and *relevant* to the offense for which probation is being granted. Accordingly, it has been held that a probation condition that

1. Has no relationship to the crime for which the offender was convicted,
2. Relates to conduct that is not of itself criminal, or
3. Requires or forbids conduct that is not reasonably related to future criminality

does not serve the statutory ends of probation and is invalid.[24]

In the case of *Higdon v. United States*,[25] the Ninth Circuit Court of Appeals rejected a probation condition that required the probationer to do 6,200 hours of volunteer work over a three-year period. The court reasoned as follows:

> First we consider the purpose for which the judge imposed the conditions. If the purposes are permissible, the second step is to consider whether the conditions are reasonably related to the purposes. In conducting the latter inquiry the court examines the impact . . . the conditions have on the probationer's rights. If the impact is substantially greater than is necessary to carry out the purposes, the conditions are impermissible.[26]

The court held that the condition, which was essentially full-time charity work, was "much harsher than necessary."

In *Rodriquez v. State*, a Florida court placed a defendant convicted of aggravated child abuse on probation for ten years, provided she (1) not have custody of her children, (2) not become pregnant, and (3) not marry without the consent of the court. The appellate court ruled that although trial courts have broad discretion to impose various conditions of probation, a special condition of probation cannot be imposed if it is so punitive as to be unrelated to rehabilitation. Applying these criteria to the case, the court held that a condition prohibiting custody of children has a clear relationship to the crime of child abuse and is therefore valid. However, probation conditions relating to marriage and pregnancy had no relationship to the crime of child abuse, and were related to noncriminal conduct. These conditions could relate to potential for future criminality—if the marriage or pregnancy resulted in the custody of minor children, who could be abused—but the conditions were not reasonably related to future criminality, since such custody of minor children was already prohibited by the valid condition directly addressed to custody. The conditions prohibiting marriage and pregnancy did nothing to decrease the possibility of future child abuse or other criminality.[27]

In a another significant case, a defendant was placed on probation for five years on condition that he refrain from the use of all alcoholic beverages. His probation was revoked when he violated the condition. He appealed, alleging that a psychiatric examination would have shown that he was a chronic alcoholic and that he was not responsible at the time of the act. The appellate court remanded the case on the ground that the district court may have imposed an impossible condition, particularly if psychiatric testimony established that his alcoholism had destroyed his power of volition and prevented his compliance with the condition.[28]

CONSTITUTIONALLY PROTECTED ACTIVITY

Courts have generally invalidated conditions related to constitutionally protected activity. Conditions that restrain freedom of speech, religion, or association involve fundamental rights and may be judged by a higher standard than "reasonableness."[29] In *Jones v. Commonwealth,* a Virginia court held that an order of a juvenile court requiring regular attendance at Sunday school and church was unconstitutional, because "no civil authority has the right to require anyone to accept or reject any religious belief or to contribute any support thereto."[30] In a 1986 case, the United States Court of Appeals reviewed a probation condition requiring a probationer to participate in an "Emotional Maturity Instruction" program. The probationer claimed the condition violated his First Amendment freedom of religion due to the program's religious content. The court stated that:

> A condition of probation which requires the probationer to adopt religion or adopt any particular religion would be unconstitutional. . . .It follows that a condition of probation which requires the probationer to submit himself to a course advocating the adoption of religion or a particular religion also transgresses the First Amendment.[31]

Yet, in *Berrigan v. Sigler* (1973), the U.S. Parole Board's decision to deny political activists Philip and Daniel Berrigan permission to travel to North Vietnam was held not to violate their First Amendment rights.[32] The court held that the travel prohibition was directly related to the public interest and did not unreasonably infringe on the Berrigans' constitutionally protected rights.

During the 1970s and 1980s several courts held that conditions of probation and parole that required probationers or parolees to submit to searches with or without a warrant were valid. In *People v. Mason,* the court ruled that the waiver of Fourth Amendment rights can be a probation condition and that by such waiver a probationer has no reasonable expectation

Philip and Daniel Berrigan.

of privacy.[33] The *reasonableness* standard of the Fourth Amendment has generally been held to apply, however, and probation and parole officers must have reasonable grounds to believe that searches are necessary to the performance of their duties with relation to the probationer or parolee.[34] In *Griffin v. Wisconsin* (1987), the United States Supreme Court addressed the issue of searches by probation and parole officers. In *Griffin,* a probation officer searched the home of a probationer under his supervision without having obtained a search warrant. The probation officer had received a tip from a police officer that guns might be found in the probationer's home. A gun was found, and the probationer was subsequently convicted on a firearms charge. At his trial, the probationer moved to suppress the introduction of the gun as evidence on the grounds that the search was a violation of his Fourth Amendment protection from unreasonable searches and seizures. The motion was denied, and the conviction was later affirmed by the Wisconsin Supreme Court.

In making the search, the probation officer had relied on a Wisconsin probation regulation that allows the search of a probationer's home without a warrant with the approval of a supervisor. The regulation also requires that there be reasonable grounds to believe contraband is present in violation of the conditions of probation.

The Supreme Court described probation as a form of sanction, like incarceration, and as such, warrant requirements were by necessity impractical; the necessity for quick decisions would be encumbered by magistrate involvement. The Court also found that the regulation permitting the search, on which the probation officer had relied, was consistent with the Fourth Amendment's "reasonableness" requirement—being analogous to previously approved exceptions such as searches and seizures in public school settings.[35]

TERM OF PROBATION

The power to fix the **term of probation** (i. e., its length) is usually given to the sentencing authority, although maximum and sometimes minimum limits may be set by statute. These limits are often similar to the terms fixed by statute for the offense if the offender is committed to a penal institution, instead of placed on probation. The modern trend, however, has been to specify limits for probation that are less than the limits for commitment. In some states, the court is empowered to extend the length of probation during the original term. In many states, the court is given authority to terminate probation at any time in the probation period or after a certain portion of the probation period has been served. Statutes regarding early termination may or may not include provisions for setting aside the conviction and restoring the offender's civil rights.

Modern standards for probation recommend that probation terms be fixed and relatively short and that the court be given authority to terminate the probation at any time during the probated period. The Model Penal Code suggests a probation of five years on conviction of a felony and of two years on conviction of a misdemeanor or petty misdemeanor.[36] The American Bar Association *Standards relating to Probation* provides that neither supervision nor the power to revoke should be permitted to extend beyond a legislatively fixed time, which should in no event exceed two years for a misdemeanor and five years for a felony.[37] The National Advisory Commission states that a sentence of probation should be for a specific term not to exceed the maximum sentence authorized by law, except that probation for a misdemeanant may be for a period not exceeding one year.[38]

As has been noted, the court is sometimes given authority to extend a term of probation or to terminate probation before the imposed time limit has expired. The procedures that should be required for modifying probation conditions are discussed next.

Term of probation
The length of probation.

MODIFICATION OF TERM AND CONDITIONS OF PROBATION

The term and conditions of probation can be modified in two ways: in some cases the modification results in a shorter term or eased restrictions, and in other cases it extends the term or imposes additional restrictions. Authority to modify the term of probation by decreasing the term and discharging the offender before completion of the term should be placed in the court.[39] The court should likewise have authority to modify the conditions of probation on application of the probationer or the probation officer, or on its own motion. The probationer should also have free access to the court for the purpose of clarifying the probation conditions. This power of modification preserves the flexibility of probation as a correctional tool, since it allows for changing conditions and for improvement in the probationer's ability to handle his or her personal affairs—one of the major objectives of probation.

Giving the court the power to discharge the offender from probation supervision before the stated term expires recognizes the fact that many probationers do not need probation services for the full, originally set time period. It has the advantage of removing from the probation rolls offenders whose reintegration into the community is complete, or at least, complete enough to make it probable that they can manage without further intervention by the probation officer.

Probation statutes grant power to the court to enlarge as well as to decrease the term and conditions of probation. When granted, this power must generally be exercised within the time limits of the original probated term, although disappearance of the probationer may *toll*, or interrupt the running of, the term of probation. The court loses the power to modify conditions if the offender is committed to an institution or if probation has been terminated by court action or the passage of time.

The desirability of giving the court authority to modify the term and conditions of probation is generally accepted. The issues that give rise to controversy are the technical issues of determining when a probation period has ended and the policy issues of what procedures should be required before the court can exercise its authority to modify the original term and conditions of probation—particularly if the modification is to extend the term or impose more restrictive conditions.

Procedures for Modifying Term and Conditions

It can be argued, of course, that the procedures for modifying the term or conditions of probation should be at least similar to those associated with the granting of the probation. However, a little reflection shows that to require an appearance of all parties before the court, complete with counsel, in order to change the reporting day from Friday to Wednesday or to clarify the meaning of a condition for the defendant would be unnecessary and would in no way promote the objectives of probation. Changes that impose longer, harsher, or more restrictive conditions on the offender would appear to demand more formal procedures than changes that lead to relaxed supervision or an early discharge from probation.

A number of states authorize early termination without providing statutory guidelines as to when the power should be exercised. A significantly larger number permit early termination or discharge from further supervision upon the satisfaction of statutory criteria or the taking of certain procedural steps. The most frequent requirement is a showing that the probationer has satisfied the condition of probation. Presence of the probationer is a usual requirement if the modification will extend the term or impose more restrictive conditions.

When the early discharge procedures also have as their objective the prevention of a conviction with its serious consequences to the offender, or are part of a process that seeks to "wipe out" the conviction and restore the offender to the enjoyment of his or her civil rights, considerable formality and careful record keeping in the court would benefit both the state and the defendant.

The American Bar Association committee working with sentencing and probation standards gave considerable thought to these procedural problems. One of the committee's first considerations was to distinguish between modifications in probation conditions that may lead to the defendant's confinement and those that would not. The standards recommend, for example, that before a revocation of probation there should be a review of the conditions, changes where necessary or desirable, and a formal or informal conference with the probationer to reemphasize the necessity of complying with the conditions.[40] The right of the probationer to apply to the court for a clarification of a change of conditions was stated without recommendation as to a conference or hearing. A request for clarification provides an avenue for resolving disputes between probationer and probation officer about the meaning of a condition, it being assumed that such disputes generally would be resolved without court intervention.[41]

Where a modification in the terms and conditions of probation may lead to confinement, procedures should correspond to those required for revocation of probation.[42] Whether this would include the "on-site hearing" demanded by *Gagnon v. Scarpelli*[43] as well as the probation revocation hearing before the court is still an open question. If the suggested modifications are so extensive as to raise this question, the matter should probably be identified as a revocation hearing. Instead of following the procedures for a modification of term or conditions, the revocation procedures would be followed.

The whole thrust of recent "due process" cases suggests that if the modification would impose new or additional burdens on the probationer, there should be a hearing, preceded by notice, at which the defendant is given an opportunity to object to the suggested modification and refute any misstatements as to the facts on which the modification is based.[44] Appearance before the court ensures that the matter will be decided by an impartial tribunal and that the decision will be based on matters before the court. The probationer should be given a written copy of the modified conditions, and care should be taken to assure that the probationer understands the continuing requirements of the probation.

SUMMARY

Probationers typically agree to abide by a set of rules or "conditions" of release. The power to fix these conditions lies with the court. One universal condition is to obey the law. Although courts have broad powers to impose other conditions, the conditions must be reasonably related to helping the offender to avoid further criminal behavior and not unduly restrictive of his/her liberty or constitutionally protected activities, such as freedom of religion. In recent years probation supervision has been linked with conditions that require a short jail term, electronic monitoring, payment of a fine, and/or community service or restitution.

The power to fix the term (length of probation) also is usually given to the court. The modern trend is to fix a relatively short term, with the provision that the court can terminate the probation at any time during the term.

The court also has the power to modify the conditions and the term of probation. The term and conditions can both be enlarged or decreased.

Generally speaking, some due process procedure must be adhered to in modifying the terms and conditions. Where the term is increased or the conditions are made more restrictive, procedures should correspond to those required for revocation of probation.

ENDNOTES

1. Rolando del Carmen, Betsy Witt, Thomas Caywood, and Sally Layland, *Probation Law and Practice in Texas* (Huntsville, Texas: Criminal Justice Center, Sam Houston State University, 1989), p. 38.

2. Richard W. Snarr, *Introduction to Corrections,* 2nd ed. (Dubuque, Ia.: Wm. C. Brown Publishers, 1992), p. 261.

3. Larry Siegel, *Criminology,* 4th ed. (St. Paul, Minn. West, 1992).

4. 18 U.S.C.A. § 3563 (b) (11); and *Federal Sentencing Guidelines Handbook: Text, Analysis, Case Digests.* (Shepard's McGraw-Hill, 1990), p. 323.

5. Patrick A. Langan and Mark Cunniff, "Recidivism of Felons on Probation, 1986–1989," *Bureau of Justice Statistics Special Report,* February 1992.

6. *Id.* at 3.

7. Belinda Rodgers McCarthy and Bernard J. McCarthy, Jr., *Community-Based Corrections,* 2nd ed. (Pacific Grove, Calif.: Brooks/Cole, 1991).

8. Model Penal Code § 301.1(3).

9. ABA, *Standards, Sentencing Alternatives and Procedures,* § 2.4(a)iii.

10. National Advisory Commission, *Standards, Corrections,* p. 321.

11. Louis Jankowski, "Probation and Parole, 1990," BJS *Bulletin,* November 1991.

12. *Federal Sentencing Guidelines Handbook, supra* note 4, at 335.

13. *Report to the Nation on Crime and Justice* (U.S. Department of Justice, Bureau of Justice Statistics, 1988).

14. Bearden v. Georgia 461 U.S. 660, 103 S.Ct. 2064, 76 L.Ed. 2d 221 (1983).

15. *Black's Law Dictionary,* 6th ed. (St. Paul, Minn.: West, 1990), p. 1313.

16. John Ortiz Smykla, *Probation and Parole: Crime Control in the Community* (New York: Macmillan, 1984), p. 222.

17. Edwin H. Sutherland, Donald Cressey, and David F. Luckenbill, *Principles of Criminology,* 11th ed. (Dix Hills, New York: General Hall, Inc., 1992).

18. Douglas C. McDonald, *Restitution and Community Service* (Washington, D.C.: National Institute of Justice, p. 192.)

19. Langan and Cunniff, *supra* note 5, at 1.

20. Siegel, *supra* note 3, at 561.

21. Langan and Cunniff, *supra,* at 7.

22. *Id.* at 5.

23. *Id.* at 6.

24. People v. Lent, 15 Cal. 3d 481, 124 Cal. Rptr. 905,541 P.2d 545 (1975), 361.

25. 627 F. 2d 893 (9th Cir.1980).

26. *Id.* at 897.

27. Rodriguez v. State, 378 So. 2d 7 (Fla.Dist.Ct.App. 1979).

28. Sweeney v. United States, 353 F.2d 10 (7th Cir.1965).

29. Sheldon Krantz, *Corrections and Prisoner's Rights* (St. Paul, Minn.: West, 1988); and Sobell v. Reed, 327 F. Supp. 1294 (S.D.N.Y. 1971).

30. Jones v. Commonwealth, 185 Va. 335, 38 S.E.2d 444 (1946).

31. Owens v. Kelley, 681 F.2d 1362 (11th Cir. 1982).

32. 358 F. Supp. 130 (D.D.C. 1973); and discussion in Krantz, *supra* note 29, at 361.

33. 5 Cal. 3d 759, 97 Cal. Reptr. 302, 488 P.2d 630 (1971); and Krantz, *supra,* at 362.

34. Krantz, *supra*, at 362; and United States v. Scott 678 F.2d.32 (5th Cir. 1982).
35. Krantz, *supra*, at 365.
36. Model Penal Code § 301.2.
37. ABA, *Standards, Probation*, § 1.1(d), and *Standards, Sentencing Alternatives and Procedures*, § 2.4.
38. *NAC, Standards, Corrections*, Standard 5.4.1.
39. The sentencing court should have the authority to terminate probation at any time. Authority should be exercised prior to the term fixed in the original sentence if it appears that the offender has made a good adjustment and that further supervision or enforced compliance with other conditions is no longer necessary. ABA, *Standards, Probation*, § 4.2., Probation.
40. ABA, *Standards, Probation*, 5.1(b).
41. *Id.*, § 3.1(c).
42. See, generally, Chapter 7, Revocation of Probation, *infra*.
43. Gagnon v. Scarpelli, 411 U.S. 778, 93 S.Ct. 1756, 36 L.Ed.2d 656 (1973).
44. Morrissey v. Brewer, 408 U.S. 471, 92 S.Ct. 2593, 33 L.Ed.2d 484 (1972).

DISCUSSION QUESTIONS

1. Distinguish between standard and special conditions of probation. What do some suggest as the *only* standard condition for all probationers? Can you suggest some reasons for this?

2. When would imposition of special conditions of probation be justified under federal probation statutes?

3. What are the most common special conditions of probation? According to the Bureau of Justice Statistics study of 79,000 probationers, what percentage of probationers have special conditions of (a) drug testing; (b) drug treatment; (c) restitution; (d) community service; (e) alcohol treatment?

4. What are the potential benefits of "shock probation"? What are its possible negative consequences?

5. Explain electronic monitoring. What are its benefits and its possible negative consequences?

6. How might fines be made more equitable? Do you believe fines should be imposed on most property offenders? Why or why not?

7. Discuss community service and restitution as conditions of probation. What are the benefits and possible negative consequences of each? Do you think that these special conditions of probation will continue to be popular as probation conditions?

8. According to court decisions, what are the three elements of a reasonable and relevant condition of probation?

9. Discuss at least three cases involving constitutionally protected activities as conditions of probation.

10. List and discuss the issues relating to the term of probation.

11. With respect modifying the term and conditions of probation, two sets of circumstances must be differentiated. What are these, and what issues are raised in the chapter?

12. Discuss modifying the conditions of probation with regard to the issue of "due process."

Probation and Parole Conditions: Recent Court Decisions

CONDITIONS HELD VALID

MARKLEY V. STATE
507 So.2D 1043 (ALA.CT.CRIM.APP.4/14/87)

The defendant, a priest, was found guilty of burglary and criminal mischief because of incidents involving his participation in an anti-abortion demonstration. The trial court suspended the imposition of sentence and placed the defendant on probation. Among the special conditions of probation was a condition that the defendant refrain from knowingly going within 500 yards of any clinic that performed abortive surgery. The defendant was subsequently found in violation of this condition and he appealed, claiming that the condition infringed upon his First Amendment rights.

The condition of the defendant's probation that he not participate in anti-abortion protests was valid and did not infringe on his First Ammendment rights.

Rejecting the defendant's claim, the court cited *Persall v. State*, 16 So.2d 332 (1944) for the proposition that a defendant has the right to accept the terms and conditions of probation or to reject them and serve out his sentence. In this case, by accepting the conditions of probation, the defendant was bound by the terms of that probation. While conditions of probation must serve the dual objectives of rehabilitation and public safety, there is no presumption that limitations on constitutional rights are impermissible. *United States v. Consuelo-Gonzalez*, 521 F.2d 259 (1975). Furthermore, a convicted criminal may be subjected, as a condition of his probation, to restrictions on his expression and associations. *Malone v. United States*, 502 F.2d 554 (9th Cir.1974), cert. denied, 419 U.S. 1124, 95 S.Ct. 809, 42 L.Ed.2d 824 (1975). In line with the above cases, the court found no violation whatsoever of the appellant's constitutional rights.

As a second matter, the court went on to find that the trial court carefully scrutinized the appellant's actions in light of his First Amendment rights. The appellant was not precluded from attending church or, indeed, going near certain places of worship, provided he was not at the same point engaged in some type of activity which had been restricted. His testimony at the revocation hearing indicated that the appellant was knowingly in violation of the terms of his probation and had participated in abortion protest activities without hesitation.

The revocation was affirmed.

PEOPLE V. MILLER
265 CAL.RPTR.587 (CAL.APP.FEB.1989).

After being convicted of committing lewd and lascivious acts upon a child under the age of fourteen, the defendant was placed on probation. One of the conditions of probation was that he have no contact with the victim or any other minor females unless in the presence of the minor's parent or with the express approval of his probation officer. It was further required that he submit to a polygraph examination at the direction of his probation officer. The probation officer asserted that the polygraph condition was necessary to monitor the defendant's compliance with other conditions of probation, especially the condition forbidding his unsupervised contact with young girls. The defendant's appeal claimed that the polygraph requirement violated his privilege against self-incrimination.

The condition requiring the defendant to submit to polygraph testing at the request of his probation officer was not unconstitutional.

On review by the California Court of Appeals, the court disagreed. The mere requirement of taking the test in itself did not constitute an infringement of the privilege. Although the defendant had a duty to answer the polygraph examiner's questions truthfully, unless he invoked the privilege or demonstrated a realistic threat of self-incrimination and was nevertheless required to answer, there would be no violation of his right against self-incrimination.

Nor could the court agree that the defendant would be entitled to *Miranda* warnings prior to the administration of the polygraph examination. Stated the court [footnotes omitted]:

> The polygraph condition is designed to help evaluate the truthfulness of defendant's reports and "[t]he purpose and objectives of probation would be frustrated if a convicted defendant could maintain . . . a right of silence at the time of his . . . report to the probation officer. . . ." (*People v. Hamilton* (1968) 260 Cal.App.2d 103, 105, 66 Cal.Rptr.831.)

> When subject to a polygraph examination as an investigative tool alone, a probationer is not placed in any worse position than he would otherwise be were there no polygraph condition. In either case, the probation officer may fully investigate the probationer's compliance with conditions whether or not the polygraph is used.

> The trial court did not abuse its discretion by including the polygraph requirement as a condition of probation for the limited use as an investigative tool.

The judgment of the trial court was affirmed.

United States v. Cothran
855 F.2d 749 (U.S. 11th Cir. Sept.1988)

The condition which required the defendant to stay out of a certain county for the first two years of his probation unless he received prior permission from his probation officer was not invalid. A district court is given wide discretion under 18 U.S.C. § 3651 to impose specific conditions of probation so long as these conditions reasonably relate to the rehabilitation of the offender.

Condition that probationer stay out of a certain county valid.

Owens v. Kelley
681 F.2d 1362 (11th Cir.1982)

The defendant was convicted of two felony charges regarding the possession of controlled substances and was placed on probation under various conditions.

Among the conditions imposed were the requirements that the probationer participate in a specific rehabilitation program, that he submit to warrantless searches and seizures by probation authorities or police officials, and that he submit to periodic polygraph or psychological stress evaluations (PSE). The probationer brought a civil rights action under Section 1983 making the following claims: (1) the program entitled Emotional Maturity Instruction violated his First Amendment rights, because it consisted of "religious" instruction; (2) the condition regarding the Fourth Amendment waiver was improper and overboard; and (3) the polygraph/P.S.E. requirement violated his right to be free from self-incrimination. The district court granted summary judgment in favor of the defendants, and appeal was taken.

First, Fourth, and Fifth Amendment violations claimed by probationer. Court held conditions valid.

On appeal the court held first that summary judgment in relation to the probationer's religious claim was improper. Summary judgment is only appropriate where there are no material facts in dispute. While the actual program in the instant case may not have contained "religious" material, the probationer had testified that instruction within the program was often based on Biblical teachings. Finding it clear that a probation condition could not require the adoption or practice of a particular religion, and finding that material facts were in dispute in the instant case, the court held that summary judgment was improper. Stated the court:

> In searching for the proper teaching of an EMI course, it is probably difficult to locate one who can teach morality without reference to religion, but that is the task which must be accomplished. We recognize that there is a fine line between rehabilitation efforts which encourage lawful conduct by an appeal to morality and the benefits of moral conduct to life of the probationer, and efforts which encourage lawfulness through adherence to religious belief. Nevertheless, this is the line that must not be overstepped. It will be the function of the District Court on remand to determine whether Owens has been placed in a program that does overstep this line.

Turning to the Fourth Amendment claims, the court found that while the claim was one of first impression in the 11th Circuit, other courts had addressed the issue with mixed results. In *United States v. Tonry*, 605 F.2d 144 (5th Cir.1979), the court fashioned a test for the propriety of probation conditions. That test follows:

> The conditions must be "reasonably related" to the purposes of the Act. Consideration of three factors is required to determine whether a reasonable relationship exists: (1) the purposes sought to be served by probation; (2) the extent to which constitutional rights enjoyed by law-abiding citizens should be accorded to probationers; and (3) the legitimate needs of law enforcement.

Noting that Georgia statutes did not specifically delineate the purposes of probation, the court found that Georgia case law established two essential purposes: the rehabilitation of the offender and the protection of the public. The court held that the condition in the instant case reasonably related to rehabilitation because it sought to dissuade the probationer from the illegal possession of controlled substances and it provided supervising officials with a mechanism to determine whether or not rehabilitation was actually occurring. While the information obtained as a result of a search could be used as a basis for revocation, it could also be used to determine supervision and counseling levels. Furthermore, the condition advanced the purpose of protecting the public by deterring future illegal conduct and enhancing law enforcement ability to detect illegal conduct.

Turning to the second *Tonry* factor, the rights that should be accorded probationers, the court found that while Fourth Amendment protections applied to the probation setting, the state had a compelling interest in setting some limitations upon probationers. Furthermore, probationers have a diminished expectation of privacy because of their conviction. Because the state has an interest in rehabilitation and protection of the public and because probationers enjoy a diminished expectation of privacy, the court found the condition to be proper. The court went on to reject the propositions that probation searches must be based on probable cause or even the lesser standard of reasonable suspicion. Citing *Latta v. Fitzharris*, 521 F.2d 246 (9th Cir.1975), for the position that a probation or parole officer should know more about a probationer or parolee than anyone else, with the exception of perhaps his family, and noting language

from *Latta* which indicated a probation search could be conducted on a mere "hunch," the court held that to impose a stricter standard would subvert the goals of rehabilitation and public protection. Acknowledging that probation searches must be "reasonable" and carried out in furtherance of the purposes of probation, the court held that a search that was intimidating or harassing and performed for reasons totally unrelated to the conviction or rehabilitation were improper. Concluded the court:

> Owens and amicus finally argue that if warrantless searches are to be permitted we should only allow such searches by probation supervisors and not by law enforcement officers. We are not convinced, however, that such a distinction should be drawn. While the primary task of supervising Owens'[s] probation rests with the state probation supervisors, law enforcement officers can lend legitimate assistance by conducting searches pursuant to the probation condition. As noted earlier, such searches are lawful so long as they are in fact conducted for probationary purposes. They cannot be conducted as "a subterfuge for criminal investigations." *United States v. Consuelo-Gonzalez*, 521 F.2d at 267.

Regarding the probationer's Fifth Amendment claims, the court found the claim to be without merit. The probationer was not required to "answer" incriminating questions and he could assert his Fifth Amendment privilege against self-incrimination if he so desired. Furthermore, there was nothing in the condition which indicated that the results would be used as a basis for probation revocation. Indeed, the court found that such a practice was impermissible under *State v. Chambers*, 240 Ga. 76, 239 S.E.2d 324 (1977). The court went on to hold that such a condition was no more intrusive than a requirement that a probationer answer all reasonable inquires by his probation officer.

As a final matter, the court found that the trial judge imposing the condition was immune to liability under Section 1983, because the complaint had not demonstrated that the actions taken were outside the judge's capacity as a judge. However, the county could be held liable were the district court to find, on remand, that the rehabilitative program violated the appellant's First Amendment rights.

The order granting summary judgment was reversed, and the matter was remanded for further proceedings.

STATE V. MORGAN
389 SO.2D 364 (LA.SUP.CT.1980)

The appellant contested the condition of her probation which required her to stay out of the French Quarter in New Orleans during the time of her probation, claiming that said conditions amounted to banishment. The defendant had been convicted of attempted prostitution, and this was a second offense.

Probationer alleged condition amounted to banishment.
Court found no merit to claim.

Reviewing the above issue the court stated as follows:

Other states have invalidated conditions requiring that a probationer leave a particular city, county, or state. See, for example, *Hoggett v. State*, 101 Miss. 269, 57 So. 811 (1912); *People v. Baum*, 251 Mich. 187, 231 N.W. 95 (1930); *In re Scarborough*, 76 Cal.App.2d 648, 173 P.2d 825 (1946); and *Weigand v. Commonwealth*, 397 S.W.2d 780 (Ky., 1965). However, the French Quarter is a small geographical area; [a]n historical district of New Orleans with carefully delineated boundaries. In addition to antiquity, it is noted for night life, drinking, and prostitution. A restriction against entering a relatively small geographical area of one city can hardly be equated with loss of citizenship or banishment from a city, county or state. Compare *State v. Chestnut*, 11 Utah 2d 142, 356 P.2d 36 (1960); *State v. Collett*, 232 Ga. 668, 208 S.E.2d 472 (Ga., 1974); and *Wilson v. State*, 151 Ga.App. 501, 260 S.E.2d 527 (Ga., 1979). Moreover, the condition of probation is reasonably related to Ms. Morgan's rehabilitation.
LSA-C.Cr.P. art. 895.A provides:
"A. When the court suspends the imposition or execution of sentence and places a defendant on probation, it shall require the defendant to refrain from criminal conduct and it may impose any specific conditions reasonably related to his rehabilitation, including any of the following:
"That the defendant shall:
* * *
"(8) Refrain from frequenting unlawful or disreputable places or consorting with disreputable persons; . . . ." A trial judge has wide latitude in imposing conditions of probation. *State v. Credeur*, 328 So.2d 59 (La., 1976). The proviso that defendant remain out of the French Quarter is apparently based upon the theory that Ms. Morgan's rehabilitation would best be served by removing her from an environment in which offenses of pros-

titution are frequently committed. The condition is reasonable and within the trial judge's discretion.

Finding no merit to the defendant's claims, the court affirmed the conviction of sentence.

BROWN V. STATE
406 SO.2D 1262 (FLA.DIST.CT.APP.1981)

It was not improper for the court to impose a condition that defendant "stay away from bars."

It was not improper for the trial court to impose as a condition of the defendant's probation that the defendant "stay away from bars." Stated the court:

The record reflects that appellant has a lengthy history of varied involvement in crime, including association with drug dealers. During prior probationary periods he was often unemployed and was considered to be generally lazy by his probation officer. Apparently, the trial judge felt hanging around bars with the associations often found there was not conducive to appellant's rehabilitation and to the protection of the public from future criminal activity in which appellant might, as a result, become involved.

The judgment of the trial court was affirmed.

VENTO V. STATE
724 S.W.2D 948 (TEX.CT.APP.2/17/87)

Probation officer may prescribe implementation of a condition imposed by court if so designated to do so by the court.

The appellant was convicted of the misdemeanor offense of driving while intoxicated. He was placed on probation on the condition that he attend and successfully complete an educational program on alcoholism and on the condition that he submit himself for testing and evaluation to determine whether or not he had a drug or alcohol dependence condition. This latter condition required the defendant to submit to such testing if requested by the Adult Probation Office. The defendant appealed, claiming that the conditions were an improper and impermissible delegation of judicial authority to the Adult Probation Office.

Rejecting the defendant's contentions, the court held that the conditions were sufficiently clear as to the cooperation required of the appellant. The fact that the court chose to allow its Adult Probation Office to prescribe an implementation of these conditions fell far short of allowing the Probation Office to impermissibly designate an additional condition. See *Salmons v. State,* 571 S.W.2d 29 (Tex.Crim.App.1978).

The judgment of the trial court was affirmed.

MEREDITH V. RAINES
131 ARIZ.244, 640 P.2D 175 (SUP.CT.1982)

May parole be revoked on the basis of a special condition orally imposed by the probation officer?

Arizona court approved revocation of parole for violation of special condition orally imposed by probation officer. No violation of due process.*

Answering in the affirmative, the court noted that while probation conditions must be written as set forth by the court, the parole situation is a different matter. Stated the court:

A parolee, however, is still considered to be in the custody of the State Department of Corrections, a part of the executive branch of government. The rules of procedure before the Board of Pardons and Paroles were promulgated under the authority of A.R.S. § 31-401, et seq. Even though we may require all conditions of probation to be in writing, it does not follow that the Board of Pardons and Paroles must do likewise so long as minimum standards of due process and equal protection are maintained. *Morrissey v. Brewer,* 408 U.S. 471, 92 S.Ct. 2593, 33 L.Ed.2d 484 (1972).

Defendant points to the United States Supreme Court, which has held that due process requires a written record be made of prison disciplinary proceedings. *Wolff v. McDonnell,* 418 U.S. 539, 94 S.Ct. 2963, 41 L.Ed.2d 935 (1974). We believe that there are, however, substantial differences between due process requirements in a prison disciplinary hearing described in *Wolff,* supra, and the requirement of written conditions of parole. Although we might believe that difficulty could be avoided by requiring written conditions, where, as here, there is no question as to the conditions imposed, that Meredith had the right to refuse them, R5-4-202(d)(2), Arizona Administrative Rules and Regulations, and that he admittedly violated such conditions, there can be no prejudice to the parolee due to the fact the conditions were verbal rather than written.

The parole board has wide discretion in performing its duty to determine the worthiness of a particular parolee to continue in that status. The conditions of supervision provided for in R5-1-312, Arizona Administrative Rules and Regulations, are broad enough to allow the parole board a great deal of discretion in revocation decisions, and yet still provide a parolee with the minimum notice that his conduct is violative of those conditions. Written conditions would be preferable, but they are not required to insure adequate notice.

In the instant case the probation officer orally imposed a condition of nonassociation with a woman who had complained of harassment by the parolee. After information indicated that the condition had been violated, a hearing was held wherein the parolee admitted the violation. Though he did not specifically agree to the condition imposed, the court noted that he did remain at liberty after it was imposed. Under these circumstances, the court found no violation of due process.

*A 1979 Arizona case, *State v. Salazar,* 595 P.2d 196 (1979), also approved an oral order by a probation officer. A 1977 Florida case, 344 So.2d 913 (Fla.Dist.Ct.App.1977), held that the court had the sole authority to impose conditions.

GAUNTLETT V. KELLEY
849 F.2D 213 (U.S. 6TH CIR. JUNE 1988)

After the defendant was successful in his attack on the condition of probation requiring chemical castration, it was not improper for the trial court to impose a term of confinement in place of that condition.

The convicted child molester was placed on probation on condition, among others, that he submit to "chemical castration" by a series of treatments with the drug Depo-Provera. The defendant appealed his sentence, and on remand, the trial judge set aside this condition and imposed a jail term of five to fifteen years. The defendant again sought review, claiming that this increase in his sentence was improper.

On review by the Sixth Circuit Court of Appeals, the court disagreed. The defendant had no legitimate expectation of finality in the original sentence imposed. Indeed, the court noted that it was he, not the State, that challenged the sentence. Stated the court:

At least one other fact militates against a finding that Gauntlett had a legitimate expectation of finality in the first sentence. Judge Borsos amended his original probation order before an appeal was taken. The amending order of February 17, 1984, added the following language:

> It was the intent of this Court that Depo-Provera medication be an essential and an integral part of the probationary order in order to give reasonable assurance that throughout the five-year probationary term that defendant would not be a danger to young children. It was *not* the intent of this Court to give probation with jail without this medical protection to the public.
>
> If, for any reason, it is not possible to carry out a course of treatment with Depo-Provera whether because of [conditions listed], or if some appellate court should determine that such a course of treatment making use of Depo-Provera to be [sic] inappropriate, unlawful, excessive, not within the trial court's power to give, or not a proper term of probation, or shall set it aside for any other reason; then the entire probation shall be set aside for failure of the condition on which it was based and the defendant then be resentenced by this judge, his successor, or by some other judge appointed to do so.

Finding that defendant was on notice that the very term of probation that he attacked as unlawful was considered to be a critical sentencing factor, the court affirmed the judgment of the district court which denied the defendant relief.

UNITED STATES v. RESTOR
529 F.SUPP. 579 (W.D.PA.1982)

A condition of probation which required air traffic control union officials, convicted of contempt in relation to their participation in work stoppage, to perform eight hours of community service per week was not improper. Stated the court [footnotes omitted]:

> The court has been unable to find any case in the Third Circuit dealing with the question of the legality of community service work as a condition of probation. However, several courts in other circuits have approved the concept as a proper approach to rehabilitation in appropriate situations where the probation conditions in total are reasonably related to the rehabilitation of the offender and the protection of the public. *Higdon v. United States*, 627 F.2d 893 (9th Cir.1980); *United States v. Pastore*, 537 F.2d 675 (2d Cir.1976). The Fourth Circuit has commented that:
>
> > We do not suggest that compelling charitable service is an appropriate condition of probation in every case,

but we think it an acceptable one here. Certainly the rehabilitative potential of such service is greater than the rehabilitative program of most prisons. The donation of charitable services to the community is both a deterrent to other potential offenders and a symbolic form of restitution to the public for having breached the criminal laws. *United States v. Arthur,* 602 F.2d 660, 664 (4th Cir.), *cert. denied,* 444 U.S. 992, 100 S.Ct. 524, 62 L.Ed.2d 422 (1979).

Community service restitution allowed as condition of probation.

Dealing with the situation in the instant case, the court stated:

> We believe that in the instant cases community service is particularly appropriate. The defendants were officers of a labor organization consisting of individuals whose job it was to assist in air traffic control to promote the safety and efficiency of air commerce. They were employees of the government and hence paid by all taxpayers. When defendants became dissatisfied with the status of the contract negotiations through which they were seeking improved working conditions and higher wages, they attempted to force the government to accede to their demands by engaging in what was patently an illegal work stoppage. Not only was the strike a violation of their oath, their contract, and the civil laws, but it was also in violation of the criminal code and a direct order of this court. Defendants were attempting through illegal means to extract from their fellow citizens employment benefits including wage increases, which defendants were unable to obtain through lawful collective bargaining.

The court went on to note that even though a probation condition may have incidental punitive effects, such circumstance did not render the condition illegal.

The request for a stay was denied.

CONDITIONS HELD INVALID

HUFF v. STATE
554 SO.2D 616 (FLA.DIST.CT.APP.DEC.1989)

The conditions prohibiting the defendant from living with a member of the opposite sex who was not a relative and from being within three blocks of a known "high drug area" as determined by his probation officer were invalid.

Defendant was convicted of burglary and was placed on probation. One of the conditions of probation required that he not live with a member of the opposite sex who was not his relative. The defendant was subsequently charged with various violations of probation. The trial court revoked probation and sentenced the defendant to nine years in prison followed by six years' probation. The trial court then reimposed the condition of probation that appellant not live with a member of the opposite sex who was not his relative. Another condition required that appellant not be within three blocks of a known "high drug area" as determined by the probation officer. Neither of these conditions was announced at the sentencing hearing.

On review, the court held that the conditions were invalid. Stated the court:

> The condition that Appellant not live with a member of the opposite sex has been held to be invalid because it relates to noncriminal conduct. See *Brodus v. State,* 449 So.2d 941 (Fla.2d DCA 1984); *Wilkinson v. State,* 388 So.2d 1322 (Fla. 5th DCA 1980).
>
> We find that the condition that Appellant not be within three blocks of a "high drug area" as defined by his probation officer is too vague to advise Appellant of the limits of his restrictions and can be easily violated unintentionally. The validity of this condition may depend on whether or not the probation officer apprised Appellant of which areas he was to avoid prior to a violation. Since the conditions were not announced at sentencing, there is nothing in the record to suggest that these areas were defined specifically or in writing. See *Almond v. State,* 350 So.2d 810, 811 (Fla. 4th DCA 1977) (striking as too vague a condition of probation prohibiting defendant from residing in "central Florida").
>
> Further, it has not been shown that either of these conditions has any relationship to the crime of burglary or is reasonably tailored to prevent future criminal conduct by the appellant. Therefore, pursuant to *Rodriguez v. State,* 378 So.2d 7 (Fla. 2d DCA 1979) (requiring conditions of probation to be reasonably related to prevention of similar criminal acts), we strike the conditions of probation. We also strike the finding of violation based upon his cohabitation with a woman. In all other respects the judgment and sentence are affirmed.

HUSSEY V. STATE
504 SO.2D 796 (FLA.DIST.CT.APP.APR.1987)

The condition prohibiting the defendant from engaging in carnival work was not rationally related to the purposes of probation, and the fact that such work required the defendant to travel did not make the condition valid.

A condition of probation is invalid if it: (1) has no relationship to the crime of which the offender was convicted; (2) relates to conduct which is not in itself criminal; and (3) requires or forbids conduct which is not reasonably related to future criminality. *Rodriguez v. State,* 378 So.2d 7 (Fla. 2d DCA 1979). In this case the defendant was charged with the possession of a machine gun, delivery of cocaine, and carrying a concealed firearm. As conditions of probation, the trial court ordered the defendant to refrain from engaging in carnival work and ordered him to pay restitution in the amount of $3,662.44 to the Florida Department of Law Enforcement for the costs of investigating the defendant's criminal activities. The defendant sought review, claiming that this condition of probation was improper.

Agreeing with the defendant, the court did not believe that restraining the appellant from participating in the carnival business was reasonably related to the defendant's rehabilitation. The defendant had engaged in the carnival business as his sole livelihood for a considerable number of years and the defendant had no prior criminal record. Moreover, the carnival business was not related to the crimes with which the defendant was charged, and the carnival business itself was not criminal activity. Rejecting the State's claim that the peripatetic nature of carnival work made it incompatible with the concept of community control, the court noted that probationers could, upon request, have their cases transferred elsewhere.

The matter was remanded with instructions to strike the condition of probation which prohibited the defendant from working in the carnival business.

PEOPLE V. APPEL, PEOPLE V. SULLIVAN
141 A.D.2D 374, 529 N.Y.S.2D 311 (JUNE 1988),

The condition requiring the defendants to donate $1,000 to a shelter for battered women, imposed upon their conviction for assault, was improper. Section 65.10(2)(g) provides that a defendant may be required to make restitution or reparation for the loss or damage caused by his offense. The payment imposed in the instant case, to a facility that was not itself the victim of the assaultive behavior, constituted an unauthorized condition.

Condition requiring $1,000 charitable donation was not proper.

NORRIS V. STATE
383 So.2d 691 (Fla.Dist.Ct.App.1980)

Condition to "live honorably" invalid.

While the probationer's conduct in committing battery upon his wife was sufficient to sustain a violation of probation for violating the law, the condition requiring the defendant to "live honorably" was disapproved.

Revocation for failure to pay supervision cost invalid without finding that probationer was able to pay and refused.

ADAMSON V. STATE
383 So.2d 294 (Fla.Dist.Ct.App.1980)

Where, as here, the appellant had been adjudicated insolvent, it was improper to revoke probation for failure to pay supervision cost without specifically finding that the appellant was able to pay. The finding of the probation violation for the appellant's failure to pay was stricken. The revocation was affirmed on the basis of the appellant's change of residence without permission and the appellant's violation of the law.

STATE V. DEAN
102 Wis.2d 300, 306 N.W.2d 286 (Ct.App.1981)

The defendant, Dr. Alice Dean, was convicted of mail fraud and false swearing. The trial court suspended the sentence and placed her on probation on the following conditions:

1. the defendant was to reside at the Holy Family Church in Karnataka State, India, for three years and provide nursing or pediatric service to poor children;
2. the defendant was to surrender her medical license;
3. the defendant was prohibited from practicing psychiatry during probation; and
4. the defendant was ordered to make restitution in the amount of $13,285 within 90 days by selling her assets.

Condition that defendant reside in India invalid. No authority to require a probationer to leave the state.

The defendant appealed, claiming that the trial court had no authority to impose a condition of uncompensated medical service to India.

The court noted that while a trial judge has wide discretion in imposing conditions of probation, this discretion is limited by statute. The applicable limitation in the instant case was the fact that India was not a member of the Interstate Compact. Furthermore, there was no authority for the trial court to require a probationer to leave the state. Thus, the order was invalid in so far as it required the defendant to reside in India.

The matter was remanded for alternative conditions.

ORDONEZ V. STATE
408 So.2d 760 (Fla.Dist.Ct.App.1982)

It was improper to revoke appellant's probation for violation of a condition requiring him to obtain a high school or G.E.D. diploma, other factors being favorable.

It was improper to revoke the appellant's probation for his violation of a condition which required him to obtain a High School or General Equivalency diploma. While the court acknowledged that probation could have originally been revoked for the appellant's failure in this regard, in the instant case the probated conviction, breaking and entering, was approximately seven years old and the defendant had made attempts, albeit feeble, to comply. Stated the court:

The fact is, however, that appellant's probation was not revoked at the hearing in 1976. Instead, the term of probation was extended another two years, during which appellant made little progress toward fulfilling the special condition. At his next hearing in 1978, the condition not having been fulfilled, another two-year extension was negotiated.

Finally, in 1980, after six years of probation, appellant attended the hearing which resulted in the ruling and the adjudication appealed here.

Appellant stands before the court a young man of twenty-four, to be now convicted of a felony he committed seven years ago. He has not been arrested for a crime in the interim. He has steady employment and has recently been promoted to management level. His family and friends are apparently supportive of his transition to maturity and honesty, although only his mother was called upon to testify. Others were present, and we presume their testimony was to be favorable.

The special condition of probation was intended to assist in appellant's rehabilitation. Its goal was to make appellant a useful, law-abiding citizen, a valuable member of society. It appears that this goal has been reached, nothing to the contrary appearing in the record. We are thus prompted to reflect on the question of what good it would do to punish appellant for failing to accept what was intended as guidance; how would it now benefit appellant or society?

The above considerations led the court to conclude that revocation would serve no purpose at this time. The revocation was reversed.

BURCHELL V. STATE
419 SO.2D 358 (FLA.DIST.CT.APP.1982)

Condition that defendant "not father any children during probation period" struck.

The per curiam opinion follows:

We strike from the conditions of defendant's probation condition #12, which states that the defendant "[m]ust not father any children during probation period." See *Rodriguez v. State,* 378 So.2d 7 (Fla. 2d DCA 1979). Otherwise, we affirm the defendant's conviction and sentences.

UNITED STATES V. TURNER
628 F.2D 461 (5TH CIR.1980)

Reimbursement of court-appointed counsel fees is not permitted as a condition of probation.

Reimbursement of court-appointed counsel fees is not permitted as a condition of probation. *United States v. Jimenez,* 600 F.2d 1172 (5th Cir. 1979). 18 U.S.C.

§ 3651 allows for only three monetary conditions: fines, restitution, and support payments to dependents. Disagreeing with the First Circuit, in *U.S. v. Santarpio,* 560 F.2d 448, *cert. denied,* 434 U.S. 984, 98 S.Ct. 609, 54 L.Ed.2d 478 (1977), the court found that payment for court-appointed counsel could not be considered a "fine" within the meaning of the above section. Furthermore, such payments could not be considered restitution to "aggrieved parties." The conviction was affirmed; however, the condition of payment of counsel fees was deleted.

ABEL V. STATE
383 SO.2D 325 (FLA.DIST.CT.APP.1980)

Where defendant adjudicated insolvent, probation could not be revoked for failure to pay supervision fees.

Where, as here, the defendant had been adjudicated insolvent and no evidence was presented as to the defendant's ability to pay the costs of supervision, it was improper to revoke probation for the defendant's failure to pay such costs. The revocation was affirmed as to the defendant's failure to work diligently, his failure to file monthly reports, and his change of his residence without permission.

WILKINSON V. STATE
388 SO.2D 1322 (FLA.DIST.CT.APP.1980)

A condition of probation is invalid if it: (1) has no relationship to the crime for which the defendant was convicted; (2) relates to conduct which is not in itself criminal, and (3) requires or forbids conduct which is not reasonably related to future criminality. In the instant case the defendant was convicted of carrying a concealed weapon. The court found the condition that the defendant not live with a female to whom he was not married or related to be improper.

SOURCE: Reported in *Probation and Parole Law Reports* (Warrensburg, Mo.: Knehans–Miller Publications). Used with permission of the publisher.

ORGANIZATION AND ADMINISTRATION OF PROBATION SERVICES

5

Court of General Jurisdiction:

A court having unlimited trial jurisdiction, both civil and criminal, though its judgments and decrees are subject to appellate review.

Court of Record:

A court that is required to keep records of its proceedings, and that may fine and imprison.

THE PROBATION SYSTEM

The operation of a probation system is best understood when we distinguish between probation as a disposition and probation as a process. Thus we make that distinction in this chapter. The *disposition* are the aspects of probation that lead to granting and revocation of probation. The *process* of probation is the furnishing of probation services. The two functions are closely related and they frequently overlap. As we shall see, different jurisdictions have different probation systems, and there is significantly less diversity in probation as a disposition than in the way probation services are provided.

Probation as a Disposition

Probation as a disposition is court-related; that is, statutory limits laid down by the legislature place the power to grant it and to revoke it in a court. The federal government permits all courts having jurisdiction of the offenses for which probation may be used to place defendants on probation.[1] This is generally true in state jurisdictions also. Thus, if the state provides only for felony probation, **courts of general jurisdiction** with power to try felony cases have the authority to grant and revoke probation. If misdemeanor probation is provided for, courts with misdemeanor jurisdiction may grant and revoke misdemeanor probation. In a few states, the power to probate is limited to **courts of record.**

   That the authority to grant probation resides with a court is not surprising, especially when we consider that probation developed out of the court's power to sentence criminal offenders and (depending on the point of view) from either its inherent or its legislatively granted power to suspend the imposition or execution of sentence. The power to revoke probation, quite logically, accompanies the power to grant it.

   Opinions differ as to the exact nature of probation; for example, whether it is a sentence or a conviction and whether it rests on suspension of *imposition* of sentence or of *execution* of sentence, or *both*. Nonetheless, there is almost unanimous agreement that granting and revoking probation is a judicial responsibility.

Probation as a Process

The probation process encompasses the organization, administration, and delivery of probation services. The administration of probation services in the fifty states differs in philosophy, organization, and procedures. In many cases, the differences have arisen more by historical accident than anything else.

EARLY PROBATION ORGANIZATION

As the states enacted probation legislation, they did not do it uniformly. They followed Vermont's *local* organizational pattern or Rhode Island's *state* organizational pattern; some states combined *adult* and *juvenile* probation services; some states combined probation with *parole* services; they developed joint or separate agencies for *felony* and *misdemeanor* probation services; they placed probation services in the *executive* branch or the *judicial* branch of the state government. Various organizational combinations were adopted. For example, Massachusetts enacted the nation's first probation statute in 1878, although the law related only to Suffolk County (Boston). The statute gave the power to appoint the probation officer to the mayor of Boston, subject to confirmation by the board of alderman, and it placed the officer under the general control of Boston's chief of police, although the officer was paid from the county treasury. The probation officer was considered an arm of the court, however, and had the power to investigate cases and recommend probation for "such persons as may reasonably be expected to reform without punishment."[2] Two years later, a law was enacted that permitted other cities and towns in Massachusetts to appoint probation officers. Statewide probation did not begin until 1891, when a statute transferred the power of appointment from the municipalities to the courts and made such appointment mandatory, rather than permissive.[3]

Vermont was the second to pass a probation statute, adopting a county plan of organization in 1898. The county judge in each county was given the power to appoint a probation officer to serve all of the courts in the county.[4]

The following year (1899) Rhode Island adopted a statewide and state-controlled probation system.[5] A state agency, the Board of Charities and Correction, was given the power to appoint a probation officer and assistants, with the requirement that at least one of the assistants be a woman.

California enacted a probation statute in 1903 following the Vermont pattern of county-based probation administration. The California law provided for adult as well as juvenile probation.[6]

In New York, probation began in 1901 under a law that empowered all justices of courts having original criminal jurisdiction in all cities to appoint officers to investigate and report cases to the courts that might deserve mitigation of punishment by probation. The first independent commission for supervising probation was established in 1907. By 1939, the probation system was made up of probation officers appointed by the local courts and paid by local governments, but under state supervision. Later, the Division of Probation in the charge of a director of probation was located in the Department of Correction. Subsequently, New York established a state Department of Correctional Services, which has as one of its divisions the Division of Probation.

The first juvenile court (and juvenile probation) statute was passed in Illinois in 1899. Illinois did not provide for adult probation until 1911, when the circuit and city courts of Illinois were authorized to appoint probation officers and place adult offenders on probation. A state probation office was created in 1923, but it did not begin to function until 1929, and in 1933 it was abolished.[7]

ORGANIZATION OF PROBATION SERVICES IN THE 1990s

The controversy over how probation services should be organized and administered continues today. The major arguments center on the issues of (1) whether probation should be administered at the state or local level, and

FIGURE 5–1

Probation Organization in the United States

SOURCE: Randall Guynes, *Research in Action* (National Institute of Justice, August 1988).

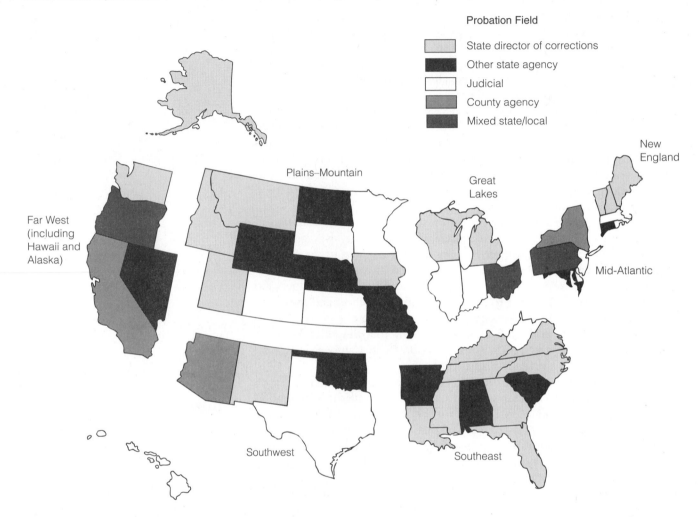

(2) whether the executive branch or the judicial branch of government should administer probation services. Figure 5–1 illustrates the situs of probation services, administration, and control in the United States today.

State versus Local Administration

Probation services in the United States are administered by more than 2,000 separate agencies. Probation is state administered in thirty-two states. Twelve states have locally administered probation services, and six others have some form of "mixed" state and local administration.

There are arguments pro and con for a statewide administration of probation services. The arguments *for* state-administered probation contend that a state-administered system is free of local political considerations and can recommend new programs without approval by local political bodies. Furthermore, a state-administered system provides greater assurance that goals and objectives can be met, and uniform policies and procedures developed. Moreover, it allows more efficiency in the disposition of resources. It is also argued that county probation agencies are small and lack thus resources for providing staff training, research programs, and services to probationers.[8]

The arguments *against* a state-administered probation system emphasize the need for local conditions and resources to be taken into account. The probationer remains in the local community and can be best supervised by a person thoroughly familiar with that community. Proponents also claim that local agencies are best equipped to experiment with new procedures and better methods because of their smaller size—mistakes are not so costly and far-reaching. They also argue that state policies are often rejected by local communities that then refuse to cooperate with the probation system, which undermines operational efficiency and success.[9]

The American Bar Association *Standards* do not favor any particular formula for allocating administrative authority for probation services between local and state governments. They agreed with the Model Penal Code[10] and the National Council on Crime and Delinquency[11] that adequate services can be developed through various approaches.[12]

The evidence on this issue appears to support state-administered probation services. Few states where probation is a local function have provided any leadership for probation services. Where probation is a local function, tremendous variations exist in the quantity and quality of services, the qualifications of probation personnel, and the emphasis on service to the court and probationers.[13]

State–County Shared Responsibility

In some jurisdictions, the system is said to be *mixed*—that is, the state and counties share responsibility for delivering probation services. This alternative arrangement usually involves a state executive-branch agency with the authority to develop standards for local probation systems that provide for a minimum acceptable level of functioning. The state agency is also responsible for establishing policies, defining statewide goals, providing staff training, assisting in fiscal planning and implementation, collecting statistics and other data to monitor the operations of local probation agencies, and enforcing changes when necessary. This organizational structure recognizes the need for local control while allowing local governments to benefit from the greater revenue-generating capacity of state government.[14] Minimum standards of service delivery and the benefits of service uniformity may thus be established and enforced under threat of withdrawal of state funds.

Judicial versus Executive

In the debate over the appropriate governmental branch for the probation system, those who favor the judicial branch argue that placing responsibility for probation in the branch that holds responsibility for other human services and correctional services is a more rational alignment. Those who favor executive-branch control point out that it allows program budgeting to be better coordinated because of that branch's greater ability to negotiate in the resource allocation process. Moreover, they claim that it facilitates a better coordinated continuum of services to offenders. These advocates of executive-branch administration argue that judges are trained in law, not administration, and are thus not equipped to administer probation services. They fear that under judicial authority, services to the court will have higher priority than services to persons.

Some independent observers support placing probation in the judicial branch. They stress that probation is more responsive to the courts, to whom it provides services, when it is administered by the judiciary. When probation is in the executive branch, it is often a branch of the department of corrections and thus probation services might have lower priority than when they are part of the judiciary. These people also argue that courts are more aware of the resource needs of probation than the executive branch, and that the relationship of probation staff to the courts provides automatic feedback on the effectiveness of probation services.[15]

The Impact of Changing Concepts of Probation on Administration

As we have noted, the nature and objectives of probation have undergone considerable change—and they continue to change. Regular probation is increasingly perceived as ineffective and as a threat to public safety. The public has had to redefine the role probation should play as a sanction for convicted felons. Increasingly, the response has been to develop intensive-supervision programs that emphasize surveillance, control, and risk management. This shift of emphasis from "routine supervision" to "intensive surveillance" has implications for probation administration and organization. Norval Morris and Michael Tonry, in their book *Between Prison and Probation,* discuss these organizational and philosophical issues.[16] Typically, they assert, the central question is, To whom is the probation officer accountable, to whom does he/she look for promotion, and thus, who has the power to influence his/her priorities?

When probation is a branch of the judiciary, the probation officer's duties are likely to be more on preparing presentence reports than on the supervising probationers, since the officer's relationship with his/her superior—the judge—is centered on the presentence function. If, however, new duties such as intensive supervision and other risk-control responsibilities are assigned, the probation department and the individual officer will be forced to devote more time and higher priority to supervising those placed under their supervision. Under the control of the judiciary, it is often difficult for the probation officer to shift priorities from servicing the court's presentencing needs to supervising the high-risk probationers. Even when the court supports and encourages the shift from service to the court to supervision, the judiciary seldom has the political clout to provide the necessary additional resources for such a change in priorities.

Placing probation administration under local executive-branch administration seldom resolves the dilemma. Except in large, prosperous counties, few local communities can provide the additional resources necessary to supervise and control the type and volume of offenders being served if intermediate punishments are to be effective. The sheer volume of offenders overwhelms the resources of most communities.

In a state probation system, however, there is at least the possibility of allocating the staff and funding necessary for the task.[17] Such placement can facilitate a more rational allocation of probation staff services, increase interaction and administrative coordination with corrections and allied human services, increase access to the budget process and establishment of priorities, and remove from the courts an inappropriate role.[18]

THE APPOINTMENT OF PROBATION OFFICERS

Depending on the situs of probation services in the judicial or executive branch of government, probation officers are appointed by the court or courts authorized to grant probation or by the director of the executive department or agency in which probation services are housed. If there is only one felony trial court in the county, the probation officer is selected by the judge that tries felony cases. Where two or more probation officers are needed, the usual pattern is that the judge or judicial body appoints a chief probation officer, who in turn selects assistants, subject to the approval of the advisory body. Salary scales are fixed, and broad policy matters are determined by the judicial body that holds the power to select the chief probation officer.

In the federal system, for example, the judges of each federal district court appoint a chief probation officer, who is under the overall supervision of the Probation Division of the Administrative Office of the United States. Collectively, the probation officers in the federal system are called *the United States Probation Service*. The chief probation officer selects the subordinate probation officers.[19] Salary and minimum qualifications are fixed by statute or determined by the Administrative Office of the United States Courts. Since the federal (United States) probation officers also supervise parolees, parolees are assigned for supervision to the appropriate chief probation officer by the United States Parole Commission,[20] the Justice Department agency that is responsible for administering the federal parole system. The assignment is based primarily on geographic considerations. The chief probation officer assigns particular parolees to individual officers on the basis of each probationer or parolee's special needs and each officer's special skills, with due consideration to caseload, geographic location, and other matters. A United States probation officer also supervises offenders at liberty under supervised release (those not released on parole), as required by the Comprehensive Crime Control Act of 1984, and those on military parole.

In a state where probation services are locally administered and parole services are statewide, there are usually two sets of supervisory officers. Parole officers are appointed by an administrative department or the board that supervises the department. Power to appoint the chief probation officer is usually in the judiciary, although it may rest with the county governing body, the governor, a state board upon nomination by a judge, or the judiciary from a list supplied by a state agency.

Where juvenile and adult probation services are administered locally and separately, the chief probation officer for adult probationers may be chosen by the judge or judges of the criminal courts, and the chief probation officer for juveniles by the juvenile judge or a juvenile board. Sometimes the juvenile board has the additional authority to designate which court is to be the juvenile court for the particular geographic area.[21]

If juvenile and adult probation are administered locally, the juvenile probation department may be assigned the responsibility for adult probation by statute, as in California.[22] Or, the judge or judges—with the approval of the juvenile board if there is one—may authorize the chief probation officer to establish a separate division of juvenile probation or the chief juvenile officer to establish a separate division of adult probation and to appoint adult probation officers as required. This is the case in Texas.[23] Actual supervision of both adult and juvenile probationers may be by the same officer,[24] or the probation officer for juveniles may be restricted from serving as probation officer for adults and vice versa.[25]

Advisory board:

Panel of citizens, judges, or other public officials who act as advisors to the judiciary in setting broad general policy or in determining other aspects of probation services and administration.

Advisory boards

The underlying reason for providing panels of judges, juvenile boards, state boards, county commissioners, or other statutory bodies is that some method of assisting the judiciary in screening potential appointees is desirable. Such bodies also act as advisors to the judiciary in setting broad general policy, salary scales, and the like.

Although the authority to appoint the chief probation officer may reside with the judge, the judge does not as a rule actually administer the probation department. That function is performed by the chief probation officer, who is given the power to appoint assistants and to handle the day-to-day work of the department.

The American Bar Association *Standards relating to Probation* sets forth what the ABA sees as the best interrelationship of the judiciary, an advisory body, and the chief probation officer in a locally administered probation system:

1. Responsibility for appointing chief probation officers in local probation departments should reside solely in the chief judge of the court or an appropriate judicial body. Consideration should be given to the creation of an agency or committee to advise in recruiting and screening chief probation officers. Such a committee should consist of representatives of government, the judiciary, the bar, and the community.
2. Chief probation officers should make all appointments of probation personnel in accordance with a merit system. After a probationary period, tenure should be granted with removal permitted only after a hearing is conducted with a civil service commission or other career service organization.

PROBATION SUBSIDY PROGRAMS

Probation subsidy programs provide financial incentives to keep and treat offenders in their local communities. The use of subsidies represents an attempt to balance state and local economic responsibility for correctional agencies. Philosophically, probation subsidies are based on the belief that probation is a more effective, more economical, and more humane correctional alternative than incarceration. Most subsidy programs today are based on the California subsidy program initiated in 1965, which was developed in response to a study that showed that 25 percent of the state's prisoners could be safely and effectively maintained in the community *if county probation systems were improved*. The California subsidy program established a base rate of commitment (prior years' commitment levels) to state correctional facilities for each county. Counties were then paid $4,000 annually (adjusted for 1967 dollars) for each person below the base rate diverted from the state correctional system.[26] Counties were to use the money to improve their services and to develop intensive supervision, drug treatment, and other community corrections programs. A number of other states soon modeled subsidy programs on the California plan—Colorado, Nevada, Ohio, Oregon, Pennsylvania, and Washington.

Probation subsidy programs have been expanded to include direct grants to counties to enhance their community correctional programs. Indiana, for instance, sets aside several million dollars annually in the form of grants to local communities for developing and improving such programs as community service, restitution, work-release, and victim assistance projects. In New York, state subsidies take the form of awards given to a probation department for complying with state-established standards and goals for service delivery. If a local county successfully complies with state standards in such areas as staff development, supervision guidelines, case monitoring, and so on, the department is eligible for the subsidy. Other jurisdictions provide reimbursement for a specific percentage of the local costs for community corrections.[27]

These and similar programs represent major commitments of state support for local correctional programs. By whatever method the subsidy is calculated, it typically involves enhancement of local correctional efforts and some *control* by the state—usually in the form of withholding funds if the program's established criteria are not met. This, of course, has major implications for probation administration.

INTERSTATE COMPACTS ON PROBATION

Our consideration of probation administration would not be complete if we failed to discuss the interstate compacts for supervising adult and juvenile probationers and parolees.

At one time, there was no means for supervising a probationer or parolee outside the state where he or she was convicted, in spite of the fact that many transient offenders are arrested and convicted far from where they have relatives and community ties. As a result, there was often no way to provide the offender with supervision in the very place that would offer the best chance for success on probation or parole. Pursuant to the Crime Control Consent Act passed by Congress in 1936, a group of states entered into an agreement by which they would supervise probationers and parolees for each other. Known as the **Interstate Compact for the Supervision of Parolees and Probationers,** the agreement was originally signed by 25 states in 1937. By 1951 it had been ratified by all the states.

Interstate Compact for the Supervision of Parolees and Probationers:

An agreement among the states to supervise probationers and parolees for each other.

109

A similar agreement, the Interstate Compact on Juveniles, provides for return of juvenile runaways, escapees, and absconders, and for cooperative supervision of juvenile probationers and parolees. An amendment to this compact provides for out-of-state confinement of juveniles. Each state enacts the compact as part of its state laws.[28]

The compacts identify the *sending state*—the state of conviction—and the receiving state—the state that undertakes the supervision. The offender must meet certain residence requirements of the receiving state. Ordinarily, the probationer or parolee must be a resident of the receiving state, have relatives there, or have employment there. The receiving state agrees to accept the offender and to provide the same supervision it accords other probationers or parolees in the state. The offender who obtains the benefits of out-of-state supervision waives extradition. The sending state may enter the receiving state to take custody of the probationer or parolee who has violated the terms of release without going through extradition proceedings, and a supplementary agreement permits the violator to be incarcerated in the receiving state at the expense of the sending state if both states agree.[29]

Parole boards usually designate one member of their number to be the "Interstate Compact Administrator." That person handles the details of arranging the supervision of parolees who are either sent out of the state for supervision or received into the state after conviction in another state. Where probation is locally administered, the compact does not work as smoothly for probation supervision as it does for parole supervision. Some exchanges take place, however, and probation supervision or detention and care of runaways and absconders is provided by the receiving state.

Problems with Interstate Compacts

Under the interstate compacts, states agree to provide "courtesy supervision" of probationers and parolees from other states. Some requests are problematic and thus are not approved. In the past, some probation and parole agencies have alleged that certain local departments and some states practiced "dumping"—transferring difficult cases to other states with little or no justification other than the desire to rid themselves of the problem individuals. In addition, some states are asked to accept far more interstate-compact supervision cases than they send out. However, the vast majority of requests for transfer of supervision are legitimate, and when it appears that a case will not unreasonably burden the receiving department, the state usually complies.

SUMMARY

Probation is both a disposition and a process. As a disposition, probation is court-related; that is, the power to grant and to revoke it is in a court. As a process, it is the organization, administration, and delivery of probation services. There is little uniformity to probation organizational patterns in the United States. Probation services may be combined with parole, or kept separate. Adult and juvenile probation may be combined, or entirely separate. Probation may be administered by the executive branch of government or by the judiciary. Probation services may be organized at the state level or at the local level. There are arguments for and against each of these organizational schemes. Generally, however, the evidence seems to support state executive-branch control of probation services as the most effective and efficient approach. The provisions for selecting probation officers, the use of probation subsidies, and interstate agreements for supervision are also discussed in relation to the issue of probation administration.

ENDNOTES

1. 18 U.S.C.A. § 3651.
2. Cited in Howard Abadinsky, *Probation and Parole: Theory and Practice,* 4th ed. (Englewood Cliffs, N.J.: Prentice Hall, 1991), p. 24.
3. *Attorney General's Survey: Probation,* vol. 2 (Washington: U.S. Department of Justice 1939), p. 24.
4. *Id.* at 22–23, n. 75.
5. *Id.* at 25.
6. *Id.* at 105–106.
7. *Attorney General's Survey, Digest,* pp. 299–300.
8. Paraphrased from National Advisory Commission, *Standards, Corrections,* pp. 315–316.
9. *Id.*
10. Model Penal Code § 401.12, comment at 147.
11. National Council on Crime and Delinquency, Standard Probation and Parole Act §§ 3.3, 7.7.
12. ABA, *Standards, Probation,* commentary, pp. 75–76.
13. National Advisory Commission on Criminal Justice Standards and Goals, *Report on Corrections* (Washington, D.C.: Government Printing Office, 1973).
14. John Ortiz Symkla, *Probation and Parole: Crime Control in the Community* (New York: Macmillan, 1984), p. 90.
15. NAC, *supra.* See also E. Kim Nelson, Howard Ohmart, and Nora Harlow, *Promising Strategies in Probation and Parole* (Washington, D.C.: Government Printing Office, 1978).
16. Norval Morris and Michael Tonry, *Between Prison and Probation: Intermediate Punishments in a Rational Sentencing System* (New York: Oxford University Press, 1990).
17. *Id.* at 230–231.
18. *Id.* at 314.
19. The selection is, however, subject to the approval of the Chief U.S. District Judge of the judicial district, who officially appoints all U.S. probation officers.
20. The U.S. Parole Commission was abolished by the Comprehensive Crime Control Act of 1984. Although the Commission was scheduled to be phased out by 1992, it was extended for an additional 5 years.
21. This is the situation in Texas. Tex.Fam.Code Ann. § 51.04 (Vernon).
22. Cal.Welf. & Inst.Code § 1760.7 (West). This is true except for two counties, which have separate juvenile and adult probation departments.
23. Tex.Code Crim.Proc. art. 42.12, § 10 (Vernon).
24. The usual situation in California.
25. The Texas statute so provides.
26. For example, if a county had a base rate of 100 commitments to state correctional facilities in a year, it would receive $4,000 for each commitment under 100. If the commitment rate in a year was 50 following the initiation of the subsidy program, the

county would receive $200,000 (50 × $4,000) to maintain those 50 offenders in the community.

27. Marilyn D. McShane and Wesley Krause, *Community Corrections* (New York: Macmillan, 1993), p. 72.

28. See, for example, Interstate Parole Reciprocal Agreement, Ill.Ann.Stat. ch. 38, §§ 123-5, 123-6 (Smith-Hurd).

29. California Interstate Compact on Juveniles, Cal.Welf. & Inst.Code §§ 1300–1308 (West).

DISCUSSION QUESTIONS

1. Distinguish between probation as a disposition and as a process.

2. Early probation legislation followed one of the two existing organizational plans—that of Vermont or Rhode Island. How were these two organizational structures different?

3. What are the major patterns of administering probation services?

4. What are the advantages and disadvantages of placing responsibility for probation in the executive branch of government?

5. What are the advantages and disadvantages of administering probation services at the state level, rather than the local level?

6. What is a "mixed" organizational structure, and what are its advantages?

7. According to Morris and Tonry the trend in probation is toward the development of intermediate sanctions such as intensive supervision programs. How might this trend affect probation administration?

8. What are the major roles of advisory boards in probation?

9. What is the purpose of the interstate compacts?

10. What are probation subsidies, and why are they used? How might a state exert control over local probation services through the use of subsidies?

Issues in Administration of Probation and Parole Administration

American probation and parole systems now face an increasingly difficult clientele despite less than adequate resources. Despite greater financial resources, personnel increases are not keeping pace with rising caseloads of clients with serious problems. These are some of the major findings of a survey of state and local probation and parole officers conducted as part of the National Assessment Program (NAP) sponsored by the National Institute of Justice.

OPERATIONS AND PROCEDURES

Agencies were asked questions about their needs to improve operations and procedures in five general categories: classification, community resources, scheduling, management information systems, and private sector contracting. As explained in the sections that follow, the last three are the most salient concerns for the respondents.

CLASSIFICATION. When asked to list projects that have improved classification, almost half the respondents stated that they had developed an evaluative technique incorporating risk. Less than 40 percent of each respondent group indicated a need to improve initial and subsequent classification of offenders' risks or needs.

SCHEDULING. Since field services organizations are dependent on others to complete many of their tasks, it was hypothesized that scheduling with other criminal justice agencies might be a problem. Respondents were asked to rate the degree to which scheduling is a problem for each of the following groups or activities:

- Court hearings (sentence and revocation hearings).
- Prison officials (investigations).
- Timing for sentence investigations.
- Clerk of court (fines and fees).

From this list, only scheduling problems with regard to sentencing and revocation hearings were rated high. More than 50 percent of local directors and 47 percent of state directors noted this as a problem. Combined agencies indicated this was a more severe problem (68 percent) that the other agencies.

MANAGEMENT INFORMATION SYSTEMS. The analysis of the questions on management information systems suggests that the use of these systems is limited. Only about 15 percent of the agencies have automated systems to support classification. The overwhelming majority of respondents either (1) did not have a system in place, (2) were just in the process of developing such a capability, or (3) limited the use of their system to minor applications such as word processing.

Respondents generally wanted historical data, such as criminal record and substance abuse information on their clients, to be computerized. The computerized system would further enhance the classification procedures and make the client information readily available for other uses. A need was also expressed for information on referrals for service to be used in the ongoing management of cases. Greater concern for referral information was reported by probation offices in the New England, Mid-Atlantic, and Far West areas. Interestingly, most groups did not place a priority on improving information on management supervision assignments and levels.

The needs expressed for management information reflected different collection strategies. Historical data on criminal records and substance abuse generally depended on information from other criminal agencies and the clients, supplemented by information from families and friends. In contrast, referrals for service and associated dates could generally be found within the agency—at least during the supervision period—and were easier to maintain within a system.

COMMUNITY RESOURCES.   Probation and parole rely on public and private resources outside their agencies to supply many services to offenders. Directors were asked to rate the degree to which they see the need to improve or create nine types of community services (Table 1). In general, parole agencies rated the items as more significant needs than the other groups.

One-half or more of the directors reported that the number of residential options were not keeping pace with offenders' needs, and at least three out of four believed increased supervision requirements were contributing to caseload management problems. Given the higher levels of supervision now required, one respondent from the Northeast argued that halfway houses and other options were needed to "restore probation and parole as legitimate sanctions." In addition to current needs for residential programs, one director noted that the challenge of the next three years will be "development of new programs to divert those currently in jails awaiting transfer to prison custody—to the extent that the community is not jeopardized."

Other differences appeared to reflect the stage of the criminal justice process at which offenders were referred. For example, 80 percent of parole agencies reported a need for housing referral services, compared to about 62 percent of other field offices. In contrast, there were few differences among agencies regarding the need for job readiness training, which was cited by 65 to 73 percent of the field offices. Vocational education services were reported as a need by 74 percent of parole and 61 percent of probation agencies, and 56 percent of combined agencies.

There were several regional variations in perceived need for improved or expanded community resources. Although adult basic education was the lowest priority for everyone, directors in the Great Lakes, Mid-Atlantic, and Southwest rated the problem considerably higher than their colleagues. Drug programs were of more concern to parole directors in the Mid-Atlantic, Southwest, and Far West than in other parts of the country. Probation offices in New England (83 percent) and the Far West (91 percent) reported a greater need for mental health services than probation offices overall (60 percent).

CONTRACTED SERVICES.   Residential, drug, job readiness, and mental health programs can be provided internally or through arrangements with public or private service providers. Recent attention given to contracting in corrections and the reduction in government-supported social service programs suggests that the demand for privately sponsored arrangements may increase. Probation and parole officials were asked to indicate whether they currently purchase none, some, most, or all of eight specific services.

The most prevalent service currently provided under contract is staff training. At least four-fifths of the respondents contract for some or all of their staff training. In contrast, emergency food is provided under contract to fewer than one-third of parole agencies and in less than 15 percent of other field offices.

The private sector is used less overall in the Southeast than in other regions. All local directors in the Southeast report fewer purchases of drug testing and

TABLE 1

Needs for New or Improved Community Resources

COMMUNITY RESOURCES	STATE AGENCIES	PROBATION AGENCIES	PAROLE AGENCIES	COMBINED AGENCIES
Residential programs	80%	72%	83%	73%
Housing referral services	57	63	80	62
Job readiness training	65	68	73	69
Mental health services	72	60	71	67
Drug programs	81	63	79	· 62
Employment referral services	50	70	66	61
Alcohol programs	62	50	73	54
Vocational education	62	61	74	56
Adult basic education	31	33	60	33

medical services. Single-function agencies contract for staff training less frequently than combined agencies. Only 7 percent of local parole offices and a lower percentage of combined agencies use the private sector for residential centers or emergency housing.

Fewer than 35 percent of Great Lakes parole directors contract for any staff training, urinalysis, mental health services, emergency food, or housing. Approximately the same percentage of probation agencies in the Great Lakes, Mid-Atlantic, and Plains–Mountain regions contract for medical services. Only about two-fifths of the Far West offices responsible for both probation and parole purchase any medical or halfway house services. *

Staff Recruitment and Retention

Staff shortages were rated high as a problem by all three groups of agencies. The results from the recruitment and retention sections of the survey provided insights into this problem.

Recruitment. Among the most significant recruitment problems are low salaries, locating qualified professional staff, shortages of qualified minority applicants, hiring freezes, and poor image of corrections work.

In general, state directors saw fewer recruitment problems than did local officers and considered a shortage of minority applicants the most important recruitment issue (Table 2). In contrast, 50 percent of the local probation directors, 53 percent of the parole directors, and 68 percent of the combined agency directors considered low salaries an important recruitment problem. Approximately 45 percent of local agencies reported problems recruiting minorities.

Restrictions on hiring significantly affect recruitment for more than 47 percent of local probation directors, but only 38 percent of their counterparts in parole. In contrast, the poor image of corrections work was a significant problem for 43 percent of local parole agencies.

Retention. Agency directors were asked to rate the degree to which seven items contribute to staff turnover: salary increases, burnout, inability to use leave time, poor image of corrections work, substance abuse, inadequate career incentives, and excessive overtime. Career incentives were considered the number-one staff retention issue by state directors (58 percent), local parole (70 percent), probation (60 percent), and combined agencies (71 percent). Salary increases and burnout were cited as serious by 40 percent or more of all four groups, with the remaining problems receiving substantially lower ratings. The salary problem was considered a major issue by 68 percent of the combined agencies.

Forty-seven percent of the probation offices and 67 percent of both parole field offices and combined agency directors rated burnout as a serious retention problem. "Burnout" is used to encompass a variety of situations, from personal crises unrelated to occupation, through systemic dysfunctions in organizations, to uncertain environmental conditions. Its causes may be personal, organizational, environmental, or (more frequently) a combination. Within the limits of this survey, it was not possible to determine the specific causes of burnout at the local level. Interestingly, from other survey responses, burnout is apparently not being caused by excessive overtime (rated as a problem by only one respondent in five) or employee substance

TABLE 2
Recruitment Problems

ISSUE	STATE AGENCIES	PROBATION AGENCIES	PAROLE AGENCIES	COMBINED AGENCIES
Low salaries	33%	50%	53%	68%
Shortage of minority applicants	48	44	41	50
Locating qualified staff	31	46	52	49
Hiring freeze	29	47	38	40
Poor image of corrections	21	27	43	37
Entrance requirements too high	17	22	28	19

abuse (rated as a problem by less than 2 percent of all respondents).

RESPONSES. It is clear that compensation, including "career incentives," is perceived as essential for both attracting and holding probation and parole staff. What is unclear is whether salaries are considered inadequate relative to similar occupations and other public service jobs in terms of skill levels required and risks involved. Addressing these staffing issues tests the ingenuity of agencies facing increased demands with constrained resources. Few agencies, for example, cite new funding as the way they are trying to solve their personnel problems. Instead, evaluation and reorganization of workload are used as the major way of alleviating staffing burdens. Frequently cited recruitment methods (reported by over one-half of all those responding) included special minority recruiters and outreach in the community and at colleges.

TRAINING. Respondents were asked to rate their agencies' interest in several training topics (Table 3). Consistent with the finding that "increased supervision needs" increased caseload problems, at least 76 percent of all groups reported they need to upgrade staff skills to handle special problem offenders. Six other topics interested at least half of all local agencies: offender monitoring techniques, counseling, stress management, legal liability, report writing, and caseload management.

While overall training needs were high (with parole reporting the highest overall), responses varied substantially by agency function. Consistent with high burnout, stress management training was a greater

need in parole and combined agencies, with almost 70 percent of agencies significantly interested. Probation agencies rank handling special offenders highest (80 percent), followed by case management (63 percent), offender monitoring (57 percent), and liability (57 percent).

There were also interesting differences between state and local perceptions of training needs. State directors reported a somewhat greater degree of interest in training in counseling techniques (61 percent) than did local offices (about 50 percent). Forty-one percent of state directors favored training in report writing, compared to 53 percent of local directors. Caseload management skills were among the most wanted training for local respondents, but among the least significant for state directors. If training policy and resource allocation were influenced primarily by state officials, these results suggested a need to reconcile local and state perspectives.

There are also some notable regional variations. Report writing was considered significant by parole in the Mid-Atlantic region and by parole and combined agencies in the Plains–Mountain states. Sixty-seven percent of directors responsible for both probation and parole in the Great Lakes region considered training in investigative techniques a significant need.

Legal liability training was deemed more serious by both probation and parole in the Plains–Mountain, Southwest, and Far West, where from 83 to 100 percent of agency directors considered this an important training topic.

What makes these results more striking is that monitoring, counseling, and report writing are fundamental to probation and parole functions. Along with

T A B L E 3

Training Needs

TRAINING AREA	STATE AGENCIES	PROBATION AGENCIES	PAROLE AGENCIES	COMBINED AGENCIES
Handling special problem offenders	79%	80%	86%	76%
Caseload management	49	63	71	61
Offender monitoring	57	57	58	58
Liability issues	53	57	67	55
Report writing	41	54	63	53
Stress management	54	52	68	69
Counseling techniques	61	52	56	57

investigations (a high priority only for parole respondents), there are the set of activities generally labeled "case management." Yet, probation and parole officials generally reported a significant need for training in these basic skills areas.

When acute basic skills deficiencies are considered along with workload, recruitment, and retention problems, they make a gloomy scenario for probation and parole. Staffing levels are not keeping pace with a growing caseload. At the same time, supervision needs are increasing. Recruitment is made difficult by low salaries that will not attract enough qualified applicants, and, once hired, employees are discouraged by poor career incentives, small salary increases, and burnout.

CONCLUSION

In broad strokes, the NAP survey painted a picture of America's probation and parole systems as facing unprecedented challenges. Despite recent budget increases of more than 20 percent for many agencies and major improvements in risk management, more than 75 percent of all agencies said staff increases are not keeping pace with the number of offenders.

Compounding this increase in staff-to-client ratio is the fact that at least three-fourths of the respondents believe offenders' supervision needs are greater now than in the past. Thus, not only are the numbers larger, the offenders are also a more difficult group to manage.

Fifty to sixty-eight percent of all local probation and parole offices report that salaries are too low to attract qualified applicants. Once hired, personnel did not find financial and other incentives sufficient to stay in positions where burnout is a major problem.

Employees in general have extremely high training needs, even in such basic skills as counseling, report writing, offender monitoring, and caseload management. Fifty-five to seventy-five percent of all local directors rate one or more of these as a significant need. In addition to training in basic skills, training in handling special problem offenders, stress management, and legal liabilities are also needed by the majority of respondents.

Unlike institutions, probation and parole agencies depend on a supply of community resources to carry out their core responsibilities. Today, over half the local offices report a need to expand or improve all types of community resource efforts, including drug programs, residential programs, housing referral services, vocational education, job readiness training, and mental health services.

Over the last 15 years, probation and parole agencies have expanded their domain from primarily presentence investigations and offender supervision to pretrial diversion, halfway houses, alleviating institutional crowding, and a host of other activities. "Dealing with an increased number and variety of alternative programs in an effective manner" was cited by one director as the most serious management problem over the next few years.

Data submitted by these 388 professionals suggested that not only must this type of growth stop or slow dramatically, but also that serious questions must be raised about the system's present capacity to absorb additional offenders. Large and difficult caseloads coupled with a lack of staff and a shortage of community resources reflect a criminal justice subsystem strained to its limits.

SOURCE: Reprinted from *Research in Action* (National Institute of Justice, August 1988).

This Supplemental Reading is excerpted from the report of a National Institute of Justice–funded study conducted by the Institute of Law and Justice, Inc., of Alexandria, Virginia. Written by Randall Guynes, the report describes the results of a survey of 49 state probation and parole directors and 339 local probation and parole offices. The primary aim of the study was to identify key needs and problems of state and local criminal-justice practitioners. Selected portions of the report are reprinted here.

SUPERVISION IN PROBATION AND PAROLE

6

KEY TERMS

Supervision
Casework model
Brokerage model
Community resource
   management team model
Justice model
Integrated model
Classification
Risk assessment
Collateral Contract
Special Intensive Parole Unit
   (SIPU)
San Francisco Project
Specialized caseloads

Supervision

The oversight a probation and/or parole officer exercises over those who are placed in his/her charge during a term of probation or parole.

Casework model

The traditional supervision strategy in which the probation/parole officer serves primarily as a counselor, dispensing "treatment" to "clients" in a one-on-one therapeutic relationship.

INTRODUCTION

Supervision is the element that differentiates probation from suspended sentence and parole from other forms of early release. In this chapter we discuss both probation and parole supervision, distinguishing between them when necessary. Some authorities believe that parole supervision requires more intense supervision, because parolees are more serious offenders—in that they have been to prison. Furthermore, the transition from rigidly controlled prison life to life in the "free world" requires major living adjustments not usually faced by probationers.

Others, however, consider probationers and parolees essentially alike. Some probationers *have* been to prison as a result of earlier crimes. Others *could have* been sentenced to prison for their crimes, had they not plea-bargained (i.e., pleaded guilty in exchange for a reduced penalty.) Further, parolees have had a "taste of prison" and may exert extra effort while on supervision in order to remain free. Accordingly, with some exceptions, the supervision process is identical. In many states and in the federal system, the same officers supervise both probationers and parolees.

In its simplest terms, **supervision** may be defined as the oversight that an officer exercises over those committed to his or her custody. Whether, in practice, it is more effective than mere oversight depends on many conditions. Few offenders can be expected to transform themselves into law-abiding citizens without some assistance. However, probation or parole cannot be a constructive force in the administration of criminal justice if supervision amounts only to discipline directed toward holding in check antisocial tendencies during the period of supervision. Merely observing conditions of release or managing not to be arrested for new offenses does not indicate that an offender has been transformed. It is the element of *constructive* supervision that distinguishes probation and parole from both leniency and punishment. The concept of supervision has undergone much change in the past 50 years.

CHANGING CONCEPTS OF SUPERVISION

The Casework Era

In 1939, the *Attorney General's Survey of Release Procedures* defined supervision as follows:

> In the conventional attitudes of the criminal law, it is a form of punishment, but the purpose of it is reformative, reconstructive, and educational; to use a scientific term, it is therapeutic.[1]

This philosophy of supervision flourished for the next 30 years. The supervision process was oriented toward **casework,** providing services to probationers or parolees (often referred to as *clients*) in an effort to assist them to live productively in the community. Probation and parole officers frequently viewed themselves as "caseworkers" and the term *agent of change* was popular as a description of their role. The literature of probation and parole supervision during this period is fraught with medical/psychiatric terminology—such terms as *treatment* and *diagnosis,* for example. The National Advisory Commission on Criminal Justice Standards and Goals, reviewing the casework era, stated:

> The literature discussed the development of social work skills in interviewing, creating therapeutic relationships with clients, counseling, providing insight, and modifying behavior.[2]

A leading textbook of the period, *Probation and Parole in Theory and Practice,* reflected this orientation with chapters entitled "Social Casework," "Case Study and Diagnosis," and "Casework as a Means of Treatment."[3] The probation officer was viewed as a social worker engaged in a therapeutic relationship with the probationer "client."

Supervision as Brokerage of Services

In the early 1970s the casework approach began to break down. The National Advisory Commission on Criminal Justice Standards and Goals reported in 1973 that probation had failed to realize many of its goals.[4] The Commission pointed out that many of the services needed by probationers and parolees could be more readily and effectively provided by specialized community agencies that provide mental health, employment, housing, education, private welfare, and other services. The Commission report stated:

> Probation also has attempted to deal directly with such problems as alcoholism, drug addiction, and mental illness, which ought to be handled through community mental health and other specialized programs.[5]

This alternative strategy for delivering probation and parole services recommended by the National Advisory Commission is referred to as the **brokerage of services** approach. The "service broker" type of probation or parole officer does not consider him/herself as the primary agent of change as in the casework approach. Instead, he or she attempts to determine the needs of the probationer or parolee and locates and refers the "client" to the appropriate community agency. Thus, an unemployed parolee might be referred to vocational rehabilitation services, employment counseling, or the state employment office. Rather than attempting to counsel a probationer with emotional problems, the "broker of services" officer would locate and refer the probationer to agencies whose staff were skilled in working with problems such as those faced by the probationer. In this supervision strategy, developing linkages between the "clients" and appropriate agencies is considered one of the probation or parole officer's most important tasks. The National Advisory Commission recommended that probation and parole officers should differentiate between services that can be provided internally—by the probation officer—and those that need to be obtained from other social institutions. The Commission specified:

> Generally, the kinds of services to be provided directly to probationers through the probation system should:
>
> ■ relate to the reasons the offender was brought into the probation system,
> ■ help him adjust to his status as a probationer,

Brokerage model
Supervision strategy in which the probation/parole officer attempts to determine the needs of the probationer/parolee and refers him/her to the appropriate community agency for services. Also called the *community resource management model.*

■ provide information and facilitate referral to needed community resources,
■ help create conditions permitting readjustment and reintegration into the community as an independent individual through full utilization of all available resources.

The Commission concluded that probationers' needs related to employment, training, housing, health, and so on, are the responsibility of other social agencies and should be provided by them.[6] By the mid to late 1970s the brokerage approach to probation and parole supervision was firmly entrenched.

Community Resource Management Team (CRMT)

Community resource management team (CRMT) model

A form of "brokerage" model in which caseloads of probationers/parolees are "pooled" and served by more than one officer, each specializing in one or more areas, such as drug/alcohol services or employment. The officer specializing in a particular area develops linkages to the community agencies that provide those services.

Another approach to supervision, closely allied to the brokerage approach, is that of the **community resource management team (CMRT) model.** Using the CMRT strategy, individual probation and parole officers develop skills and linkages with community agencies in one or two areas only. One officer might be designated the drug abuse specialist, and another the employment specialist. The CMRT concept recognizes that the diverse needs of the probation or parole caseload cannot be adequately satisfied by one individual. Thus the caseload is "pooled," and the probationer might be assisted by not one, but several officers. For example, Officer Mary Smith might assess the probationer's needs for drug treatment and refer him/her to the appropriate agency for assistance. Officer Sam Jones might work with him/her in obtaining job training and employment from other community social agencies. Each officer applies his or her particular skills and linkages in the community to serve the needs of the offender.

The Justice Model of Supervision

Justice model

A supervision strategy in which supervision is geared to helping offenders comply with the conditions of their release. The traditional rehabilitative function is voluntary and is brokered through the appropriate community agencies.

In recent years a new model of probation and parole supervision has come to dominate supervision philosophy. It is the **justice model,** which advocates an escalated system of sanctions corresponding to the social harm resulting from the offense and the offender's culpability. The justice model repudiates the idea that probation is a sanction designed to rehabilitate offenders in the community and, instead, regards a sentence of probation as a proportionate punishment that is to be lawfully administered for certain prescribed crimes.[7]

In the justice model of probation, the probationary term is not viewed as an alternative to imprisonment, but rather as a valid sanction in itself. The popular view that probation is an alternative to incarceration has led the public to regard probation as an expression of leniency, and the public often feels that the offender is "getting off." There is no question that justice and the community's welfare are best served when *some* offenders are imprisoned. But for the *majority,* who can safely remain in the community, the public must feel that appropriate penalties are imposed. Therefore, the "justice" philosophy regards probation as a separate, distinct sanction requiring penalties that are graduated in severity and duration corresponding to the seriousness of the crime.[8]

THE ROLE OF THE JUSTICE MODEL PROBATION OFFICER. A **justice-model** probation penalty specifies:

1. some degree of deprivation of personal liberty, and
2. reparation to the victim or the community.[9]

Advocates of the justice model hold that practices of counseling, surveillance, and reporting accomplish very little and have minimal impact on recidivism. On the other hand, they favor probation that consists of monitoring court orders for victim restitution or community service and that ensures that the imposed deprivation of liberty is carried out.[10]

Justice-model probation specifically gears offender assistance to helping probationers comply with the condition of their probation. Other services such as mental health counseling, alcohol, and drug treatment, and such, should be available for probationers who express a need or desire for them, and should be brokered through social agencies in the community. As already noted, the primary responsibility of the probationer is to complete the conditions imposed by the court satisfactorily. Likewise, the primary task of the probation officer is to assist the probationer in satisfactorily completing the conditions. The probation agency, however, should be prepared to assist those individuals who *voluntarily* request rehabilitative assistance.[11]

Most probation and parole agencies in the United States now subscribe to the general tenets of the justice model. For example, the 1991 edition of the Federal Probation System supervision manual, *Supervision of Federal Offenders,* states:

> The primary objectives of supervision are to enforce compliance with the conditions of release, to minimize risk to the public, and to reintegrate the offender into a law-abiding life style.[12]

As recently as eight years earlier, the federal probation system's supervision philosophy had been a "community-resource-manager" approach. The 1983 edition of the supervision handbook stated:

> The most important goal of the supervision process is to engage the available community resources or provide assistance directly to aid offenders in organizing their lives to successfully meet the challenges of life in conformity with law.[13]

The shift in philosophy in probation and parole systems throughout the country was obvious and abrupt. The primary impetus for this change can be traced to the philosophical and political movements of the late 1970s and early 1980s that placed greater emphasis on punishment[14] and the failure of corrections to live up to its "promises" to rehabilitate, reintegrate, and restore offenders to productive, law-abiding lives. One particular event contributed more than any other to the shift to a more punitive role for probation and parole: the publication by Robert Martinson and his associates of a national study of treatment programs. In Martinson's study, more than 200 correctional treatment programs were carefully evaluated and declared failures.[15] The work was persuasive, and it was soon followed by other studies that reported similar results.[16] As Larry Siegel states:

> These less than enthusiastic reviews of correctional rehabilitation helped develop a more conservative view of corrections, which holds that prisons are places of incapacitation and punishment and should not be used for treatment.[17]

Supervision Objectives and Duties of Federal Probation Officers

The primary objectives of supervision are to enforce compliance with the conditions of release, to minimize risk to the public, and to reintegrate the offender into a law-abiding lifestyle. To accomplish these objectives, the officer has the following specific responsibilities.

DISCHARGE STATUTORY DUTIES. To comply with the requirements of 18 U.S.C. section 3603, probation officers shall [see Ch. IV. A.1A]:

- instruct the person under supervision as to the conditions specified by the sentencing court and provide him or her with a written statement clearly setting forth all such conditions;
- keep informed concerning the compliance with any condition of supervision and report thereon to the court or Parole Commission;
- keep informed as to the conduct and condition of a person under supervision and report his or her conduct and condition to the sentencing court or Parole Commission:
- use all suitable methods, consistent with the conditions specified by the court, to aid a person under supervision and to bring about improvements in his or her conduct and condition; and
- keep a record of the officers' work.

PROTECT THE COMMUNITY. To provide this most vital aspect of community supervision, the probation officer should [see Ch. IV.A.1B]:

- establish a plan of supervision consistent with the level of risk posed by the offender to the community;
- utilize risk control supervision activities, including verification of employment and sources of income, financial investigation, monitoring of associates, record checks, urinalysis, and restrictions on travel;
- request modification of the conditions of supervision if necessary to reduce risk. Such modifications may include home detention, community confinement, provisions for search and seizure, and requirements for financial disclosure; and
- systematically review the conduct and condition of offenders and revise supervision plans in accordance with changes in risk levels.

ADDRESS RELEVANT PROBLEMS OF OFFENDERS. To assist the offender in becoming a law-abiding and productive member of the community, the probation officer should [see Ch. IV. A.1C]:

- assess the relevant problems of the offender that are likely to be associated with further criminal conduct and develop a supervision plan to address those problems;
- utilize community resources to provide the offender with the opportunity to participate in substance-abuse and/or mental-health treatment, employment assistance, and educational opportunities; and
- ensure that the offender's response to treatment is consistent with risk-control supervision.

SOURCE: *Supervision of Federal Offenders,* monograph no. 109 (Washington: Probation and Pretrial Services Division, Administrative Offices of the U.S. Courts, June 1991).

The so-called "medical model" of corrections which stressed diagnosis and treatment ended with the "nothing works" findings by Martinson and others—a more conservative approach which stressed "deserved punishment," incapacitation, and reparation to the victim.

Thus, we now find ourselves in a conservative era of criminal justice history. Probation and parole are at a crossroads, redefining their mission and role from "therapeutic correctional treatment" toward control, deserved punishment, and risk management.

AN INTEGRATED MODEL OF SUPERVISION

In practice, probation and parole supervision usually lies between the two extremes of the casework approach and the justice model. Effective supervision has elements of control *and* treatment; neither will suffice alone. The justice model of corrections has been, we believe, correctly described as "a solution . . . of despair, not hope."[18] Because we cannot show that treatment programs have been successful in bringing about long-term change in the offender, we have assumed that they have no value, and that a strategy that emphasizes control and punishment is therefore more efficacious. However, research has not shown the justice model approach to be any more successful in reducing recidivism than the approach it replaced.

Control and treatment are not mutually exclusive in supervision, and we can draw an analogy to child-rearing practices. In their widely acclaimed 1990 book, *A General Theory of Crime,* Michael Gottfredson and Travis Hirschi attribute crime to deficiencies in self-control. They explored the nature and sources of self-control, locating it largely in family child-rearing practices. They then went on to use self-control as the basis for a general theory of crime.[19] They reported that low self-control tends to ensue in the absence of nurturance, discipline, and training.[20] Good child-rearing practices—which develop self-control—contain elements of all three. It is not too great an intellectual step to move from child-rearing practices to probation and parole supervision strategies. Many authorities have commented on the commonalities of behavior between criminals and children; namely, the pursuit of immediate pleasures, lack of ability to defer gratification, immature judgment, impulsiveness, and short attention span. Discipline, nurturance, and training socialize the child and develop the self-control and maturity of judgment necessary for successful integration into society. A child who experiences only discipline is not likely to develop into a mature, contributing member of society. So too, the child who is nurtured and trained, but not disciplined, is equally unlikely to become a contributing member of society. Probation and parole supervision, too, must contain all three. Current philosophy does not negate the nurturing and training elements; it merely assigns them much less priority than the discipline (control) element.

The strategy we recommend involves an active treatment function (nurturing and training) within a broad framework of control (discipline). This is referred to as an **integrated model.** We recall an argument between the Director of Treatment and the Director of Security in large state prison on the subject of the relative importance of rehabilitation and institutional security. The treatment director charged that the institution's security regulations undermined his efforts to treat and rehabilitate the inmates. The head of security, an Assistant Warden of many years' experience, drawled, "Doctor, no matter how good your programs are, you can't treat 'em if we can't keep 'em." It is in this context that we view probation and parole supervision.

Integrated model

A supervision strategy in which an active treatment function is contained within a broad framework of control.

The Surveillance Function in Supervision

Supervision must first involve surveillance, which is defined as "a watch kept over a person, group, etc."[21] Probation and parole are expected to provide a means of ascertaining whether those released live up to the conditions imposed by the court or the parole board. Failure to maintain proper surveillance can only bring the officer and the system into disrepute. Furthermore, an officer's failure to require the offender to adhere to the terms of release complicates the officer's task. Supervision cannot exist in a lax, haphazard manner without arousing the contempt of the offender. In addition, public support and cooperation are difficult to obtain for any probation or parole system that does not assure the community of at least minimum protection against renewed criminal activities by those under supervision.

The federal probation system guidelines for supervision specify three supervision objectives:

1. to enforce compliance with the conditions of release,
2. to minimize risk to the public, and
3. to reintegrate the offender into a law-abiding lifestyle.[22]

The third objective, to reintegrate the offender, cannot possibly be accomplished unless the first two objectives are satisfied.

The Treatment Function in Supervision

The rehabilitative function of supervision includes both nurturing and training. Treatment-oriented supervision, conducted within a context of discipline and control, must be directed toward removing or reducing individual and social barriers that may result in recidivism. Carrying out a supervisory process that can accomplish this end is an extraordinarily difficult task. Offenders can be dealt with effectively only if on an individual basis and according to their special conditions and needs. Much of the effectiveness of supervision depends on the personal relationship between the officer and the offender. An honest, direct relationship between the officer and the offender is the most effective means of promoting change and ensuring successful completion of the term of probation. The authoritative nature of the relationship should be made clear to the offender, but the spirit of encouragement and helpfulness should also be apparent. Most probationers and parolees have problems they must overcome if they are to succeed in complying with the terms and conditions of release and remaining crime free. Among the most critical problems are employment and drug and/or alcohol abuse.

EMPLOYMENT SERVICES.   It is not unreasonable to suggest that meaningful employment is the most important issue for most probationers and parolees. Not only does employment provide financial support for the offender and his/her family, but it is also crucial for establishing and maintaining self-esteem and personal dignity—qualities that are seen by most authorities as essential to successful reintegration into the community.[23] Joy Davidoff-Kroop, in a study of employment services provided by the New York State Division of Parole, concluded:

> Two recent parole follow-up studies showed a high rate of unemployment amongst parolees returned to prison.[24]

Experienced probation and parole officers know this to be true, and most probation and parole conditions require the offender to maintain employment during the period of supervision. However, finding and maintaining employment is not a simple task. Offenders are often the last to be hired and the first to be terminated. Many of them are unskilled, and many have poor work habits. Some are barred from employment in their chosen fields due to regulatory and licensing laws that preclude persons with a criminal conviction.

Because of the very critical relationship between success on parole or probation supervision and meaningful employment, it is incumbent of the supervising officer to assess the employment status of each person under his/her supervision and to work with them to locate a job. In many cases the probationer or parolee will require a vocational assessment to determine his/her employability, interests, capabilities, and any barriers to employment. Many will require vocational or job-readiness training before they can seek a job. Ideally, these services are obtained from external agencies and organizations such as state employment offices or vocational rehabilitation services. The probation or parole officer's job is to locate the existing service, refer the supervisee to the service, assist him/her in obtaining the service, and monitor progress and participation. Ideally, the probation or parole agency would have funds available for purchasing these services if they are not available otherwise.

DRUG AND ALCOHOL ABUSE SERVICES. Drug and alcohol abuse have a negative effect on every aspect of an offender's life; they contribute to employment, marital, and other personal and social problems. For many, if not most, substance abuse contributed directly or indirectly to the crime(s) that led to their conviction. Recent studies show that approximately 51 percent of inmates in the United States Bureau of Prisons were incarcerated for drug-related offenses.[25] The Bureau of Justice Statistics reported that in 1988 more than half of all state prisoners had been using drugs or alcohol or both at the time of the offense for which they were serving time.[26] Because these findings are obtained primarily from self-reports, they should be interpreted conservatively. The true figure is likely much higher.

In light of these data, probation and parole officers must consider drug and alcohol monitoring and treatment as a major aspect of their job. None of the goals of supervision can be met when the releasee is using and abusing alcohol and/or drugs. The federal probation manual, *The Supervision Process,* states:

> In the United States alcohol is the principal drug of abuse. Alcoholism represents a unique problem in the supervision of offenders in that often alcohol is not identified as a primary problem having a direct effect on all other aspects of an individual's life. A probation officer may address an offender's lack of employment, marital difficulties, or other social problems when, in fact, they are all secondary to the problem of alcoholism.[27]

and,

> One of the most important functions of the probation officer is the identification of drug abuse from available historical data, recognition of physical symptoms, and urinalysis.[28]

As in the case of employment problems, few probation and parole officers possess the expertise necessary to provide drug and alcohol assessment, urinalysis monitoring, and/or treatment. Once again, the releasee should have ready access to external agencies and organizations. To carry out his/her duties, the probation/parole officer helps the probationer/parolee obtain the needed services by assessing the needs, being aware of available community resources, contacting the appropriate resources, referring the probationer for services, and monitoring compliance.

A Typology of Probation Officer Work Styles

University of Delaware criminologist Carl Klockars found that the broadest component of probation supervision is the role that officers set for themselves and the logic and rationale they develop to explain what they do or what they ought to do. Klockars developed a typology of probation officers that defines four basic work styles on the "probation *is not* casework" versus "probation *is* casework" continuum:[29]

The Law-Enforcer

At the "probation is not casework" pole are officers who stress the legal authority and enforcement aspects of the position. These officers' philosophies dictate firmness, authority, and rule-abidance as essentials of social life. Of prime importance to such officers are the court order, authority, and decision-making power.

The Time-Servers

Time-serving officers are nearly the functional equivalent of the law enforcers. They see their jobs as fulfilling certain requirements until their retirement and they have little aspiration to improve their skills. Their conduct on the job is to abide by the rules, and they meet their job responsibilities minimally but methodically. Rules and regulations are upheld but unexamined. They don't make the rules; they just work there.

The Therapeutic Agent

At the other pole are officers who consider themselves therapeutic agents. They see their role as administering a form of treatment, introducing the probationer or parolee to a better way of life, and motivating patterns of behavior that are constructive. They give guidance and support to those who are unable to solve their problems by themselves and provide them an opportunity to work through their ambivalent feelings. The philosophy of the therapeutic agent may be summarized as follows:

1. I take conscious pains in every contact with offenders to demonstrate my concern for them and my respect for them as human beings.
2. I seize every opportunity to help offenders come to understand the nature of the shared problem solving, aiding the process by actually experiencing it.
3. I recognize, bring into the open, and deal directly with offenders' negative attitudes toward me as the representative of social authority.
4. I partialize the total life problems confronting offenders.

5. I help individuals perceive the degree to which their behavior has and will result in their own unhappiness.

The Synthetic Officer

The fourth and final work style in Klockar's typology is distinguished by recognition of both the treatment and law-enforcement components of probation officers' roles. These officers' attempts at supervision reflect their desire to balance the needs for therapy and law-enforcement. Thus, they set for themselves the task of combining the paternal, authoritarian, and judgmental with the therapeutic. Theirs is a dilemma–combining treatment and control–that is found throughout the field of corrections.

From the foregoing, it is obvious that probation and parole supervision is a multifaceted problem that depends not only on the quality of the particular administrative organization and the officers' education and experience, but also—and to a great degree, more importantly—upon the way in which the officers view their job and their role within the system. The Supplemental Reading "The Five Faces of Probation" at the end of the chapter analyzes probation officers' perceptions of their role.

CLASSIFICATION: THE FIRST STEP IN SUPERVISION

The first step in the supervision process is to classify the offender's case. **Classification** consists of assessing the risks posed by the offender, identifying the supervision issues, and selecting the appropriate supervision strategies. Most probation and parole agencies have devised some form of caseload classification as a guide for risk control, allocating their officers' time, and measuring their officers' work loads.

Case classification is the initial phase of case management planning. Specific objectives to be achieved by the offender and the agency should be identified. Ideally, such planning involves the officer responsible for case supervision, the first-line supervisor, any specialists involved in the case assessment, and the offender.

Case classification should also determine control requirements, treatment needs, and the administrative categorization of the case.

Control requirements can specify restrictions on the offender's movement, residence, and associations; the frequency of his/her contact with the probation or parole officer; and reporting requirements.

Treatment needs frequently exist for employment, training, education, residence, and finances and for counseling and guidance to address drug or alcohol abuse or other psychological or emotional problems.

Administrative categorization of the case determines the extent and nature of time to be allocated to the offender by the staff and assesses the degree of risk posed by the offender. In this classification, it is essential to identify strategies and resources that will meet the offender's needs.

Classification

Determination of the level of needed supervision (usually in terms of minimum, medium, maximum, etc.) based on the probationer/parolee's risk of recidivism and need for services.

Classification is an ongoing process. It should provide for periodic review (probably quarterly) of actions initiated and completed by both the offender and the agency. Reviews provide opportunity for reclassifying the offender or changing plans in response to changing circumstances or reassessments of needs. Achievement of defined objectives should trigger a reduction in controls and restraints, as well as of staff time allocations, and should look toward the earliest possible release from supervision that is consistent with public safety.

Objective norms or guidelines for categorizing risk and level of supervision can permit more consistent handling of cases and provide a more rational basis for determining staff time requirements. The development and consistent use of a logical classification process provides a basis for rational management of probation or parole caseloads; in fact, it is a prerequisite for determining the needs for staff and other resources.

The elements of an effective probation and parole classification system include:

■ classification based on risk of continued criminal activity and the offender's need for services
■ a parallel case management classification system designed to help officers develop effective case plans and select appropriate casework strategies
■ a management information system designed to enhance planning, monitoring, education, and accountability
■ a work load system to allow the agency to equitably, effectively, and efficiently allocate limited resources

Risk Assessment

Risk assessment

Determination of an offender's risk of recidivism and appropriate classification and case management strategies. This is most often accomplished by using actuarial prediction scales based on variables shown to be empirically correlated with success or failure on probation or parole.

Not only does the assessment of risk and needs provide a measure of the client's propensity to further criminal activity; it also indicates the level of agent intervention that will be required to deal with the client's problem. It does not, however, indicate the appropriate supervision strategy. Most **risk assessment** strategies are based on the system developed in Wisconsin in the late 1970s and adopted by the National Institute of Corrections (NIC). Two factors are considered in Wisconsin model: (1) the degree of risk of recidivism posed by the offender and (2) the amount of assistance the offender requires from the probation or parole agency. Together, these variables predict the level of supervision the offender needs.

Most jurisdictions have developed some form of risk prediction scale to assist them in developing supervision plans and in caseload classification. The federal probation system employs the Risk Prediction Scale (RPS) for classifying and developing supervision plans for probationers; see Figure 6–1. The RPS is based on variables that have been correlated empirically with probation success or failure. For example, two variables have been found to predict a low level of required supervision. The probationer is automatically assigned to "low-activity" supervision if he or she has completed high school *and* has a history free of opiate usage. If the offender is not automatically assigned to low-activity supervision, the officer assigns points for the presence of five risk variables:

Risk Prediction Scale (RPS 80)

NAME	PROBATION OFFICER	DATE

I. Automatic Assignment

If "yes" is checked for both A and B, place in Low-Activity Supervision.

A. Individual has completed high school education.　　YES ☐　NO ☐

B. Individual has history free of opiate usage.　　YES ☐　NO ☐

II. Risk Score Determination

If not automatically assigned, use items C through G to determine risk score and supervision activity level.

C. Twenty-eight years or older at time of instant conviction .... (7) _____

D. Arrest-free period of five (5) or more consecutive years.. (4) _____

E. Few prior arrests (none, one, or two) ....(10) _____

F. History free of opiate usage... (9) _____

G. At least four (4) months' steady employment prior to arraignment for present offense...... (3) _____

SUM OF POINTS (33) _____

RISK SCORE RANGE　　　　　　　　　　　　　　　SUPERVISION LEVEL

Automatic Assignment
or　　　　>————————————————————▶　　Low Activity ☐
20–33

0–19　　　>————————————————————▶　　High Activity ☐

FIGURE 6–1
Risk Prediction Scale

SOURCE: United States Probation Service Administration-Office of the United States Courts.

1. twenty-eight years or older at time of instant offense; 7 points
2. arrest-free for five or more consecutive years; 4 points
3. few prior arrests (none, 1, or 2); 10 points.
4. history free of opiate use; 9 points
5. at least four months' steady employment prior to arraignment for present offense; 3 points

The maximum possible score is 33 points. An offender is automatically assigned to low-activity supervision if his or her score is 20–33 points. A score of 0–19 points places the offender in high-activity supervision.

While objective, statistics-based devices such as the RPS provide "educated" predictions of risk, the federal system uses an additional, *subjective* method to assist the probation officer in determining whether the risk posed by the offender is greater than that predicted by the risk prediction instrument. If the offender has already been identified as a risk, this subjective method helps to identify the type of risk involved. Such indications include:

■ substance abuse related to criminal conduct
■ current or prior violent behavior and/or use of weapons
■ participation in continuing criminal conspiracies (e.g., wholesale drug distribution or organized crime)
■ unexplained assets or current lifestyle incompatible with reported income
■ pattern of similar criminal conduct
■ serious mental health problems[30]

The supervision handbook, *Supervision of Federal Offenders,* concludes:

> The combination of the risk prediction score and the existence or absence of the offense or offender characteristics . . . will assist the officer in determining to what extent the case plan and supervision activities must address risk control activities.[31]

Most state probation and parole systems utilize risk/needs prediction instruments. These instruments differ in some respects, but all of them place offenders in groups with a known *statistical probability* of committing new crimes or violating the conditions of supervision. Pennsylvania, for example, assesses 11 risk variables to determine the level of supervision required by the offender. Pennsylvania also assesses 13 needs variables that provide a standardized means of discerning problem areas that should be addressed in the supervision process; see Figure 6–2. The probationer is assigned to one of several levels of supervision on the basis of these two scores.

Levels of Supervision

Although various names are used to differentiate the levels of supervision, most are essentially restatements of the traditional *maximum, medium,* and *minimum* supervision classes. Some systems place almost all new cases in the highest supervision class. Others categorize primarily on the basis of the seriousness of the offense and the offender's prior record. Occasionally, the kind and extent of services required is the basis. Practically all classification systems specify contact requirements for each level. Unfortunately, these requirements are almost universally specified in terms of number of contacts

FIGURE 6-2

Pennsylvania's Initial Client Assessment Form

COMMONWEALTH OF PENNSYLVANIA
BOARD OF PROBATION AND PAROLE
PBPP-20 (1/85)

INITIAL CLIENT ASSESSMENT

CLIENT NAME (Last, First, Middle Initial)	PAROLE NO.	AGENT NAME	OFFICE	DATE

RISK ASSESSMENT

1. Age at First Conviction: (or juvenile adjudication)
- 24 or older 0
- 20-23 2
- 19 or Younger 4

2. Number of Prior Probation/Parole Revocations: (adult or juvenile)
- None 0
- One or more 4

3. Number of Prior Felony Convictions: (or juvenile adjudications)
- None 0
- One 2
- Two or more 4

4. Convictions or Juvenile Adjudications for:
(Select applicable and add for score. Do not exceed a total of 5. Include current offense.)
- Burglary, theft, auto theft, or robbery 2
- Worthless checks or forgery 3

5. Number of Prior Periods of Probation/Parole Supervision:
(Adult or Juvenile)
- None 0
- One or more 4

6. Conviction or Juvenile Adjudication for Assaultive Offense within Last Five Years: (An offense which involves the use of a weapon, physical force or the threat of force.)
- Yes. 15
- No 0

7. Number of Address Changes in Last 12 Months:
(Prior to incarceration for parolees)
- None 0
- One 2
- Two or more 3

8. Percentage of Time Employed in Last 12 Months:
(Prior to incarceration for parolees)
- 60% or more 0
- 40%-50% 1
- Under 40% 2
- Not applicable 0

9. Alcohol Usage Problems: (Prior to incarceration for parolees)
- No interference with functioning 0
- Occasional abuse; some disruption of functioning . 2
- Frequent abuse; serious disruption; needs treatment . 4

10. Other Drug Usage Problems: (Prior to incarceration for parolees)
- No interference with functioning 0
- Occasional abuse; some disruption of functioning . 1
- Frequent abuse; serious disruption; needs treatment . 2

11. Attitude:
- Motivated to change; receptive to assistance ... 0
- Dependent or unwilling to accept responsibility . 3
- Rationalizes behavior; negative; not motivated to change ... 5

TOTAL [ ]

INITIAL ASSESSMENT SCALES

Risk Scale		Needs Scale
0-5 .... Reduced Supervision .... -8-10		
6-18 .... Regular Supervision 1-10		
19-30 .... Close Supervision 11-25		
31 & above ...... Intensive Supervision .... 26 & above		

SCORING AND OVERRIDE

Score Based Supervision Level ..... Intensive ... [ ]   Regular ..... [ ]
.... Close .... [ ]   Reduced..... [ ]

Score Override .... No .... [ ]   Yes .... [ ]

FINAL GRADE OF SUPERVISION .... Intensive .. [ ]   Regular .... [ ]

Override Explanation: .... Close ...... [ ]   Reduced..... [ ]

NEEDS ASSESSMENT

1. Academic/Vocational Skills
- High school or above skill level .... -1
- Adequate skills; able to handle everyday requirements ... 0
- Low skill level causing minor adjustment problems ... +2
- Minimal skill level causing serious adjustment problems ... +4

2. Employment
- Satisfactory employment for one year or longer ... -1
- Secure employment; no difficulties reported; or homemaker, student or retired ... 0
- Unsatisfactory employment; or unemployed but has adequate job skills ... +3
- Unemployed and virtually unemployable; needs training ... +6

3. Financial Management
- Long-standing pattern of self-sufficiency; e.g., good credit rating -1
- No current difficulties 0
- Situational or minor difficulties .... +3
- Severe difficulties; may include garnishment, bad checks or bankruptcy ... +5

4. Marital/Family Relationships
- Relationships and support exceptionally strong . -1
- Relatively stable relationships 0
- Some disorganization or stress but potential for improvement ... +3
- Major disorganization or stress .... +5

5. Companions
- Good support and influence .... -1
- No adverse relationships 0
- Associations with occasionally negative results . +2
- Associations almost completely negative .... +4

6. Emotional Stability
- Exceptionally well adjusted; accepts responsibility for actions .. -2
- No symptoms of emotional instability; appropriate emotional responses ... 0
- Symptoms limit but do not prohibit adequate functioning; e.g., excessive anxiety ... +4
- Symptoms prohibit adequate functioning; e.g. lashes out or retreats into self ... +7

7. Alcohol Usage
- No interference with functioning 0
- Occasional abuse; some disruption of functioning . +3
- Frequent abuse; serious disruption; needs treatment . +6

8. Other Drug Usage
- No interference with functioning 0
- Occasional substance abuse; some disruption of functioning ... +3
- Frequent substance abuse; serious disruption; needs treatment . +5

9. Mental Ability
- Able to function independently 0
- Some need for assistance; potential for adequate adjustment; mild retardation ... +3
- Deficiencies severely limit independent functioning; moderate retardation ... +6

10. Health
- Sound physical health; seldom ill 0
- Handicap or illness interferes with functioning on a recurring basis +1
- Serious handicap or chronic illness; needs frequent medical care. +2

11. Sexual Behavior
- No apparent dysfunction 0
- Real or perceived situational or minor problems . +3
- Real or perceived chronic or severe problems ... +5

12. Recreation/Hobby
- Constructive 0
- Some constructive activities .... +1
- No constructive leisure-time activities or hobbies ... +2

13. Agent's Impression of Client's Needs
- Minimum .... -1
- Low 0
- Medium .... +3
- Maximum .... +5

TOTAL [ ]

---

per month or other time interval and by the type or location (i.e., home, office, telephone, or collateral). Few specify the quality or content of the contact.

In most instances, the work plan optimistically looks toward gradual reduction of the level of supervision if the client manages to avoid further transgressions of rules or laws (at least, avoids *apprehension* for any transgressions). In many instances, the final, minimum level is that of no supervision or a level of assistance other than that specifically requested by the client or necessitated by rearrest.

Collateral contact

A contract by the probation officer with an individual other than the probationer such as his/her spouse, employer or other person who might have knowledge of the probationer's activities.

Typical Contact Standards by Supervision Level

MAXIMUM/INTENSIVE SUPERVISION

■ One face-to-face contact and one collateral contact monthly.

■ Monthly report; one home visit; one face-to-face (in addition to home visit); one employment verification; one special condition.

■ Two face-to-face contacts monthly; one collateral contact monthly; one home visit every forty-five days.

■ Four face-to-face contacts monthly; one collateral contact monthly; one home call within thirty days of placement on caseload and within two weeks after each reported move; verification of residence every three months; criminal history check after first year of supervision.

■ Two face-to-face contacts monthly, one of which must be in the field; two collateral contacts per month.

MEDIUM/MODERATE SUPERVISION

■ One face-to-face contact monthly and one collateral contact per quarter.

■ One home visit (per quarter); one monthly report; one residence verification; one face-to-face contact; one employment verification; one special condition, if applicable.

■ One face-to-face contact and one collateral contact monthly; one home visit every ninety days.

■ Two face-to-face contacts monthly with unemployed offenders; one contact if verified full-time employment/training; one collateral contact per month; home call within thirty days of placement on caseload and within two weeks after each reported move; verification of residence every three months and employment/training monthly; criminal history check after first year of supervision.

■ One face-to-face contact per month; one collateral contact monthly; one field visit every three months.

MINIMUM SUPERVISION

■ One face-to-face semiannual contact and collateral contact quarterly.

■ One home visit, as needed, one monthly report; one face-to-face (per quarter); one employment verification (per quarter).

■ One face-to-face contact monthly, unless quarterly reporting.

■ One face-to-face contact monthly: verification of residence once every three months.

■ Mail-in report monthly; one face-to-face contact every three months; one collateral contact every three months.

SOURCE: Edward E. Rhine, William R. Smith, and Ronald W. Jackson, *Paroling Authorities: Recent History and Current Practice* (Laurel, Md.: American Correctional Association, 1991). Reprinted with permission of the American Correctional Association.

Classification of caseload or work load is ideally a management tool to aid in setting priorities within the agency and caseload. Classification, then, is an aid to supervision, not a substitute for it. It is not a crystal ball for accurately predicting an individual's future behavior. Nonetheless, it enables an officer to quickly and consistently "get a handle on" an individual case when information is limited and to focus on the degree to which an individual's behavior fits a behavioral profile that corresponds to a prescribed level of supervision. The initial assessment is subsequently expanded into a more detailed supervision plan that is regularly reassessed and modified.

Development of Casework Strategy

In many cases an officer needs considerable experience with a client in order to formulate an appropriate casework strategy. This can create problems when clients are involuntary and time is limited, because the first few months of supervision are often critical to achieving successful completion of probation and parole. Therefore, a means for reducing the time required to develop casework strategies can be beneficial. To this end, the Wisconsin model includes a process (termed *client-management classification*) that uses a 45-minute semistructured interview and a forced-choice rating instrument. Clients' responses to the questionnaire assign them to one of four supervision techniques:

1. selective intervention
2. casework/control
3. environmental structuring
4. limited setting

This classification process helps officers anticipate the behavior and problems clients may present and provides recommendations for dealing with each type of client. It does not prescribe a level of supervision; it deals generally with how a particular client can best be supervised. Maximum, medium, and minimum supervision clients may be found in all four client-management classification categories.

Wisconsin's Management Information System

A unique feature of the Wisconsin program is the incorporation of classification data in the management information system. The information system contains data collected on probationers and parolees at admission, at reevaluation, and at termination. A comprehensive client profile is entered in the system for each offender at the time of admission to probation or parole. Data collected at reevaluation and termination are then merged with admission data, providing a "before, during, and after" record of each client.

Data is analyzed to provide routine reports to management, evaluation of the system, and answers to special requests. Comprehensive periodic reports are prepared for various levels of management, and these are used to identify trends, project populations, examine usage of community resources, and set priorities for future purchases of services.

CASELOADS AND WORK LOAD COMPUTATION

Traditionally, 50 "units" has been considered the ideal caseload for a probation officer. However, there is no empirical evidence to show that this number is ideal or that it is regarded as such any longer. In 1967 the President's Commission on Law Enforcement Standards and Goals recommended supervision caseloads of 35 or less.[32] Edward Rhine and his associates reported in 1991 that average adult-parole caseloads ranged from 25 in one state to 307 in another, with pronounced variation among states. More specifically, they found that:

> Five jurisdictions reported average caseloads of fifty or less, while nineteen reported caseloads averaging between fifty-one and seventy-five. In eighteen states, the average caseload ranged from 76 to 100. Finally, four states had average caseloads

between 102 and 125, while one state reported an average caseload of 162, and another, 307.[33]

The Special Intensive Parole Unit (SIPU) Study

In the 1960s the California Division of Adult Parole developed a research project known as the **Special Intensive Parole Unit (SIPU).**[34] The research-ers set up experimental caseloads of 15 men, pairing them with control groups of regular caseloads of 90 men. The 15-man caseloads were supervised closely and intensely for the first three months after release—presumably the most vulnerable period for failure. After three months, these intensive caseload parolees were reassigned to regular 90-man caseloads. Examination of the progress data for the two groups did not show that the 15-man intensive supervision units were more effective in reducing the failure rate than the 90-man caseloads.

Subsequent SIPU studies tested 30-man caseloads for periods of six months, 35-man caseloads for twelve months, and 30-man caseloads for twenty-four months, respectively. The project as a whole did not show significantly better success rates with the experimental intensive caseloads.[35]

The San Francisco Project

In a study of federal probation in the Northern District of California referred to as the **San Francisco Project,** an attempt was made to determine the relative effectiveness of minimum, regular, ideal, and intensive caseloads.[36]

The "minimum" caseload, numerically the largest, called for reporting by mail and service upon demand. The "regular" caseload consisted of 85 units, the "ideal" caseload of 50 units, and the "intensive" caseload of 25 units.

New probationers were randomly assigned to the caseload groups. At the end of two years, the performance of the minimum caseload groups was not significantly different from that of the regular caseload groups. The regular and ideal caseloads showed violation rates of 22 percent and 24 percent, respectively. The intensive caseload groups' violation rate was 38 percent. This inflated rate contained a high proportion of technical violations, presumably a consequence of the higher level of supervision. If technical violations were excluded from the analysis, there were *no significant differences* in violation rates for the minimum, regular, ideal, and intensive caseload groups.

All of the studies conducted in caseload size point to one of the most frequently voiced criticisms of early research: that when caseloads were reduced, the supervising officers were given no direction on what to do with the extra time available to them. The conclusions drawn in the San Francisco Project to explain why intensive supervision did not seem to reduce the rate of violation included the speculation that it may not be the number of contacts, but rather, the *quality of work* that is vital. The authors stated,

> If at the outset of supervision, a climate of trust and confidence is established, it seems more likely the clients will seek the assistance of a probation officer before permitting their personal adjustment to deteriorate to the point of probation or

parole violation. No available evidence documents that routine contacts without goals will increase such a possibility. Clearly needed is a closer attention to understanding and measuring the quality, not the quantity of supervision.[37]

More recent research has indicated that the client-to-agent ratio is an inadequate method of staff deployment, because it assumes that all "units" are equal. The number and difficulty of presentence reports a probation officer must write, the number of drug or alcohol offenders in a caseload, and a caseload's geographic distribution all mitigate against standardized caseload size.[38] One author of this textbook, while working as a U.S. Probation Officer in the Western District of Texas during the 1970s, supervised a caseload dispersed geographically from San Antonio to Midland, a distance of more than 300 miles. At the same time, one of his New York City colleagues was able to visit his entire caseload within the confines of twelve city blocks. Similarly, a caseload consisting of drug addicts differs greatly from one of white-collar tax evaders or violators of Securities and Exchange Commission rules. An effective classification system identifies differences in offenders that will impact on the amount of supervision they require. It is then possible to ascertain the total *work load* of probation or parole officers, as opposed to the total caseload.[39]

Specialized Caseloads

The use of specialized caseloads has proven to be effective in improving supervision quality and effectiveness. Offenders with certain characteristics can often benefit from supervision by a specialist, a probation or parole officer who has special education, training, or experience in the particular area. These **specialized caseloads** are used with such groups as youthful offenders, drug addicts, alcoholics, dangerous offenders, sex offenders, and emotionally disturbed offenders.[40] Rhine, Smith, and Jackson found that specialized parole supervision caseloads were being used in 25 states by 1990. Fourteen states were using specialized caseloads for sex offenders; twelve states, for drug offenders; ten jurisdictions, for offenders with mental disabilities; five, for "career criminals"; and two states, for violent criminals.[41] Specialized caseloads for DWI (Driving While Intoxicated) offenders were established in Texas in 1983, and now they exist in virtually every medium-to-large probation department. Although there are few empirical studies of the efficacy of specialized caseloads, anecdotal reports support the concept.

THE CASE RECORD

An essential aspect of supervision is maintaining an accurate and valid case record of chronological anecdotal entries. The case record is a conveniently organized, readily accessible accumulation of all data related to the study and treatment of each offender. It constitutes a permanent file of pertinent information about the client that the probation or parole officer has gathered from the time of the preliminary investigation until the period of supervision is terminated. This record should contain information that will help the officer to determine the problems and needs of probationers, to determine the types of services and help that are required, and to evaluate the results of the services rendered. Information about family relations, religious interest and expression, health, education, finances, employment, the client's character and personality, and the client's attitudes and outlook is essential for developing a program of reintegration and change. The quality of the probation and parole officer's work in helping the client is reflected in the facts, observations, and situations that the officer documents in the anecdotal case record.

Each entry should include:

1. the purpose, nature, and circumstances of the contact and the action taken
2. the probationer or parolee's problem and needs at the time of the interview, how the probationer or parolee is affected by them, and how they are being met
3. the specific action taken to help resolve the client's needs
4. an evaluation of the progress or success achieved as a result of earlier contacts
5. any needed modification in the treatment plan for adapting to the client's changing needs.

The probation or parole officer should record as objectively and as accurately as possible what transpired during the interplay of the personalities of the officer and the client during the interview, what decisions were reached and in what manner, and what accomplishments were achieved. Objective and accurate recording of the client's emotional makeup, attitudes, wishes, desires, aspirations, prejudices, likes and dislikes, predispositions, conflicts, and sense of values is essential to understanding the client's problems and needs. Skills in observation, vocabulary, and clear written expression are required for recording these relatively subjective elements of the probationer or parolee's character and personality well.

The case record should be summarized and evaluated periodically. This encourages the officer to apply diagnostic thinking to his or her work and to reflect on the progress of the case to date. It is particularly useful in cases under supervision for periods of a year or more and is helpful in gaining a quick summary of the case. A periodic summary should show what actions have been attempted but failed, what has been accomplished, and what plan for the future is indicated.

One of the Supplemental Readings following this chapter is a typical chronological case record.

SUMMARY

The most vital aspect of the probation and parole process in the criminal justice system is supervision. In its simplest terms, supervision is the oversight that is exercised over those who have been placed on probation or parole. A supervisory process that is highly individualized and purposefully reconstructive can meet the needs of an adequate probation or parole system. The personality, training, and experience of the supervising officer largely determines the adequacy of the process. Lax supervision and failure to deal firmly with those who persistently violate the terms of release can bring an entire system into disrepute. Adequate probation or parole supervision must deal with all phases of the offender's life, including the offender's family and the community in which he or she lives. Although probation and parole professionals may disagree on the value and propriety of many specific techniques of supervision, all recognize the need for a plan of treatment that is based on the needs, capacities, and limitations of each offender. The physical and mental health, capacities, and limitations of the offender; the offender's home and family; his or her leisure time activities, education, vocational training, economic status, and work habits; and the offender's capacity for discipline and self-control must all be considered by those who are attempting to him or her to become a law-abiding citizen.

In order to deal affirmatively with all aspects of the probationer or parolee's life that require aid, the officer cannot act entirely alone. The officer must, whenever possible, endeavor to secure the assistance and cooperation of community agencies and facilities. Responsibility for securing the assistance and monitoring and evaluating the results of these agencies rests with the probation and parole officer. This is an indispensable part of an officer's duty; if it is neglected, the officer's work will remain unsatisfactory.

Probation and parole supervision necessitate frequent and continuous contact with the offender. This contact should be characterized by a positive relationship of mutual respect and trust and the officer's willingness to see his or her role as multi-faceted, not as a singularly therapeutic or enforcement-oriented role.

Good probation service is not easily accomplished when officers are compelled to carry too many cases. A supervision caseload of fifty offenders per officer has been suggested as desirable. Research has indicated, however, that the total work load, based on a properly classified caseload, should determine the ratio of clients to agent.

Our discussion of supervision in probation and parole may be summarized by paraphrasing from the American Bar Association's Standards for Criminal Justice project's *Standards relating to Probation:*

> The basic idea underlying probation and parole is to help the offender learn to live productively in the community that has been offended.[42]

ENDNOTES

1. *Attorney General's Survey; Probation,* vol. 2 (Washington: U.S. Department of Justice 1939), p. 261.

2. National Advisory Commission on Criminal Justice Standards and Goals, *Report on Corrections* (1973), cited in George Killinger and Paul Cromwell, eds., *Corrections in the Community,* 2nd ed. (St. Paul: West, 1978), p. 108.

3. Helen D. Pidgeon, *Probation and Parole in Theory and Practice* (New York: National Probation and Parole Association, 1942), reported in NAC, *Corrections, supra* note 2.

4. NAC, *Corrections, supra*

5. Cited in "Probation Standards and Goals," in Killinger and Cromwell, *Corrections, supra* note 2, pp. 107–108.

6. *Id.* p. 115.

7. Robert J. Gemignani, "Rethinking Probation," *Change* 5 (1983), no. 4.

8. *Id.* at 2.

9. *Id.*

10. *Id.* at 3.

11. *Id.*

12. *Supervision of Federal Offenders,* monograph no. 109 (Washington: Administrative Offices of the U.S. Courts, Probation and Pretrial Services Division, June 1991), p. 2.

13. *The Supervision Process,* publication no. 106 (Administrative Office of the U.S. Courts, Probation Division, April 1983), p. 2.

14. See Robert G. Culbertson and Thomas Ellsworth, "Treatment Innovations in Probation and Parole," in Lawrence W. Travis III, ed., *Probation, Parole, and Community Corrections* (Prospect Heights, Ill.: Waveland Press, 1985).

15. D. Lipton, Robert Martinson, and Judith Wilks, *The Effectiveness of Correctional Treatment: A Survey of Treatment Evaluation Studies* (New York: Praeger, 1975).

16. Charles Murray and Louis Cox, *Beyond Probation: Juvenile Corrections and the Chronic Delinquent* (Beverly Hills: Sage, 1979).

17. Larry J. Siegel, *Criminology,* 4th ed. (St Paul: West, 1992), p. 575.

18. Willard Gaylin and David Rothman, "Introduction," in Andrew von Hirsch, *Doing Justice: The Choice of Punishments* (New York: Hill and Wang, 1976), pp. xxi–xli.

19. Michael R. Gottfredson and Travis Hirschi, *A General Theory of Crime* (Stanford, Calif.: Stanford University Press, 1990), p. xv.

20. *Id.* at 95.

21. *The Random House College Dictionary* (New York: Random House, 1973).

22. *Supervision of Federal Offenders, supra* note 12 at 2.

23. *The Supervision Process, supra* note 13. Materials in this section rely heavily on "Systematic Approach to Supervision Responsibilities" in this manual.

24. Joy Davidoff-Kroop, *An Initial Assessment of the Division of Parole's Employment Services.* (Albany: New York State Division of Parole, 1983), p. 1.

25. Donald W. Murray, "New Initiatives in Drug Treatment in the Federal Bureau of Prisons," *Federal Probation,* June 1991, p. 35.

26. Steven D. Dillingham and Lawrence A. Greenfeld, "An Overview of National Correctional Statistics," *Federal Probation,* June 1991, p. 31.

27. *The Supervision Process, supra* note 13, at 29.

28. *Id.* at 32.

29. Carl B. Klockars, Jr., *Journal of Criminal Law, Criminology, and Police Science* 63 (1974), no. 4.

30. *Supervision of Federal Offenders, supra* note 12, pp. 16–17.

31. *Id.,* p. 17.

32. President's Commission on Law Enforcement Standards and Goals, *The Challenge of Crime in a Free Society* (Washington, D.C.: Government Printing Office, 1967).

33. Edward E. Rhine, William R. Smith, and Ronald W. Jackson, *Paroling Authorities: Recent History and Current Practice* (Laurel, Md.: American Correctional Association, 1991), p. 112.

34. Stuart Adams, "Some Findings from Correctional Caseload Research," *Federal Probation,* December 1967.

35. *Id.* at 54.

36. Joseph V. Lohman, G. Albert Wahl, and Robert M. Carter, *The San Francisco Project,* (Berkeley: University of California, April 1965).

37. William P. Adams, Paul M. Chandler, and M. G. Neithercutt, "The San Francisco Project: A Critique," *Federal Probation,* December 1971.

38. Rhine et al., *supra* note 33.

39. Much of the foregoing discussion of the Wisconsin model is based on articles in the professional literature by S. Christopher Baird, particularly "Probation and Parole Classification: The Wisconsin Model," *Corrections Today,* May–June 1981.

40. See Howard Abadinsky, *Probation and Parole: Theory and Practice,* 3rd ed. (Englewood Cliffs, N.J.: Prentice Hall, 1987), p. 341

41. Rhine et al., *supra,* p. 112.

42. ABA Project on Standards in Criminal Justice, *Standards related to Probation,* approved draft (1970), p. 1.

Discussion Questions

1. Discuss how the concept of supervision has changed over the past half-century. What factor(s) brought about the changes?

2. How do the "casework" and "brokerage of services" supervision models differ?

3. What are the probation officer's major functions in the justice model?

4. What change in the federal system's philosophy of supervision is evidenced by comparing the 1983 and 1991 federal supervision manuals? What are some factors that may have brought about the change?

5. What is case classification? Upon what factors are cases classified? Why is classification important?

6. Discuss the use of risk prediction scales. What is their purpose? How might they be used in case management? What appear to be the most important variables in risk prediction?

7. Discuss the concept of work load or caseload computation? What is the traditional position? What factors must be considered in addition to the number of cases supervised?

8. What was the SIPU study, and what did it tell us about caseload size?

9. What did the San Francisco study find with regard to the relative effectiveness of various caseloads? What conclusions can be drawn from the findings?

10. How does a specialized caseload differ from traditional caseloads? Is there any evidence to suggest that specialized caseloads are more effective than others?

11. Explain the analogy between child rearing and probation supervision. What is the lesson to be learned from the analogy?

12. Discuss the "surveillance" and "treatment" functions in supervision. How are they related?

13. Discuss Carl Klockar's typology of probation officers. Relate this typology to the "probation grid" explained in the first Supplemental Reading for this chapter.

14. Why is it critical for probation and parole officers to assess clients' needs regarding substance abuse and employment? How are they related the other needs and risks in probation supervision?

SUPPLEMENTAL READINGS

The Five Faces of Probation

In seeking to meet the challenge of crime and delinquency, the modern probation officer finds himself caught up in a peculiar double bind. He must serve the needs of his probationers, on one hand, and the needs of the community, on the other. This two-sided facet of the probation officer's function is a result of evolutionary changes in both the conception and scope of probation. It represents corrections' attempt to discover the most effective means of accomplishing humane but realistic treatment of offenders.

The law mandates that probationers should be "helped" to overcome or neutralize their antisocial behaviors. At the same time probation is aimed as "protecting" the community from those same overt behaviors. The dilemma this poses is well known to probation officers who must put this dual task into some manageable perspective in their work. Too often, the training of correctional personnel shows features of choosing one goal over the other. Depending on whether one's orientation comes from psychology, sociology, criminology, social work, counseling, etc., probation styles tend to treat the dual goals as somewhat mutually exclusive.

Out of this duality emerges what may be termed the "five faces of probation." This is taken to mean that probation officers manifest certain strategies, approaches, or styles of "probationing" that reflect their degrees of concern for meeting the stated goals of help and protection. Each of these styles "shows its face" to the probationer and starts the interaction that leads to five differential outcomes in probation officer–probationer relationships.

This set of relationships can be examined and clarified in terms of a Probation Grid. The grid concept stems from Blake and Mouton's[1] well-known "Managerial Grid," used so successfully by them for training managerial personnel. Such a construct has been applied to other content areas like decisionmaking,

change, and leadership. This article proposes to explicate a Probation Grid stemming directly from the probation objectives of helping individuals and protecting the community.

These objectives will be expressed as the probation officer's concern for effective *control* over his client's illegal behaviors, and the probation officer's concern for satisfactory *rehabilitation* of his probationer. These concerns, for analytical purposes, are seen as independent of each other, though in practice, probation officers may impose a relationship on them that manifests the five faces of probation. Therefore in the grid model, the two dimensions are oriented at right angles to each other. The horizontal axis of the Probation Grid represents the goal of control experienced by officers, and the vertical axis reflects his concern for rehabilitation of the probationer.

This article is interested in the degree to which a probation officer is concerned about the two grid dimensions. Therefore, as in the Blake–Mouton grid, each axis is scaled from 1 to 9 to reflect degree of concern. The value 1 denotes low or minimal "concern for," while 9 symbolizes high or maximal "concern for." By arranging the concerns at right angles to each other and by providing a scalar arrangement, the probation faces of probation officers can be assessed from the frame of reference they bring to the relationship between the concerns. "Concern for" is not a static term rooted only in the officer's attitude. What is significant is how that officer is concerned about control, or about rehabilitation, or about how these concerns fuse.

The Probation Grid is presented in the figure. Three faces of probation in the grid assume that concerns for control and rehabilitation are in basic conflict with each other and are mutually exclusive. The officer who has this frame of reference finds himself choosing one concern over the other, but not both, as his probation focus. The probation faces that result from this forced choice, reading in grid fashion (right and up), are the

[1] Robert Blake and Jane Mouton, *The Managerial Grid* (Houston: Gulf Publishing Co., 1964).

9/1, 1/9, and 1/1. Each of these faces will be evaluated according to its primary characteristics in probation counseling.

Control is defined as a condition in which the probationer is under close behavioral surveillance by his probation officer and is not violating probation rules. *Rehabilitation* is defined as a condition obtained when the probationer is not violating his probation rules, is not under close surveillance, and apparently has internalized some prosocial behaviors.

THE 9/1 FACE

The lower right-hand corner of the grid represents a maximal concern for control and a minimal concern for rehabilitation. This frame of reference is based on the assumption that probationers will respond only when they have to, under coercive surveillance with swift penalties when they do not conform. It is not suggested that probation officers with a 9/1 face have no interest in their clients, but rather that this interest becomes manifested only under rigid control variables.

The 9/1 officer sincerely believes that probationers need a strict leader who governs their otherwise hedonistic tendencies.

A 9/1 officer believes that control is rehabilitation and that his most crucial obligation is to protect community interests via strict limits placed on his clients. If the community is properly protected, a kind of *fait accompli* effect is produced in the probationer whose illegal behaviors are blocked through control. Such a system of enforced cooperation induces clients to accept probationary conditions without having to internalize them. Interaction between probation officer and probationer tends to be formal, official, and largely a question of "one upsmanship" on the side of the probation officer.

This one-dimensional probation face may be effective. It could also lead to false security that a client is under control when, in fact, his compliance is only superficial. Kelman[2] has demonstrated that conformity

[2]Herbert C. Kelman, "Compliance, Identification, and Internalization: Three Processes of Attitude Change," *Journal of Conflict Resolution* 2 (1958), pp. 51–60.

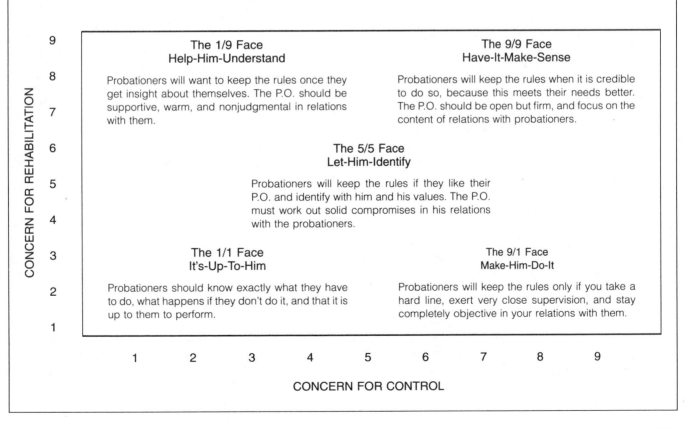

behavior that occurs under conditions of high power remains intact only so long as there is surveillance. Removal of close monitoring results in a decrease of conformity behavior and a return to more prepotent modes of acting, which may well be antisocial. Combined with the hostility and resentment a 9/1 probation face often produces in others, this approach represents an unstable form of behavior management.

The probation officer's 9/1 face says to the probationer, "I expect you to keep these probationary conditions. I'll do what I can to help you, but you will have to 'toe the mark,' and there is no room for error."

THE 1/9 FACE

The 1/9 is designated by the upper left-hand grid position, which indicates high probation officer concern for rehabilitating his probationer and small concern for controlling him. In this approach the probation officer's overriding motivation is based on the assumption that individuals are basically good and will seek appropriate, legal behaviors once they are helped to understand themselves. This self-knowledge will promote growth, foster prosocial attitudes, and terminate in satisfactory observance of probationary rules.

The 9/1 face is rejected as constituting an effort by the community to impose its own values of correct behavior on the probationer. This is seen as antithetical to the free choice condition needed if the client is to foster his own adaptation to the orders of the court. The face projected to the probationer in this framework is a warm, supportive, and nonjudgmental countenance. The probation officer tends to emerge primarily as a therapist who facilitates insight on the client's part. He learns to form a close relationship with the probationer and refines a repertoire of clinical skills aimed at rehabilitation.

Unlike the 9/1, a 1/9 face produces probationary supervision under conditions of freedom, mutuality, and a high level of client decisionmaking. The psychodynamics of individual probationers emerge as more potent than the social determinants of crime or delinquency. This also poses a dilemma for probation officers. A 1/9 face lends itself to manipulation, a perception that is permissive and that there is some likelihood of being "conned."

The probation officer's 1/9 face says to the probationer, "I hope that you will understand the need for these probationary conditions. I will support you in every way I can and help you make your own decisions in a way that you will find contentment and not feel threatened by me."

THE 1/1 FACE

The lower-left grid location refers to probation officers who manifest minimal concerns for both control and rehabilitation. In this face, probationers are thought of as autogenous and, therefore, will change or fail to do so as a result of their own motivation. No conscious or systematic probation strategy will be effective, because circumstances, spontaneous occurrences, and genetic chance are the important variables. If individual probationer tendencies for illegal behaviors are in conflict with external probationary attempts to alter them, the probation officer must set up a situation to evaluate what happens. His role is to appraise and advise his client about failure to conform, keep the court informed on the probationer's observance of the rules, and operate as an observer of progress rather than initiator of behavioral change.

Considerable energy is invested into the logistics of probation. Records are well-maintained, reports are current, and probationer contacts are regular. However, the limited affective involvement with clients and a mechanical approach to probation leave this officer with no dynamic probation face. It should be noted that such an outcome is not necessarily due to the officer's personality. A 1/1 probation program or administration might well promote status quo values that frustrate aggressive probation officers, who then revert to "reporting" procedures as a way to fill the role assigned in their work.

The probation officer's 1/1 face says to his probationer, "I'm sure you understand these conditions of probation. It's up to you to stick to them. No one can do it for you. If you need me, be sure to contact me."

THE 5/5 FACE

In the grid center is found the 5/5 probation officer who proceeds on the assumption that both control and rehabilitation are necessary but that full concern cannot be given to both. This face demonstrates a belief that probationers need leadership; they have not benefited from sound identification figures in the past; in fact, their very alignment with deviant models probably induced their earliest extralegal actions. Individuals have strong needs for positive affiliations with others, and probation officers provide this opportunity for probationers.

The 5/5 face must have and display the personal, psychological, social, and culturally valued qualities that probationers can learn to assume. The probation officer works hard at gaining trust and respect by demonstrating a "regular guy" face that can be trusted to understand the "real" problems encountered by probationers.

A positive relationship between probation officer and client has always been central to good probation but not necessarily with the view of maintaining the personal charisma of the officer. In the 5/5 face this likeableness becomes crucial. If the probationer likes his probationer officer and attempts, therefore, to please him, then the likelihood of his breaking court orders is less. By implication, this helps to secure some control while also helping the individual probationer to alter some of his antisocial predispositions.

Some work completed in recent years by attraction theory psychologists suggests that a 5/5 face holds promising components for the probation officer–probationer relationship. Aronson,[3] for example, thinks that increasing rewards and punishments from a person have more impact on his attractiveness than constant, invariant rewards and punishments. For the probation officer who must so often "start from scratch" with his probationer, Aronson's minitheory seems to be significant for developing 5/5 attractiveness in his work.

The probation officer's 5/5 face suggests to probationers that "you and I will work together in keeping these probation rules. I know how you must be feeling and thinking, and if you stick with me you can make it."

THE 9/9 FACE

By orienting the concern for control and the concern for rehabilitation at right angles to each other, it is possible to clarify probation faces reflected to individuals who are on probation. The countenances postulated so far indicate an orientation toward an incompatibility of the dual concerns. This dichotomization has bedeviled corrections for decades.

The 9/9 face seeks to integrate concerns for control and rehabilitation. The 9/9 probation officer brings full concern for both dimensions of the grid at the same time. This means he creates conditions that help a probationer help himself but that are limited by the reality of probationary conditions. This means that he stresses goals, rather than personality traits of his probationer. These traits are treated as important but not necessarily in cause and effect fashion. Instead, the probationer is helped to select from goals calculated to meet his needs more effectively within a legal framework. The 9/9 face organizes legitimate choices and, through a collaborative relationship, induces the client to act in accord with prosocial expectations.

Underlying a 9/9 face is the notion that probationers are more likely to exert control over themselves and become rehabilitated when they can internalize what is expected of them.

> Internalization can be said to occur when an individual accepts influence because the content of the induced behavior—the ideas and actions of which it is composed—is intrinsically rewarding.[4]

Put another way, it may be said that clients change when it makes sense to do so because there is some kind of "pay off." Their needs are met in better fashion. In the 9/1 face, probationers tend to see resentment or fear; in a 1/9 face, they are inclined to see chances to manipulate their probation officer; in a 1/1 face, probationers may read apathy; in a 5/5 profile a tenuous balance of charisma shows up. The 9/9 face projects credibility and says to the probationer, "Let's put our heads together, take a look at what needs to be done, how we may be able to go about doing it, and determine the best way of finishing a realistic probation program."

It seems reasonable to assert that probation officers reflect all of these faces with various probationers under different circumstances. Each carries with it a

---

[3]Elliot Aronson, "Who Likes Whom and Why," *Psychology Today*, August 1970, 48–50, 74.

[4]Kelman, *supra*, at 54.

different set of probable outcomes. This article suggests that a basic 9/9 face is more likely to give equitable attention to concerns for both control and rehabilitation. If true, we may hypothesize that this set of conditions is most likely to meet the needs of both probationers and community.

SOURCE: From Louis Tamaino, *Federal Probation* 39, no. 4 (Dec. 1975), pp. 37–41.

Supervising Alcohol- and Drug-Abusing Probationers and Parolees

ALCOHOL ABUSE

In the United States alcohol is the principal drug of abuse. Alcoholism represents a unique problem in the supervision of offenders in that often alcohol abuse is not identified as a primary problem having a direct effect on all other aspects of an individual's life. A probation officer may address an offender's lack of employment, marital difficulties, or other social problems when, in fact, they are all secondary to the problem of alcoholism. Numerous reports have documented a close association with drinking and crime. When the abuse of alcohol can be reasonably linked with failure to abide by the conditions of supervision, the probation officer has the responsibility to insist that treatment is pursued.

Alcoholism was recognized by the American Medical Association in 1956 as a disease. The degenerative qualities of the disease are recognized as progressive in nature, adversely affecting an individual's physical, emotional, and social well-being. Viewing alcoholism as a disease emphasizes the compulsiveness of alcoholic behavior, characterized by the repeated inability to refrain from drinking. By definition, then, an *alcoholic* is any person who is addicted to the use of alcohol.

The causes of alcoholism are complex and involve biological, cultural, and psychological factors. Frequently, the alcohol abuser is the second- or third-generation family member to drink to excess. Characteristically the abuser suffers from low self-esteem and an inability to cope effectively with problems. Determining why a particular individual becomes an alcoholic, if that were possible, should not be the focus of the probation officer. Although the alcoholic offender exhibits feelings such as depression, inferiority, anxiety, or loneliness, which may appear treatable, it is more important to address the reality that once a person develops a physical dependency on alcohol, alcoholism has a life of its own which produces increasing physical and social deterioration.

IDENTIFICATION OF ALCOHOLISM. Active alcoholics usually deny affliction with the disease. Thus the identification of symptoms of alcoholism must come from a variety of sources including the presentence investigation report, other social history documents, arrest records, observation, and interviews with family and friends. Local police reports may reveal family problems, neighborhood complaints, runaway children, and spouse abuse. There may also be records of drunk driving and/or drunk and disorderly conduct that may or may not have been prosecuted. Employment records may indicate poor work histories, unexplained discharges, and frequent periods of unemployment. Additionally, employers may describe a worker with a declining level of performance. Medical records frequently include stomach, liver, and kidney problems. The observant probation officer may also notice physical symptoms of advanced drinking such as hand tremors, bloodshot eyes, and blotchy facial appearance. Additionally, the alcoholic may report memory losses and blackouts.

Unlike other diseases such as diabetes or tuberculosis, alcoholism carries the social stigma of being "different," "mentally unfit," or "the town drunk," contributing to the alcoholic's denial and alibi system. Typically, elaborate systems of justification are constructed in an attempt to convince others and themselves that they have no problem. Denial of the problem in the form of alibis and excuses frequently includes the following: minimizing the consequences of drinking; attributing drinking to causes no longer present; suggesting the use of "weaker" drinks; self-pity; clinging to resentment or blaming others; and avoiding treatment by exhibiting a disparaging attitude toward those who do seek help. While the alcoholic continues to deny the problem of drinking, the family adjusts to its damaging consequences. Frequently the family of the drinker has assumed responsibility for the negative behavior that has come about as a result of the offender's drinking. This attempt to compensate and cover up for the alcoholic is exhibited by the spouse who frequently calls the employer and makes excuses as to why the alcoholic cannot work when, in fact, he or she is "hungover."

SUPERVISION PLANNING WITH ALCOHOLICS. Probation officers may not have the expertise or be in the best position to function as a primary treatment source for the offender. The probation officer will be most effective by preparing the alcoholic and family members for referral to Alcoholics Anonymous, Alanon, community treatment programs, and supportive counseling.

If alcoholism has not been formally diagnosed in the case history, yet sufficient information from other reliable sources (employers, observation, family members) clearly represents a pattern of problem drinking, the probation officer must confront the offender directly. Questions should focus on the effect continued drinking has had on the offender's life. Labeling the offender an alcoholic is not a desirable approach. It is essential to build an arena where the effects of alcohol abuse can be discussed frankly. Empathy and respect for the individual must be exhibited.

The first and foremost objective in treating alcoholism is sobriety. Lecturing or ordering the alcoholic to stop drinking will simply perpetuate a denial system that has continued to operate in spite of obvious chaos. The method chosen to achieve sobriety is dependent upon the degree of debilitation. Sobriety may need to be reached by voluntary or involuntary detoxification at nearby hospitals or institutions, particularly if the offender becomes violent to himself or others while intoxicated. Assaultive or aggressive behavior represents a danger that should not be tolerated.In most cases alcohol abuse can be dealt with on an outpatient basis. Underlying problems that contribute to alcohol abuse cannot be addressed until sobriety begins, therefore a top priority is getting the person engaged in an abstinence program. Since alcoholism is a disease for which there is no cure and because alcoholics will resist help, obtaining a special condition of supervision for treatment is usually necessary.

A highly successful treatment modality is Alcoholics Anonymous. Most recovering alcoholics hold the view that it takes another alcoholic to treat the rationalizations, denial, and manipulative techniques (or con) of an alcoholic; in short, a person who has "been there." Although no member is in a position to discuss other members, all Alcoholics Anonymous meetings have secretaries who will sign a report of attendance without a Release of Information consent form. Alcoholics Anonymous holds that whether an individual wants to go to Alcoholics Anonymous or not is unimportant; once present, the person cannot help but listen and hopefully, sooner or later a story, scene, incident, or person they meet will facilitate a desire for the termination of drinking. Alcoholics Anonymous is a support system that works. Attendance at an open Alcoholics Anonymous meeting is a recommended experience for probation officers.

Although the family may recognize and discuss the problems caused by the offender's alcohol abuse, this is not to be confused with their willingness to seek the necessary help. The family must be persuaded that they are incapable of helping the alcoholic with home remedies such as hiding the bottle. Their efforts are likely to be injurious and they should be encouraged to seek help from Alanon, a fellowship of relatives and friends of alcoholics. The effect alcoholism has on the spouse and children should not be underestimated. The interpersonal dynamics within the family frequently become guarded, leaving no access to a healthy atmosphere for expression of feelings. Perhaps due to embarrassment, rage, pity, or other unresolved feelings, the family attempts to conceal the negative impact of the drinker to the outside world. The probation officer's ability to change the relationship within the family is limited. Frequently, the more attention and help given to family members, the greater the punishment inflicted upon them by the alcoholic. As with the narrowly focused goal of sobriety for the alcoholic, the probation officer needs to be a patient, empathetic listener to the concerns of the family and refer them to Alanon or supportive therapy.

Probation officers should avoid the tendency to be trapped in the "rescuer syndrome." This is a phenomenon in which the helper (probation officer) believes that he or she can cure the excessive drinker and "save him from himself" and alcohol. Trying to help the alcoholic by "saving him" from the responsibility and consequences of drinking behavior is unhelpful. Understanding the abuser's behavior is important; however, excusing it is detrimental. Giving up something as powerful as alcohol is difficult. The abuser may undergo many relapses on the road to sobriety. A probation officer should understand that relapses are a part of recovery as long as the periods of sobriety are longer than the periods of relapse. The most valuable aspect in managing the abuser is being realistic about what can be accomplished in the battle against alcohol abuse. A sense of humor is one of the most important aspects of maintaining a healthy balance in working with alcohol abusers. Keeping a personal and professional perspective is extremely important in the face of great emotional and personal tragedy encompassing the alcohol abuser and family.

Individual, group, and family psychotherapy have gained wide recognition in the treatment of alcoholism. Frequently, various types of psychotherapy are used in combination with AA. Other treatment modalities include: the use of medically supervised Antabuse, a drug that sensitizes persons to alcohol so that they become violently ill when drinking; employment assistance programs established by many large companies to provide treatment while on the job; outpatient clinics; Alateen, a support group for children of alcoholics; halfway houses; biofeedback; and others. Probation officers must be fully knowledgeable about the variety of services offered within their community so that a range of resources can be brought to

bear in the treatment of alcoholism. Regardless of the treatment modality, the struggle for sobriety for the alcoholic is a continuous process in which the person is never cured but, rather, maintained in the act of recovering.

Drug-Abusing Offenders

Two terms are used in the Federal Probation System to describe drug abusers: *drug addict* (21 USC 802(16)) refers to one who habitually uses opium, opiates, opium derivatives, cocaine, and certain extracts of the coca leaves; *drug dependent* is defined in title 18 USC 3651 and 4203 as a person who uses substances controlled by law (42 USC 201(9)) and is in a state of psychic or physical dependency, or both, arising from the use of that substance on a continuing basis. The controlled substances include marihuana, barbiturates, amphetamines, and hallucinogens, but not alcohol. Drug dependency is characterized by behavior that includes a strong compulsion to take a substance on a continuing basis in order to experience its psychic effects or to avoid the discomfort caused by its absence.

Considering the large number of illegal drugs that have varying physical, emotional, and social consequences, probation officers must determine the seriousness of an offender's abuse in order to design the appropriate method of treatment. The first factor is the extent of dependency caused by the drug. Drugs that induce compulsive use, creating a physical or psychological dependency, and those that produce tolerance, requiring a higher intake to achieve the same effect, require a greater treatment intervention.

The extent of adverse consequences of drug use to individuals is the second factor to be considered in determining the seriousness of an offender's abuse. Direct consequences can be physical illness, chronic brain disease, and death. Psychological reactions can be violent behavioral changes, paranoia, extreme anxiety, apathy, and depression. Social consequences of drug use include the need to support drug habits by crime, the inability to maintain a lawful means of support, and dependence upon various health and welfare institutions.

Based on the criteria contained in the Domestic Council's Report to the President, *White Paper on*

Drug Abuse, September 1975, heroin is ranked as the most severe drug of abuse with high dependency liability, severe personal and social consequences, and large number of dependent individuals. Amphetamines, particularly those injected intravenously, also ranked high, followed by barbiturates, cocaine, hallucinogens and inhalants, and, finally, marihuana.

Many drug abusers create entire systems of rationalization, deceit, denial, and hostility toward anything that is incompatible with the use of drugs. Many abusers see their drug use simply as a means of getting high and, since their subculture supports this activity, resistance to intervention in this lifestyle is to be expected.

IDENTIFYING DRUG PROBLEMS.   One of the most important functions of the probation officer is the identification of drug abuse from available historical data, recognition of physical symptoms, and urinalysis.

Historical Data. The presentence investigation report and other case material reflecting offense behavior, arrest history, family and health, and employment history must be examined for evidence of a history of drug abuse. Arrests for possession, distribution, or conspiracy involving drugs may indicate drug abuse. The nature of previous charges may provide clues as to drug usage. For instance, offenses such as burglary, theft, shoplifting, and prostitution may have been committed for the purpose of supporting a drug habit. Awareness of drugs of local preference assists in identifying drug abuse.

Family members and associates provide valuable information about an offender's drug use, although this information will often be expressed in terms of complaints about the offender's inability to hold a job, disruptive behavior at home, thefts from the home, and poor choice of associates. A history of arrests and convictions for drug-related offenses by other family members is also significant.

Information available to the probation officer may reflect that the offender has had contact with social and health agencies for treatment of diseases and illnesses that may be related to drug abuse. If the offender has been incarcerated, a medical evaluation is usually available to the probation officer.

The offender may have acknowledged drug usage, although this admission generally comes only after the abuse is obvious. Unfortunately even if admitted, offenders are frequently deceptive about drug abuse, downplaying or exaggerating the frequency and extent of abuse for manipulative purposes.

Physical Symptoms. The probation officer can detect drug abuse by identifying:

- fresh or healed injection marks (track marks) along vein lines in any part of the body
- lesions, abscesses, and abscess scars
- discoloration of upper arm areas from tourniquet use
- cigarette burns on upper torso and hands
- aggravated pustular acne
- rhinorrhea (runny nose) from inhaling substances
- reddened, constricted, or dilated pupils
- eye sensitivity to light
- occurrences of pneumonia, hepatitis, hemorrhoids, staphylococcia septacemia, bacterial endocarditis (heart membrane inflammation), edema of lungs, and the cessation of menstrual period in women
- other physical manifestations such as enlarged or puffy hands or loss of motor control of the wrist that result from injections.

Urinalysis. Urinalysis is an appropriate method to confirm suspected use of illicit drugs. In the presence of historical data noting abuse of drugs, physical or emotional indicators, or offenses directly or indirectly associated with drug abuse, the probation officer should resolve questions of potential drug usage through urinalysis testing. Such tests can be requested of the offender without a specified condition of supervision. Positive results for the presence of illicit drugs or refusal to submit to urinalysis signal the need for an additional condition for drug abuse treatment and urinalysis. The identification of the types of drug abused and the frequency of use is important to the subsequent treatment process.

Urinalysis is also used as an adjunct to treatment that enables the probation officer to determine whether a person under supervision has refrained from or returned to the use of controlled substances. A phased urine-collection program has been established for all drug-dependent persons under supervision. The phases have been structured with scheduled and unscheduled urine collections to prevent a person from timing the use of controlled substances to avoid detection.

Collection and testing is accomplished in three stages in accordance with the following *minimum* guidelines:

Phase I—Six Collections Monthly

At least 6 samples per month are collected. This initial stage lasts approximately 6 months. At a minimum, 2 samples in each month are on a "surprise" basis, with no more than a 24-hour advance notice. If a person is found to have a positive urine sample, more frequent urine collections are required.

Phase II—Four Collections Monthly

After a period of approximately 6 months of negative test results, the frequency of urine testing may be reduced to a weekly schedule. At least two of these samples a month are unscheduled. If a urine sample is found to be positive, more frequent samples are collected.

Phase III—Two Collections Monthly

After a period of approximately 3 months of negative test results, the frequency of collection is reduced to a biweekly schedule on a "surprise" basis. If the person continues to remain drug-free, collection becomes less frequent at the discretion of the probation officer.

The urine-collection phase should be recorded in the Classification and Initial Supervision Plan and changes in collection phases set forth in the Case Review. *Revocation or modification of conditions of release should be based on a pattern of positive test results corroborated by physical evidence, observed behavior, arrest information, or an admission of drug abuse.*

DRUG TREATMENT PHILOSOPHY.   It is the policy of the Administrative Office that treatment services are to be provided to drug dependent federal offenders through the use of available community resources, by treatment provided directly by U.S. probation staff, by the use of contract services, or by any combination thereof.

The goal of this treatment is abstinence from illegal drug use and the reintegration of the offender into society as a law-abiding and contributing member. To accomplish this goal, treatment modalities favor an abstinence approach over those that use medication as the primary treatment tool. Two tenets serve as the philosophical underpinning of this approach: (1) a drug abuser is not emotionally or intellectually amenable to treatment while actively using drugs; and (2) treatment relies upon the least restrictive modality, ranging from outpatient supportive counseling to the most restrictive residential treatment modality. Methadone maintenance is used only as a last resort before revocation and only after abstinence methods have been exhausted.

TREATMENT MODALITIES.   There are a number of drug aftercare facilities available to offenders in most metropolitan areas of the country. These programs offer a variety of services and enjoy varying reputations. In providing drug aftercare services for individuals under supervision the probation officer must provide services directly or act as a broker within the community to acquire the necessary resources.

Within the community setting there are at least three categories of treatment programs: (1) nonresidential treatment programs, (2) residential treatment programs, and (3) detoxification and methadone maintenance.

Determining the appropriate program is a difficult task. The foundation of this decision rests on many variables, which include: (a) drug abuse history, (b) criminal record, (c) previous treatment, (d) residential, employment, and social stability, and (e) motivation for treatment.

Nonresidential Treatment Program. The determination to place an individual in a nonresidential treatment program is based on evidence that the drug abuser can remain drug-free while receiving treatment. Generally, such persons will not have a recent drug history in excess of 2 years or heroin addiction of more than 1 year. The person should be able to maintain employment or attend school and learn to interact as a member of a stable peer group. An individual participating in this type program should be able to function under community supervision with assistance and support from the treatment facility. In addition, they should not have any incapacitating character deficiencies or be homicidal or suicidal. Treatment may consist of individual counseling complemented by services such as group and family counseling, vocational testing, training and placement, physical examination, temporary housing, transportation, and emergency financial assistance. Individuals in nonresidential treatment should be motivated to act and function in the community.

Frequently the drug abuser will exhibit behavior disorders too extensive to be treated by counseling.

Thus, psychotherapy provided by a psychiatrist or psychologist may be necessary. For this approach to be successful the abuser must be willing to explore sources of his problem behavior, adhere to a rigorous appointment schedule, and be willing to make behavioral changes.

Regardless of the treatment source, the probation officer is to work in conjunction with the provider to develop an individual treatment program plan that defines the services and the role the probation officer is to take in the treatment process. It is essential the probation officer have an active role in the treatment process and monitor the offender's progress.

Residential Treatment Programs. Residential treatment programs are necessary when individuals demonstrate that they cannot function in a community environment without continued drug abuse. Generally, these persons lack motivation and have dropped out of or failed in other drug-treatment programs. Many individuals appropriate for residential treatment have a history of opiate addiction or other drug abuse spanning several years. There are three basic types of residential treatment programs:

1. *Community Treatment Centers (Halfway Houses).* The community treatment center provides a structured residential setting to assist the offender in successfully managing a debilitating life crisis. Such centers provide a variety of services, including supportive counseling, job development and placement, financial planning for reintegration back into the community, and reestablishing communication with persons outside the drug culture. The community treatment center placement is used prior to release on parole to assist the former drug abuser in making a satisfactory reintegration into the community. Where the community treatment center provides sufficient control to maintain drug abstinence, it may be used at the time of sentencing as an alternative to more restrictive forms of incarceration. As a consequence of relapse into drug abuse, community treatment centers can be used for a limited period of time to remove the offender from the drug culture and redirect him to a responsible drug-free lifestyle. When a drug abuser is placed in a community treatment center, the probation officer continually works with the staff of the center to set objectives to be met during the offender's residence.

2. *Therapeutic Community.* A therapeutic community is a highly structured 24-hour-a-day treatment approach designed for major behavioral and value changes. In this setting, individuals may receive a full range of social, education, and therapeutic interventions. In either short- or long-term placements, the goal is to engage the abuser in an intensive and all-inclusive treatment program.

3. *Hospitalization.* Some drug abusers are treated in private or public hospitals offering a wide range of services. Such placements may be the result of related medical or psychiatric problems. A hospital can provide short-term, comprehensive psychiatric and medical treatment that usually requires community treatment following release.

DETOXIFICATION AND METHADONE MAINTENANCE. *Detoxification.* Because treatment goals cannot be accomplished while an offender is actively dependent on drugs, probation officers have an obligation to insist upon detoxification. Detoxification involves the immediate or gradual withdrawal from drugs and should take place under medical supervision. If the offender cannot voluntarily detoxify without assistance from others, a formal nonresidential or residential intervention is necessary. For opiate abusers, methadone is frequently used to aid the detoxification. Federal regulations define *methadone detoxification* as the use of methadone in decreasing doses for no longer than 21 days.

Methadone Maintenance. Methadone maintenance is defined by federal regulations as the administration of methadone in excess of 21 days. The use of methadone maintenance programs to treat offenders should be considered only as a last resort and when abstinence methods have failed. Individuals referred to community treatment facilities offering this type of service should have been drug-addicted for more than 2 years, be at least 18 years of age, and have a history of repeated failures in other drug problems. Individuals admitted to a maintenance program should also have displayed a history of law violations that closely correlate with opiate use, such as shoplifting, mail theft, forgery, or drug possession.

SOURCE: Excerpted from *Supervision of Federal Offenders,* monograph no. 109 (Washington: Probation and Pretrial Services Division, Administrative Offices of the U.S. Courts, June 1991).

A Typical Chronological Case Record

LONG, DAVID CHRONOLOGICAL RECORD

8/25/82 P-OV* Mr. Long and his parents were interviewed after he was placed on probation this date. Conditions of probation were explained and discussed with Long and signed. He was given a copy of the conditions. Mr. Long stated he recently was accepted at the Skills Center for their training program for building maintenance. He appears to be enthusiastic about this training and employment in this trade. We also discussed his $150 restitution obligation. We provided him with specific written instructions regarding payments that are to be made to the clerk of the court. He understood these directions and added that he will begin making payments as soon as he begins making money. Family difficulties were discussed with Mr. Long and his parents, and they were referred to the Family Service Agency for an evaluation. They agreed to go there within the next 2 weeks to discuss possible counseling. We also discussed his difficulties with negative peer associations in the past, and he indicated that his experience in the present case has taught him a lesson and he intends to disassociate himself from these people in the future. Mr. Long does not represent a "third-party risk"—Supervisor Jones concurs.   mjk

8/30/82 C-T Memo forwarded to our Clerk's Office apprising them of Mr. Long's $150 restitution and giving them the name of the victim, John McKinley, and his address in Westfield, Connecticut. Also advised them that Mr. Long has been given appropriate payment instructions.   mjk

9/7/82 C-T Mr. Greene, Skills Center (692-1234). Counselor verified that Mr. Long has enrolled in their building maintenance program. The probationer has been attending classes regularly since starting on August 30, 1982. Initially he appears to be applying himself to training, and the counselor feels that he will be a very good student.   mjk

9/8/82 C-T Family Service Agency, Mr. Rogers (684-1000), contacted. Had first meeting with Long and his parents last night. The family has agreed to a contract with the Family Service Agency to see Mr. Rogers two times a month on alternating Wednesday evenings for a total of 2 months.   mjk

9/15/82 P-HV Probationer and parents seen. Mr. Long reports attending class at the Skills Center regularly. He stated that he likes the program and feels he is accomplishing a great deal. The parents are more satisfied with his adjustment, and this seems to be related to his progress in school. The report that he seems to have shut himself off from former negative peer associations. The family stated they had attended two counseling sessions at the Family Service Agency and that these sessions have been helpful. They also noted that the problems have lessened on their own. They will attend 1 more month, but feel that if things continue to be stable, they will drop the counseling program.   mjk

10/13/82 P-HV Mr. Long and family seen. No changes since last contact. Still going to Skills Center and feels he is progressing toward completion of the program. Family is still in counseling, but plan to drop after completion of four meetings with the counselor. The family situation seems much improved. The probationer will establish his own residence once employed. The family seems closer, and there appears no rush for his change of residence at this time.   mjk

10/27/82 C-T Mr. Greene at Skills Center. Reported that Mr. Long had progressed well and is halfway through the program. He has only missed 1 day of the training since enrolled, due to illness. mjk

10/28/82 C-T   Mr. Rogers, Family Service Agency. The probationer, parents, and counselor have agreed to terminate counseling due to resolution of family problems.   mjk

11/16/82 T   The probationer states his relationship with his parents is very good now, but he still wants to move out on his own. He feels that he should because of his age and because of his desire to be responsible for himself. The probation officer agreed with this and intends to promote this plan in the future. The probationer feels that his parents would like to see him stay on at the house, but he intends to move as soon as he is employed and can support himself. He has a new girlfriend, Jo Kramer. She resides at her parents' home located at 552 South Lebanon Street, telephone 968-2232. Mr. Long states that he sees her a lot and spends most of his free time with her.   mjk

12/15/82 C-T   Mr. Greene at the Skills Center. Long will complete training on December 17, 1982. He has already had several referrals for placement through the Center's job referral office. Mr. Greene feels that the probationer may soon be employed after his graduation from the building maintenance program. He described the probationer as having been an excellent student.   mjk

12/16/82 P-HV   Long reported that he had several good job leads. He stated he will interview tomorrow at the Serene Development Company as an apartment maintenance man. This company operates several large complexes in this area. The parents were seen briefly and they seemed very satisfied with the subject's progress toward gaining employment.   mjk

12/23/82 T   Telephoned probation officer to notify that he landed a job with the Serene Company. He will work at their West Terrace Apartments maintaining 200 units. They will provide him an apartment at a reduced rate in order for him to live on the premises. The starting gross salary is $600 a month. He starts

the job after Christmas, but may move into his apartment sooner than that. Told him to provide us with appropriate documentation relative to his income and rent.   mjk

12/27/82 T   Mr. Long reported that he just moved into his apartment at 444 Terrace Drive, Number 210. He can be reached during the day at 888-6310. He starts the job January 2.   mjk

1/10/83 T   Mr. Long likes his work. The manager of the apartment refers maintenance problems to him, and then he works on his own to complete them. He pays $200 a month rent on an apartment that normally rents for $450 a month, furnished. Mr. Long states the apartment manager, James Jones, is aware of his probation status. Advised Mr. Long to report to my office first week in March and reminded him to bring salary and rent verification. Also, we directed him to make a restitution payment of at least $25 to the Clerk's Office and continue with such payments on a biweekly basis.   mjk

2/2/83 C-T   With mother. Parents pleased over the probationer's adjustment. They like his new girlfriend, and the mother feels that they may be getting serious in their relationship. They visit regularly with the probationer and have not seen any old friends around him.   mjk

2/21/83 C-T   Received notice from Clerk's Office that Long made $50 restitution payment on 2/18/83. Probationer now has $100 restitution balance. Probation office is encouraged by this relatively large initial payment. At this point we anticipate no problems with probationer satisfying this restitution obligation within the near future.   mjk

SOURCE: *The Supervision Process,* monograph 109 (Washington: Probation Division, Administrative Office of the U.S. Courts, April 1983).

*Key to abbreviations: P-HV (Personal-Home Visit), P-OV (Personal-Office Visit), C-T (Collateral-Telephone), T (Telephone).

REVOCATION OF PROBATION

7

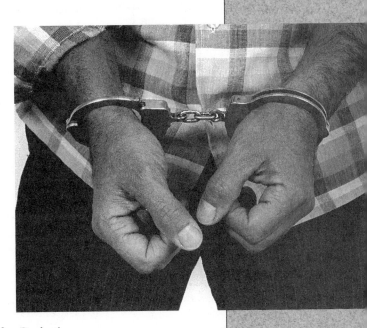

KEY TERMS

Revocation
Technical violation
Technical conditions
Modification of conditions
Jail therapy
Proof beyond a reasonable doubt
Preponderance of the evidence
On-Site hearing
Revocation hearing
Right to counsel
Sufficiency of notice
Sending state
Extradition
Receiving state

In 1985, the RAND Corporation, a highly respected research organization, reported findings from a study of felony probation in California. They found that over a 40-month period, 65 percent of a sample of felony probationers were rearrested, and 34 percent received a new jail or prison term.[1] In 1992, Patrick Langan and Mark Cunniff released the results of research using a sample of 79,000 felons sentenced to probation in 1986.[2] They reported that 43 percent had been rearrested for a felony within three years of being placed on probation. An additional 19 percent had a disciplinary hearing for violating the conditions of their supervision (technical violations). In sum, their findings closely corresponded with those of the earlier Rand study. Figure 7–1 illustrates the outcome of 100 felony probations based on the Langan and Cunniff study.

From these and other research findings, it is apparent that probation is often unsuccessful. In such cases, the probation officer must take steps to revoke probation or to modify the conditions of supervision. The focus of this chapter is on the revocation of probation. In our discussion of revocation of probation, we will consider several distinct but overlapping and interrelated aspects of the process: the *decision* to revoke probation, which includes the decisions of the probation officer to recommend and of the court to order revocation; the *legal procedures* for revoking probation, which are governed by several recent court decisions and involve technical legal matters that should be understood by the probation officer; the problems of sentencing or resentencing after revocation of probation; and appeals and other legal proceedings the probationer may take after revocation in attempting to get the revocation or the sentence set aside.

THE DECISION TO REVOKE

As we have seen, release on probation is a *conditional* release; that is, the probationer's liberty is not absolute, because it is subject to his or her compliance with certain specified requirements. Violation of the requirements, or *conditions*, can result in revocation of probation and incarceration of the offender. Needless to say, revocation of probation is a serious matter to the probationer.

Although a probationer's right to be at liberty in the community is subject to certain restrictions imposed both by law and the court order that grants probation, the probationer's status is in many fundamental ways equal to that enjoyed by persons who have not been charged or convicted of an offense. The probationer can continue to live free in the community, can work at suitable employment, can enjoy the association of family and friends, can participate in community activities, and can generally enjoy the benefits that a free society offers its members.

Perceptions of Revocation by the Probation Officer

Revocation of probation is a serious matter to the probation officer as well as to the probationer. The probation officer's particular supervision orientation determines how he or she perceives it, however.

FIGURE 7-1

100 Felons Tracked through Their First 3 Years of Probation

SOURCE: Patrick Langan and Mark Cuniff, *Recidivism of Felons on Probation, 1986-1989* Washington, D.C.: Bureau of Justice Statistics, 1992.

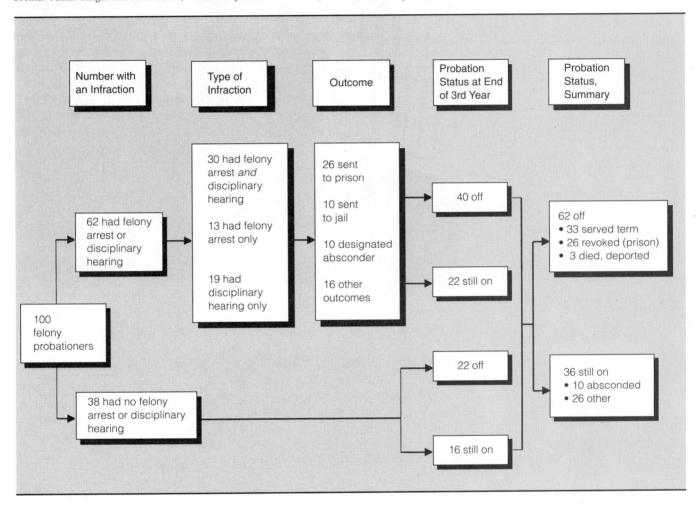

The *traditional* probation officer is very apt to view revocation of probation as a "failure."[3] Before the probation officer–probationer relationship has deteriorated to the point where revocation is considered, the officer has invested considerable time and effort to rehabilitate the probationer. The probation officer has probably developed a genuine interest in the probationer and become acquainted with his or her family. The officer may feel strongly that commitment will mitigate against, rather than facilitate, the probationer's ultimate adjustment to society and will be concerned about the commitment's impact on the family.

The *community resource manager* type of probation officer will see probation revocation in terms of his or her own inability to locate and arrange for the probationer's needs, or as the community's failure to provide the necessary resources.

Probation officer interviewing inmates.

The *justice model* probation officer will attribute the revocation decision to the probationer's failure to live up to the terms of the contract or agreement with the court. This officer knows that despite probation officers' conscientious efforts, a percentage of probationers will fail. These are not failures of the system, the community, or the probation officer, but rather the failure of probationers to put forth effort to succeed and adjust in free society.

Revocation and the Community

Revocation of probation is also a serious matter to the community. Commitment of the offender will increase the cost to the community, since keeping an offender under probation supervision costs much less than providing him or her care and treatment in a correctional institution. Commitment of breadwinners may force their families to go on relief or to make greater demands on the community's welfare resources. On the other hand, revocation offers the community protection in the case of a probationer who continues to commit criminal acts and violate the terms of his or her probation.

Violations of Probation Conditions

Revocation of probation thus is not treated lightly, and not every violation of probation conditions results in revocation. Sometimes the probation officer will permit a whole series of minor violations before taking the offender before the court; when there, the officer may recommend modifying the

Revocation

The withdrawal of either probation or parole because the behavior of the offender was in violation of the conditions agreed upon. Revocation requires the offender to begin or continue serving his or her sentence.

imposed conditions in hopes that a change in the conditions will increase the chance of successful adjustment. The federal guidelines for reporting violations of probation conditions—which are similar to those in many state jurisdictions—require the probation officer (except for certain specified serious incidents) to "consider whether or not a modification of the conditions of supervision would bring the offender into compliance and serve the relevant purposes of sentencing."[4]

Authority to Revoke Probation

It must be kept clearly in mind that although the probation officer or the probation department can recommend revocation, only the court has authority to revoke probation. This authority remains with the court that granted the probation,[5] unless the case has been transferred to another court that is given the same powers as the sentencing court.[6] The federal probation statute and all state statutes provide for transfer of jurisdiction in appropriate cases to allow the probationer, with the court's permission, to change residence. This change of residence may be from one part of the state to another or, in the case of the federal offender, from one part of the country to another. The transfer of *jurisdiction* to another court is distinguished from the provision of interstate compacts for the transfer of responsibility for *supervision only* to another state's probation department. When transfer is under the interstate compact, authority to modify the conditions of probation, revoke probation, or terminate probation remains with the court in the sending state.

WHEN PROBATION CAN BE REVOKED

Probation may be revoked by the court if the probationer either commits a new crime or violates a "technical" condition of probation.

Technical Violations

Technical violations are infractions that do not involve law violations. **Technical conditions** are those that require the offenders to report regularly to the probation or parole officer, not move from or leave the jurisdiction without obtaining permission, support dependents, refrain from excessive use of alcohol, work regularly at a lawful occupation, pay a fine or restitution, and so on. As a general rule, probation is not revoked for occasional violation of technical conditions. Probation officers are encouraged to address these violations promptly and to take whatever action is necessary to ensure compliance. Revocation, however, is the last resort for dealing with technical violations. Revocation policy in most jurisdictions is generally consistent with the federal guideline, which states:

> When a violation is detected, the officer is to respond with the least restrictive measures necessary to bring the offender into compliance in light of the seriousness

Technical violation

Infraction of probation or parole condition not involving violation of a law.

Revocation: "The Good Old Days"

Probation and parole officers, like anyone else, are prone to a bit of nostalgic reflection now and then. At training sessions and conferences the astute eavesdropper can tune in to countless "remember when" stories. Occasionally one hears a longing for the time when things were "simpler." "You know, back when we didn't have to fight with a lawyer at every turn of the supervision process." One might be prone to agree with our wistful officer on any number of topics, but when it comes to the procedural protections applicable to the supervision and revocation process, one has to ask, "The good old days to whom?" While the procedural protections attendant to probation and parole revocation are clearly a bane to the P.O.'s existence, from the prospective of the probationer or parolee, the "good old days" were anything but.

Prior to 1972, the procedures for probation and parole revocation varied greatly depending on where you were. In many jurisdictions, a simple order of revocation with an opportunity for allocution was all that was necessary to send a probationer on his way to prison. A parolee, often subject to more summary proceedings, was fortunate if he got some sort of formal notice of the reason he was arrested and returned to the penitentiary. To be sure, not all jurisdictions were so cavalier with regard to the revocation process. A few did extend what could roughly be called a "hearing," but even these "hearings" were little more than an opportunity for the probationer or parolee to give his personal version of events. So lacking in procedural protections was the revocation process that one observer was prompted to write that "there is no other area of law, except perhaps the civil commitment of the mentally ill, where the lives of so many people are so drastically affected by officials who exercise a virtually absolute, unreviewed discretion." See Cohen, *Sentencing, Probation, and the Rehabilitative Ideal,* 47 Texas Law Review 1 (1968).

The sixties saw considerable expansion of procedural protections in the context of "criminal prosecutions." Once a defendant had been "convicted," however, the general view was that the "criminal prosecution" had terminated and the procedural protections attendant thereto no longer applied. If the Court had difficulty deciding precisely when a "criminal prosecution" commenced for Sixth Amendment–right to counsel purposes [see *Kirby v. Illinois,* 404 U.S. 1055 (1972), and *United States v. Ash,* 413 U.S. 300 (1973)], it had no such difficulty in determining where a "criminal prosecution" ended. In *Mempa v. Rhay,* 389 U.S. 128 (1967), the Court drew the line at sentencing. Thus, the petitioners in *Mempa,* having been placed on probation without being sentenced, were entitled to counsel at the revocation hearing, not because the hearing itself was a critical stage in the prosecution, but because the hearing would involve the imposition of sentence. Those probationers who had been sentenced and then placed on probation, and all parolees, were not entitled to representation by counsel under the Sixth Amendment to the United States Constitution.

Enter *Morrissey v. Brewer,* 408 U.S. 471(1972). The petitioner in *Morrissey* launched a new attack on parole revocation proceedings. Rather than claiming that the procedural protections attendant to criminal trial were applicable, he claimed that he was entitled to "some" procedure designed to assure the fairness of the parole revocation proceeding. The Court agreed.

The Court rejected the state's claim that, because parole was a privilege, no procedural protections were applicable. Rather, because parole release vested an inmate with some "expectation" of continued liberty so long as the conditions of parole were observed, some procedure was constitutionally compelled before the state could revoke parole. The Court then set forth the procedures it considered minimally necessary to comport with fundamental fairness in the parole revocation process.

Given the discretion afforded the parole officer in the arrest and detention decision, the Court held that some type of preliminary "probable cause" inquiry should be held as soon as possible after arrest or detention. This hearing was to be conducted by a "neutral and detached" officer, someone not connected with the original investigation of the alleged violations or the decision to arrest or detain. This preliminary revocation hearing was to examine the factual basis for the alleged violations to assure that further detention was not without cause. Furthermore, a second or "final" parole revocation hearing was required. Two issues would be addressed at this hearing: whether the facts supported the violations alleged and, if the facts of the alleged violations were established, whether the circumstances warranted revocation. At both hearings the parolee was entitled to the following: (1) sufficient advance notice of the alleged violations; (2) an opportunity to present evidence on his own behalf; (3) an opportunity to confront and cross-examine adverse witnesses, unless the hearing officer made a determination of "good cause" for not allowing confrontation; and (4) notice of the decision of the hearing body, including the evidence relied on.

In *Gagnon v. Scarpelli*, 411 U.S. 778 (1973), the Court found that the same basic procedures outlined in *Morrissey* were applicable to the probation revocation process. However, the Court also found it necessary to address an additional claim: Was there a due process right to counsel in revocation proceedings?

Rejecting the petitioner's claim that a right to counsel should "always" attend the revocation process, the Court chose instead a more "flexible" approach. The right to counsel in probation and parole revocation proceedings was to be de-cided on a case-by-case basis, in the exercise of the sound discretion of the state authority "charged with the responsibility for administering the probation and parole system." However, even under this "flexible" approach, the Court cautioned that, in certain circumstances, the assistance of appointed counsel might be "required" as a matter of fundamental fairness. Stated the Court:

> Presumptively, it may be said that counsel should be provided in cases where, after being informed of his right to request counsel, the probationer or parolee makes such a request, based on a timely and colorable claim (i) that he has not committed the alleged violation of the conditions upon which he is at liberty; or (ii) that, even if the violation is a matter of public record or is uncontested, there are substantial reasons which justified or mitigated the violation and make revocation inappropriate and that the reasons are complex or otherwise difficult to develop or present. In passing on a request for the appointment of counsel, the responsible agency should consider, especially in doubtful cases, whether the probationer appears to be capable of speaking effectively for himself. In every case in which a request for counsel at a preliminary or final hearing is refused, the grounds for refusal should be stated in the record.

The lower court decisions that have interpreted *Morrissey* and *Gagnon* since 1973 number in the thousands. While the results reached by these courts on specific issues such as the timeliness of a hearing or the "good cause" necessary for not allowing confrontation are often conflicting, what remains is a fairly uniform process designed to assure the proper exercise of discretion in the probation and parole revocation process. These procedures are worth noting as we reflect on "the good old days."

SOURCE: Dane Miller, *Probation and Parole Law Reports* 10 (1988), pp. 1-3. Reprinted with permission from Knehans-Miller Publications. January 1988.

of the violation, its implications for public safety, and the type and frequency of supervision strategies that were being employed at the time of the violation.[7]

The "measures" contemplated by the guideline range from a simple admonition from the probation officer to revocation and incarceration.

ALTERNATIVES TO REVOCATION.   Probation officers are given considerable discretion to handle technical violations without referral to the court so long as the infractions do not develop into a pattern or result in a threat to public safety. Carl Klockars suggests that much probation work is conducted by threats of revocation.[8] For most probationers, a warning or admonition is sufficient. In some jurisdictions, it is common practice to bring the probationer back before the court to show cause why the probation should not be revoked, but with an understanding between the probation officer and the court that revocation is not desired. This return to court, to face the judge, has a more sobering effect on the defendant than a simple admonition in the probation officer's office.

Another alternative, one that is the subject of intense controversy, is that of jail therapy. **Jail therapy** consists of placing a probationer in jail without holding a subsequent revocation hearing. The period of incarceration (in jurisdictions where the practice is allowed) is usually short, and the "therapy" has two basic purposes: (1) to impress upon the probationer the seriousness of the offense and the possible consequences of continued violation, and (2) to provide a realistic comparison between life in the community and life in jail. Opponents of jail therapy reject it as being punitive in nature and as not contributing to the probationer's ultimate rehabilitation. They also believe that the relationship between the probation officer and the probationer may be permanently destroyed by such an action.

In other cases, circumstances might warrant modification of conditions that appear to be impossible to meet, unreasonable, or inappropriate. The federal probation rule states:

> Except where mandatory provisions control or when other compelling factors exist, the officer should consider whether or not a modification of the conditions of supervision would bring the offender into compliance and serve the relevant purpose of sentencing.[9]

REVOCATION UPHELD FOR TECHNICAL VIOLATIONS. Although guidelines and policies regarding technical violations of probation (or parole) do not encourage revocation, courts have upheld revocation for technical violations under a wide variety of circumstances. These are representative:

- engaging in a scuffle with campus police during a demonstration in violation of the condition that the probationer not participate in demonstrations[10]
- failure to pay off civil judgments for fraud although probationer was able to pay[11]
- failure to make child support payments[12]
- failure to report[13]
- failure to pay supervision fees although financially able[14]
- associating with persons who were not "law-abiding"[15]
- driving a motor vehicle when condition specified license to drive was suspended.[16]

Violations of Condition to Obey All Laws

Even when the offender commits a new crime, revocation is not automatic. Most courts require the probation officer to report any violation of law and to make a recommendation regarding the issuance of a warrant and initiation of revocation proceedings.

Federal policy, set out in *Supervising Federal Offenders*, states:

> A violation of any federal, state, or local law that is punishable by any term of imprisonment must be reported immediately to the court or Parole Commission. In making a recommendation regarding issuance of a warrant, the officer must consider the risk posed by the new offense behavior. *If it appears that the violation*

represents a significant threat to community safety or signals a risk of flight, the officer should recommend the issuance of a warrant. [Emphasis added.][17]

STANDARD OF PROOF IN REVOCATION HEARINGS

When a revocation warrant alleges that the probationer committed a new crime, the decision to revoke does not require that the probationer be found guilty of the new offense. **Proof beyond a reasonable doubt,** the standard of proof required in criminal cases, is *not* needed for the court to find that the probationer violated the conditions of probation. All that is needed is a **preponderance of the evidence,** evidence that is of greater weight or that is more convincing than the evidence that is offered in opposition to it. This is the level of proof necessary in a civil trial. Furthermore, evidence that would not be admitted in a criminal trial (such as hearsay or uncorroborated accomplice testimony) is admissible in a revocation hearing. Judges may also consider evidence such as employment history, efforts at drug/alcohol treatment, and other information that would not be considered at a criminal trial.

Proof beyond a reasonable doubt

Fully satisfied, entirely convinced, or satisfied to a moral certainty. The level of proof required in a criminal case.

Preponderance of the evidence

A standard of proof in civil cases (and revocation hearings) defined as evidence that is of greater weight or more convincing than the evidence offered in opposition to it.

National Standards for Revocation

The American Bar Association *Standards relating to Probation* and the National Advisory Commission *Standards* provide that revocation of probation based solely on the commission of another crime should await the disposition of that charge,[18] except that the court should have the discretionary authority to detain the probationer without bail. "Disposition of the charge" probably would include a plea of guilty or a finding of guilt and sentence, but would not extend to final disposition, which in some cases would wait for the action of the superior court upon an appeal.

REVOCATION AFTER TERM OF PROBATION HAS EXPIRED

Some probationers are arrested for committing new crimes, and either detained or released on bail pending disposition of the new charges. If the original period of probation expires during this waiting interval, the court's right to revoke probation is not affected if the defendant is convicted of the new crime. This is so if the revocation warrant is issued (and, if possible, executed) before the probation expires.[19]

Probation may also be revoked after the term of probation has expired, if the probationer has absconded supervision before the completion of the sentence. It is usual for probation statutes to provide that the term of probation is "tolled" if the defendant is either charged with a violation of probation or flees the jurisdiction (or cannot be found) and a warrant is issued. To *toll* the running of a sentence or a period of time limitation is to interrupt it, to "stop the clock." The Illinois statute, for example, provides that when a petition is filed charging a violation of a probation condition, the court may order a summons for the offender to appear or a warrant for the offender's arrest:

> The issuance of such warrant or summons shall toll the sentence of probation or of conditional discharge until the final determination of the charge, and the term of probation or conditional discharge shall not run so long as the offender has not answered the summons or warrant.[20]

DUE PROCESS: *MORRISSEY* AND BEYOND

In 1972, the United States Supreme Court in *Morrissey v. Brewer*[21] (a case that concerned a revocation of parole) declared that before parole could be revoked, the parolee was entitled to minimum due-process safeguards. At a parole revocation hearing these minimum safeguards were stated as:

1. written notice of the claimed violations of parole,
2. disclosure to the parolee of evidence against him or her,
3. opportunity to be heard in person and to present witnesses and documentary evidence,
4. the right to confront and cross-examine adverse witnesses (unless the hearing officer specifically finds good cause for not allowing confrontation),
5. a neutral and detached hearing body such as a traditional parole board, the members of which need not be judicial officers or lawyers, and
6. a written statement of the fact finders as to the evidence relied on and reasons for revoking parole.

The Court stated:

> We turn therefore to the question of whether the requirements of due process in general apply to parole revocations. As Mr. Justice Blackmun has written recently, this Court now has rejected the concept that constitutional rights turn upon whether a governmental benefit is characterized as a right or as a privilege . . . Whether any procedural protections are due depends upon the extent to which an individual will be condemned to suffer grievous loss . . . The question is not merely the "weight" of the individual's interest, but whether the nature of the interest is one within the contemplation of the "liberty or property" language of the Fourteenth Amendment. . . .[22]

The Court spelled out a two-step procedure that includes an **on-site hearing** and a **revocation hearing.** The on-site hearing is conducted at or near the site of the alleged violation, usually at the jail or detention facility where the arrested parolee is being held. The on-site hearing is for the purpose of determining whether there is probable cause or reasonable grounds to believe that the arrested parolee committed the alleged act(s) which would constitute a violation of parole conditions. The on-site hearing is somewhat informal and may be conducted by a parole officer who is not involved in the case against the parolee. On request of the parolee, adverse witnesses must be made available for questioning in the parolee's presence. Based on the information presented at the on-site hearing the hearing officer determines if there is reason to warrant the parolees continued detention pending a revocation hearing.

The second stage of the process is a formal revocation hearing. The *Morrissey* Court held that the parolee must be provided certain "minimum due process" rights which include: (a) written notice of the claimed violation of parole; (b) disclosures to the parolee of the evidence against him; (c) opportunity to be heard in person and to present witnesses and documentary evidence; (d) to confront and cross-examine adverse witnesses; (e) to be heard by neutral and detached hearing body which may be a traditional parole board but need not be judicial officers or lawyers; and, (f) a written statement by the fact finders as to the evidence relied on and reasons for revoking parole.

California was the first state to consider a *probation* revocation in light of the decision of *Morrissey v. Brewer.* In *People v. Vickers,* the California Supreme Court held that proceedings for revocation of probation granted after a conviction and imposition of sentence were bound by the United States Supreme Court's decision in *Morrissey* to the extent that the decision established minimal due process requirements on parole revocation, since probation proceedings cannot be distinguished in principle insofar as demands of due process are concerned. However, the California court decided that the proceedings for probation revocation need not be identical to those established in *Morrissey* for parole revocation, provided that they assure equivalent due-process safeguards. Accordingly, the California court recognized the validity of a summary termination of an absconding probationer's status if that probationer were accorded a hearing conforming to the *Morrissey* standards after being taken into custody. The court said:

> A different situation is presented, however, when a parolee's right to liberty is the subject of proceedings had before his arrest or actual deprivation of his conditional liberty. Such a situation commonly develops when a parolee unilaterally elects to escape the restraints imposed on his liberty and severs the lines of communication with those assigned to supervise him; in effect, he absconds. Should he remain at liberty without proceedings had against him he could conceivably complete his term and the Authority would lose jurisdiction in the matter * * * Due process does not require that the defendant profit by such wrongdoing and we read *Morrissey* as applicable only in those instances wherein an actual seizure of the individual has occurred. It is this loss of liberty which compels the procedures set forth in *Morrissey.* Accordingly, a summary termination of his status through revocation while the parolee remains at liberty and unavailable to the authorities does not fall within the prescription of *Morrissey.* Once taken into custody, however, due process requires that he be accorded both preliminary and formal hearings which conform to *Morrissey* standards. The purpose of the hearings would not be to revoke parole as such revocations would have already been summarily ordered, but rather to afford the defendant an opportunity to require the Authority to establish that the alleged violations did in fact occur and justify the revocation.
>
> For the same reasons we had held that *Morrissey* is applicable to probation, as well as parole revocation proceedings, we conclude that a summary termination of probationary status in the case of an absconding probationer comports with due process requirements if he is accorded a hearing which conforms to *Morrissey* standards after being taken into custody.[23]

Right to Counsel

On the question of right to counsel—a determination not made in *Morrissey*—the California court announced *as a judicially declared rule of criminal process* that a probationer is entitled to the representation of retained or appointed counsel at formal proceedings for the revocation of probation, or following such summary revocation in appropriate cases [emphasis added].[24] However, the California court refused to apply *Morrissey,* or its decisions in *Vickers,* retroactively.[25]

In May 1973, the United States Supreme Court, in *Gagnon v. Scarpelli,* extended to probationers the right to preliminary and final revocation hearings under the conditions specified in *Morrissey v. Brewer.* It further mandated a case-by-case determination of the need for counsel in the sound discretion of the state authority responsible for administering the probation and parole system. If the probationer's or parolee's version of a disputed issue can fairly be represented only by trained counsel, appointment of counsel for the indigent probationer or parolee should be made, "although participation by counsel will probably be both undesirable and unnecessary in most revocation hearings."[26]

Sufficiency of Notice

In accordance with developing due process concepts, recent cases are demanding an increasing degree of specificity in notices of intended revocation of probation. The allowance of sufficient time for preparation of a defense is also being mandated. In a Texas case, for example, the defendant was served with a notice of a motion to revoke probation on the day of the hearing and was told orally that one of the bases for the revocation would be "theft by false pretext" instead of "felony theft" as set out in the written notice. It was held that the defendant had been denied rudiments of due process by the court's failure to give him adequate and prior notice to prepare his defense.[27] In another Texas case, the state's motion to revoke probation alleged that the defendant had "violated paragraphs (a), (b), and (c) of his Conditions of Probation." The defendant claimed the pleadings were insufficient. The denial of his motion by the trial court was reversed on appeal. The appellate court stated that the state's pleadings were not sufficient to give the defendant fair notice of the conduct or acts for which the state intended to offer evidence to prove a violation of the conditions of probation.[28]

Nature of Hearing

The requirements of minimum due process in a revocation hearing have not changed the basic character of the probation revocation hearing. In *Morrissey v. Brewer* the court said, "We begin with the proposition that the revocation of parole is not part of a criminal prosecution, and thus the full panoply of rights due a defendant does not apply to parole revocation." Thus, a hearing on probation revocation is still a hearing and not a trial. As such, it is not governed by the rules concerning formal criminal trials.[29] It is not necessary that all the technical provisions in criminal procedure be followed. The result of a probation hearing is not a conviction, but a finding upon which the trial court may exercise discretion by revoking or continuing probation.[30] The defendant is not entitled to a jury trial on revocation of probation.[31]

Early cases that held that the defendant need not be present for revocation of probation have probably not been overruled if the hearing at which the defendant is not present is a summary hearing to revoke the probation of an absconding defendant, and the defendant is given a proper due-process hearing after arrest and before commitment. However, cases that announce a general rule that the defendant need not be present at a revocation hearing have been overruled.

PROCEEDINGS FOLLOWING REVOCATION

In cases where a sentence has been imposed and its execution is suspended, the defendant whose probation has been revoked is committed to begin the service of sentence. In the event that *imposition* of sentence has been suspended, statutes commonly give the court the authority to sentence the defendant as though no probation had been granted.[32]

The American Bar Association *Standards relating to Probation* provides that, "Sentence should be imposed following a revocation according to the same procedures as are applicable to original sentencing proceedings.[33]

Special Problems under Interstate Compacts

Special problems arise after the probation of a probationer who is under supervision in a state other than the state of conviction is revoked. The Interstate Compact for the Supervision of Parolees and Probationers provides that any state that has signed the compact will accept supervision of a parolee or probationer who meets the residence requirements set forth in the compact, and will supervise the probationer at the same level of supervision that it gives to its own cases. The **sending state** may retake a person being supervised in another state simply by having its officer present appropriate credentials and proving the identity of the person to be retaken. On requesting and accepting out-of-state supervision, the probationer waives **extradition** prior to leaving the sending state, although formal extradition procedures may be resorted to if necessary.

It is well established that the sending state can retake a probation violator being supervised under the compact without resorting to formal extradition procedures. The **receiving state** is bound to surrender the probationer unless a criminal charge is then pending against the individual in the receiving state. In such a case, the probationer cannot be retaken without the receiving state's consent until he or she is discharged from prosecution or from any imprisonment for such offense. The practical effect is that the sending state cannot retake the probationer into custody until all local charges are disposed of. Some states admit a probationer to bail pending disposition of charges for revocation of probation. Other states hold that the right to bail does not apply to persons who have been tried and convicted.

The validity of the waiver of extradition has been upheld against a challenge that it violated the parolee's constitutional rights and was invalid because it would not become operative until some future date. It is also generally held that the sending state alone has authority to determine upon what basis a

Sending state

The state that initiates a transfer of supervision under the Interstate Compacts.

Extradition

The surrender on demand by one state to another of a person accused or convicted of an offense outside its own jurisdiction and with in the jurisdicition of another.

Receiving state

The state that accepts transfer of supervision under the interstate compacts.

violator may be returned and that the reasons for return are not reviewable by the receiving state.[34]

SUMMARY

Probation is not always successful. Whenever probationers commit new offenses or violate the technical conditions of their supervision, probation revocation may have to be considered. The decision to revoke probation has consequences for the probation officer, the probationer, and for society and thus is not treated lightly. Where the violation is of a technical condition—such as failure to report, leaving the jurisdiction without permission, or excessive use of alcohol—the probation officer may take whatever action is necessary to encourage observance of the conditions. However, most states encourage probation officers to respond to such violations with the least restrictive measures necessary to bring the offender into compliance. Probation officers may admonish the probationer, counsel him/her, or reevaluate the supervision strategy to determine if the conditions require modification. Revocation is the last resort.

When the violation is a new criminal offense, most jurisdictions require that the sentencing court be notified. Although the probation officer can recommend revocation, the authority to revoke lies entirely with the court.

Probation revocation requires a two-step procedure that includes an on-site hearing to determine probable cause and a revocation hearing to evaluate any contested relevant facts and consider whether the facts warrant revocation. This procedure is governed by the United States Supreme Court's decisions in *Morrissey v. Brewer* (1972) and *Gagnon v. Scarpelli* (1973).

ENDNOTES

1. Joan Petersilia, Susan Turner, James Kahan, and Joyce Peterson, *Granting Felons Probation: Public Risks and Alternatives* (Santa Monica, Calif.: The RAND Corporation, 1985).

2. Patrick Langan and Mark Cunniff, "Recidivism of Felons on Probation," *Special Report* (Washington, D.C.: Bureau of Justice Statistics, February 1992).

3. The traditional officer's attitude toward these revocation decisions reflects the rehabilitative rather than punitive focus of the probation/parole system. For example, here is a quote from Gagnon v. Scarpelli, 411 U.S. 778, 93 S.Ct. 1756, 36 L.Ed.2d 656 (1973): "Revocation is, . . . if anything, commonly treated as a failure of supervision. While presumably it would be inappropriate for a field agent never to revoke, the whole thrust of the probation/parole movement is to keep [individuals] in the community, working with adjustment problems there, and using revocation only as a last resort where treatment has failed or is about to fail."

4. *Supervision of Federal Offenders,* monograph no. 109 (Washington: Administrative Offices of the U.S. Courts, Probation and Pretrial Services Division, 1991), pp. 39–40. The guidelines require mandatory revocation for possession of a firearm or controlled substances.

5. Authority to grant probation lies with the court having jurisdiction to try the offense. 18 U.S.C.A. § 3561. State statutes are similar.

6. *Id.,* § 3563. The court to which transfer is made has all the power previously possessed by the court from which transfer is made, except that the period of probation cannot be changed without the consent of the sentencing court.

7. *Supervision of Federal Offenders, supra* note 4, at 37.

8. Carl Klockars, "A Theory of Probation Supervision," *Journal of Criminology, Criminal Law, and Police Science* 63 (1972), no. 4, pp. 550–557.

9. *Supervision of Federal Offenders, supra,* at 39–40.

10. People v. King, 267 Cal.App.2d 814, 73 Cal.Rptr. 440 (1968), cert. den. 396 U.S. 1028, 90 S.Ct.. 576, 24 L.Ed.2d 524 (1970).

11. People v. McClean, 130 Cal.App.2d 439, 279 P.2d 87 (1955).

12. Olivas v. State, 168 Tex.Crim. 437, 328 S.W.2d 771 (1959).

13. House v. State, 166 Tex.Crim. 41, 310 S.W.2d 339 (1958).

14. Rinto v. State, 628 S.W. 2d 159 (Tex. Ct. App., 1982).

15. United States v. Furukawa, 596 F.2d 921 (9th Cir. Ct. App., 1979).

16. Baker v. State, 428 So. 2d 684 (Fla. Dist. Ct. App., 1983).

17. *Id.* at 39. For federal probationers, two offenses, possession of a firearm and possession of controlled substances, result in mandatory revocation.

18. ABA, *Standards relating to Probation,* § 5.3; National Advisory Commission *Standards* § 5.4.5.

19. United States v. Blunt, 680 F.2d 1216 (8th Cir., 1982).

20. Ill. Unified Code of Corrections § 1005-6-5(2).

21. Morrissey v. Brewer, 408 U.S. 471, 92 S.Ct. 2593, 33 L.Ed.2d 484 (1972).

22. *Id.*

23. People v. Vickers, 25 Cal. App. 3d 1080: 102 Cal.Rptr. 418 (1972).

24. *Id.*

25. People v. Nelson, 25 Cal.App.3d 1075, 102 Cal.Rptr. 416 (1972).

26. Gagnon v. Scarpelli, 411 U.S. 778, 93 S.Ct. 1756, 36 L.Ed.2d 656 (1973). *But see* Lane v. Attorney General, 477 F.2d 847 (5th Cir.1973); appointment of counsel required where statute permitted retained counsel on parole revocation. *See also* Cottle v. Wainwright, 477 F.2d 269 (5th Cir.1973).
In Pannell v. Jones, 2 Prison Law Reporter 347 (Erie County, N.Y.Sup.Ct., April 13, 1973), a hearing and representation by counsel were required to revoke aftercare status of a narcotics addict.

27. Kuenstler v. State, 486 S.W.2d 367 (Tex.1972).

28. Burkett v. State, 485 S.W.2d 578 (Tex.1972).

29. People v. Sweeden, 116 Cal.App.2d 891, 254 P.2d 899 (1953).

30. Soliz v. State, 171 Tex.Crim. 376, 350 S.W.2d 566 (1961).

31. People v. Price, 24 Ill.App.2d 364, 164 N.E.2d 528 (1960). People v. Larson, 17 Ill.App.2d 417, 150 N.E.2d 224 (1958).

32. Cal.Penal Code § 1203.2 (West). Ill.Ann.Stat. ch. 38, § 117-3 (Smith-Hurd). N.Y. Penal Law § 60.10 (McKinney).

33. ABA, *Standards, Probation,* § 5.4(1).

34. Gagnon v. Scarpelli, 411 U.S. 778, *Standards Relating to Probation* 6, 36 L.Ed.2d 656 (1973).

Discussion Questions

1. How successful is probation? What percentage of probationers violate the conditions of their supervision?

2. How might a "traditional" probation officer view revocation? Why?

3. How might a "community resource manager" probation officer view probation revocation? Why?

4. Contrast the "justice model" officer's perception of revocation with those of the "traditional" and "community resource manager" officer's. Which is your view? Why?

5. For what reasons is probation revocation a serious concern of the community and society?

6. Why do you think the federal supervision manual suggests that the probation officer should consider the "least restrictive" course of action when dealing with a probation violation?

7. Compare and contrast the two categories of probation violation.

8. What is "jail therapy"? What are its positive and negative aspects?

9. Compare probation violation hearings and criminal trials with regard to due process (i.e., standard of proof, right to counsel, etc.). Why are the two procedures different?

10. What is the rule of law in *Morrissey v. Brewer? Gagnon v. Scarpelli? People v. Vickers?*

11. What problems arise with probation revocation under the Interstate Compact?

SUPPLEMENTAL READING

Recidivism of Felons on Probation

INTRODUCTION

Probation supervision in the community accounts for about 60% of the 4.3 million adults serving a sentence on a given day in the United States. Offenders convicted of felonies comprise about half of the probation population nationwide. While convicted felons on probation outnumber the populations of San Diego or Detroit, little research across multiple jurisdictions has examined possible public-safety consequences of felony probation.

This report describes subsequent arrests and levels of compliance with court-ordered requirements of a sample of felony probationers drawn from 17 states. Within 3 years of sentencing nearly 2 in 3 had been either arrested for a new felony or charged with violating their supervision requirements. Among those discharged from supervision, about half with financial obligations had not fully paid, and about a third of those ordered to fill special conditions had failed to satisfy those conditions. Overall, the data suggest that a relatively small fraction of felony probationers fully comply with all of the orders of the court.

FINDINGS

State courts in 32 counties across 17 states sentenced 79,000 felons to probation in 1986. Within 3 years of sentencing, while still on probation, 43% of these felons were rearrested for a felony. Half of the arrests were for a violent crime (murder, rape, robbery, or aggravated assault) or a drug offense (drug trafficking or drug possession).

These findings are from the nation's largest follow-up survey of felons on probation, using a sample that represented a fourth of the total 306,000 felons sentenced to probation in 1986. Survey findings are based on criminal history records and information from probation agency files. The other findings include the following:

■ Sixty-two percent of the probationers followed either had a disciplinary hearing for violating a condition of their probation or were arrested for another felony.
■ Within 3 years, 46% of all probationers had been sent to prison or jail or had absconded (meaning their whereabouts were unknown or they had failed to report).
■ A probation department often recommends in writing an appropriate sentence to the judge, who may accept or reject the recommendation. Of the 79,000 probationers in the follow-up survey, 21% had *not* been recommended for supervision in the community.
■ The 21% of probationers who were not recommended for probation were nearly twice as likely to have their sentence revoked and to be sent to prison (37%) as those recommended for probation (22%).
■ As a condition of their freedom, 53% of all felony probationers had a special condition to satisfy and 84% had a financial penalty to pay.
■ The most commonly imposed special conditions required drug testing (31%), drug treatment (23%), or alcohol treatment (14%).
■ Types of financial penalties included victim restitution (29%), court costs (48%), and probation supervision fees (32%).
■ The average financial penalty was $1,800: victim restitution with an average of $3,400; court costs, $560; and supervision, $680.
■ Among probationers completing their probation term within the 3-year period covered in the survey, 69% of those with special conditions had fully satisfied all conditions, and 47% of those with a financial penalty had paid their penalty in full.

A goal of intensive supervision is to reduce the likelihood of continued criminal activity. Yet, probationers under intensive supervision had the highest arrest rate of any supervision level (56%).

The follow-up data cannot account for the higher arrest rate. The rate may reflect supervision failure or the fact that probationers normally assigned to intensive supervision are high-risk offenders. For example, among those under intensive supervision, 39% had a prior felony conviction, and 75% were drug abusers; among all probationers, corresponding percentages were 26% and 53%. Even taking into account these risk characteristics, probationers in intensive supervision were arrested more frequently than those under less scrutiny. But it is still possible that considering more characteristics would eliminate the difference or even reveal that probationers under intensive supervision did better than expected.

What Happened to Probationers after Felony Arrest.   Rap sheets revealed that 75% of the probationers were convicted after their first felony arrest (64% had a felony conviction and 11% had a misdemeanor conviction). Of those convicted, 88% were sentenced to incarceration—to prison in 42% of cases and to jail in 46%. The total percentage of those sentenced to incarceration upon conviction after a second or third arrest rose only slightly above 88%. However, the likelihood of a sentence to prison changed markedly: prison sentences comprised 42% of sentences after the first arrest, 49% after the second, and 70% after the third.

Probation Status Three Years Later.   Three years after being placed on probation, 38% of the felons were still under supervision, and 62% had left probation. Those on probation included 10% who had absconded and 28% who had not. The offenders off probation included 33% who had completed their sentence, 26% who had gone to prison, and 3% who had died or had been deported.

PROBATION STATUS AFTER 3 YEARS	PERCENT
Total	100%
Still on probation	38%
Absconded	10
Other	28
Off probation	62%
Served term	33
Revoked (prison)	26
Died or deported	3

The 33% completing their term had served an average of $2\frac{1}{4}$ years on probation, or 90% of their $2\frac{1}{2}$ year average sentence. (Three and a half years was the average sentence for all those in the follow-up.)

While those who completed their term did better than many others in the follow-up, most nevertheless got into trouble:

- 28% had at least one felony arrest on probation
- 24% had at least one disciplinary hearing
- 13% had both an arrest and hearing
- 16% had at least one sentence to jail
- 31% of those with a special condition had not satisfied the condition in full
- 53% of those with a financial penalty had not paid the penalty in full.

In short, only 39% of those who had served their sentence were trouble-free.

The Effect of Drug Testing and Treatment in Reducing New Arrests.   Based upon probation department records in the sampled counties, most probationers in the follow-up had a drug abuse problem (53%), characterized by either occasional (22%) or frequent use (31%) of illegal drugs. Drug abusers were more likely than nonabusers to have had a subsequent arrest during the follow-up period:

DRUG ABUSE	PERCENT OF PROBATIONERS ARRESTED
Nonabuser	36%
Occasional abuser	44
Frequent abuser	55

Probation records reveal that among those with known drug problems, 42% were *not* required by the judge to be tested periodically or to participate in drug treatment. The evidence is inconclusive whether testing or treatment helps to reduce the likelihood of subsequent arrest among those with a known drug problem. If the frequency of drug use is held constant, half of all drug abusers ordered to be tested or treated and half of all drug abusers not so ordered were rearrested during their probation.

The probationer's compliance with special conditions of drug testing or treatment—not just whether testing or treatment had been ordered—does provide possible evidence of a lower likelihood of rearrest. Those who had satisfied the condition or were making progress toward satisfying the condition (together comprising 54% of all drug abusers ordered to be tested or treated) were less likely to have a new arrest (38%) than either those who had made no progress (66%) or those drug abusers who had not been ordered to be tested or treated (48%).

	PERCENT OF PROBATIONERS ARRESTED ON PROBAITON		
	Total	Satisfied Condition or Made Progress	Neither Satisfied Condition nor Made Progress
DRUG TESTING/TREATMENT			
Testing *or* treatment	51%	38%	66%
Testing *and* treatment	51	36	65
Testing only	53	34	67
Treatment only	47	42	67
None	48	-	-

THE EFFECT OF INTENSIVE SUPERVISION IN REDUCING NEW ARRESTS. Many probation departments assign an entering probationer to a level of supervision based upon the criminal and social history documented in the PSI. The assigned supervision level generally specifies the required frequency of contact between the probation officer and the offender. The distribution of contact levels among probationers in the follow-up is shown below:

INITIAL SUPERVISION LEVEL	PRESCRIBED NUMBER OF CONTACTS	PERCENT OF SAMPLE
Intensive	9 per month	10%
Maximum	3 per month	32
Medium	1 per month	37
Minimum	1 per 3 months	12
Administrative	None required	9

Whether probationers were actually seen as frequently as their supervision level prescribed could not be determined from the probation records in the sampled jurisdictions.

The 34,000 felony probationers with subsequent arrests were arrested for a felony 64,000 times during the follow-up period. Among those with new felony arrests, 54% had one new arrest, 24% had two, and the remaining 22% had three or more. Robbers (55%),

those convicted of drug possession (52%), and burglars (49%) had among the highest rearrest rates. By contrast, about 20% of the felons sentenced to probation for murder or rape were arrested for a new crime during the follow-up period.

Felons on probation for murder (including nonnegligent manslaughter) were the ones most likely to be rearrested for murder (5%). Rapists were the ones most likely to be rearrested for rape (3%). This pattern—a tendency for offenders to repeat the crime they were previously convicted of—was evident for each offense type. Even with the overall pattern, the vast majority of arrested probationers were not rearrested for the same offense for which they were serving probation. For example, 21% of murderers on probation were rearrested—5% for a new murder and the remaining 16% for a different offense. Furthermore, about 96% of the 340 arrests for murder were of persons not on probation for murder. Of the 247 felons on probation for murder, 12 (or 5%) of them were rearrested for murder. Therefore, of the 340 probationers arrested for murder, 12 of them were felons on probation for murder.

An estimated 9% of probationers, or 6,700 felons, were arrested for a violent crime: murder (0.8%), rape (0.6%), robbery (3.5%), or aggravated assault (3.6%) (Table 1). The 6,700 arrested for a violent crime were 20% of the total 34,000 arrested. The felony probationers with new arrests reflected a higher percentage of violent offenders (20%) than was true for the entire sample (12%). The percentage of drug and property offenders among those with new arrests paralleled the composition of the felony probation sample:

	PERCENT OF PROBATIONERS	
OFFENSE	Sample	New Arrests
Total	100%	100%
Violent	12	20
Property	34	34
Drugs	34	33
Other	20	13
Number	79,043	34,000

COMPLIANCE WITH THE CONDITIONS OF SUPERVISION. Violating the conditions of probation did not always result in prolonging release or in an imposition of time in prison or jail. For every 100 probationers who had been discharged as "successful" after completion of their probation term, 48 had one or more conditions to satisfy as part of their sentence. Probation records indicate that about 33 satisfied those conditions, 5 partially satisfied them, and 10 failed to satisfy or to make progress toward satisfying any of them. Among the 10 of every 100 "successful" discharged probationers who failed to satisfy the conditions of supervision, 2 served a term of confinement. Records for the other eight provide no evidence of a penalty for their failure.

FELONY ARRESTS AND DISCIPLINARY HEARINGS FOR PROBATIONERS. Within 3 years from sentencing, 62% of probationers in the follow-up were either arrested for a new felony or charged at a hearing with violating a condition of supervision. The overall estimate of 62% consisted of 30% who had both a subsequent felony arrest and a disciplinary hearing, 13% who had just an arrest, and 19% who had just a hearing.

Over the 3 years, 43% of the sample had a subsequent felony arrest, and 49% had a disciplinary hearing for violating a condition of supervision. Outcomes of an arrest or a disciplinary hearing range from dismissing the charge and continuing the felon on probation to revoking probation and sending the felon to prison or jail. In addition, absconding from the jurisdiction during the probationary period may result in the issuance of a bench warrant. Absconding, new felony arrests and convictions that result in a sentence to confinement, and revocation of the conditional sentence to probation all represent unsuccessful outcomes.

Absconders and those sent to prison or jail after either conviction for a new offense or revocation of probation comprised 46% of all felony probationers in the followup. Within 3 years of sentencing, 26% of the felony probationers were sent to prison, another 10% were sent to jail, and an additional 10% were designated absconders with unknown whereabouts.

Imposition of a jail or prison term usually followed more than the probationer's just failing to perform community service, missing a meeting with the probation officer, or committing some other technical violation of supervisory conditions. An estimated 86% of unsuccessful probationers sent to prison and 79% of those sent to jail had at least one new felony arrest during the follow-up period. Felony probationers with new arrests (66%) were about twice as likely as those with only technical violations (35%) to be sent to prison or jail during the 3-year follow-up.

TYPE OF INFRACTION	PERCENT OF PROBATIONERS SENTENCED TO INCARCERATION		
	Total	Prison	Jail
Arrest	66%	47%	19%
Technical violation only	35	24	11

FELONY ARREST OFFENSES. The follow-up gathered information on felony arrests from two sources: probation department files and state criminal-history repositories. The second source, most often maintained by state police departments, contains records of arrest and prosecution known as "rap sheets." The quality of recidivism data from the two sources differed. Probation departments could not locate 20% of the probation files. Among cases with files that were located, the probation department records showed 50% fewer probationers arrested than actually were arrested, according to the combined sources. This finding suggests that probation officers did not know of half of all the arrests of probationers under their supervision.

Together, probation department files and rap sheets revealed that within 3 years of their sentence, 43% of probationers were rearrested for a felony within the state. The estimate of recidivism would have been higher had out-of-state arrests been included. Moreover, some probationers were not available for arrest during the full 3 years because they were in jail under a split sentence, were deported, had absconded, or had died.

Adapted from Patrick A. Langan and Mark A. Cunniff, "Recidivism of Felons on Probation," *Special Report* (Washington, D.C.: Bureau of Justice Statistics, February 1992).

SUPPLEMENTAL READING

Morrissey v. Brewer*

JOHN J. MORRISSEY and
G. DONALD BOOHER, Petitioners
v. LOU B. BREWER, Warden, et al.
408 U.S. 471, 33 L.Ed.2d 484, 92 S.Ct. 2593
[No. 71-5103]
Argued April 11, 1972. Decided June 29, 1972.

SUMMARY

Two Iowa convicts whose paroles were revoked by the Iowa Board of Parole filed habeas corpus petitions in the United States District Court for the Southern District of Iowa, alleging that they were denied due process because their paroles were revoked without a hearing. The District Court denied the petitions on the ground that due process did not require a prerevocation hearing, and the United States Court of Appeals for the Eighth Circuit affirmed (443 F.2d 942).

On certiorari, the United States Supreme Court reversed and remanded the case to the Court of Appeals for return to the District Court with directions to make findings on the procedures actually followed by the Parole Board in the two parole revocations. In an opinion by BURGER, Ch. J., expressing the views of six members of the court, it was held that the minimum requirements of due process in revoking paroles include (a) written notice of the claimed parole violations; (b) disclosure to the parolee of evidence against him; (c) opportunity to be heard in person and to present witnesses and documentary evidence; (d) the right to confront and cross-examine adverse witnesses (unless the hearing officer specifically finds good cause for not allowing confrontation); (e) a neutral and detached hearing body such as a traditional parole board, members of which need not be judicial officers or lawyers; and (f) a written statement by the fact finders as to the evidence relied on and reasons for revoking parole. The court further held that a preliminary hearing officer's determination that there is probable cause to hold a parolee for the parole board's final decision on parole revocation warrants the parolee's continued detention pending the final decision; but the court expressly permitted the question whether a parolee is entitled, in a parole revocation proceeding, to the assistance of retained counsel or to appointed counsel if he is indigent.

BRENNAN, J., joined by MARSHALL, J., concurred in the result on the ground that due process also requires that the parolee be allowed the assistance of retained counsel at his revocation hearings.

DOUGLAS, J., dissented on the grounds that a parolee who does not commit a new offense should not be arrested or jailed until his parole is revoked, and that a parolee is entitled to counsel in parole revocation proceedings.

BURGER, C. J., delivered the opinion of the Court, in which STEWART, WHITE, BLACKMUN, POWELL, and REHNQUIST, JJ., joined; BRENNAN, J., filed an opinion concurring in the result, in which MARSHALL, J., joined, *post*, p. 490, 33 L.Ed.2d p. 500. DOUGLAS, J., filed an opinion dissenting in part, *post*, p. 491, 33 L.Ed.2d p. 500.

APPEARANCES OF COUNSEL

W. DON BRITTIN, Jr., argued the cause for petitioners.

LARRY S. SEUFERER argued the cause for respondents.

Briefs of Counsel, p. 962, *infra*.

OPINION OF THE COURT

[408 U.S. 472]

Mr. Chief Justice BURGER, delivered the opinion of the Court.

[1] We granted certiorari in this case to determine whether the Due Process Clause of the Fourteenth Amendment requires that a State afford an individual some opportunity to be heard prior to revoking his parole.

Petitioner Morrissey was convicted of false drawing or uttering of checks in 1967 pursuant to his guilty plea, and was sentenced to not more than seven years' confinement. He was paroled from the Iowa State Penitentiary in June 1968. Seven months later, at the direction of his parole officer, he was arrested in his home town as a parole violator and incarcerated in the county jail. One week later, after review of the parole officer's written report, the Iowa Board of Parole revoked Morrissey's

[408 U.S. 473]

parole, and he was returned to the penitentiary located about 100 miles from his home. Petitioner asserts he received no hearing prior to revocation of his parole.

The parole officer's report on which the Board of Parole acted shows that petitioner's parole was revoked on the basis of information that he had violated the conditions of parole by buying a car under an assumed name and operating it without permission, giving false statements to police concerning his address and insurance company after a minor accident, obtaining credit under an assumed name, and failing to report his place of residence to his parole officer. The report states that the officer interviewed Morrissey, and that he could not explain why he did not contact his parole officer despite his effort to excuse this on the ground that he had been sick. Further, the report asserts that Morrissey admitted buying the car and obtaining credit under an assumed name, and also admitted being involved in the accident. The parole officer recommended that his parole be revoked because of "his continual violating of his parole rules."

The situation as to petitioner Booher is much the same. Pursuant to his guilty plea, Booher was convicted of forgery in 1966 and sentenced to a maximum term of 10 years. He was paroled November 14, 1968. In August 1969, at his parole officer's direction, he was arrested in his home town for violation of his parole and confined in the county jail several miles away. On September 13, 1969, on the basis of a

written report by his parole officer, the Iowa Board of Parole revoked Booher's parole and Booher was recommitted to the state penitentiary, located about 250 miles from his home, to complete service of his sentence. Petitioner asserts he received no hearing prior to revocation of his parole.

[408 U.S. 474]

The parole officer's report with respect to Booher recommended that his parole be revoked because he had violated the territorial restrictions of his parole without consent, had obtained a driver's license under an assumed name, operated a motor vehicle without permission, and had violated the employment condition of his parole by failing to keep himself in gainful employment. The report stated that the officer had interviewed Booher and that he had acknowledged to the parole officer that he had left the specified territorial limits and had operated the car and had obtained a license under an assumed name "knowing that it was wrong." The report further noted that Booher had stated that he had not found employment because he could not find work that would pay him what he wanted—he stated he would not work for $2.25 to $2.75 per hour—and that he had left the area to get work in another city.

After exhausting state remedies, both petitioners filed habeas corpus petitions in the United States District Court for the Southern District of Iowa alleging that they had been denied due process because their paroles had been revoked without a hearing. The State responded by arguing that no hearing was required. The District Court held on the basis of controlling authority that the State's failure to accord a hearing prior to parole revocation did not violate due process. On appeal, the two cases were consolidated.

The Court of Appeals, dividing 4 to 3, held that due process does not require a hearing. The majority recognized that the traditional view of parole as a privilege rather than a vested right is no longer dispositive as to whether due process is applicable; however, on a balancing of the competing interest involved, it concluded that no hearing is required. The court reasoned that parole is only "a correctional device authorizing service of sentence outside the penitentiary," 443 F.2d

[408 U.S. 475]

942, 947; the parolee is still "in custody." Accordingly the Court of Appeals was of that view that prison officials must have large discretion in making revocation determinations, and that courts should retain their traditional reluctance to interfere with disciplinary matters properly under the control of state prison authorities. The majority expressed the view that "non-legal, non-adversary considerations" were often the determinative factors in making a parole revocation decision. It expressed concern that if adversary hearings were required for parole revocation, "with the full panoply of rights accorded in criminal proceedings," the function of the parole board as "an administrative body acting in the role of parens patriae would be aborted", id., at 949, and the board would be more reluctant to grant parole in the first instance—an apprehension that would not be without some basis if the choice were between a full-scale adversary proceeding or no hearing at all. Additionally, the majority reasoned that the parolee has no statutory right to remain on parole. Iowa law provides that a parolee may be returned to the institution at any time. Our holding in Mempa v. Rhay, 389 U.S. 128, 19 L.Ed.2d 336, 88 S.Ct. 254 (1967), was distinguished on the ground that it involved deferred sentencing upon probation revocation, and thus involved a stage of the criminal proceeding, whereas parole revocation was not a stage in the criminal proceeding. The Court of Appeals' decision was consistent with many other decisions on parole revocations.

[2] In its brief in this Court, respondent asserts for the first time that petitioners were in fact granted hearings after they were returned to the penitentiary. More generally, respondent says that within two months after the Board revokes an individual's parole and orders him returned to the penitentiary, on the basis of the parole officer's written report it grants the individual a hearing before the Board. At that time, the Board goes over "each of

[408 U.S. 476]

the alleged parole violations with the returnee, and he is given an opportunity to orally present his side of the story to the Board." If the returnee denies the report, it is the practice of the Board to conduct a further investigation before making a final determina-

tion either affirming the initial revocation, modifying it, or reversing it.[1] The State asserts that Morrissey, whose parole was revoked on January 31, 1969, was granted a hearing before the Board on February 12, 1969. Booher's parole was revoked on September 13, 1969, and he was granted a hearing on October 14, 1969. At these hearings, the State tell us—in the briefs—both Morrissey and Booher admitted the violations alleged in the parole violation reports.

Nothing in the record supplied to this Court indicates that respondent claimed, either in the District Court or the Court of Appeals, that petitioners had received hearings promptly after their paroles were revoked, or that in such hearing they admitted the violations; that information comes to us only in the respondent's brief here. Further, even the assertions that the respondent makes here are not based on any public record but on interviews with two of the members of the parole board. In the interview relied on to show that petitioners admitted their violations, the board member did not assert he could remember that both Morrissey and Booher admitted the parole violations with which they were charged. He stated only that, according to his memory, in the previous several years all but three returnees had admitted commission of the parole infractions alleged

[408 U.S. 477]

and that neither of the petitioners was among the three who denied them.

[3] We must therefore treat this case in the posture and on the record respondent elected to rely on in the District Court and the Court of Appeals. If the facts are otherwise, respondent may make a showing in the District Court that petitioners in fact have admitted the violations charged before a neutral officer.

I

Before reaching the issue of whether due process applies to the parole system, it is important to recall the function of parole in the correctional process.

1. The hearing required by due process, as defined herein, must be accorded *before* the effective decision. *See* Armstrong v. Manzo, 380 U.S. 545, 15 L.Ed.2d 62, 85 S.Ct. 1187 (1965). Petitioners assert here that only one of the 540 revocations ordered most recently by the Iowa Parole Board was reversed after hearing. Petitioners' Reply Brief 7, suggesting that the hearing may not objectively evaluate the revocation decision.

[4, 5] During the past 60 years, the practice of releasing prisoners on parole before the end of their sentences has become an integral part of the penological system. Note, *Parole Revocation in the Federal System*, 56 Geo.L.J. 705 (1968). Rather than being an ad hoc exercise of clemency, parole is an established variation on imprisonment of convicted criminals. Its purpose is to help individuals reintegrate into society as constructive individuals as soon as they are able, without being confined for the full term of the sentence imposed. It also serves to alleviate the costs to society of keeping an individual in prison.[2] The essence of parole is release from prison, before the completion of sentence, on the condition that the prisoner abide by certain rules during the balance of the sentence. Under some systems, parole is granted automatically after the service of a certain portion of a prison term. Under others, parole is granted by the discretionary action of a board, which evaluates an array of information about a prisoner

[408 U.S. 478]

and makes a prediction whether he is ready to reintegrate into society.

To accomplish the purpose of parole, those who are allowed to leave prison early are subjected to specified conditions for the duration of their terms. These conditions restrict their activities substantially beyond the ordinary restrictions imposed by law on an individual citizen. Typically, parolees are forbidden to use liquor or to have associations or correspondence with certain categories of undesirable persons. Typically, also they must seek permission from their parole officers before engaging in specified activities, such as changing employment or living quarters, marrying, acquiring or operating a motor vehicle, traveling outside the community, and incurring substantial indebtedness. Additionally, parolees must regularly report to the parole officer to whom they are assigned and sometimes they must make periodic written reports of their activities. Arluke, *A Summary of Parole Rules—Thirteen Years Later*, 15 Crime & Delinq. 267, 272-273 (1969).

2. *See* Warren, *Probation in the Federal System of Criminal Justice*, 19 Fed. Prob. 3 (Sept. 1955); *Annual Report*, (Ohio Adult Parole Authority 1964/65), 13-14; Note, *Parole: A Critique of Its Legal Foundations and Conditions*, 38 N.Y.U.L.Rev. 702, 705-707 (1963).

[6] The parole officers are part of the administrative system designed to assist parolees and to offer them guidance. The conditions of parole serve a dual purpose; they prohibit, either absolutely or conditionally, behavior that is deemed dangerous to the restoration of the individual into normal society. And through the requirement of reporting to the parole officer and seeking guidance and permission before doing many things, the officer is provided with information about the parolee and an opportunity to advise him. The combination puts the parole officer into the position in which he can try to guide the parolee into constructive development.[3]

The enforcement leverage that supports the parole conditions derives from the authority to return the parolee

[408 U.S. 479]

to prison to serve out the balance of his sentence if he fails to abide by the rules. In practice, not every violation of parole conditions automatically leads to revocation. Typically, a parolee will be counseled to abide by the conditions of parole, and the parole officer ordinarily does not take steps to have parole revoked unless he thinks that the violations are serious and continuing so as to indicate that the parolee is not adjusting properly and cannot be counted on to avoid antisocial activity.[4] The broad discretion accorded the parole officer is also inherent in some of the quite vague conditions, such as the typical requirement that the parolee avoid "undesirable" associations or correspondence. *Cf.* Arciniega v. Freeman, 404 U.S. 4, 30 L.Ed.2d 126, 92 S.Ct. 22 (1971). Yet revocation of parole is not an unusual phenomenon, affecting only a few parolees. It has been estimated that 35%-45% of all parolees are subject to revocation and return to prison.[5] Sometimes revocation occurs when the parolee is accused of another crime; it is often preferred to a new prosecution because of the procedural ease of

3. Note, *Observations on the Administration of Parole*, 79 Yale L.J. 698, 699-700 (1970).

4. *Ibid.*

5. President's Commission on Law Enforcement and Administration of Justice, Task Force Report: Corrections 62 (1967). The substantial revocation rate indicates that parole administrators often deliberately err on the side of granting parole in borderline cases.

recommitting the individual on the basis of a lesser showing by the State.[6]

Implicit in the system's concern with parole violations is the notion that the parolee is entitled to retain his liberty as long as he substantially abides by the conditions of his parole. The first step in a revocation decision thus involves a wholly retrospective factual question: whether the parolee has in fact acted in violation of one or more conditions of his parole. Only if it is determined that

[408 U.S. 480]

the parolee did violate the conditions does the second question arise: should the parolee be recommitted to prison or should other steps be taken to protect society and improve chances of rehabilitation? The first step is relatively simple; the second is more complex. The second question involves the application of expertise by the parole authority in making a prediction as to the ability of the individual to live in society without committing antisocial acts. This part of the decision, too, depends on facts, and therefore it is important for the board to know not only that some violation was committed but also to know accurately how many and how serious the violations were. Yet this second step, deciding what to do about the violation once it is identified, is not purely factual but also predictive and discretionary.

If a parolee is returned to prison, he usually receives no credit for the time "served" on parole.[7] Thus, the returnee may face a potential of substantial imprisonment.

II

[7] We begin with the proposition that the revocation of parole is not part of a criminal prosecution and thus the full panoply of rights due a defendant in such a proceeding does not apply to parole revocations. *Cf.* Mempa v. Rhay, 389 U.S. 128, 19 L.Ed.2d 336, 88 S.Ct. 254 (1967). Parole arises after the end of the

criminal prosecution, including imposition of sentence. Supervision is not directly by the court but by an administrative agency, which is sometimes an arm of the court and sometimes of the executive. Revocation deprives an individual, not of the absolute liberty to which every citizen is entitled, but only of the conditional liberty properly dependent on observance of special parole restrictions.

[408 U.S. 481]

[8-11] We turn, therefore, to the question whether the requirements of due process in general apply to parole revocations. As Mr. Justice Blackmun has written recently, "this Court now has rejected the concept that constitutional rights turn upon whether a governmental benefit is characterized as a 'right" or as a 'privilege.' " Graham v. Richardson, 403 U.S. 365, 374, 29 L.Ed.2d 534, 543, 91 S.Ct. 1848 (1971). Whether any procedural protections are due depends on the extent to which an individual will be "condemned to suffer grievous loss." Joint Anti-Fascist Refugee Committee v. McGrath, 341 U.S. 123, 168; 95 L.Ed. 817, 852, 71 S.Ct. 624 (1951) (Frankfurter, J., concurring), quoted in Goldberg v. Kelly, 397 U.S. 254, 263; 25 L.Ed.2d 287, 296; 90 S.Ct. 1011 (1970). The question is not merely the "weight" of the individual's interest, but whether the nature of the interest is one within the contemplation of the "liberty or property" language of the Fourteenth Amendment. Fuentes v. Shevin, 407 U.S. 67, 32 L.Ed.2d 556, 92 S.Ct. 1983 (1972). Once it is determined that due process applies, the question remains what process is due. It has been said so often by this Court and others as not to require citation of authority that due process is flexible and calls for such procedural protections as the particular situation demands. "[C]onsideration of what procedures due process may require under any given set of circumstances must begin with a determination of the precise nature of the government function involved as well as of the private interest that has been affected by governmental action." Cafeteria & Restaurant Workers Union v. McElroy, 367 U.S. 886, 895; 6 L.Ed.2d 1230, 1236; 81 S.Ct. 1743 (1961). To say that the concept of due process is flexible does not mean that judges are at large to apply it to any and all relationships. Its flexibility is in its scope once it has been determined that some process is due; it is a

6. *See* Morrissey v. Brewer, 443 F.2d 942, at 953-954, n. 5 (C.A.8 1971) (Lay, J., dissenting); Rose v. Haskins, 388 F.2d 91, 104 (C.A.6 1968) (Celebrezze, J., dissenting).

7. Arluke, *A Summary of Parole Rules—Thirteen Years Later,* Crime and Delinquency 267, 271 (1969); Note, *Parole Revocation in the Federal System,* 56 Geo.L.J. 705, 733 (1968).

recognition that not all situations calling for procedural safeguards call for the same kind of procedure.

We turn to an examination of the nature of the interest

[408 U.S. 482]

of the parolee in his continued liberty. The liberty of a parolee enables him to do a wide range of things open to persons who have never been convicted of any crime. The parolee has been released from prison based on an evaluation that he shows reasonable promise of being able to return to society and function as a responsible, self-reliant person. Subject to the conditions of his parole, he can be gainfully employed and is free to be with family and friends and to form the other enduring attachments of normal life. Though the State properly subjects him to many restrictions not applicable to other citizens, his condition is very different from that of confinement in a prison.[8] He may have been on parole for a number of years and may be living a relatively normal life at the time he is faced with revocation.[9] The parolee has relied on at least an implicit promise that parole will be revoked only if he fails to live up to the parole conditions. In many cases, the parolee faces lengthy incarceration if his parole is revoked.

[12] We see, therefore, that the liberty of a parolee, although indeterminate, includes many of the core values of unqualified liberty and its termination inflicts a "grievous loss" on the parolee and often on others. It is hardly useful any longer to try to deal with this problem in terms of whether the parolee's liberty is a "right" or a "privilege." By whatever name, the liberty is valuable and must be seen as within the protection of the Fourteenth Amendment. Its termination calls for some orderly process, however informal.

Turning to the question what process is due, we find that the State's interests are several. The State has found the parolee guilty of a crime against the people. That finding justifies imposing extensive restrictions on the individual's liberty. Release of the parolee before the end of his prison sentence is made with the recognition that with many prisoners there is a risk that they will not be able to live in society without committing additional antisocial acts. Given the previous conviction and the proper imposition of conditions, the State has an overwhelming interest in being able to return the individual to imprisonment without the burden of a new adversary criminal trial if in fact he has failed to abide by the conditions of his parole.

Yet, the State has no interest in revoking parole without some informal procedural guarantees. Although the parolee is often formally described as being "in custody," the argument cannot even be made here that summary treatment is necessary as it may be with respect to controlling a large group of potentially disruptive prisoners in actual custody. Nor are we persuaded by the argument that revocation is so totally a discretionary matter that some form of hearing would be administratively intolerable. A simple factual hearing will not interfere with the exercise of discretion. Serious studies have suggested that fair treatment on parole revocation will not result in fewer grants of parole.[10]

This discretionary aspect of the revocation decision need not be reached unless there is first an appropriate determination that the individual has in fact breached

[408 U.S. 484]

the conditions of parole. The parolee is not the only one who has a stake in his conditional liberty. Society has a stake in whatever may be the chance of restoring him to normal and useful life within the law. Society thus has an interest in not having parole revoked because of erroneous information or because of an erroneous evaluation of the need to revoke parole, given the breach of parole conditions. *See* People *ex rel.* Menechino v. Warden, 27 N.Y.2d 376, 379 and n. 2; 267 N.E.2d 238, 239 and n. 2 (1971) (parole board has less than full picture of facts). And society has a further interest in treating the parolee with basic fairness: fair treatment in parole revocations will en-

---

8. "It is not sophistic to attach greater importance to a person's justifiable reliance in maintaining his conditional freedom so long as he abides by the conditions of his release, than to his mere anticipation or hope of freedom." United States *ex rel.* Bey v. Connecticut Board of Parole, 443 F.2d 1079, 1086 (C.A.2 1971).

9. *See, e.g.,* Murray v. Page, 429 F.2d 1359 (C.A.10 1970) (parole revoked after eight years; 15 years remaining on original term).

10. Sklar, *Law and Practice in Probation and Parole Revocation Hearings,* 55 J.Crim.L.C. & P.S. 175, 194 (1964) (no decrease in Michigan, which grants extensive rights); Rose v. Haskins, 388 F.2d 91, 102 n. 16 (C.A.6 1968) (Celebrezze, J., dissenting) (cost of imprisonment so much greater than parole system that procedural requirements will not change economic motivation).

hance the chance of rehabilitation by avoiding reactions to arbitrariness.[11]

[13] Given these factors, most States have recognized that there is no interest on the part of the State in revoking parole without any procedural guarantees at all.[12] What is needed is an informal hearing structured to assure that the finding of a parole violation will be based on verified facts and that the exercise of discretion will be informed by an accurate knowledge of the parolee's behavior.

III

We now turn to the nature of the process that is due, bearing in mind that the interest of both State and

[408 U.S. 485]

parolee will be furthered by an effective but informal hearing. In analyzing what is due, we see two important stages in the typical process of parole revocation.

[14] (a) *Arrest of Parolee and Preliminary Hearing.* The first stage occurs when the parolee is arrested and detained, usually at the direction of his parole officer. The second occurs when parole is formally revoked. There is typically a substantial time lag between the arrest and the eventual determination by the parole board whether parole should be revoked. Additionally, it may be that the parolee is arrested at a place distant from the state institution, to which he may be returned before the final decision is made concerning revocation. Given these factors, due process would seem to require that some minimal inquiry be conducted at or reasonably near the place of the alleged parole violation or arrest and as promptly as convenient after arrest while information is fresh and sources are available. *Cf.* Hyser v. Reed, 115 U.S.App.D.C. 254, 318 F.2d 225 (1963). Such an inquiry should be seen as in the nature of a "preliminary hearing" to determine whether there is probable cause or reasonable ground to believe that the arrested parolee has committed acts that would constitute a violation of parole conditions. *Cf.* Goldberg v. Kelly, 397 U.S. at 267-271; 25 L.Ed.2d at 298-300.

[15] In our view, due process requires that after the arrest, the determination that reasonable ground exists for revocation of parole should be made by someone not directly involved in the case. It would be unfair to assume that the supervising parole officer does not conduct an interview with the parolee to confront him with the reasons for revocation before he recommends an arrest. It would also be unfair to assume that the parole officer bears hostility against the parolee that destroys his neutrality; realistically the failure of the parolee is in a sense a

[408 U.S. 486]

failure for his supervising officer.[13] However, we need make no assumptions one way or the other to conclude that there should be an uninvolved person to make this preliminary evaluation of the basis for believing the conditions of parole have been violated. The officer directly involved in making recommendations cannot always have complete objectivity in evaluating them.[14] *Goldberg v. Kelly* found it unnecessary to impugn the motives of the caseworker to find a need for an independent decision-maker to examine the initial decision.

[16] This independent officer need not be a judicial officer. The granting and revocation of parole are matters traditionally handled by administrative officers. In *Goldberg*, the Court pointedly did not require that the hearing on termination of benefits be conducted by a judicial officer or even before the traditional "neutral and detached" officer; it required only that the hearing be conducted by some person *other* than one initially dealing with the case. It will be sufficient, therefore, in the parole revocation context, if an evaluation of whether reasonable cause exists to believe that conditions of parole have been violated is

---

11. *See* President's Commission on Law Enforcement and Administration of Justice, Task Force Report: Corrections 83, 88 (1967).

[13] 12. *See* n. 15, *infra.* As one state court has written, "Before such a determination or finding can be made it appears that the principles of fundamental justice and fairness would afford the parolee a reasonable opportunity to explain away the accusation of a parole violation. [The parolee] . . . is entitled to a conditional liberty and possessed of a right which can be forfeited only by reason of a breach of the conditions of the grant." Chase v. Page, 456 P.2d 590, 594 (Okla.Crim.App.1969).

13. Note, *Observations on the Administration of Parole,* 79 Yale L.J. 698, 704-706 (1970) (parole officers in Connecticut adopt role model of social worker rather than an adjunct of police, and exhibit a lack of punitive orientation).

14. This is not an issue limited to bad motivation. "Parole agents are human, and it is possible that friction between the agent and parolee may have influenced the agent's judgment." 4 Attorney General's Survey on Release Procedures: Parole 246 (1939).

made by someone such as a parole officer other than the one who has made the report of parole violations or has recommended revocation. A State could certainly choose some other independent decision-maker to perform this preliminary function.

[17, 18] With respect to the preliminary hearing before this officer, the parolee should be given notice that the hearing

[408 U.S. 487]

will take place and that its purpose is to determine whether there is probable cause to believe he has committed a parole violation. The notice should state what parole violations have been alleged. At the hearing the parolee may appear and speak in his own behalf; he may bring letters, documents, or individuals who can give relevant information to the hearing officer. On request of the parolee, persons who have given adverse information on which parole revocation is to be based are to be made available for questioning in his presence. However, if the hearing officer determines that the informant would be subjected to risk of harm if his identity were disclosed, he need not be subjected to confrontation and cross-examination.

[19, 20] The hearing officer shall have the duty of making a summary, or digest, of what occurs at the hearing in terms of the responses of the parolee and the substance of the documents or evidence given in support of parole revocation and of the parolee's position. Based on the information before him, the officer should determine whether there is probable cause to hold the parolee for the final decision of the parole board on revocation. Such a determination would be sufficient to warrant the parolee's continued detention and return to the state correctional institution pending the final decision. As in *Goldberg*, "the decision-maker should state the reasons for his determination and indicate the evidence he relied on . . ." but it should be remembered that this is not a final determination calling for "formal findings of fact and conclusions of law." 397 U.S. at 271; 25 L.Ed.2d at 300. No interest would be served by formalism in this process; informality will not lessen the utility of this inquiry in reducing the risk of error.

[21] (b) *The Revocation Hearing.* There must also be an opportunity for a hearing, if it is desired by the parolee, prior to the final decision on revocation by the parole

[408 U.S. 488]

authority. This hearing must be the basis for more than determining probable cause; it must lead to a final evaluation of any contested relevant facts and consideration of whether the facts as determined warrant revocation. The parolee must have an opportunity to be heard and to show, if he can, that he did not violate the conditions, or, if he did, that circumstances in mitigation suggest that the violation does not warrant revocation. The revocation hearing must be tendered within a reasonable time after the parolee is taken into custody. A lapse of two months, as the State suggests occurs in some cases, would not appear to be unreasonable.

[22, 23] We cannot write a code of procedure; that is the responsibility of each State. Most States have done so by legislation, others by judicial decision usually on due process grounds.[15] Our task is limited to deciding the

[408 U.S. 489]

minimum requirements of due process. They include (a) written notice of the claimed violations of

15. Very few States provide no hearing at all in parole revocations. Thirty States provide in their statutes that a parolee shall receive some type of hearing. *See* Ala.Code, Tit. 42, § 12 (1959); Alaska Stats. § 33.15.220 (1962); Ariz.Rev.Stats.Ann. § 31-417 (1956); Ark.Stat.Ann. § 43-2810 (Supp.1971); Del.Code.Ann., Tit. 11, § 4352 (Supp.1970); Fla.Stats.Ann. § 947.23(1) (Supp.1972); Ga.Code Ann. § 77-519 (Supp.1971); Haw.Rev.Stats. § 353-66 (1968); Idaho Code §§ 20-229, 20-229A (Supp.1971); Ill.Ann.Stat. §§ 204(e), 207 (Supp.1972); Ind.Ann.Stats. § 13-1611 (Supp.1972); Kan.Stat.Ann. § 22-3721 (1971); Ky.Rev.Stats.Ann. § 439.330(1)(e) (1962); La.Rev.Stats.Ann. § 15:574.9 (Supp.1972); Me.Rev.Stats.Ann., Tit. 34, § 1675 (Supp.1970-1971); Md.Ann.Code, Art. 41, § 117 (1971); Mich.Comp.Laws § 791.240a, Mich.Stats.Ann. § 28.2310(*l*) (Supp.1972); Miss.Code Ann. § 4004-13 (1956); Mo.Ann.Stats. § 549.265 (Supp.1971); Mont.Rev.Codes §§ 94-9838, 94-9835 (1969); N.H.Rev.Stats.Ann. § 607:46 (1955); N.M.Stat.Ann. § 41-17-28 (1972); N.Y.Correc.Law § 212, subd. 7 (Supp.1971); N.D.Cent.Code § 12-59-15 (Supp.1971); Pa.Stats.Ann., Tit. 61, § 331.21a(b) (1964); Tenn.Code Ann § 40-3619 (1955); Texas Code Crim.Proc. Art. 42.12, § 22 (1966); Vt.Stat.Ann., Tit. 28, § 1081(b) (1970); Wash.Rev.Code §§ 9.95.120 through 9.95.126 (Supp.1971); W.Va.Code Ann. § 62-12-19 (1966). Decisions of state and federal courts have required a number of other States to provide hearings. *See* Hutchison v. Patterson, 267 F.Supp. 433 (Colo.1967) (approving parole board regulations); United States *ex rel.* Bey v. Connecticut State Board of Parole, 443 F.2d 1079 (C.A.2 1971) (requiring counsel to be appointed for revocation hearings); State v. Holmes, 109 N.J.Super. 180, 262 A.2d 725 (1970); Chase v. Page, 456 P.2d 590 (Okla.Crim.App.1969); Bearden v. South Carolina, 443 F.2d 1090 (C.A.4 1971) (North Carolina and Virginia also subject to fourth circuit rule); Baine v. Beckstead, 10 Utah 2d 4, 347 P.2d 554 (1959); Goolsby v. Gagnon, 322 F.Supp. 460 (E.D.Wis.1971). A number of states are affected by no legal requirement to grant any kind of hearing.

parole; (b) disclosure to the parolee of evidence against him; (c) opportunity to be heard in person and to present witnesses and documentary evidence; (d) the right to confront and cross-examine adverse witnesses (unless the hearing officer specifically finds good cause for not allowing confrontation); (e) a "neutral and detached" hearing body such as a traditional parole board, members of which need not be judicial officers or lawyers; and (f) a written statement by the fact finders as to the evidence relied on and reasons for revoking parole. We emphasize there is no thought to equate this second stage of parole revocation to a criminal prosecution in any sense. It is a narrow inquiry; the process should be flexible enough to consider evidence including letters, affidavits, and other material that would not be admissible in an adversary criminal trial.

We do not reach or decide the question whether the parolee is entitled to the assistance of retained counsel or to appointed counsel if he is indigent.[16]

[408 U.S. 490]

[24] We have no thought to create an inflexible structure for parole revocation procedures. The few

---

16. The Model Penal Code § 305.15(1) (Proposed Official Draft 1962) provides that "[t]he institutional parole staff shall render reasonable aid to the parolee in preparation for the hearing and he shall be permitted to advise with his own legal counsel."

basic requirements set out above, which are applicable to future revocations of parole, should not impose a great burden on any State's parole system. Control over the required proceedings by the hearing officers can assure that delaying tactics and other abuses sometimes present in the traditional adversary trial situation do not occur. Obviously a parolee cannot relitigate issues determined against him in other forums, as in the situation presented when the revocation is based on conviction of another crime.

In the peculiar posture of this case, given the absence of an adequate record, we conclude the ends of justice will be best served by remanding the case to the Court of Appeals for its return of the two consolidated cases to the District Court with directions to make findings on the procedures actually followed by the Parole Board in these two revocations. If it is determined that petitioners admitted parole violations to the Parole Board, as Iowa contends, and if those violations are found to be reasonable grounds for revoking parole under state standards, that would end the matter. If the procedures followed by the Parole Board are found to meet the standards laid down in this opinion that, too, would dispose of the due process claims for these cases.

We reverse and remand to the Court of Appeals for further proceedings consistent with this opinion.

Reversed and remanded.

Gagnon v. Scarpelli

JOHN R. GAGNON,
Warden, Petitioner, v.
GERALD H. SCARPELLI
411 US 778, 36 L Ed 2d 656, 93 S Ct 1756
[No. 71-1225]
Argued January 9, 1973. Decided May 14, 1973.

SUMMARY

After the petitioner had pleaded guilty to a charge of armed robbery in Wisconsin and the trial court had sentenced him to 15 years' imprisonment, the judge suspended sentence, placed the petitioner on probation for 7 years in the custody of the Wisconsin Department of Public Welfare, and authorized him to reside in Illinois, where, pursuant to an interstate compact, he was accepted for supervision by Illinois probation authorities. Subsequently, he and a companion were arrested in Illinois for a burglary. Several days later, the Wisconsin Department, without affording him either a hearing or counsel, revoked his probation on the grounds that by being involved in and arrested for the burglary, and by associating with his companion, a known criminal, he had violated his probation. Shortly thereafter, he was incarcerated in a Wisconsin prison to begin serving his 15-year sentence. In habeas corpus proceedings in the United States District Court for the Eastern District of Wisconsin, the petitioner contended that the revocation of his probation without affording him a hearing or counsel was a denial of due process. The District Court agreed with this contention and granted a writ of habeas corpus (317 F Supp 72), and the Court of Appeals for the Seventh Circuit affirmed (454 F2d 416).

On certiorari, United States Supreme Court affirmed in part, reversed in part, and remanded the case. In an opinion by **Powell, J.,** it was held (1) expressing the unanimous view of the court, that the petitioner was entitled to both a preliminary hearing to determine whether there was probable cause to believe that he had violated his probation and a final hearing prior to the ultimate decision whether his probation should be revoked, and (2) expressing the view of eight members of the court, that the state was not under a constitutional duty to provide counsel for indigents in all probation revocation cases, but that the decision as to the need for counsel must be made on a case-by-case basis in the exercise of a sound discretion by the state authority charged with responsibility for administering the probation system, and that certain general guidelines as to whether the assistance of counsel was constitutionally necessary should be applied in the first instance by those charged with conducting the revocation hearing.

OPINION OF THE COURT

[411 US 779]

Mr. Justice **Powell** delivered the opinion of the Court.

This case presents the related questions whether a previously sentenced probationer is entitled to a hearing when his probation is revoked and, if so, whether he is entitled to be represented by appointed counsel at such a hearing.

I

Respondent, Gerald Scarpelli, pleaded guilty in July 1965, to a charge of armed robbery in Wisconsin. The trial judge sentenced him to 15 years' imprisonment, but suspended the sentence and placed him on probation for seven years in the custody of the Wisconsin Department of Public Welfare (the Department).[1] At

---

1. The Court's order placing respondent on probation provided, among other things, that "[i]n the event of his failure to meet the conditions of his probation he will stand committed under the sentence all ready [sic] imposed." App. 10. The agreement specifying the conditions of the probation, duly executed by respondent, obligated him to "make a sincere attempt to avoid all acts which are forbidden by law. . . ." App 12. of his

[411 US 780]

in the course of the burglary of a house. After being apprised of his constitutional rights, respondent admitted that he and Kleckner had broken into the house for the purpose of stealing merchandise or money, although he now asserts that his statement was made under duress and is false. Probation was revoked by the Department on September 1, without a hearing. The stated grounds for revocation were that:

"1. [Scarpelli] has associated with known criminals, in direct violation of his probation regulations and his supervising agent's instructions;"

"2. [Scarpelli] while associating with a known criminal, namely Fred Kleckner, Jr., was involved in, and arrested for, a burglary . . . in Deerfield, Illinois." App 20.

On September 4, 1965, he was incarcerated in the Wisconsin State Reformatory at Green Bay to begin serving the 15 years to which he had been sentenced by the trial judge. At no time was he afforded a hearing.

Some three years later, on December 16, 1968, respondent applied for a writ of habeas corpus. After the petition had been filed, but before it had been acted upon, the Department placed respondent on parole.[2] The District Court found that his status as parolee was sufficient custody to confer jurisdiction on the court and that the petition was not moot because the revocation carried "collateral consequences," presumably including the restraints imposed by his parole. On the merits, the District Court held that revocation without a hearing and counsel was a denial of due process. 317 F Supp 72 (ED Wis 1970). The Court of Appeals affirmed sub nom. Gunsolus v. Gagnon, 454 F2d 416 (CA 7 1971),

[411 US 781]

and we granted certiorari, 408 US 921, 33 L Ed 2d 331, 92 S Ct 2490 (1972).

---

probation and a "Travel Permit and Agreement to Return" allowing him to reside in Illinois, with supervision there under an interstate compact. On August 5, 1965, he was accepted for supervision by the Adult Probation Department of Cook County, Illinois. that time, he signed an agreement specifying the terms

On August 6, respondent was apprehended by Illinois police, who had surprised him and one Fred Kleckner, Jr.

2. Respondent was initially paroled to a federal detainer to serve a previously imposed federal sentence arising from another conviction. He was subsequently released from federal custody, but remains a parolee under the supervision of the Department.

II

Two prior decisions set the bounds of our present inquiry. In Mempa v Rhay, 389 US 128, 19 L Ed 2d 336, 88 S Ct 254 (1967), the Court held that a probationer is entitled to be represented by appointed counsel at a combined revocation and sentencing hearing. Reasoning that counsel is required "at every stage of a criminal proceeding where substantial rights of a criminal accused may be affected," id., at 134, 19 L Ed 2d 336, and that sentencing is one such stage, the Court concluded that counsel must be provided an indigent at sentencing even when it is accomplished as a part of subsequent probation revocation proceeding. But this line of reasoning does not require a hearing or counsel at the time of probation revocation in a case such as the present one, where the probationer was sentenced at the time of trial.

Of greater relevance is our decision last Term in Morrissey v Brewer, 408 US 471, 33 L Ed 2d 484, 92 S Ct 2593 (1972). There we held that the revocation of parole is not a part of a criminal prosecution.

"Parole arises after the end of the criminal prosecution, including imposition of sentence. . . . Revocation deprives an individual, not of the absolute liberty to which every citizen is entitled, but only of the conditional liberty properly dependent on observance of special parole restrictions." Id., at 480, 33 L Ed 2d 484.

Even though the revocation of parole is not a part of the criminal prosecution, we held that the loss of liberty entailed is a serious deprivation requiring that the parolee be accorded due process. Specifically, we held that a parolee is entitled to two hearings, one a

[411 US 782]

preliminary hearing at the time of his arrest and detention to determine whether there is probable cause to believe that he has committed a violation of his parole and the other a somewhat more comprehensive hearing prior to the making of the final revocation decision.

[1] Petitioner does not contend that there is any difference relevant to the guarantee of due process between the revocation of parole and the revocation of

probation, nor do we perceive one.[3] Probation revocation, like parole revocation, is not a stage of a criminal prosecution, but does result in a loss of liberty.[4] Accordingly, we hold that a probationer, like a parolee, is entitled to a preliminary and a final revocation hearing, under the conditions specified in *Morrissey v Brewer, supra.*[5]

[411 US 783]

III

The second, and more difficult, question posed by this case is whether an indigent probationer or parolee has a due process right to be represented by appointed counsel at these hearings.[6] In answering that question, we draw heavily on the opinion in *Morrissey.* Our first point of reference is the character of probation or parole. As noted in *Morrissey* regarding parole, the "purpose is to help individuals reintegrate into society as constructive individuals as soon as they are able. . . ." 408 US, at 477, 33 L Ed 2d 484. The duty and attitude of the probation or parole officer reflect this purpose:

> While the parole or probation officer recognizes his double duty to the welfare of his clients and to the safety of the general community, by and large concern for the client dominates his professional attitude.

[411 US 784]

The parole agent ordinarily defines his role as representing his client's best interests as long as these do not constitute a threat to public safety.[7] Because the probation or parole officer's function is not so much to compel conformance to a strict code of behavior as to supervise a course of rehabilitation, he has been entrusted traditionally with broad discretion to judge the progress of rehabilitation in individual cases, and has been armed with the power to recommend or even to declare revocation.

In *Morrissey,* we recognized that the revocation decision has two analytically distinct components:

> "The first step in a revocation decision thus involves a wholly retrospective factual question: whether the parolee has in fact acted in violation of one or more conditions of his parole. Only if it is determined that the parolee did violate the condition does the second question arise: should the parolee be recommitted to prison or should other steps be taken to protect society and improve chances of rehabilitation?" *Morrissey v. Brewer, supra,* at 479-480, 33 L Ed 2d 484.[8]

---

3. Despite the undoubted minor differences between probation and parole, the commentators have agreed that revocation of probation where sentence has been imposed previously is constitutionally indistinguishable from the revocation of parole. *See, e.g.,* Van Dyke, *Parole Revocation Hearings in California: The Right to Counsel,* 59 Calif L Rev 1215, 1241-1243 (1971); Sklar, *Law and Practice in Probation and Parole Revocation Hearings,* 55 J Crim LC & PS 175, 198 n. 182 (1964).

4. It is clear at least after Morrissey v. Brewer, 408 US 471, 33 L Ed 2d 484, 92 S Ct 2593 (1972), that a probationer can no longer be denied due process, in reliance on the dictum in Escoe v. Zerbst, 295 US 490, 492, 79 L Ed 2d 1566, 55 S Ct 818 (1935), that probation is an "act of grace."

5. Petitioner argues, in addition, that the Morrissey hearing requirements impose serious practical problems in cases such as the present one in which a probationer or parolee is allowed to leave the convicting State for supervision in another State. Such arrangements are made pursuant to an interstate compact adopted by all of the States, including Wisconsin. Wis.Stat.Ann. § 57.13 (1957). Petitioner's brief asserts that as of June 30, 1972, Wisconsin had a total of 642 parolees and probationers under supervision in other States and that incomplete statistics as of June 30, 1971, indicated a national total of 24,693 persons under out-of-state supervision. Brief for Petitioner.

Some amount of disruption inevitably attends any new constitutional ruling. We are confident, however, that modifications of the interstate compact can remove without undue strain the more serious technical hurdles to compliance with *Morrissey.* An additional comment is warranted with respect to the rights to present witnesses and to confront and cross-examine adverse witnesses. Petitioner's greatest concern is with the difficulty and expense of procuring witnesses from perhaps thousands of miles away. While in some cases there is simply no adequate alternative to live testimony, we emphasize that we did not in *Morrissey* intend to prohibit use where appropriate of the conventional substitutes for live testimony, including affidavits, depositions, and documentary evidence. Nor did we intend to foreclose the States from holding both the preliminary and the final hearings at the place of violation or from developing other creative solutions to the practical difficulties of the *Morrissey* requirements.

6. In *Morrissey v Brewer,* we left open the question "whether the parolee is entitled to the assistance of retained counsel or to appointed counsel if he is indigent." 408 US, at 489, 33 L Ed 2d 484. Since respondent did not attempt to retain counsel but asked only for appointed counsel, we have no

occasion to decide in this case whether a probationer or parolee has a right to be represented at a revocation hearing by retained counsel in situations other than those where the State would be obliged to furnish counsel for an indigent.

7. F. Remington, D. Newman, E. Kimball, M. Melli and H. Goldstein, Criminal Justice Administration, Materials and Cases 910-911 (1969).

8. The factors entering into these decisions relate in major part to a professional evaluation, by trained probation or parole officers, as to the overall social readjustment of the offender in the community, and include consideration of such variables as the offender's relationship toward his family, his attitude toward the fulfillment of financial obligations, the extent of his cooperation with the probation officer assigned to his case, his personal associations, and—of course—whether there have been specific and significant violations of the conditions of the probation. The importance of these considerations, some factual and others entirely judgmental, is illustrated by a Wisconsin empirical study which disclosed that, in the

[411 US 785]

The parole officer's attitude toward these decisions reflects the rehabilitative rather than punitive focus of the probation/parole system:

"Revocation . . . . is, if anything, commonly treated as a failure of supervision. While presumably it would be inappropriate for a field agent *never* to revoke, the whole thrust of the probation-parole movement is to keep men in the community, working with adjustment problems there, and using revocation only as a last resort when treatment has failed or is about to fail."[9]

[2] But an exclusive focus on the benevolent attitudes of those who administer the probation/parole system when it is working successfully obscures the modification in attitude which is likely to take place once the officer has decided to recommend revocation. Even though the officer is not by this recommendation converted into a prosecutor committed to convict, his role as counsellor to the probationer or parolee is then surely compromised.

When the officer's view of the probationer's or parolee's conduct differs in this fundamental way from the latter's own view, due process requires that the difference be resolved before revocation becomes final. Both the probationer or parolee and the State have interests in the accurate finding of fact and the informed use of discretion—the probationer or parolee to insure that his liberty is not unjustifiably taken away and the State to make certain that it is neither unnecessarily interrupting a successful effort at rehabilitation nor imprudently prejudicing the safety of the community.

[411 US 786]

[3, 4] It was to serve all of these interests that Morrissey mandated preliminary and final revocation hearings. At the preliminary hearing, a probationer or parolee is entitled to notice of the alleged violations of probation or parole, an opportunity to appear and to present evidence in his own behalf, a conditional right to confront adverse witnesses, an independent decision maker, and a written report of the hearing. *Morrissey v.*

sample studied, probation or parole was revoked in only 34.5% of the cases in which the probationer or parolee violated the terms of his release. S. Hunt, *The Revocation Decision: A Study of Probation and Parole Agents' Discretion* 10 (unpublished thesis on file at the library of the University of Wisconsin 1964), cited in Brief for Petitioner, Addendum 106.

9. Remington, Newman, Kimball, Melli and Goldstein, *supra*, n. 7, at 910.

Brewer, supra, at 487, 33 L Ed 2d 484. The final hearing is a less summary one because the decision under consideration is the ultimate decision to revoke rather than a mere determination of probable cause, but the "minimum requirements of due process" include very similar elements:

(a) written notice of the claimed violations of [probation or] parole; (b) disclosure to the [probationer or] parolee of evidence against him; (c) opportunity to be heard in person and to present witnesses and documentary evidence; (d) the right to confront and cross-examine adverse witnesses (unless the hearing officer specifically finds good cause for not allowing confrontation); (e) a "neutral and detached" hearing body such as a traditional parole board, members of which need not be judicial officers or lawyers; and (f) a written statement by the factfinders as to the evidence relied on and reasons for revoking [probation or] parole. *Morrissey v. Brewer, supra,* at 489, 33 L Ed 2d 484.

[5] These requirements in themselves serve as substantial protection against ill-considered revocation, and petitioner argues that counsel need never be supplied. What this argument overlooks is that the effectiveness of the rights guaranteed by *Morrissey* may in some circumstances depend on the use of skills which the probationer or parolee is unlikely to possess. Despite the informal nature of the proceeding and the absence of technical

[411 US 787]

rules of procedure or evidence, the unskilled or uneducated probationer or parolee may well have difficulty in presenting his version of a disputed set of facts where the presentation requires the examining of cross-examining of witnesses or the offering or dissecting of complex documentary evidence.

[6] By the same token, we think that the Court of Appeals erred in accepting respondent's contention that the State is under a constitutional duty to provide counsel for indigents in all probation or parole revocation cases. While such a rule has the appeal of simplicity, it would impose direct costs and serious collateral disadvantages without regard to the need or the likelihood in a particular case for a constructive contribution by counsel. In most cases, the probationer or parolee has been convicted of committing another crime or has admitted the charges against him.[10] And while in some cases he may have a justifiable excuse for the violation or a convincing reason why revocation is not the appropriate disposition, mitigating evidence of this kind is often not susceptible of proof or is so simple as not to require either investigation or exposition by counsel.

The introduction of counsel into a revocation proceeding will alter significantly the nature of the proceeding. If counsel is provided for the probationer or parolee, the State in turn will normally provide its own counsel; lawyers, by training and disposition, are advocates and bound by professional duty to present all available evidence and arguments in support of their clients' positions and to contest with vigor all adverse evidence and views. The role of the hearing body itself, aptly described in *Morrissey* as being "predictive and discretionary" as well as factfinding, may become more akin to that of a judge at a trial, and less attuned to the

[411 US 788]

rehabilitative needs of the individual probationer or parolee. In the greater self–consciousness of its quasi-judicial role, the hearing body may be less tolerant of marginal deviant behavior and feel more pressure to reincarcerate rather than to continue nonpunitive rehabilitation. Certainly, the decision-making process will be prolonged, and the financial cost to the State—for appointed counsel, counsel for the State, a longer record, and the possibility of judicial review—will not be insubstantial.[11]

[5, 7] In some cases, these modifications in the nature of the revocation hearing must be endured and the costs borne because, as we have indicated above, the probationer's or parolee's version of a disputed issue can fairly be represented only by a trained advocate. But due process is not so rigid as to require that the significant interests in informality, flexibility and economy must always be sacrificed.

In so concluding, we are of course aware that the case-by-case approach to the right to counsel in felony prosecutions adopted in Betts v Brady, 316 US 455, 86 L Ed 1595, 62 S Ct 1252 (1942), was later

rejected in favor of a per se rule in Gideon v Wainwright, 372 US 335, 9 L Ed 2d 799, 83 S Ct 792, 93 ALR 2d 733 (1963). *See also* Argersinger v Hamlin, 407 US 25, 32 L Ed 2d 530, 92 S Ct 2006 (1972). We do not, however draw from *Gideon* and *Argersinger* the conclusion that a case-by-case approach to furnishing counsel is necessarily inadequate to protect constitutional rights asserted in varying types of proceedings: there are critical differences between criminal trials and probation or parole revocation

[411 US 789]

hearings, and both society and the probationer or parolee have stakes in preserving these differences.

In a criminal trial, the State is represented by a prosecutor; formal rules of evidence are in force; a defendant enjoys a number of procedural rights which may be lost if not timely raised; and, in a jury trial, a defendant must make a presentation understandable to untrained jurors. In short, a criminal trial under our system is an adversary proceeding with its own unique characteristics. In a revocation hearing, on the other hand, the State is represented, not by a prosecutor, but by a parole officer with the orientation described above; formal procedures and rules of evidence are not employed; and the members of the hearing body are familiar with the problems and practice of probation or parole. The need for counsel at revocation hearings derives, not from the invariable attributes of those hearings, but rather from the peculiarities of particular cases.

[8, 9] The differences between a criminal trial and a revocation hearing do not dispose altogether of the argument that under a case-by-case approach there may be cases in which a lawyer would be useful but in which none would be appointed because an arguable defense would be uncovered only by a lawyer. Without denying that there is some force in this argument, we think it a sufficient answer that we deal here, not with the right of an accused to counsel in a criminal prosecution, but with the more limited due process right of one who is a probationer or parolee only because he has been convicted of a crime.[12]

10. *See* Skar, *supra*, n. 3, at 192 (parole), 193 (probation).

11. The scope of the practical problem which would be occasioned by a requirement of counsel in all revocation cases is suggested by the fact that in the mid-1960's there was an estimated average of 20,000 adult felony parole revocations and 108,000 adult probation revocations each year. President's Commission on Law Enforcement and Administration of Justice, Task Force Report: The Courts 56 n. 28 (1967).

12. *Cf. In re* Gault, 387 US 1, 18 L Ed 2d 527, 87 S Ct 1428 (1967), establishing a juvenile's right to appointed counsel in a delinquency proceeding which while denominated civil, was functionally akin to a criminal trial. A juvenile charged with violation of a generally applicable statute is differently situated from an already-convicted probationer or

[411 US 790]

[10] We thus find no justification for a new inflexible constitutional rule with respect to the requirement of counsel. We think, rather, that the decision as to the need for counsel must be made on a case-by-case basis in the exercise of a sound discretion by the state authority charged with responsibility for administering the probation and parole system. Although the presence and participation of counsel will probably be both undesirable and constitutionally unnecessary in most revocation hearing, there will remain certain cases in which fundamental fairness—the touchstone of due process—will require that the State provide at its expense counsel for indigent probationers or parolees.

[11, 12] It is neither possible nor prudent to attempt to formulate a precise and detailed set of guidelines to be followed in determining when the providing of counsel is necessary to meet the applicable due process requirements. The facts and circumstances in preliminary and final hearings are susceptible of almost infinite variation, and a considerable discretion must be allowed the responsible agency in making the decision. Presumptively, it may be said that counsel should be provided in cases where, after being informed of his right to request counsel, the probationer or parolee makes such a request, based on a timely and colorable claim (i) that he has not committed the alleged violation of the conditions upon which he is at liberty; or (ii) that, even if the violation is a matter of public record or is uncontested, there are substantial reasons which justified or mitigated the violation and make revocation inappropriate, and that the reasons are complex or otherwise difficult to develop or present. In passing on a request for the

parolee, and is entitled to a higher degree of protection. *See In re* Winship, 397 US 358, 25 L Ed 2d 368, 90 S Ct 1068 (1970) (the standard of proof in a juvenile delinquency proceeding must be "proof beyond a reasonable doubt").

appointment of counsel, the responsible agency also should consider,

[411 US 791]

especially in doubtful cases, whether the probationer appears to be capable of speaking effectively for himself. In every case in which a request for counsel at a preliminary or final hearing is refused, the grounds for refusal should be stated succinctly in the record

IV

[13, 14] We return to the facts of the present case. Because respondent was not afforded either a preliminary hearing or a final hearing, the revocation of his probation did not meet the standards of due process prescribed in *Morrissey*, which we have here held applicable to probation revocations. Accordingly, respondent was entitled to a writ of habeas corpus. On remand, the District Court should allow the State an opportunity to conduct such a hearing. As to whether the State must provide counsel, respondent's admission to having committed another serious crime creates the very sort of situation in which counsel need not ordinarily be provided. But because of respondent's subsequent assertions regarding that admission, see supra, at 780, 36 L Ed 2d at 660, we conclude that the failure of the Department to provide respondent with the assistance of counsel should be re-examined in light of this opinion. The general guidelines outlined above should be applied in the first instance by those charged with conducting the revocation hearing.

Affirmed in part, reversed in part, and remanded.

Mr. Justice **Douglas,** dissenting in part.

I believe that due process requires the appointment of counsel in this case because of the claim that respondent's confession of the burglary was made under duress. See Morrissey v. Brewer, 408 US 471, 498, 33 L Ed 2d 484, 92 S Ct 2593 (opinion of Douglas, J.)

II

PAROLE

AT PRESENT, FORTY-ONE STATES HAVE some form of parole statutes and procedures for the discretionary release of most adult felony offenders from prisons and correctional institutions. Almost all jurisdictions have at least nominal programs for supervising offenders released to the community and procedures for their return to incarceration should they fail in community adjustment.

The structure of the paroling process—including the composition and selection of the parole board, caseloads, training, and authority of field staff and procedures used for the parole grant or revocation—varies considerably from jurisdiction to jurisdiction. The same is true for the *use* of parole. Some states parole virtually all adult prisoners, while in others legislative action has abolished discretionary release on parole.

These variations in the structure and use of the parole process, as well as the accompanying variations in sentencing structures from one jurisdiction to another, account in good part for the lack of agreement about the legal status of parole across the country. Where parole is the common, almost universal means of release from prison, it comes to be viewed as a right. Where it is granted reluctantly and rarely, and in jurisdictions with long statutory sentences and no other alternatives to mitigation of sentences, parole becomes crucially important to inmates.

This section focuses on parole as a subsystem of the entire field of criminal justice. The history and philosophy of parole are discussed in detail, as are current practices and legal issues and attempts to clarify the contemporary controversies involving parole and other forms of early release from incarceration. Parole is viewed in its relationship to sentencing, imprisonment, and other aspects of the correctional continuum.

THE HISTORY AND CONCEPT OF PAROLE

KEY TERMS

Mandatory release
Probation
Pardon
Parole d'honneur
Transportation
Ticket-of-leave
Ticket-of-leave man
Mark system
Alexander Maconochie
Sir Walter Crofton
The Irish system
Norfolk Island
Indeterminate sentence
Zebulon R. Brockway

Mandatory release

Conditional release to the community that is automatic at the expiration of the maximum term of sentence *minus* any credited time off for good behavior.

THE CONCEPT OF PAROLE

The procedure now known as *parole* was first tried in the United States at Elmira Reformatory in 1876. Since then, its use has extended to all parts of the country and it is now the major device by which offenders are released from prisons and correctional institutions. Even after a century of use, there is much misapprehension and misunderstanding about parole, much of which arises from a confusion in terminology. The general public often considers parole to be based on clemency or leniency and seldom distinguishes it from probation and pardon. The terms *parole, probation,* and *pardon* are used indiscriminately not only by the public, but even by officials, judges, and in some state statutes. Because of this confusion in terminology and administration, parole is often charged with all the shortcomings of other release procedures, for which it is in no way responsible. It is evident, therefore, that a clear definition of the term is essential to any analysis of parole. **Parole** *is the conditional release, by an administrative act, of a convicted offender from a penal or correctional institution, under the continued custody of the state, to serve the remainder of his or her sentence in the community under supervision.*

Parole versus Mandatory Release

Mandatory release differs from parole in that mandatory releasees enter supervision in the community *automatically* at the expiration of their maximum term *minus* credited time off for good behavior. In many jurisdictions where parole-board authority has been abolished, most released prisoners return to the community via mandatory release. As with parole, mandatory release may be revoked for failure to comply with the conditions of release.

Parole as Distinguished from Probation

Probation and parole are different methods of dealing with offenders, although their terms are often used interchangeably. Whereas parole is a form of release granted to a prisoner who has served a portion of a sentence in a correctional institution, **probation** is granted an offender without requiring incarceration. Parole is an administrative act of the executive or an executive agency, whereas probation is a judicial act of the court. Therefore, so-called bench parole—which is nothing more than a suspension of sentence without supervision—is not parole at all, but a form of probation; and the use of the word *parole* in this connection is improper, and misleading and should thus be eliminated.

Parole as Distinguished from Pardon

Wilcox distinguished between **pardon** and parole as follows:

Pardon involves forgiveness. Parole does not. Pardon is a remission of punishment. Parole is an extension of punishment. Pardoned prisoners are free. Parolees may be arrested and re-imprisoned without a trial. Pardon is an executive act of grace; parole is an administrative expedient.[1]

The distinction between parole and pardon was clearly drawn in an address before the American Prison Association in 1916:

> The whole question of parole is one of administration. A parole does not release the parolee from custody; it does not discharge or absolve him from the penal consequences of his act; it does not mitigate his punishment; it does not wish away the stain or remit the penalty; it does not reverse the judgment of the Court or declare him to have been innocent or affect the record against him. Unlike a pardon, it is not an act of grace or of mercy, of clemency or leniency. The granting of parole is merely permission to a prisoner to serve a portion of his sentence outside the walls of the prison. He continues to be in the custody of the authorities, both legally and actually, and is still under restraint. The sentence is in full force and at any time he does not comply with the conditions upon which he is released, or does not want to conduct himself properly, he may be returned, for his own good and in the public interest.[2]

It has been pointed out that there is no similarity between pardon and parole, except that both involve release from an institution.[3] Release on parole is not based on any concept of clemency. Nor is it regarded as a lenient treatment of prisoners, even though they are released prior to the expiration of their sentence. Parole, as it functions today, is an integral part of the total correctional process. As such, it is a method of selectively releasing offenders from the institution and placing them under supervision in the community, whereby the community is afforded continuing protection while the offender is making adjustments and beginning to contribute to society.

Pardon

An executive act of clemency that absolves an individual from the legal consequences of a crime and conviction. A pardon is an act of grace or a remission of guilt. A *full* pardon freely and unconditionally absolves the party from the consequences of the crime and conviction. A *conditional* pardon becomes operative when the grantee has performed some specified act, or it becomes void after the occurrence of some specified event, or it remits only a portion of the penalties that are the legal consequences of a crime and conviction.

THE ORIGINS OF PAROLE

The English word *parole* is derived from the French *parole d'honneur*, meaning "word of honor." This choice of word was very unfortunate, inasmuch as most people would distrust a released prisoner's word of honor. It is not surprising, therefore, that the French themselves prefer the term *conditional liberation* to the one we borrowed from their language.

In penal philosophy, parole is a part of the general nineteenth-century trend in criminology from punishment to reformation. In 1791, during the French Revolution, the Comte de Mirabeau (Honoré-Gabriel Rigueti) anticipated modern penal theories when he published a report based on the idea of reformation and emphasizing the principles of labor, segregation, rewards under a mark system, conditional liberation, and aid on discharge.[4] Another Frenchman, Bonneville de Marsangy, public prosecutor of Versailles published a book in 1847 in which he discussed a pardoning power, conditional liberation, police supervision of discharged convicts, aid upon discharge, and rehabilitation. This book was distributed by the government to the members of both chambers of Parliament. In 1864, in a further work on this subject, he used the following simile in his argument for what is now called *parole:*

Parole d'honneur

French for "word of honor," from which the English word *parole* is derived.

As a skillful physician gives or withholds remedial treatment according as the patient is or is not cured, so ought the expiatory treatment imposed by law upon the criminal to cease when his amendment is complete; further his detention is inoperative for good, an act of inhumanity, and a needless burden to the state. Society should say to the prisoner, "Whenever you give satisfactory evidence of your genuine reformation, you will be tested, under the operation of a ticket of leave; thus the opportunity to abridge the term of your imprisonment is placed in your own hands."[5]

Parole, *as a practice*, originated almost simultaneously with three European prison administrators: A Spaniard, Montesinos; a German, Obermaier; and an Englishman, Maconochie.

Montesinos

In 1835, Col. Manuel Montesinos was appointed governor of the prison at Valencia, Spain, which held about 1,500 convicts. He organized the institution on the basis of semimilitary discipline and encouraged vocational training and primary education of the prisoners. The novelty of his plan was that there were practically no guards to watch the prisoners, who nevertheless, made few, if any, attempts to escape. The main reason for this was probably that each could earn a one-third reduction in the term of his sentence by good behavior and positive accomplishments. The number of recommitments while Montesinos was governor fell from 35 percent to "a figure which it would be imprudent to name, lest it should not be believed."

The law that allowed this program was subsequently repealed, and the system collapsed. Montesinos resigned, and in a pamphlet published in 1846 drew the following conclusions from his experiment:

What neither severity of punishment nor constancy in inflicting them can secure, the slightest personal interest will obtain. In different ways, therefore, during my command, I have applied this powerful stimulant; and the excellent results it has always yielded, and the powerful germs of reform which are constantly developed under its influence, have at length fully convinced me that the most inefficacious methods in the prison, the most pernicious and fatal to every chance of reform, are punishments carried to the length of harshness. The maxim should be constant and of universal application in such places, not to degrade further those who come to them already degraded by their crimes. Self-respect is one of the most powerful sentiments of the human mind, since it is the most personal; and he who will not condescend, in some degree, according to circumstances, to flattery of it, will never attain his object by any amount of chastisement; the effect of ill treatment being to irritate rather than to correct, and thus turns from reform instead of attracting to it. The moral object of penal establishments should not be so much to inflict punishment as to correct, to receive men idle and ill-intentioned and return them to society, if possible, honest and industrious citizens.[6]

Obermaier

When Georg Michael Obermaier became governor of a prison in Munich Germany, in 1842,[7] he found approximately 700 rebellious prisoners being kept in order by more than 100 soldiers. In a short time he gained the men's confidence, removed their chains, discharged nearly all of their guards, and appointed one of them superintendent of each of the industrial shops. His success in reforming prisoners was so great that reportedly only ten percent relapsed into crime after their discharge. He was aided by two favorable circumstances: many of the men were sentenced to simple imprisonment with no fixed term; and there was thorough supervision of discharged inmates by numerous prison aid societies.

Maconochie and Crofton

Chief credit for developing early parole systems, however, goes to Alexander Maconochie, who was in charge of the English penal colony at Norfolk Island, 1000 miles off the coast of Australia, and to Sir Walter Crofton, who was director of Ireland's prisons. Crofton refined the scheme originated by Maconochie into what is known today as the *ticket-of-leave,* or *Irish system.* Inasmuch as the earliest known plan of conditional liberation was used in the Australian convict colonies, and since present-day parole is closely linked to these experiments, their tragic history is worthy of consideration. We discuss this next.

TRANSPORTATION AND TICKET-OF-LEAVE

Transportation to America

The **transportation** of English criminals to the American colonies began in the early seventeenth century. The system evolved from a 1597 law that provides for the banishment of those who appear to be dangerous. As early as 1617, reprieves and stays of execution were granted to persons convicted of robbery who were strong enough to be employed in the colonies. The government devised a plan to transport convicted felons to the American colonies as a partial solution to the shortage of labor in the colonies and the poor economic conditions and widespread unemployment in England. The London, Virginia, and Massachusetts Companies and similar organizations supported the plan. The king approved the proposal to grant reprieves and stays of execution—pardons—to convicted felons who were physically able to be employed in the colonies.

Initially, no specific conditions were imposed on those receiving pardons. Consequently, many of them evaded transportation and returned to England before their terms expired, which made it necessary to impose certain restrictions on individuals who were granted pardons. About 1655, the form of pardon was amended to include specific conditions and to provide that the pardon would be nullified if the recipient failed to abide by the conditions.

Until 1717, the government had paid a fee to contractors for each prisoner transported. Under a new procedure adopted that year, the contractor was given "property in service," and the government took no interest in the welfare or behavior of the offender unless he or she violated the conditions of the pardon by returning to England before the sentence expired. Upon arrival

Transportation

The forced exile of convicted criminals. England *transported* convicted criminals to the American colonies until the Revolution and afterward, to Australia. The foundations of the transportation system are found in the law of 1597, 39 Eliz. c.4, "An Acte for Punyshment of Rogues, Vagabonds, and Sturdy Beggars." The act declared that obdurate idlers "shall . . . be banished out of this Realm . . . and shall be conveyed to such parts beyond the seas as shall be . . . assigned by the Privy Council."

in the colonies, the "services" of the prisoner were sold to the highest bidder, and thereafter the prisoner was an indentured servant.

The system of indenture dates to 1512, and it originally had no relation to persons convicted of crimes. It usually applied to the indenture of apprentices to masters for a number of years. The indenture consisted of a contract stipulating the conditions of the relationship and was somewhat similar to the parole agreement of today.

Transportation to Australia and Ticket-of-Leave

The Revolutionary War brought an end to the practice of transporting criminals to America, but the transportation law was not repealed. Detention facilities in England became overcrowded, resulting in a more liberal granting of pardons. During a serious crime wave, the English public demanded enforcement of the transportation law, and Australia was designated as a convict settlement, with the first shipload arriving there in January 1788. Transportation to Australia differed from transportation to the American colonies in that the government incurred all expenses of transportation and maintenance, and the prisoners remained under government control instead of being indentured. The governor was given "the property and service" for the prisoners, and he assigned them to the free settlers, who assumed the property and service agreement. As early as 1790, the governor of New South Wales had the right to grant conditional pardons. He could set the convicts free and give them grants of land, afterward even assigning newly arrived convict laborers to them. Such was the original **ticket-of-leave** system that was regulated by statute in 1834. Originally there were no provisions for governmental supervision of **ticket-of-leave men and women.**

In 1811, a policy was adopted that required prisoners to serve specific periods of time before becoming eligible to receive ticket-of-leave. Strict enforcement of the policy was not seen until 1821, when an eligibility scale was formulated. Prisoners serving a sentence of seven years became eligible for the ticket-of-leave after serving four years; those serving sentences of fourteen years, after serving six years; and those serving life sentences, after eight years.

In 1837, **Alexander Maconochie,** a former British naval captain and geographer, proposed to the House of Commons a system whereby the duration of the sentence would be determined not by time, but by the prisoner's industry and good conduct. He proposed a **mark system** by which "marks" or credits would be credited to the prisoner daily in accordance with the amount of labor performed and his or her conduct. His system saw the prisoners passing through a series of stages from strict imprisonment, through conditional release, to final and complete restoration of liberty, with promotions being based on marks accredited.

Maconochie was given the opportunity to test his "mark system" in 1840, when he was appointed governor of the notorious penal colony on **Norfolk Island,** a thousand miles off the eastern coast of Australia. Under his mark system there, prisoners were able to progress through stages of custody, each less restrictive than the previous one:

Ticket-of-leave

A license or permit given to a convict as a reward for good conduct, which allowed him to go at large and labor for himself before his sentence expired, subject to certain restrictions and revocable upon subsequent misconduct. A forerunner of parole.

Ticket-of-leave man

A convict who has obtained a ticket-of-leave.

Mark system

Credits for good behavior and hard work. In Alexander Maconochie's mark system on Norfolk Island, convicts could use the credits or *marks* to purchase either goods or time (reduction in sentence). In this system the prisoner progressed through stages from strict imprisonment, through conditional release, to final and complete restoration of liberty, with promotion being based on the marks accredited. One of the historical foundations of parole.

1. strict custody
2. labor in work gangs
3. freedom in certain areas of the island
4. conditional release—"ticket-of-leave"
5. complete freedom

Vocal and powerful detractors in Australia and in England railed against Maconochie's system, however. It was seen as "radical" and too "liberal" by many influential colonists in Australia, who believed that convicts should be kept in irons and not given any relief from their sentences. They lobbied the colonial governor of Van Dieman's Land (now Tasmania), who had appointed Maconochie to his post, for his dismissal. The governor was torn between his hope that Maconochie's experiment would succeed and his fear of the political power of the colonists who opposed the project. Finally, however, partly due to the controversy over his methods and partly because of pressure in England to cut the costs of the transportation system, Maconochie was dismissed in 1844, and the "noble experiment" came to an end.

As the free settlers in Australia increased in number, they protested the use of the country as a dumping ground for prisoners. In response to the protest, England initiated a selection system whereby prisoners would undergo an eighteen-month training program before being transported to Australia. The selection experiment failed, but it was the first use of trained, experienced individuals for selecting prisoners who have profited by a training program. Three prison commissioners were appointed to make the selections, which may well have set the precedent for the three-member parole boards later established by prison reformers in America. In 1867, transportation of prisoners to Australia was terminated.

England's Experience with Ticket-of-Leave

Although England did not stop transporting prisoners to Australia until 1867, the English Penal Servitude Act of 1853, pertaining to English and Irish prisoners, substituted imprisonment for transportation. In accordance with the act, prisoners sentenced to 14 years or less were to be committed to prison, but the judge was given the option of ordering transportation or imprisonment for prisoners with sentences of more than 14 years. The law also specified the length of time prisoners must remain incarcerated before becoming eligible for conditional release on ticket-of-leave. This act legalized the ticket-of-leave system.

Prisoners released on a ticket-of-leave in England were to be subject to three general conditions:

1. The power of revoking or altering the license of a convict will most certainly be exercised in the case of misconduct.
2. If, therefore, he wishes to retain the privilege, which by his good behavior under penal discipline he has obtained, he must prove by his subsequent conduct that he is really worthy of Her Majesty's clemency.
3. To produce a forfeiture of the license, it is by no means necessary that the holder should be convicted of a new offense. If he associates with notoriously bad characters, leads an idle or dissolute life, or has no visible means of

obtaining an honest livelihood, etc., it will be assumed that he is about to relapse into crime, and he will at once be apprehended and recommitted to prison under his original release.[8]

The British policy assumed that the prison program would be reformative; that the prisoners released on ticket-of-leave would have responded positively to prison training programs, and that those released would be adequately supervised. Such was not the case. The three years following the enactment of the Servitude Act saw an outbreak of serious crime attributed to a lack of supervision of the ticket-of-leave men. The British public thus came to regard the ticket-of-leave system as a menace to public safety and an absolute failure.

A series of prison riots in 1862, accompanied by another serious crime wave, again focused attention on prison administration and the ticket-of-leave system. A Royal Commission was appointed to investigate both areas. The commission's final report blamed poor training programs for the problems and gave the opinion that prisoners were released on ticket-of-leave without giving reliable evidence of their reformation. The Royal Commission's report resulted in policemen being given responsibility for supervising released prisoners. Later, a number of prisoners' aid societies, supported in part by the government, were established. These agencies aligned their methods of supervision with the method that had proven effective in Ireland.

SIR WALTER CROFTON AND THE IRISH SYSTEM OF TICKET-OF-LEAVE

Sir Walter Crofton, who had studied Maconochie's innovations on Norfolk Island, became the administrator of the Irish Prison System in 1854, one year after the Penal Servitude Act was passed. He believed that the intent of the law was to make the penal institution more than just a house of incarceration. Crofton felt that prison programs should be directed more toward reformation and that tickets-of-leave should be awarded only to prisoners who had shown definite achievement and positive attitude changes.

Under Crofton's administration, the **Irish system** became renowned for its three classes of penal servitude: strict imprisonment, indeterminate sentence, and ticket-of-leave. Each prisoner's classification was determined by the marks he or she had earned for good conduct and achievement in industry and education, a concept borrowed from Maconochie's experience on Norfolk Island. So-called indeterminate sentences were employed, and institutional conditions for this class were made as near to normal as possible, the restraint exercised over the prisoner being no more than what was required to maintain order. The ticket-of-leave system was different from the one in England. The general written conditions of the Irish ticket were supplemented with instructions designed for closer supervision and control and thus resembled the conditions of parole in the United States today.

Ticket-of-leave men and women residing in rural areas were under police supervision, but those living in Dublin were supervised by a civilian employee called the *Inspector of Released Prisoners.* These persons had the responsibility of securing employment for the ticket-of-leave man, visiting the residence, and verifying employment. It was the Inspector of Released Prisoners or the designated local police officer to whom the ticket-of-leave man periodically reported. The Irish system of ticket-of-leave had the confidence and support of the public and of the convicted criminal.

DEVELOPMENT OF PAROLE IN THE UNITED STATES

Three concepts underlie the development of parole in the United States: (1) a reduction in the length of incarceration as a reward for good conduct, (2) supervision of the parolee, and (3) imposition of the **indeterminate sentence.**

Release as a result of a reduction in the time of imprisonment was always accompanied by a written agreement in which the prisoner agreed to abide by the conditions specified by the authority authorizing the release. These documents would now be considered parole agreements. The agreement normally stipulated that any violation of the conditions would result in a return to the institution. The first legal recognition of shortening the term of imprisonment as a reward for good conduct in the United States was the 1817 "Good Time" Law in New York.

Supervision of those released from prison was originally accomplished by volunteers. Members of prison societies were also among the first volunteer supervisors of adult offenders. The Philadelphia Society for Alleviating the Miseries of Public Prisons recognized the importance of caring for released prisoners as early as 1822. In 1851, the society appointed two agents to assist those prisoners discharged from the Philadelphia County Prison and the penitentiary. The first public employees paid to assist released prisoners are believed to have been appointed by the State of Massachusetts in 1845.

Indeterminate sentence

A sentence to imprisonment in which the duration is not fixed by the court but is left to be determined by some other authority (typically a parole board or other agency) after some minimum period is served. The basis of parole.

Zebulon R. Brockway and the Elmira Reformatory

By 1865, American penal reformers were well aware of the reforms achieved by conditional-release programs in the European prison systems, particularly in the Irish system. As a result, an indeterminate sentence law was passed in Michigan in 1869 at the instigation of **Zebulon R. Brockway.** (This law was subsequently declared unconstitutional, however.) Brockway later became superintendent of the newly constructed Elmira Reformatory in New York and he succeeded in getting an indeterminate-sentence law adopted in that state in 1876. The first parole system in the United States had come into being.

The system established at Elmira included grading inmates on their conduct and achievement, compulsory education, and careful selection for parole. Volunteer citizens, known as *guardians,* supervised the parolees. A condition of parole was that the parolee report to the guardian the first day of each month. Written reports became required and they were submitted to the institution after being signed by the parolee's employer and guardian.

Parole legislation spread much more rapidly than did indeterminate-sentence legislation. By 1901, twenty states had parole statutes, but only eleven had indeterminate-sentence laws. By 1944, however, every U.S.

Reformatory at Elmira, New York

jurisdiction had adopted some form of parole release, and indeterminate sentencing had become the rule rather than the exception.[9]

Summary

Parole is different from other forms of release and community supervision, but yet the term *parole* is often used interchangeably with *probation, pardon,* and *mandatory release*. The misunderstanding and misapprehensions about parole today are to some extent due to this semantic confusion.

Parole has origins in the work of penal reformers in Germany, Spain, France, and on Norfolk Island in the early decades of the 19th century. The Norfolk Island experiments with "ticket-of-leave" and the "mark system" by a former British naval officer, Alexander Maconochie, constitute the origins of parole as we know it in the United States. Walter Crofton, head of the Irish Prison System, studied Maconochie's work on Norfolk Island and implemented his ideas in Ireland. Crofton's efforts were noticed by the U.S. prison reformer Zebulon R. Brockway, and Brockway adopted them in 1876 at the Elmira Reformatory in New York. This program was the first use of parole in the United States.

Endnotes

1. Claire Wilcox, *Theory of Parole,* (1927), p. 20; quoted in *Attorney General's Survey of Release Procedures; Parole,* vol. 4 (Washington: U.S. Department of Justice, 1939).
2. Warren F. Spaulding, *Proceedings,* American Prison Association, 1916, p. 548.
3. Justin Miller, "Evils of Confusion between Pardon and Parole," *Proceedings,* American Prison Association, 1932.
4. *Attorney General's Survey, supra* note 1, p. 6.

5. Quoted in Fredrick H. Wines, *Punishment and Reformation,* Crowell (1895), p. 219.

6. *Id.* at 194.

7. *Id.* at 195.

8. Parker, *Parole: Origins, Development, Current Practices, and Statutes,* American Correctional Association, Corrections—Parole-MDT-Project, resource document no. 1, 1972.

9. The historical discussions in this chapter relied on three documents: *Attorney General's Survey, supra* note 1; Charles L. Whitehead, *Adult Parole in Texas,* unpublished M.A. thesis (Huntsville, Texas: Sam Houston State University, May 1975); and Robert Hughes, *The Fatal Shore: The Epic of Australia's Founding* (New York: Vintage, 1986).

Discussion Questions

1. Define *parole* and *pardon,* and distinguish between them.

2. Distinguish between *parole, mandatory release,* and *probation.*

3. Discuss the founders of parole and their contributions.

4. What is the "mark system," and what is its relationship to the origins of parole?

5. What was a "ticket-of-leave," and what is its relationship to the origins of parole?

6. What was transportation? What is the connection between transportation and parole?

7. What were the five stages in Maconochie's mark system? How did his system differ from the English practice of ticket-of-leave?

8. How did parole develop in the United States? Be sure to include discussions of the Irish System, Zebulon Brockway, the Elmira Reformatory, and the indeterminate sentence in your explanation.

Alexander Maconochie and the Origins of Parole

ALEXANDER MACONOCHIE wanted to shift the focus of penology from punishment to reform. Of course, the state could and must punish crime, but punishment on its own, he argued, was a socially empty act without checks built into it: "Our penal science is . . . without precise rule, a mere balancing between conflicting impulses, severity for the supposed good of society on one hand, and leniency for the supposed good of the criminal on the other, in both frequently running into error." He saw no sense in punishing a criminal for his past while not training him with incentives for his future.

Because it was fixated on punishment alone, the Old System had produced mainly crushed, resentful, and embittered men and women in whom the spark of enterprise and hope was dead. So Maconochie argued. Exemplary punishment was only vindictive; it ran wild, degrading both convict and jailer. Terms like *mercy* and *remission of punishment* were to be dropped. "Let us offer our prisoners, not favors, but *rights*, on fixed and unalterable conditions."[25]

But how was this to be done? How to stop the corrosion of despair, the leakage of human possibility? Maconochie never claimed to be an original penal thinker, but he had what more "original" men like Jeremy Bentham lacked—firsthand experience of prison and humane understanding of its inmates. The basic idea for his system had first been raised by the Cambridge theologian William Paley in his *Moral and Political Philosophy* (1785). In this early Utilitarian text, Paley suggested that the punishment of criminals should be measured, not by raw time, but by work, "in order both to excite industry, and to render it more voluntary."

Within a few years, this idea of punishment by task and not by time was rooted in America. It found another advocate in Richard Whately, soon to be appointed Archbishop of Dublin. In the *London Review* in 1829, Whately urged that convicts be sentenced to give the state a measurable amount of labor in expiation of their sins, so that the quicker and better they worked, the sooner they would be free: "With each additional step they took on the treadmill they would be walking out of prison—by each additional cut of the spade they would be cutting a way to return to society."

Such ideas reached the Quaker missionaries James Backhouse and George Walker and went from them to Maconochie. They, too, advocated task rather than time punishment, and argued that, as most convicts were morally childish, the penal reformer might take a cue from the discipline of "enlightened" schools, which offered rewards for good conduct rather than punishment for bad. At each monthly muster, the diligent convict would get a "ticket," and the lazy would lose one or more; getting three tickets would shorten one's sentence by a month.

Such ideas of discipline by the carrot, not the stick, were the germ of Alexander Maconochie's "Mark System." Maconochie argued that sentences should be indefinite—no more stretches of seven, ten, fourteen years or life. Instead, the convicts would have to earn a certain number of "marks," or credits for good behavior and hard work, before they got free. Six thousand marks would be the equivalent of a seven-year sentence, seven thousand would correspond to ten years, ten thousand to life. They would buy their way out of prison with these marks. To buy, they must save.

Hence the length of his sentence was, within limits, up to the convict himself. Marks could be exchanged for either goods or time. The prisoner could buy "luxuries" with his marks from the jail administration—extra food, tobacco, clothing, and the like. They were "just wages, and will equally stimulate to care, exertion, economy, and fidelity." Maconochie hoped to abolish rations, "whose moral effect is always bad, by taking the care of a man's maintenance out of his own hands." Ideally, the convict would pay for everything beyond a bare subsistence diet of bread and water with the marks he earned.

Maconochie believed his Mark System would be objective. As things stood, prisoners were at the mercy of their overseers for "indulgences," which "corrupt and debilitate the mind." Official freedom to remit sentences led the convicts to lie and curry favor. It made them servile or evasive, and usually both. Only measurable actions could measure reform:

> The term "remission of sentence" should be banished. . . . There should, in truth, be none whatever; but the duration of the sentences being made measurable by conduct under them, and not by time at all . . . no power should anywhere even exist in a subordinate authority to remit a fraction of it; but on the other hand, there should not be less certainty in the result of good conduct. *The fate of every man should be placed unreservedly in his own hands. . . . There should be no favour anywhere.*

As soon as a convict entered the system, then, he would begin his Pilgrim's Progress with a short harsh stretch of confinement with hard labor and religious instruction. This was a moral aperient, punishment for the past.

The next phase, rehabilitation, for the future, would begin with his advance through the stages of the Mark System, where everything he had was bought with his labor and obedience, translated into marks and entered in the commandant's incorruptible ledgers. As the convict's behavior improved and the moral lesson of the Mark System—nothing for nothing—sank in, so his environment altered by stages: first, solitary or separate imprisonment; then, "social labor" through the day and separate confinement at night; next, "social treatment both day and night"; and so on. He rose from one grade to the next automatically, with no interference from commandant or magistrates, depending on his total credit of marks. Some, of course, would slide back, losing marks or wasting them, which only reinforced the metaphor of real life. However, just as there would be no favors under Maconochie's system, so the only punishment would be the loss of marks—the mild, inescapable, all-seeing accountancy that drew its attentive parallels between time and money, units of labor and moral worth.

Once the prisoner was trained to see the relation between morality and self-interest, he stood ready for the third stage of the Mark System: group therapy. Maconochie wanted to put "developed" prisoners in groups of six. They would work together and mess together. Each man in the group would be responsible for the marks of others as well as his own. If one backslid and lost marks, all would. In this way the prisoners would learn mutual dependence and social responsibility.

Nobody in England or America, let alone penal Australia, had tried such therapies on convicts before. This idea of prison as a moral hospital would not win full acceptance until well into the twentieth century. The details of Maconochie's system—that prisoners should have direct access to the commandant, through an ombudsman, for instance, or that officials should take a personal interest in individual convicts—were a century ahead of their time.

SOURCE: Excerpted from The Fatal Shore by Robert Hughes copyright © 1985 by Robert Hughes. Reprinted by permission of Alfred A. Knopf, Inc.

PAROLE IN TRANSITION

Medical model

The concept that given proper care and treatment, criminals can be changed into productive, law-abiding citizens. This approach suggests that people commit crimes due to influences beyond their control, such as poverty, injustice, and racism. Also called the *rehabilitation model.*

Indeterminate sentence

A sentence imposed by a court that specifies a minimum and maximum period of imprisonment, the exact length of the term being fixed by action of exective authority (usually a parole board) at a later time.

PAROLE AND THE MEDICAL MODEL

For fifty years, the predominant goal of corrections has been to rehabilitate the offender. This **rehabilitative ideal,** the so-called **medical model,** assumed that criminal behavior had its roots in environmental and psychosocial aspects of the offender's life and that corrections could, in fact, correct it. Inherent within the medical model of corrections is the **indeterminate sentence** and the concept of parole. Indeterminacy of sentencing provides the flexibility and discretion for the rehabilitative ideal to function. The judge at the time of sentencing can "tailor-make" a sentence to the particular needs of the offender and provide, by means of an indeterminate sentence, an opportunity for release at the optimum time in the rehabilitative process. The release decision is thus shared between the court, which sets a minimum and a maximum period of incarceration, and the correctional system—typically a parole board. The parole board's responsibility is to determine, with the assistance of prison authorities, the optimal release moment—the time at which the inmate is most ready to reenter the community as a responsible citizen.

This philosophy assumes that correctional specialists have the ability to diagnose an offender's problems and develop a means of curing those problems. Since one cannot know at the time of "diagnosis" how long it will take to effect a "cure," the indeterminate sentence makes it possible, in theory at least, to confine an offender as long as is necessary and to follow up that confinement with community supervision.

Indeterminate Sentencing

Through almost consensual use of indeterminate sentencing in the United States since the middle 1930s, parole has played a major role in the U.S. correctional system. Once an offender is sentenced to prison, it is largely the parole authorities who determine when he or she will be released and under what conditions, and whether his/her conduct after release warrants continued freedom or imprisonment.

The motives behind the development of parole were varied. They were partly humanitarian, to offer some mitigation of lengthy sentences; partly to control in-prison behavior by holding out the possibility of early release; and partly rehabilitative, since supervised reintegration into the community is more effective and safer than simply opening the gates. (See Chapter 8, History and Concept of Parole.)

Changing Public Opinion

Although parole has generally drawn support from many sources and has a history of consensual acceptance, it has occasionally been subject to vigorous criticism and reexamination. In the early twentieth century, particularly after World War I, parole administration came under attack. Critics claimed that parole was not fulfilling its promise. Antiparole groups believed that parole release was used primarily as a means of controlling inmates and that it failed to produce the desired lasting changes in their behavior and attitudes. This was a severe criticism at a time of increasing acceptance of the "rehabilitative ideal" with its emphasis on treatment and cure in criminal corrections.[1]

Other critics of the system pointed out that release was granted after only a cursory review of the inmates' records and that paroling authorities had no criteria by which to measure rehabilitation and on which to base release decisions.

These criticisms led to two major changes in parole administration and organization. First, more emphasis was placed on postrelease supervision, and the number of parole conditions was increased. Second, there was a shift in parole authority from prison personnel to parole boards with independent authority and statewide jurisdiction.[2]

By the mid 1930s the parole system's continuance as a viable part of the justice system again was being scrutinized. The Attorney General's Survey of Release Procedures, a monumental study of the correctional process, was established to review the efficacy of parole. The survey report stated:

> While there has never been a time when the functions and purpose of parole have been clearly understood, at no period has the entire institution been the object of so much controversy and attack or viewed with as much suspicion by the general public as it has been during the past four or five years.[3]

Mounting prison populations and rising recidivism rates aggravated the general uneasiness concerning early release via parole. Questions involving the value of rehabilitation as a goal of corrections arose, and without the philosophical underpinnings of reform and rehabilitation as purposes of punishment, parole has no function in the criminal justice system.

Both the concept of rehabilitation and the practice of parole survived the criticism, and in 1940, President Franklin D. Roosevelt declared, "We know from experience that parole, when it is honestly and expertly managed, provides better protection for society than does any other method of release from prison."[4]

Perhaps a bit optimistically, New York Parole Commissioner (later, Director of the U.S. Bureau of Prisons) Sanford Bates, in a 1941 speech entitled "The Next Hundred Years," stated:

> Parole, as a method of release, will soon have become an indispensable part of this correctional process. We shall speak more accurately of *subjecting* a prisoner to parole than of *granting* him parole. We shall learn to speak of recidivists not as parole failures, but as unreformed inmates. We shall not shrink from the word, *parole*, as something involving weakness or venability, but shall recognize institution aftercare and supervision as a necessary sequel to a prison term. *Nevermore shall we talk about abolishing parole* any more than about abolishing police or commitment or discipline. [Emphasis added.][5]

Thus the "medical" model of corrections was born during these years of the late 1930s and early 1940s. This rehabilitative ideal viewed corrections as corrective and reformative, as opposed to punitive.

The years between World War II and 1970 saw the advent and development of classification systems, vocational training, academic training, group and individual therapy, conjugal visitation in some prisons, work release, and numerous other reforms. By 1967 (at the height of the reformative era), a

Halfway house for recent parolees.

Harris Poll of a nationwide sample found that 77 percent of the population believed that prisons should be *mainly corrective,* while only 11 percent believed they should be *mainly punitive.*[6] The belief that criminals could be changed if they were given the opportunity and if sufficient skills, funds, and personnel were available, was the central philosophy of the rehabilitative model of corrections. Parole was once again considered a viable and necessary aspect of the American system of corrections.

A Philosophical Change

In the middle 1970s, with a suddenness remarkable in social change, there was a dramatic turnabout. Individualism, rehabilitation, sentence indeterminacy, and parole all seemed to fall from grace and, indeed, appeared to be on their way out.[7] By 1978, a Law Enforcement Assistance Administration publication stated: "One of the movements we are currently witnessing in the criminal justice field is the trend toward the establishment of **determinate** or 'fixed' **sentencing** of criminal offenders."[8]

The correctional system's failure to reduce the steadily increasing crime rate and its obvious inability to reduce recidivism, rehabilitate offenders, or make predictive judgments about offenders' future behavior brought about public disillusionment, disappointment, and resentment. The pendulum began to

Determinate sentence

A sentence to imprisonment for a fixed period of time as specified by statute; also known as *flat, fixed,* or *straight* sentence.

208

swing, and by the late 1970s it seemed to have moved 180 degrees from the rehabilitative ideal to the "just deserts" approach to criminal correction.

In contrast to the rehabilitative ideal, the **just deserts** or **justice model** denies the efficacy of rehabilitation and changes the focus of the system from the offender to the offense. The September 1977 issue of *Corrections Magazine,* for example, was devoted to the debate regarding the justice model and determinate sentencing. Even a brief review of the contents of this journal indicates that determinate sentencing and the abolition of parole were embraced by liberals and conservatives alike. Prison reformers and police chiefs seemed to be in almost complete agreement.

The general aim of those favoring determinate sentencing was to abolish, or at least to tightly control, discretion. This included the discretion of the prosecutor to choose charges and plea-bargain, the discretion of judges to choose any sentence within a broad range of time, the discretion of prison administrators to decide what kind of treatment a prisoner needed in order to become law-abiding, and the discretion of parole boards to release or not to release prisoners without having to justify their decision or render their decisions consistent. Determinate sentencing was the reformers' answer to this problem.[9] The proposals of the mid 1970s called for clear, certain, uniform penalties for all crimes, either through legislative action or the promulgation of guidelines to which prosecutors, judges, and parole boards would be required to adhere.

Just deserts

The concept that the goal of corrections should be to punish offenders because they *deserve* to be punished, and that punishment should be commensurate with the seriousness of the offense.

Justice model

The correctional practice based on the concept of "just deserts." The justice model calls for fairness in criminal sentencing, in that all persons convicted of a like offense will receive a like sentence. Prisons are viewed as a place of even-handed punishment, not rehabilitation. This model of corrections relies on determinate sentencing and abolition of parole.

ORIGINS OF MODERN CONCEPTS OF DETERMINACY

Where did all this talk of determinate sentencing begin? John Irwin, an ex-prisoner and now an author and college professor, contends that inmates themselves, particularly inmates in California prisons in the 1960s, were the original advocates of determinacy.[10] California, Irwin believes, had the most indeterminate of all indeterminate sentencing structures and a parole board that was very "stingy with its favors." The situation in California prisons prompted the formation of a working group of the American Friends Service Committee, which produced the book *Struggle for Justice* in 1971. In it the group denounced the very existence of U.S. prisons as well as the rehabilitative model of corrections, declaring coercion of prisoners for any purpose to be immoral. Although *Struggle for Justice* declared that all prisons should be shut down, it recognized that such a proposal was unrealistic. The book declared that the least that should be done was to repeal all indeterminate sentencing laws and design a system in which offenders convicted of similar crimes served roughly equal terms in prison.

David Greenberg, one of the primary authors of *Struggle for Justice,* was also a member of a group called the Committee for the Study of Incarceration. Together with Andrew von Hirsch, the committee's executive director, Greenberg persuaded the committee that the most important subject to study was not the conditions of incarceration, but the haphazard and irrational manner in which offenders ended up—or did not end up—in prison, and the equally chaotic system of release. The committee's final report was published in 1976 under the title *Doing Justice: The Choice of Punishments.* Written by von Hirsch, it was a heavily philosophical monograph whose thesis was that the motives underlying the treatment of criminal offenders at the time were all wrong.

The principal goals of the correctional system at the time were to rehabilitate and restrain offenders based on predictions of their future criminality or dangerousness. As a result, the sanctions prescribed for particular crimes had little to do with the severity of criminal behavior. In fact, large numbers of widely disparate crimes were often punished with the same indeterminate term, with the actual setting of a release date left to parole boards, which made judgments about particular offenders' potential rehabilitation and dangerousness.

Doing Justice pointed out that the goal of sentencing should be to punish offenders, that it is proper to punish the criminal because he or she "deserves" to be punished, and that each punishment should be commensurate with the gravity of the last offense or series of offenses. The committee recommended the adoption of a **presumptive sentence** for each crime or category of crimes, with the presumptive sentences graded according to the severity of the crime. The severity of the crime would be graded on two scales: the harm done by the offense, and the offender's culpability. The judgment of the degree of culpability would be based partly on the offender's prior record. The reasoning behind this was that a succession of criminal acts would imply calculation or deliberate defiance of the law, thus making the offender more culpable for the current offense.

Having proposed punishment as the main goal of sentencing, the committee then ruled out prison as the punishment for all but the most serious offenses, those in which bodily harm is threatened or done to the victim. The committee proposed alternatives such as periodic imprisonment, increased use of fines, and other lesser sanctions. In those cases where prison is deemed necessary, the committee recommended that no prison sentence exceed five years except in some murder cases.

At about the same time *Doing Justice* was making the academic rounds, another determinate sentencing model was published in David Fogel's book *". . . We are the Living Proof . . ." The Justice Model for Corrections*. Fogel, former Minnesota Commissioner of Corrections, former head of the Illinois Law Enforcement Commission, and then a university professor, is considered by many the "father of determinate sentencing." As early as 1970, he had been actively urging a narrowing of sentencing and parole discretion and had been among the most influential of the determinate-sentencing advocates in the drafting of legislation in various states.

One of the main goals of Fogel's sentencing reforms was to humanize the internal operation of correctional institutions by extending much more freedom to inmates and "unhooking" their release date from their progress or participation in programs. He advocated the abolition of parole boards and the establishment of "flat-time" sentencing—a single sentence for each class of felonies that could be altered slightly if there were aggravating or mitigating circumstances.[11]

In June 1977, then University of Chicago Law School Dean Norval Morris, speaking at a symposium on criminal sentencing, addressed the issues of determinacy and parole by asking, "Should the indeterminacy of parole discretion be preserved?" Morris responded to the six most common justifi-

Presumptive sentence

A statutorily determined sentence convicted offenders will *presumably* receive if convicted. Offenders convicted in a jurisdiction with presumptive sentences will be assessed this sentence unless mitigating or aggravating circumstances are found to exist.

cations for the parole board, rather than the judge, fixing the precise release date; that the parole board is able to:

1. find the optimum moment for release;
2. provide an incentive for rehabilitation;
3. facilitate prison control and discipline;
4. share sentencing responsibility to maximize deterrence while reducing the time served;
5. control the size of the prison population; and
6. rectify unjust disparity in sentencing.[12]

Morris stated that the first justification—the parole board's ability to predict the optimum moment for release—has repeatedly failed to be proved empirically. The second justification, provision of an incentive for the offender's rehabilitation, has as its net effect the reliance on compulsory rehabilitation in the prison setting. "This type of coerced curing of crime is ineffective," Morris said, "and is wasteful of resources. We don't know enough to make that second purpose work." The third justification, facilitating prison control and discipline, is an important, latent, pragmatic justification of parole, but it is vulnerable to attack on grounds of injustice. The fourth claimed justification of parole is the sharing of sentencing responsibility between the court and the parole board in order to maximize deterrence. Although it is true that parole allows for judicial pronouncements of larger punishments that are in fact served, the charade, Morris claims, is so well known that court systems compensate for it. Judges and juries (where jury sentencing is applicable) routinely take parole laws into consideration when handing down sentences, knowing that, in most cases, the offender will serve less time than the sentence publicly announced. There still exists the question, however, of whether the parole experience has increased or reduced times served in the United States. The fifth justification, the ability to control the prison population, has occasionally been useful. Generally speaking, however, in times of community anxiety about crime and the pressures for law and order, there has been great pressure on the parole boards to be more conservative in granting parole. When this has occurred, parole boards, rather than attempting to solve the problem by releasing more prisoners, have compounded the problem by tightening requirements for parole. To the last claimed justification of parole, that of rectifying unjust sentencing disparities, Morris responds:

> In Illinois, and I believe the same is true in many states, crime for crime and criminal for criminal, sentences imposed by courts in Chicago are subsequently less severe than those imposed in downstate, small-town, and rural areas. The Illinois Parole Board, not incorrectly, in my view, exercises its releasing discretion so as to minimize the grosser disparities—it moves toward a regression to the mean.[13]

A question arises, however; should we not develop other mechanisms for serving that purpose in place of parole? Morris believes we should, and he views the ultimate abolition of parole as inevitable. What alternatives are available, and what problems do these alternatives pose?

The trend of the 1978 symposium and of the public attitude prevalent at the time seemed inevitably to point to increasing determinacy in sentencing and ultimately to abolishing parole as a release mechanism. However, many theorists of the sentence reform movement urged caution before abolishing parole outright and instituting "real time" sentences in its place. In the book *The Question of Parole,* Andrew von Hirsch and Kathleen Hanrahan warned:

> Our culture has historically thought of prison time in huge quantities, and this has made it harder to justify the more modest actual confinements meted out by parole boards. The long-run objective should be the creation of a system that speaks in terms of moderate real sentences and banishes the long, fictional prison terms— through a gradual, slow phase-out of parole release.[14]

Their message was not heeded. Between 1976 and 1982, at least fifteen states passed determinate sentencing legislation. Other states increased penalties, passed mandatory sentencing, and career-criminal laws. One observer wrote, "Even though no model came to predominate, the impact on parole, especially discretionary parole release, was dramatic."[15] In some states both parole release and postrelease supervision were abandoned. In other states, parole release was abandoned but supervision was retained. In still other states, parole guidelines were established to reduce and structure release decision making.

Parole, however, did not disappear from the correctional scene. Indeed, in most states today, the parole board retains the power to alter the amount of time served in prison by releasing prisoners to community supervision before the completion of the maximum sentence. The legislature has limited the releasing power of the parole board in some jurisdictions by requiring that prisoners serve a flat minimum or some proportion of the maximum sentence before becoming eligible for parole. In other jurisdictions, parole board discretion is extensive—relatively unconstrained by law or not constrained at all.

At this writing, forty-one states and the federal system allow the parole board some discretion in the release of prisoners. The *American Corrections Association's Standards* continues to consider parole the preferred release mechanism and to recommend that such power be given to:

> . . . [a] single authority provided by statute which has parole decision-making power with respect to all offenders convicted of a felony who are sentenced to a term of imprisonment and are eligible for discretionary parole.[16]

The very active movement toward determinacy and abolition of parole lost momentum in the 1980s, but by no means disappeared. By 1990, twelve states had abolished parole or severely curtailed its discretionary power (California, Colorado, Connecticut, Delaware, Florida, Illinois, Indiana, Maine, Minnesota, New Mexico, North Carolina, and Washington). In addition, the U.S. Parole Commission was abolished (to be phased out by 1992) by the Comprehensive Crime Control Act of 1984. In these jurisdictions parole was replaced by some type of determinate sentencing scheme. Prisoners receive fixed sentences, which they must serve in full, minus any reductions for good behavior.

Parole boards in most jurisdictions, continue to handle revocations, and in some jurisdictions, they also handle good-time decisions. Discretionary paroling may continue in these jurisdictions to a limited extent, for persons sentenced to life imprisonment, persons sentenced before the current structure went into effect, or for youthful offenders.

A Reprieve and a New Role for Parole

The abolition of discretionary parole release did not prove to be the panacea some had expected. During the 1970s and 1980s the nation's prison population grew dramatically—partly fueled by the reduction in parole discretion and the harsher sentences that came with determinate and mandatory sentencing. In 1970, there were 196,429 prisoners in state and federal prisons, with the rate of incarceration at 96 per 100,000. By 1980 the rate of incarceration had risen to 139 per 100,000. By June 30, 1990, the U.S. prison population had reached 755,425, and the incarceration rate was 289 per 100,000—a 300 percent increase since 1970.[17] Table 9–1 documents this trend.

In some jurisdictions the rapid increase in prison populations brought about a reappraisal of the abolition decision. Since 1976, Maine has had to build four new prisons to handle the increased population resulting from parole abolition. Other states have faced similar problems. Idaho adopted a hybrid scheme that permitted judges to impose either *fixed* sentences with no parole eligibility or indeterminate sentences, with the parole board setting release dates.[18] The U.S. Parole Commission, scheduled to be phased out by 1992, was given an "extension" until 1997. In 1985, Colorado reinstated parole, six years after abolition. North Carolina, which had placed severe limitations of the use of parole, has since allowed more discretion. Florida,

TABLE 9–1

Prisoners in State Institutions and on Release

YEAR	TOTAL Prison Population	Releases	Parole	PERCENTAGE Mandatory Release	Expiration of Term	Other
1975	240,593	106,742	68.3	5.1	19.1	7.5
1976	262,833	106,928	68.9	5.8	19.2	6.0
1977	278,141* 285,456*	115,213	71.9	5.9	16.1	6.1
1978	294,396	119,796	70.4	5.8	17.0	6.8
1979	301,470	128,954	60.2	16.9	16.3	6.7
1980	329,821	136,968	57.4	19.5	14.9	8.2
1981	369,930	142,489	54.6	21.4	13.9	10.1
1982	413,806	157,144	51.9	24.4	14.4	9.3
1983	437,248	191,237	48.1	26.9	16.1	8.9
1984	464,567	191,499	46.0	28.7	16.3	9.0
1985	502,507	203,895	43.2	30.8	16.9	.1
1986	545,133	230,672	43.2	31.1	14.8	10.8
1987	581,609	270,506	40.6	31.2	16.2	12.0
1988	627,402	301,378	40.3	30.6	16.8	12.3
1989	633,787	364,434	39.1	30.5	16.0	14.4
1990	690,157	394,682	40.5	29.6	13.1	16.8

Source: Adapted from A. Keith Bottomley, "Parole in Transition," in Michael Tonry and Norval Morris, eds. *Crime and Justice: A Review of Research*, vol. 12 (Chicago: University of Chicago Press, 1990). p. 343.

*Before 1977, only prisoners in the *custody* of state and federal correctional institutions were counted; after 1977, all prisoners under state and federal *jurisdictions* were counted. Both figures are given to facilitate comparison.

which adopted sentencing guidelines in 1983 and abolished parole, recently returned the function under a new name, *Controlled Release Authority.*[19]

Prison Population Control

Parole boards have always been the "back door-keeper" of America's prisons, often serving as the operators of safety valves to relieve crowded institutions.[20] Although this function is not consistent with the philosophy of parole as a tool of rehabilitation, and most paroling authorities do not believe that the management of prison populations is (or should be) their primary responsibility,[21] it has become a *de facto,* if not a *de jure* function. Recent years, however, have witnessed an institutionalization of this function. In a report for the National Institute of Corrections, Peggy Burke noted:

> There is no longer any question of whether paroling authorities will become involved in population issues, but rather . . . when.[22]

Some states have given legislative authority and direction to their parole boards to control prison populations. Others have done so through informal agreements among the governor, the director of corrections, and the parole board. Boards in states such as Michigan, Georgia, and Texas have become actively involved in prison population management out of necessity; prison populations in those states had risen to levels that threatened the correctional authorities' ability to maintain control of their institutions. In Georgia the governor cited an "atmosphere of tension, and potentially explosive violence."[23] Federal court orders established "caps" on the prison populations in Texas and Michigan. Through a variety of formal and informal methods, parole boards in each of these jurisdictions have been utilized in efforts to reduce and maintain the prison population, with varying and arguable degrees of success.

Most authorities agree, however, that it is not feasible, in the long term, to control prison populations by parole-board action. The reductions achieved in those states that so use their paroling power, are at best, temporary—and have often achieved those results to the detriment of effective postrelease supervision due to escalating caseloads. In their report on the ACA Parole Task Force survey, Rhine, Smith, and Jackson concluded that where parole boards are used as the "backdoor" for overcrowded prisons, the population crisis is often simply transferred from the institutional component of corrections to the community component. They report that many jurisdictions have increased and expanded community correctional facilities—such as halfway houses, work release centers, house arrest-electronic monitoring, and intensive supervision—to monitor the offenders who are granted early release. Furthermore,

> In some states the continuing escalation in prison populations has had another, albeit unanticipated effect on the ability of parole officers to revoke parole for anything other than serious criminal violations. In Georgia and Texas, parole officers have experienced difficulty in revoking parolees for technical violations of the conditions of supervision, even when there are indications of deteriorating behavior on the part of the parolee. In 1984, approximately 52 percent of those revoked in Texas represented technical violators. . . . In 1988 this figure fell to less than 5 percent.[24]

POSTRELEASE SUPERVISION

Postrelease supervision has been maintained in most jurisdictions, even in those states that have effectively abolished the parole board's discretion in release decisions. Only a very few jurisdictions have abolished postrelease supervise altogether. Others have limited postrelease supervision to a short period after release, generally one to three years.

Kevin Krajick points out that in Maine and Connecticut, many judges, unhappy with the abolition of postrelease supervision, began sentencing large numbers of prisoners to **split sentences**—that is, terms of jail or imprisonment to be followed by probation—in an effort to assure that inmates would not be released without some kind of supervision.[25] In Maine, the proportion of split sentences has doubled since the abolition of parole supervision.[26]

This means of circumventing the legislation was forecast by former U.S. Parole Board Chairman Maurice Sigler in 1975 when he spoke of the criminal justice system as having "hydraulic properties."[27] Sigler stated that "when discretion is artificially compressed at one level of the system, it is increased at another level in order that the decision makers, be they policemen, prosecutors, judges, or parole boards, are capable of individualizing justice and reducing injustice caused by ill-conceived laws."[28] Sigler spoke of a state that had introduced a mandatory sentence for nighttime burglary. Within the next year the filings by police and prosecutors for daytime burglary had increased by 90 percent, and nighttime burglary had all but disappeared. Had the burglars, in response to the new legislation, changed their nocturnal habits, or were the police and prosecutors maintaining their discretion by filing the cases as daytime burglary? The danger in such a situation is that the discretion, formerly out in the open, becomes less visible and not subject to scrutiny.

The supervision component was retained in other states that abolished parole by allowing release dates to be determined by **good-time** laws, with supervision for the period of the sentence. At the federal level, the Sentencing Reform Act (1987), which implemented sentencing guidelines and paved the way for the abolition of parole, created a new form of postrelease supervision, **supervised release.** Courts may impose a term of supervised release as a part of a sentence that includes imprisonment at the time of the initial sentencing. Unlike parole, supervised release does not replace a portion of the sentence of imprisonment. Rather, it orders supervision in addition to any term of imprisonment. The conditions of supervised release are the same as those of probation or parole.[29]

GOOD-TIME POLICIES

Most of the new laws have retained policies for **good time,** which award prisoners days off their minimum or maximum terms for maintaining good behavior or participating in various prison activities or programs. The amount of "good time" that can be accrued varies widely among states—ranging from 5 days to *more than 30 days per month* off an inmate's time in prison. Because a good-time policy can result in major reductions of sentenced terms, it can be a real incentive for cooperative behavior.

Good time

Reduction in sentence for institutional good conduct.

Good-time policies are written into many states' statutes, but they may also be nonstatutory, systemwide correctional policies. Good-time is typically awarded and administered by a state's department of corrections or by individual prison wardens. Typically, this credit is automatically awarded and subtracted from a prisoner's sentenced term at the time of prison entry and then rescinded in whole or in part for unsatisfactory behavior. In Oregon, good-behavior credit is subtracted from the maximum sentence and does not affect a prisoner's parole eligibility date or actual time served unless the prisoner is not paroled and serves the maximum term. More typically, however, the minimum sentence is reduced by good time, so that good-time policies are a significant element in prison-term length. This is particularly true in states that have eliminated discretionary parole release.

A few states award good-time credit in ways that do not reduce sentence length. In New Hampshire, for example, a number of disciplinary days are automatically added to the minimum term, and it is from this number that good-behavior days are subtracted. If the prisoner accrues all of his or her "good time," the disciplinary days will cancel out, and the parole eligibility date will occur, as scheduled, on the completion of the minimum sentence. Otherwise, the prisoner is penalized by a delay in the eligibility date.

Good-time reductions based on prisoners' positive actions are in effect in thirty-three states and the federal system. These reductions result from participating in various programs (such as work, school, rehabilitative counseling, medical research, or blood donation) or from meritorious conduct (including success under minimum security). In January 1983, the California Department of Corrections eliminated automatic time off for good behavior; prisoners sentenced after that date must earn all their good-time credit through work or school participation.

SUMMARY

Although the 1990s finds the criminal justice system embroiled in controversy, engaged in self-examination, and subjected to scrutiny by the public and the courts, the issues involved—prison overcrowding, the efficacy of probation and parole, sentencing disparity, parole-release decision making, and indeed, the very continued existence of parole–are not new, and neither are the proposed solutions. The inertia of the criminal justice system is as great as is its failure to learn the lessons of history.

More than a century ago, the leading penologists of the time met in Cincinnati to form the National Prison Association, now the American Correctional Association. The main objective of that first meeting in 1870 was to attempt to resolve the conflict between those who advocated the punishment-centered Pennsylvania and Auburn Prison Systems and those who advocated a progressive, new system recently imported from Ireland. The new system, which appealed to progressive prison administrators, had three main factors: trade training, the indeterminate sentence, and parole.

What emerged was the remarkable "Declaration of Principles," a blueprint for the future of U.S. corrections. The concepts of vocational training, indeterminate sentencing, and parole were established, and for the most part embraced by the leadership of the newly emerging discipline of corrections.

Since that time, these same issues have been scrutinized, rejected, embraced, modified, codified, outlawed, and reincarnated under new labels. Over a period of fifty years, Presidential commissions have alternatively recommended the extension of parole and indeterminacy of sentencing and the outright abolition of the same. The optimal solution is not yet at hand. History has taught us that all too often the unanticipated and unintended consequences of reform have aggravated, rather than mitigated the problems they sought to solve. Prudence in reform efforts is advisable, and such lessons as can be learned from past efforts should be carefully evaluated.

ENDNOTES

1. Lawrence F. Travis III and Vincent O'Leary, *Changes in Sentencing and Parole Decision Making, 1976–1978* (Washington: National Institute of Corrections, 1979). A publication of the National Parole Institutes and Parole Policy Seminars.

2. *Id.* at 6.

3. *Attorney General's Survey of Release Procedures: Parole,* vol. 4 (Washington: U.S. Department of Justice, 1939).

4. Quoted by Sanford Bates in his speech, "The Next Hundred Years," at the Thirty-Fifth Annual Conference of the National Probation Association, Atlantic City, N.J., 1941.

5. Sanford Bates, then Commissioner of Parole for the State of New York, became the Director of the U.S. Bureau of Prisons. Bates reorganized the Bureau of Prisons, introduced psychologists and psychiatrists into the system, and is often recognized as the father of "the new prison."

6. "Harris Poll," *Los Angeles Times,* Aug. 14, 1967.

7. National Advisory Commission on Criminal Justice Standards and Goals, *A National Strategy to Reduce Crime* (Washington: Law Enforcement Assistance Administration, 1973).

8. *Id.*

9. David B. Griswold and Michael D. Wiatrowski, "The Emergence of Determinate Sentencing," *Federal Probation,* June 1983.

10. Reported in Michael S. Serrill, "Determinate Sentencing: The History, the Theory, the Debate," *Corrections Magazine,* September 1977. The foregoing material on the history of the determinate sentencing movement drew liberally from this excellent paper.

11. David Fogel, *". . . We are the Living Proof . . ." The Justice Model for Corrections,* 2nd ed. (Cincinnati: Anderson Publishing Company, 1979).

12. "Conference Takes a Hard Look at Proposals," *Corrections Magazine,* September 1977, pp. 65–66.

13. *Id.* at 67.

14. Andrew von Hirsch and Kathleen Hanrahan, *The Question of Parole: Retention, Reform, or Abolition?* (Cambridge, Mass: Ballinger Publishing, 1981), p. 81

15. Edward E. Rhine, William R. Smith, and Ronald W. Jackson, *Paroling Authorities: Recent History and Current Practice* (Laurel, Md.: American Correctional Association, 1991), p. 25.

16. American Correctional Association, *supra,* at XIX.

17. Rhine et al., *supra,* at 26.

18. A. Keith Bottomley, "Parole in Transition: A Comparative Study of Origins, Developments, and Prospects for the 1990s," in Michael Tonry and Norval Morris, eds., *Crime and Justice: A Review of Research,* vol. 12. (Chicago: The University of Chicago Press, 1990). p. 342.

19. Rhine et al., *supra*, at 26.

20. *Id.* at 27.

21. Rhine et al. (*supra*, at 96), reporting on the ACA Parole Task Force survey, stated: "Regardless of the pressure to release, most parole board chairs surveyed by the Task Force do not believe that the management of prison population levels should be an important responsibility of parole boards."

22. Peggy B. Burke, *Current Issues in Parole Decision Making: Understanding the Past, Shaping the Future* (Washington: National Institute of Corrections, 1988), pp. 31–32.

23. Cited in Rhine et al., *supra*, at 90.

24. *Id.* at 97–98.

25. Kevin Krajick, "Abolishing Parole: An Idea Whose Time Has Passed," *Corrections Magazine*, June 1983.

26. *Id.*

27. Maurice Sigler, "Abolish Parole?" in speech at Law Day convocation, Culver–Stockton College, Canton, Missouri, May 1975.

28. *Id.*

29. 18 U.S.C. § 3583 (e) (3).

Discussion Questions

1. Discuss the "medical model" of corrections. How do parole and indeterminacy relate to this model?

2. Why did the medical model fall out of favor? What factors were associated with this phenomenon?

3. What is the "justice model" of corrections? What factors were associated with its emergence in the 1970s?

4. What happened to parole under the justice model? Why?

5. How and why did parole acquire a new role in the 1980s and 1990s? What is that role? How do you feel about this new role?

THE PAROLE BOARD AND PAROLE SELECTION

KEY TERMS

Paroling Authority
Institutional model of
    organization
Autonomous model of
    organization
Consolidation model of
    organization
Parole guidelines
Graduated release
Parole eligibility
Salient Factor Score
"Guiding principles"
Grace or privilege theory
Continuing custody theory
Parens patriae
Liberty interest

Paroling authority

An administrative body (usually 3–19 members) empowered to decide whether inmates shall be conditionally released from prison before the completion of their sentence, to revoke parole, and to discharge from parole those who have satisfactorily completed their terms.

THE PAROLE BOARD

The first element of parole is the decision by a duly constituted authority to determine the portion of the offender's sentence that he or she must complete before being released to complete the sentence outside the institution. This authority is granted to an executive-branch agency, a parole board (or parole commission) that is charged with administering parole policy. The board must work within the statutes of the particular jurisdiction but may adopt its own rules and regulations insofar as they do not conflict with the statutes. The scope of the board's authority and the consequences of its actions are enormous. No other part of the criminal justice system concentrates such power in the hands of so few.[1]

Parole boards have two basic functions: to select prisoners for parole and to determine when revocation and return to prison is necessary. In twelve states the parole board also has the responsibility to supervise and provide continuing control of parolees in the community. In most jurisdictions, however, supervision of parolees is carried out by parole officers under the supervision of the department of corrections. These officers are responsible for enforcing the conditions of parole established by the parole board. Figure 10–1 illustrates the variety of functions carried out by parole boards and the percentage of jurisdictions where that function is the responsibility of the parole board.

ELEMENTS OF AN EFFECTIVE PAROLE SYSTEM

Parole boards vary widely in their power and responsibility, but all effective parole systems have certain characteristics. The American Correctional Association regards the essential elements of an effective parole system to be:[2]

1. flexibility in sentencing and parole laws
2. a qualified parole board
3. a qualified parole staff
4. freedom from political or improper influences
5. workable position in the governmental administrative structure
6. proper procedures
7. prerelease preparation within the institution
8. proper public attitude toward parole
9. research and statistics on effectiveness

We discuss each of these elements in this section.

Flexibility in Sentencing and Parole Laws

An effective parole system requires an indeterminate-sentencing environment and that the release decision for most offenders be made by the paroling authority. This does not preclude statutes that require a minimum term to be served before eligibility for certain offenses or statutes that prohibit parole for some offenses. Public safety and accountability require some constraints on parole boards' discretion, particularly for violent offenders and those with

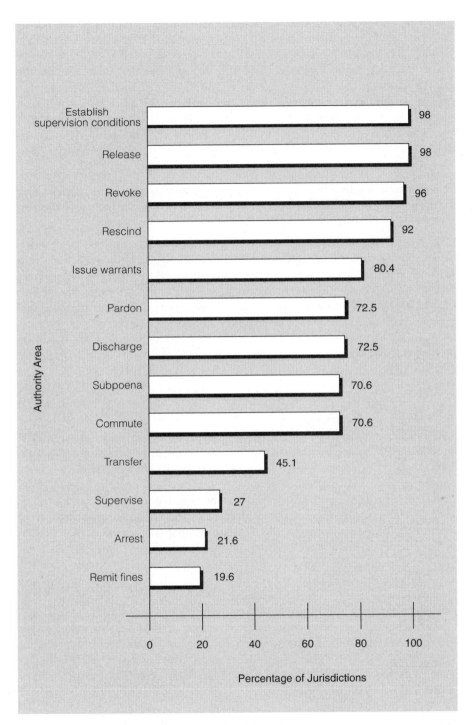

F I G U R E 10–1

Statutory Jurisdiction of Paroling Authorities

SOURCE: Edward E. Rhine, William R. Smith, and Ronald W. Jackson, *Paroling Authorities: Recent History and Current Practice* (Laurel, Md.: American Correctional Association, 1991).

long criminal histories and previous incarcerations. Most incarcerated offenders, however, are not violent and are not recidivists. Parole serves an important correctional purpose for these offenders in allowing for consideration of their individual circumstances, reducing unnecessary confinement, and ameliorating inequities in sentencing.

It is not possible to obtain agreement on a form of sentencing and parole law that would permit the release of a prisoner at the optimum time. Wide latitude and discretion was advocated in the past. Since the 1970s, however, there has been a movement toward the use of objective guidelines in the release decision. The National Advisory Commission reported, "The absence of written criteria by which decisions are made constitutes a major failing in virtually every parole jurisdiction."[3] The commission recommended that parole decisions be made visible and that parole authorities be made accountable for their decisions through the use of explicit parole-selection policies. The American Correctional Association (ACA) recommends:[4]

> The criteria which are employed by the parole authority in its decision making are available in written form and are specific enough to permit consistent application to individual cases (Standard 2-1082).

In an attempt to make parole-selection decisions more rational and consistent, many paroling jurisdictions have established decision guidelines that serve to structure discretion without removing it. By specifying the primary factors to be considered in parole selection and the weight to be assigned to each factor, the paroling authority gives judges, the public, and the potential parolees a clearer idea of how it generally exercises its discretion.

Qualified Parole Board

The American Correctional Association concludes that parole boards should be of such integrity, intelligence, and good judgment as to command respect and public confidence. Because of the importance of their quasi-judicial functions, they must possess the equivalent personal qualifications of a high judicial officer. They must be forthright, courageous, and independent. They should be appointed without reference to creed, color, or political affiliation.

Board members should have sufficiently broad educational backgrounds that they have knowledge of those professions most closely related to parole administration—specifically, academic training that qualifies them for professional practice in fields such as criminology, education, psychiatry, psychology, law, social work, and sociology. It is essential that each member have the capacity and the desire to "round out" his or her knowledge, as effective performance depends on understanding legal processes, the dynamics of human behavior, and cultural conditions contributing to crime.

Parole board members should have previous professional experience that has given them intimate knowledge of common situations and problems confronting offenders. This might be obtained from a variety of fields, such as probation, parole, the judiciary, law, social work, a correctional institution, or a delinquency prevention agency.[5]

SELECTION AND TERM OF BOARD MEMBERS.   In most jurisdictions the governor appoints parole board members.[6] In some jurisdictions the governor shares the appointing authority with another body. In others, the secretary or commissioner of corrections appoints the parole board, and in one state, the secretary of public safety makes the appointments.[7] As a rule, parole board members are appointed for a term of years, rather than serving at the pleasure of the governor. However, the ACA Parole Task Force survey found that in six states—Georgia, Michigan, Minnesota, Ohio, West Virginia, and Wisconsin—board members are not appointed for specific terms.[8] In forty percent of the states, board members serve four-year terms, and in twenty-five percent of the states, they serve six years. Three- and five-year terms are less common.

Any parole decision is influenced by the board members' qualifications and expertise. Therefore, it is important that each member be qualified and possess expertise. Many parole officials are able and knowledgeable, whereas some have neither the qualifications nor the expertise. Statutes vary in the explicitness with which they specify the qualifications of a parole board member. A few require only that the member be of "good moral character." Rhine and his associates reported that over half of the jurisdictions had no requirement that board members possess any special professional qualifications. In these states, the governor may nominate any person without regard for education, training, or experience. Others specify specific educational or special qualifications. For example, New York statutes require that each member of the board have graduated from an accredited college or university, with a degree in criminology, criminal justice administration, law enforcement, sociology, law, social work, corrections, psychology, psychiatry, or medicine, plus five or more years of experience in one or more of those fields. Montana requires that at least one board member have "particular knowledge of Indian culture and problems."[9]

Many authorities view the part-time board of parole often found in smaller states as one of the most severe problems in corrections. Able to give only a limited amount of time to the job because of their business or professional concerns, part-timers cannot participate effectively in correctional decision making. Since the mid 1970's there has been a trend toward increasing the number of full-time boards. According to the ACA Parole Task Force survey, there are thirty-one full-time boards and seven boards with a mixture of full-time and part-time members. In the states with both full-time and part-time members, the chair is usually full-time and the other members serve on a part-time basis.[10] Table 10–1 summarizes parole board organizational characteristics.

Qualified Parole Staff

A parole officer is expected to perform three main functions:

1. to make investigations and write reports, and to evaluate, interpret, and present data for the guidance of the court, the institution, or the paroling authority
2. to keep informed about the conduct and enforcement of parolees by personal contacts and to report to the court or paroling authority any violation
3. to interpret his or her work to the community by actively participating in civic and community organizations.

In order to perform these functions, a parole officer must possess certain basic qualifications and specialized knowledge. The minimum qualifications should be

TABLE 10-1

Parole Board Characteristics

JURISDICTION	LENGTH OF TERM (YEARS)	FULL-TIME (F) OR PART-TIME (P)	NUMBER OF MEMBERS
Alabama	6	F	3
Alaska	5	P	5
Arizona	5	F	7
Arkansas	5	P	5
California	4	F	9
Colorado	3	F	5
Connecticut	4	F/P	11
Delaware	4	F/P	5
District of Columbia	5	F	5
Florida	4	F	6
Georgia	7	F	5
Hawaii	4	F/P	3
Idaho	5	P	5
Illinois	6	F	12
Indiana	4	F	5
Iowa	4	F/P	5
Kansas	4	F	3
Kentucky	4	F	7
Louisiana	4	F	5
Maine	4	P	5
Maryland	6	F	7
Massachusetts	5	F	7
Michigan	7	F	7
Minnesota	7	F/P	2
Mississippi	4	F/P	5
Missouri	6	F	5
Montana	4	P	4
Nebraska	6	F	5
Nevada	4	F	5
New Hampshire	5	P	5
New Jersey	6	F	7
New Mexico	4	F	3
New York	6	F	19
North Carolina	4	F	5
Ohio	7	F	7
Oklahoma	4	P	5
Oregon	4	F	5
Pennsylvania	6	F	5
Rhode Island	3	P	5
South Carolina	6	P	7
South Dakota	4	P	3
Tennessee	6	F	5
Texas	6	F	18
Utah	6	F/P	6
Vermont	5	P	5
Virginia	4	F	5
Washington	5	F	7
West Virginia	7	F	3
Wisconsin	7	F	7
Wyoming	6	P	5

SOURCE: Edward E. Rhine, William R. Smith, and Ronald W. Jackson, *Paroling Authorities: Recent History and Current Practice* (Laurel, Md.: American Correctional Association, 1991). Used with permission of the American Correctional Association.

■ a working knowledge of the principles of human behavior,
■ knowledge of the laws of the jurisdiction in which he or she will work and of the powers and limitations of the position, and
■ familiarity with the operation of related law-enforcement agencies in the particular jurisdiction.

The minimum standards for employment as a probation or parole officer should include:

■ a bachelor's degree from a college or university with coursework in the social sciences,
■ one year of paid full-time experience in employment for the welfare of others, or one year of graduate work beyond the baccalaureate, and
■ good character and a well-balanced personality.

Freedom from Political or Improper Influences

A parole system should be entirely free from political control, manipulation, or influence and also from improper influences of pressure groups of any type. The law should forbid parole board or staff participation in partisan political activities and coerced contributions to party campaign funds, and should give the parole authorities the independence and security of tenure that they must have in order to resist interference successfully.[11]

Workable Position in Government

The parole system should be administered within the governmental structure that assures the most effective coordination of parole with other correctional services, such as institutional programs, and with community-based correctional agencies such as probation halfway houses, drug and alcohol treatment agencies, the courts, and police. Basically, four major parole structures exist:

1. The parole board serves as the administrative and policy-making board for a combined probation and parole system.
2. The parole board administers parole services only.
3. Parole services are administered by the department that administers the state correctional institutions.
4. Parole services are administered by the state correctional agency, which also administers the probation and institutional services.

The two dominant organizational patterns are the institutional model and the autonomous model. The **institutional model** is most prevalent in the juvenile field and centers parole decision making primarily in the institutions. The **autonomous model** prevails in the adult field and centers parole decision making in an independent authority. Advocates of the institutional model believe that because the institutional staff are most familiar with the offender and his or her response to institutional programs, they are most sensitive to the optimum time for release. They see the autonomous board as (1) unconcerned with or insensitive to problems of the institutional programs and the staff's goals, (2) too preoccupied with issues other than the rehabilitative

Institutional model of parole organization

An organizational pattern in which parole release decisions are made primarily within the institution. Advocates of the institutional model believe that because institutional staff are most familiar with the offender and his/her response to institutional programs, they are most sensitive to the optimal time for release. Most commonly used in the juvenile field.

Autonomous model of parole organization

An organizational pattern in which parole decisions are made by an autonomous body not affiliated with other agencies of the criminal justice system. Most common pattern for adult paroling authorities.

Consolidation model of parole organization

An organizational pattern in which parole decisions are made by a central authority that has independent powers but that is organizationally situated in the department of corrections.

aspects of the offender's treatment to make appropriate case decisions, (3) lending unnecessary complications to decision making, and (4) infringing on the professional judgment of competent institutional staff.

On the other hand, proponents of the autonomous model believe that the institutional staff places undue emphasis on the offender's institutional adjustment. They see the institutional board as (1) being tempted to set release policies to fit the needs of the institution, to control population size, and to rid itself of problem cases; (2) extending confinement as a penalty for petty rule violations; and (3) having decision-making procedures that are so informal and lacking in visibility that questions arise concerning the board's ability to maintain fairness or even an appearance of fairness.

Although both the institutional and autonomous models are in practice, the **consolidation model** has gained popularity. This model is a result of the trend toward consolidating all correctional services—institutional and field programs—into a single department. In the consolidation model, parole decisions are made by a central authority that has independent powers although it is organizationally situated in the department of corrections. Advocates of this model contend that it (1) promotes greater concern for the entire corrections system, (2) provides greater sensitivity to institutional programs, and (3) separates parole decisions from the institution's immediate control, thereby giving appropriate weight to parole considerations beyond management of the institution.

Regardless of the organizational or administrative structure adopted by the jurisdiction, it is essential that it facilitate close coordination between the parole decision makers and all correctional programs. In so doing, sufficient autonomy should be retained to permit the parole board to serve as a check on the system.

Proper Procedures

Under traditional parole practice, the decision about a prisoner's release is deferred until well into his or her sentence; the prisoner is given a parole hearing shortly before completion of the minimum term. If the prisoner is not granted parole at that time, another hearing is scheduled after some additional period. Consequently, a prisoner may have several parole hearings before learning whether he or she will be granted parole and when he or she will actually be released. From the perspective of the traditional rehabilitative model, this practice is both necessary and desirable, since parole decisions are to be based primarily on rehabilitative concerns. The goal of the parole release authority is to identify the optimal time for release. Thus, deferral of the release decision is necessary for enabling the prisoner's rehabilitative progress to be monitored.

Current thought has been shaped by empirical evidence. Research has failed to demonstrate that institutional rehabilitative programs are effective or that the optimal time for release can be ascertained. Behavior in prison has not been found to be a good predictor of future criminal behavior. More and more jurisdictions are moving by statute or voluntarily toward the use of

parole guidelines as explicit standards for determining the optimal length of a prison sentence without reference to the prisoner's institutional record, length of incarceration before parole, or other factors that have not been shown to correlate with prisoners' ability to live crime-free in the world outside prison.

Prerelease Preparation within the Institution

THE PAROLE PLAN.   When a tentative or definite parole date has been set by the board, a parole plan should be developed for the future parolee. This specifies what will be a satisfactory home or living arrangement for the individual and assesses his or her potential for employment. The plan is usually investigated and approved by the parole field staff.

GRADUATED RELEASE.   Direct, sudden release from confinement in a controlled environment to the free community often results in psychological and cultural shock to the releasee, and this may very well affect the person's ability to adjust. Whenever possible, the inmate should be transferred to a minimum-security or open-type institution a few months before release. In such a setting the inmate may begin to exercise the necessary self-direction for living in free society.

Work-release arrangements and furloughs are also helpful as means of gradually allowing the inmate short, yet important, opportunities to function without the strict regimen and all-encompassing discipline of the closed institution. The use of halfway houses or prerelease centers is increasing, and preliminary research indicates that inmates released to those settings are considerably less prone to recidivism.[12]

RELEASE UNDER A FIRM, HELPFUL SUPERVISOR.   Parole supervision is a continuation of the correctional process. Its effectiveness in aiding the parolee's reintegration in society relies on the knowledge and experience of the field officer. This topic is discussed in Chapter 6, "Supervision of Probationers and Parolees."

Proper Public Attitude toward Parole

The American Correctional Association states,

> The parole board and the institution have a large part to play in the matter of the parolee's return to society; however, the manner in which the public receives the parolee and the attitude it assumes is vital to that person's success.[13]

Probation and parole officers should do all they can to increase public understanding of and appreciation for probation and parole. They should take advantage of opportunities to speak to educational and community groups and to use radio and television to foster public understanding of probation and parole and to explain their responsibilities and objectives. Most media

Parole guidelines
Guidelines to be followed in making parole release decisions. Most guidelines prescribe a "presumptive term" for each class of convicted inmate depending on both offense and offender characteristics.

stories about probation and parole are of the PAROLEE ARRESTED IN HOLDUP variety. There are, however, many success stories that can and should be told.

Research and Statistics on Effectiveness.

Full public acceptance of parole as a means of release from prisons and other correctional institutions can come only from rigorous research demonstrations of its effectiveness. Virtually all subjects connected with crime and criminal justice need further research. In 1927, Felix Frankfurter observed that the subject of crime was "overlaid with shibboleths and cliches" and that it was essential to "separate the known from the unknown, to divorce fact from assumption, to strip biases of every sort from their authority."[14] This statement is no less true today. Research is needed for developing and validating parole prediction tables, recidivism outcome indices, and other instruments that aid boards in predicting the future behavior of those being considered for parole. Research into the causes of recidivism and subsequent revocation could be invaluable in equipping the parole officer with the tools necessary for aiding parolees in this area. Most importantly, research is needed on the question, What factors in inmates' backgrounds and present circumstances are predictive of success or failure on parole?

Preconceived and outmoded prejudices and concepts of parole boards and staff can be modified or eliminated in light of statistical analyses of the outcomes of board decisions. Parole authorities know that the criminal justice system needs improvement, and gathering solid research data is the first step in bringing about improvement. As a subsystem of the criminal justice process, parole is inextricably interrelated with all other aspects of the system.

THE DECISION TO PAROLE

Who is to be paroled? This question has vital importance today. The parole selection process is of serious consequence to the effectiveness, perhaps even the survival, of the entire parole system. Since the selection process determines to a great extent the character of the system as a whole, it has inevitably received more criticism than any other aspect of the system.

Eligibility for Parole

Prisoners can generally become eligible for parole at the completion of their minimum sentence. Early in their incarceration—often within the first few months—a **parole eligibility** date is fixed. The way the date is established varies from state to state. Many states require an inmate to have served one third of the imposed sentence to be eligible for *consideration* for parole; thus a 15-year sentence would require that 5 years be served before parole eligibility. However, most statutes allow for further reductions in the eligibility date through credit for time served in jail before sentencing and/or "good-time" credits.[15] Some states credit "good time" to the inmate upon arrival in prison and calculate the eligibility date by subtracting credited good time from the maximum sentence. An inmate who is serving a 15-year sentence and receiving "standard" good time of 20 days per month (50 days' credit on his or her sentence for each 30 days served), would be eligible for parole consideration after 40 months ($\frac{2}{3} \times 15 \times \frac{1}{3}$).

The Parole Release Decision

The decision to grant parole is a complicated one, and the consequences of the decision are of the gravest importance, both for society and for the inmate. A decision to grant parole results in conditional release before the expiration of the maximum term of imprisonment; a denial results in continued imprisonment. The parole release decision is often more important than the court's sentence in determining how long the prisoner actually spends incarcerated. In the absence of clear legislative or judicial guidelines for parole decisions, vast responsibility has been placed on parole boards. Parole decisions traditionally have been regarded as matters that demand special expertise, matters that involve observation and treatment of offenders and release under supervision at a time that maximizes both the protection of the public and offenders' rehabilitation. This idealistic correctional goal of protecting society while rehabilitating the offender has served as additional justification for vesting broad discretionary powers in parole authorities.[16]

Statutes have usually directed parole boards to base their decisions on one or more of these criteria:

- the probability of recidivism,
- the welfare of society,
- the conduct of the offender while in the correctional institution,
- the sufficiency of the parole plan.

Such statutory language does not lend itself to a workable decision-making scheme, so the parole boards have had to interpret and determine the best means by which to turn the legislative mandate into functioning administrative machinery. This broad discretion has brought criticism upon the paroling authority for making arbitrary, capricious, and disparate decisions. The lack of published standards to guide decision making, combined with the lack of written reasons for parole decisions, contribute to this perception.[17]

Traditional Parole Decision Making

Traditionally, the hearing stage of parole decision making was thought to provide decision makers with an opportunity to speak with and observe the prospective parolee, to search for and intuit such indications of his or her rehabilitation as repentance, willingness to accept responsibility, and self-understanding. Parole decisions were not based on formally articulated criteria or policies, but on the subjective, intuitional judgments of individual decision makers.[18] The courts, to the extent that they were willing to review the parole decision at all, agreed with the contentions of paroling authorities that to impose even minimal due-process constraints on the decisional process would interfere with the fulfillment of its duty to engage in diagnosis and prognosis.

In 1970, in *Menechino v. Oswald,* the U.S. Court of Appeals held:

> The Board has an identity of interest with [the inmate] . . . It is seeking to encourage and foster his rehabilitation and readjustment to society. . . . In making this determination the Board is not restricted by rules of evidence developed for the purpose of determining legal or factual issues. It must consider many factors of a nonlegal nature [such as] medicine, psychiatry, criminology . . . psychology and human relations.[19]

In his book *Conscience and Convenience,* David Rothman discussed the issue of discretionary decision making by parole boards. He reported that in the early twentieth century, parole boards primarily considered the seriousness of the crime in determining whether or not to release an inmate on parole. However, there was no consensus on what constituted a serious crime. "Instead," Rothman wrote, "each member made his own decisions. The judgements were personal and therefore not subject to debate or reconsideration"[20] Rothman's evaluation of early parole decision making applies equally to many jurisdictions in the late twentieth century. Both authors of this book have served on parole boards and have observed situations in which board members' biases or preconceptions mitigated for or against a release decision—with little else factored in. One decision maker of our acquaintance refused to vote to parole any person convicted of murder. Another member of the same paroling body regarded murder as a situational crime of passion and reminded his colleagues that "murderers have a very low recidivism rate." As Rothman states, ". . . one man's nightmare case did not necessarily frighten another."[21] Another board member of our acquaintance looked only at the nature and seriousness of the offense in arriving at a release decision, whereas a colleague in the very next office was primarily concerned with an inmate's adjustment and behavior since being incarcerated. She commented, "A person can't do anything about what he did to get here [in prison]. I look at what they have done to get their life in order."

Growing recognition of the lack of fundamental fairness in such situations made the need for research-based predictors of risk of recidivism obvious. In 1973 the National Advisory Commission on Criminal Justice Standards and Goals spoke to the issue of parole decision making:

> The sound use of discretion and ultimate accountability for its exercise rests largely in making visible the criteria used in forming judgments. . . . The absence of written criteria by which decisions are made constitutes a major failing in virtually every parole jurisdiction.[22]

Development of Parole Guidelines

In that same year the U.S. Board of Parole[23] took a major step in the direction recommended by the National Advisory Commission. As a part of a general reorganization plan, case decision making authority was delegated to panels of hearing examiners, using explicit parole selection guidelines established by the Board of Parole.[24] The guidelines were an attempt to structure discretion without removing it. By making explicit the primary factors to be considered in parole decisions, as well as the weight to be given to each, the Board of

Parole provided judges, the public, and inmates with a clearer idea of how it intended to exercise its discretion.

Research had shown that parole decisions could be predicted by using specific variables. Three variables were identified as explaining a large number of the board's decisions:

- the seriousness of the offense,
- the risk posed by the inmate (probability of recidivism), and
- the inmate's institutional behavior (relatively less important than the first two).

The researchers produced a chart that related seriousness of offense and risk of recidivism to suggested terms of imprisonment. Based on this chart, the parole board constructed a matrix by placing the two dimensions—seriousness of offense and risk of recidivism—on the *x*- and *y*-axes of a graph. Range of sentence length was then determined by plotting intersections of the dimensions on the graph.

THE SALIENT FACTOR SCORE.   This actuarial device was continually validated and evaluated over ten years and was revised several times, the latest in 1981. Known as the **Salient Factor Score (SFS),** it provided explicit guidelines for release decision making based on a determination of the potential risk of parole violation. The 1981 version of the SFS measures six offender characteristics and assigns a score to each. See Figure 10–2.

Note in the figure that the first offender characteristic considered in the Salient Factor Score calculation is *Prior Convictions/Adjudications.* This offender characteristic has a score range of 0 to 3. Offenders with no prior convictions are assigned a score of 3, one prior conviction results in a score of 2, and two to three prior convictions a score of 1, and so on. Each offender characteristic is scored in a similar manner and the sum of the six items yields the *predictive score.* The higher the score—maximum of 10—the less likely is the probability of recidivism.

Although the SFS provided a method of summarizing research data on the relationship between offender characteristics and the likelihood of recidivism, its use with a guidelines system did not eliminate the need for clinical judgment. No prediction device can take into account all the variations in human behavior. Thus, provision was made to allow the decision maker to override the salient factor score, but only for articulated, written reasons. If the decision maker chose to make a clinical judgment outside the guidelines, he or she was required to explain the specific factors considered in the decision to override the SFS.[25]

Following the lead of the federal parole system, many states adopted guidelines for use in release decision making. Some states adopted a *matrix* guideline system similar to the SFS, and others adopted different types of guidelines. Most of these other systems feature a list of factors to be considered in making release decisions. Rhine and associates refer to this second category of guidelines as **guiding principles.** Joan Petersilia and Susan Turner[26] compiled a list of criteria used in both types of instruments—matrix and guiding principles. It appears in Table 10–2.

Regardless of the form parole release guidelines take, they serve to structure the exercise of discretion. Parole boards are free to deviate from their

Salient Factor score

The parole guidelines developed and used by the United States Parole Commission for making parole-release decisions; served as the model for parole guidelines developed on many other jurisdictions.

F I G U R E   10–2

Salient Factor Score

Note: For purposes of the Salient Factor Score, an instance of criminal behavior resulting in a judicial determination of guilt or an admission of guilt before a judicial body shall be treated as a conviction, even if a conviction is not formally entered.

SOURCE: U.S. Parole Commission.

Item A.   PRIOR CONVICTIONS/ADJUDICATIONS (ADULT OR JUVENILE) . . . .☐
  None. . . . . = 3
  One. . . . . = 2
  Two or three . . . . = 1
  Four or more . . . . = 0

Item B.   PRIOR COMMITMENT(S) OF MORE THAN THIRTY DAYS (ADULT OR JUVENILE). . . . .☐
  None. . . . . = 2
  One or two . . . . = 1
  Three or more. . . . . = 0

Item C.   AGE AT CURRENT OFFENSE/PRIOR COMMITMENTS. . . . .☐
  Age at commencement of the current offense:
    26 years of age or more. . . . . = 2*
    20–25 years of age. . . . . = 1*
    19 years of age or less. . . . . = 0
  * EXCEPTION: If five or more prior commitments of more than thirty days (adult or juvenile), place an "x" here _____ and score this item . . . . = 0

Item D.   RECENT COMMITMENT-FREE PERIOD (THREE YEARS). . . . .☐
  No prior commitment of more than thirty days (adult or juvenile) or released to the community from last such commitment at least three years prior to the commencement of the current offense . . . . = 1
  Otherwise . . . . = 0

Item E.   PROBATION/PAROLE/CONFINEMENT/ESCAPE STATUS VIOLATOR THIS TIME . . . . = ☐
  Neither on probation, parole, confinement, or escape status at the time of the current offense; nor committed as a probation, parole, confinement, or escape status violator this time. . . . . = 1
  Otherwise . . . . = 0

Item F.   HEROIN/OPIATE DEPENDENCE. . . . . = ☐
  No history of heroin/opiate dependence. . . . . = 1
  Otherwise . . . . = 0

TOTAL SCORE . . . .☐

guidelines, but generally must give reasons for doing so. Parole authorities are guided in their decision making, while retaining broad powers; deviations from these guides are held in check by the possibility of appeal.

Research indicates that guidelines have performed one of their intended functions, that of evening out obvious disparities so that prison time is more predictable. The main argument against them is that they do not address the questions of who is to go to prison in the first place and how wide the sentence ranges should be. These questions are addressed mostly by the courts, and many critics have pointed out that court sentencing is just as capricious, unpredictable, and fraught with disparities as parole decisions ever were.[27]

Prisoners' Perceptions of Parole Selection

Whether the length of incarceration before parole is any more predictable in guideline jurisdictions is still speculative. James Beck studied prisoners'

TABLE 10-2

Criteria Used in Parole-Release-Risk Instruments

MOST COMMONLY USED ITEMS (5)

(found in over 75% of instruments identified)
Number of parole revocations
Number of adult or juvenile convictions
Number of prison terms served
Number of incarcerations served
Current crime involves violence

SECOND-MOST COMMONLY USED ITEMS (11)

(found in 50–74% of instruments identified)
Number of prior convictions
Number of previous felony sentences
Number of juvenile incarcerations
Number of jail terms served
Age at first incarceration
Commitment-free period shown
On parole at arrest
Victim injured
Current age
Drug use
Prison infractions

THIRD-MOST COMMONLY USED ITEMS (15)

(found in 25–49% of instruments identified)
Number of adult or juvenile arrests
Age at first conviction
Repeat of conviction types
Length of current term
Total years incarcerated
Current crime is property crime
Current crime involved weapon
Current crime involved forcible contact
Educational level
Employment history
Living arrangements
Alcohol use/abuse
Program participation in prison
Parole release plan formulated
Escape history

SOURCE: Joan Petersilia and Susan Turner, "Guideline-Based Justice: Prediction and Racial Minorities," in D. Gottfredson and M. Tonry, eds., *Prediction and Classification* (Chicago: University of Chicago Press, 1987).

perceptions of parole decision making in the federal parole system, which used a justice-model guideline system, and in Pennsylvania, which used a rehabilitative nonmatrix guideline system.[28] The Pennsylvania board was generally treatment-oriented and strongly considered institutional behavior, recommendations of institutional staff, and parole release plans. The federal system, as we have discussed in detail, primarily considered offense severity and offender characteristics, such as prior criminal history.

Contrary to expectations, Beck found no significant difference in the two groups' abilities to predict parole decisions, but he found that a significantly greater percentage of Pennsylvania inmates than federal-jurisdiction inmates considered the parole procedure "basically fair" (48 percent of inmates as opposed to only 20 percent of the federal inmates). The major conclusion of the study was that the "justice" approach to parole does not result in greater perceived certainty for the offender, even though the criteria are made concrete and more sharply defined. The treatment model—based on institutional adjustment—allowed the offender a greater perceived influence over the parole decision, and thus was viewed as basically more fair. Beck concluded that the justice approach to parole is still a useful tool for reducing sentence disparity and that the rehabilitation approach will remain suspect until some method of rehabilitating offenders has been proven effective. From the viewpoint of the offender, however, the rehabilitation model of parole seems to be the preferred method of deciding when an offender should be released from prison. Beck's findings do not surprise us. As former parole board members, we (the authors) have received hundreds of letters from inmates protesting the use of offense-related factors in making parole decisions. A letter one of us received from an inmate while serving on the Texas parole board illustrates this point:

> I can't do nothing about what I did. I did it and I'm sorry I did. Now I'm trying to show you people that I've changed and can be trusted out in the free world but you keep setting me off [denying parole] because of "nature and seriousness of the offense." Tell me what I can do to make parole. Please.[29]

Any system that totally ignores positive institutional behavior runs the risk of alienating the offender and increases the possibility of poor adjustment. Many, however, suggest that "career" criminals know how to "do time"; that is, they can manipulate the parole board by avoiding institutional violations and participating in "rehabilitation" programs that look good on their record when they are reviewed for parole.

So, despite criticisms leveled at the use of guidelines, this procedure appears to offer the greatest degree of fairness to the parole-granting process. By making explicit the primary factors that the board should consider in parole selection and the weight that should be given to each, the unfettered discretion traditionally allowed parole boards should, at the very least, be structured and more predictable.

Due Process

One of the most striking aspects of the traditional parole release process has been the virtual inability to review parole decisions.[30] In recent years, courts have provided some procedural protections and articulated criteria for reviewing the conditions that parole boards have set on parolees' conduct, and for revoking parole and returning parolees to prison. Until very recently, federal and state courts almost invariably rejected claims that the denial of parole was subject to review because of procedural or substantive defects in the parole release decision process.[31]

The parole grant has long been analogized by courts to the grant of executive pardon, which makes it essentially an "act of grace" or the conferring of a "privilege," neither of which gives rise to rights or expectations in need of due process.[32] In addition to the act of **grace or privilege** rationales, another theory for judicial passivity in this area has been the **continuing custody theory,** the argument that parole merely constitutes a change in the nature of custody, which places the parole decision in the area of administrative decision making.[33]

However, the theory of grace or privilege is inconsistent with the view that parole is merely a change in custody status, since the former theory recognizes that a substantial benefit of conditional freedom is being conferred. The custody theory ignores the fact that a major purpose of parole is to provide a halfway point between incarceration and total freedom in the community in order to promote rehabilitation and to protect society.[34]

Another rationale used to justify the vast and unreviewable discretion is that parole boards act as *parens patriae* with respect to the inmates. As such, the boards need be concerned only with promoting the inmates' rehabilitation through the exercise of their expert knowledge and judgment, which obviates any need for procedural protection.[35] This rationale reflects the pervasive view that release decisions were part of the rehabilitation process. In support of this view, courts have emphasized that parole boards possess an administrative expertise in evaluating "nonlegal" factors relevant to the release decision.[36] The courts acquiesced in the board's assertion that the proper moment for parole can only be determined after an inmate has been observed for a period of time and attempts have been made to treat the inmate within the rehabilitative institutional context.[37]

In *Menechino v. Oswald,*[38] a prisoner argued that the New York State Board of Parole's denial of his application for parole was illegal, because he had not received notice of the information to be considered, a fair parole hearing with a right to counsel, the right to cross-examine and to produce favorable witnesses, or a specification of the grounds and underlying facts upon which the denial was based. The court offered two reasons in holding that these due-process rights did not apply to parole release hearings. First, the court ruled that the inmate had no legally cognizable "interest" in his parole grant, since he did not enjoy a status that was being threatened or taken away. Second, the parole board's interest in the proceeding was not adverse to that of the inmate, because the board was "seeking to encourage and foster his rehabilitation and readjustment into society.[39]

Although the courts' prevailing view has been that of noninterference in parole release decisions, this has not been the only view. Abuses of discretion have been judicially reviewed, and parole boards have been found abusing their discretion, committing capricious acts, and conducting practices contrary to the general notions of fairness.[40]

In 1979 the U.S. Supreme Court addressed directly the issue of due process in parole release decision making. In *Greenholtz v. Inmates of the Nebraska Penal and Correctional Complex*[41] the inmates of a Nebraska prison brought an action alleging they had been unconstitutionally denied parole by the Nebraska Board of Parole. The inmates contested, among other things,

Grace or privilege theory

The view that parole is a privilege and a matter of grace (mercy) by the executive. Under this theory parole confers no particular rights on the recipient and is subject to withdrawal at any time.

Continuing custody theory

The view that the parolee remains in custody of either the parole authorities or the prison and that his/her constitutional rights are limited. Release on parole is merely a change in the *degree* of custody.

Parens patriae

Latin "parent of the country," refers to the traditional role of the state as guardian of persons under legal disability, such as juveniles, the insane, and incarcerated persons. The assumption is that the state acts in the best interest of those over whom the *parens patriae* relationship exists.

Supreme Court building

(1) the state's hearing process, (2) the board's practice when it denies parole of informing the inmates in what respect they fall short of qualifying for parole, and (3) a notice procedure of informing inmates of the month during which the parole hearing will be held in advance, and then posting notice of the exact time for the hearing on the day of the hearing.

After the lower federal courts held in favor of the inmates, the U.S. Supreme Court reversed the decision of the court of appeals. The Court stated:

> Like most parole statutes, it [the Nebraska statute] vests broad discretion in the Board. No ideal, error-free way to make parole release decisions has been developed. The whole question has been, and will continue to be, the subject of experimentation involving analysis of psychological factors combined with fact evaluation guided by the practical experience of the actual parole decision makers in predicting future behavior.[42]

The Court continued the trend of past decisions by discussing the "ultimate purpose of parole . . . rehabilitation,"[43] and stated:

> The fact that anticipation and hopes for rehabilitation programs have fallen short of expectations of a generation ago need not lead states to abandon hopes for those objectives; states may adopt a balanced approach in making parole determinations, as in problems of administering the correctional systems.[44]

The Court refused to require a hearing in all cases for every inmate as prescribed by the court of appeals, holding that such a requirement would provide, at best, a negligible decrease in the risk of error. In sum, the Court held that

The Nebraska procedure affords an opportunity to be heard, and when parole is denied it informs the inmate in what respect he falls short of qualifying for parole; this affords the process that is due under these circumstances. The Constitution does not require more.[45]

THE IMPORTANCE OF *GREENHOLTZ.*   Although the *Greenholtz* case did not extend due process as far as desired by the plaintiffs, nor as extensively as did the court of appeals, it did establish that some due-process protections were available in the parole-granting process. The Court held that the methods provided for in the Nebraska statute—providing the right to an initial hearing, notice of the hearing, and articulation of the reasons for denial—were sufficient. It distinguished parole-release decision making from parole-revocation decision making and refused to apply the due-process provisions of *Morrissey v. Brewer,* which prescribe a panoply of rights to a parolee in a revocation hearing. The Court concluded that parole release and parole revocation "are quite different" because "there is a . . . difference between losing what one has and not getting what one wants."[46]

Greenholtz, then, appears to require reasonable notice of a hearing, an initial hearing wherein the prisoner is allowed to present the case, and if parole is denied, a recitation of the reasons for denial. On the other hand, the requirement depends on the wording of the state or federal statute being interpreted. The Court concluded:

> We can accept respondent's view that the expectancy of release provided in this statute is entitled to some measure of constitutional protection. However, we emphasize that this statute has unique structure and language and thus any other state statute provides a protectable entitlement must be decided on a case by case basis.[47]

The American Correction Association (ACA) Standards require parole hearings to be conducted as fairly and equitably as possible with due-process conditions maintained and all procedural safeguards assured.[48] Further, ACA Standards require that the criteria for decision making are to be written in enough detail to permit consistent application in individual cases, and that the decision regarding parole release and the reasons for it are to be communicated to the prisoner orally and explained to agree with the written criteria. Applicants denied parole must be informed of an approximate future hearing date and must receive suggestions for improving their chances to receive parole by the time of the next hearing.

The ACA Standards far exceed the due-process requirements established by the courts, although it must be noted that the standards are not binding on any paroling authority; rather, they are only guidelines or models.

Since there is considerable disagreement regarding the amount and type of due process necessary at the parole-granting hearing, it is instructive to note that there was division on the Court in *Greenholtz* and that separate concurring opinions were written. Of particular interest is the separate opinion of Justice Powell. Powell agreed that the inmates had a right to some due process in the consideration of their release on parole, but he disagreed that the due process was conditioned on the wording of the state statute governing the deliberations of the parole board. Powell wrote that substantial liberty from legal restraint is at stake when the state makes decisions regarding probation or parole:

Although still subject to limitations not imposed or citizens never convicted of a crime, the parolee enjoys a liberty comparably greater than whatever minimal freedom of action he may have retained within prison walls, a fact that the Court recognized in *Morrissey v. Brewer*. . . .[49]

Because this liberty is valuable and its termination inflicts a grievous loss on the parolee, the Court concluded in *Morrissey v. Brewer*[50] that the decision to revoke parole must be made in conformity with due-process standards. Powell wrote that the prisoner should justifiably expect that parole will be granted fairly and that the mere existence of a parole system is sufficient to create a **liberty interest** in the parole-release decision protected by the Constitution.[51] Liberty interest refers to any interest recognized or protected by the due process clauses of state or federal constitutions.

Justice Marshall, joined by Justices Brennan and Stevens in dissenting, wrote:

> I must register my opinion that all prisoners potentially eligible for parole have a liberty interest of which they may not be deprived without due process, regardless of the particular statutory language that implements the parole system.[52]

Considering the lack of unanimity in the *Greenholtz* case, it is possible that future cases will further extend due process to parole-release hearings and that due process rights in *Morrissey v. Brewer* and *Gagnon v. Scarpelli* will be incorporated into the parole-selection process.

SUMMARY

The first element of parole is the decision by a duly constituted authority to determine the portion of the sentence that an inmate must complete before being released to finish his or her sentence outside the institution. This authority is granted to a parole board. The scope of the board members' authority and the consequences of their actions are enormous. No other part of the criminal justice system concentrates such power into the hands of so few.[53]

Parole boards have responsibility for selecting prisoners for parole and determining when revocation of parole and return to prison are necessary. In some states the parole board is also responsible for supervising parolees in the community. To be effective, parole boards must have certain essential elements: (1) there must be flexibility in sentencing and parole laws; (2) parole board members must be qualified for their jobs; (3) the parole staff must be qualified; (4) the parole board must be free from political interference; (5) parole must have a workable position in the government structure; (6) the board must employ proper parole procedures; (7) prerelease preparation must take place within the institution; (8) there must exist a proper public attitude toward parole; and research on the effectiveness of parole must be conducted.

Since parole selection determines the character of the organization itself, the process of selection has serious consequences to the effectiveness, and perhaps even the survival, of the entire parole system. Despite its importance to the prisoner, society, and the justice system as a whole, however, the process is a confused procedure with little consensus regarding the proper means by which decisions are made, the grounds for decisions, and whether or not minimal due process should be allowed.

From the intuitive approach of the "rehabilitative" parole board to the "justice-model" system with its guidelines and parole matrices, the system has not yet evolved a consistent decision-making base. Even the prisoners, who are at the complete mercy of the system, do not agree on which method they prefer. One study indicates that inmates may prefer mercy to justice, as they overwhelmingly favored the intuitive approach of the Pennsylvania parole system to the guidelines approach of the federal system.

The courts, too, are at odds, although at present there seems to be a rather consistent theme that due process, if allowed at all, will be minimal and determined by the statutes of the jurisdiction. It will not be protected by the Fourteenth Amendment and thus will not be a Constitutional issue.

The ACA *Manual of Correctional Standards* perhaps summarizes the issue of due process at the release hearing as well as possible:

> To an even greater extent than in the case of imprisonment, probation and parole practice is determined by an administrative discretion that is largely uncontrolled by legal standards, protections, or remedies. Until statutory and case law are more fully developed, it is virtually important within all of the correctional field that there should be established and maintained reasonable norms and remedies against the sort of abuses that are likely to develop where men have great power over their fellows and where relationships may become both mechanical and arbitrary.[54]

ENDNOTES

1. Edward E. Rhine, William R. Smith, and Ronald W. Jackson, *Paroling Authorities: Recent History and Current Practice* (Laurel, Md.: American Correctional Association, 1991), pp. 32–33.

2. American Correctional Association, *Manual of Correctional Standards* (Washington, D.C., 1966), pp. 115–116.

3. National Advisory Commission on Criminal Justice Standards and Goals, Corrections (Washington, 1973), p. 397.

4. American Correctional Association, *Manual for Adult Parole Authorities,* 2nd ed. (Washington, 1980), p. 22.

5. ACA, *supra* note 2, pp. 117, 118.

6. On some occasions this has resulted in appointments on the basis of political affiliation, rather than qualifications for making parole decisions.

7. Rhine et al., *supra* note 1, at 37.

8. *Id.* at 51.

9. Id. at.

10. *Id.* at 51. Connecticut, Delaware, Hawaii, Minnesota, and Mississippi have full-time chairs and members who serve part-time. In Iowa and Utah, the chair and at least one member are full-time, and other members serve part-time.

11. ACA, *supra* note 4, at 124.

12. George G. Killinger and Paul Cromwell, Jr., eds., *Corrections in the Community: Alternatives to Imprisonment,* 2nd ed. (St. Paul: West Publishing, 1978).

13. ACA, standards, *supra,* note 2, at 132.

14. Quoted in *The Challenge of Crime in a Free Society,* A Report of the President's Commission on Law Enforcement and Administration of Justice (1967), p. 274.

15. Good time (or "gain time") is awarded by prison authorities for institutional good conduct and reduces the period of sentence an inmate must serve before parole eligibility. Originally introduced as an incentive for inmates, it has become virtually automatic—being lost by misbehavior, rather than awarded for good behavior. The range of good-time credits is from 5 days per month to over 30 days per month. In recent years, large amounts of good time have been awarded by correctional authorities in order to reduce prison overcrowding.

16. William J. Genego, Peter D. Goldberger, and Vicki C. Jackson, "Parole Release Decision Making and the Sentencing Process," 84 *Yale L.J.* 810 (1975).

17. Elizabeth L. Taylor, *In Search of Equity: The Oregon Parole Matrix,* unpublished monograph, 1981. In 1974 the United States Court of Appeals for the 7th Circuit held that an inmate must be provided written notice of the reason for denial of parole. *King v. United States,* 492 F.2d 1337 (7th. Cir. 1974).

18. 84 *Yale L.J.* 810, 820.

19. Menechino v. Oswald, 430 F.2d 403, 407–08 (2d Cir.1970), *cert. denied,* 400 U.S. 1023, 91 S.Ct.588, 27 L.Ed.2d 635 (1971).

20. David J. Rothman, *Conscience and Convenience: The Asylum and Its Alternatives in Progressive America* (Boston: Little, Brown, 1980), p. 173.

21. *Id.* at 174.

22. NAC, *supra* note 3, at 397.

23. Later called the U.S. Parole Commission. By the Comprehensive Crime Control Act of 1984, the Commission was to be phased out over eight years, terminating completely in 1992, but was subsequently given five additional years before final abolition.

24. Peter B. Hoffman and Lucille K. DeGostin, "Parole Decision Making: Structuring Discretion," *Federal Probation,* Dec. 1974.

25. Peter B. Hoffman and Sheldon Adelberg, "The Salient Factor Score: A Nontechnical Overview," *Federal Probation,* March 1980.

26. Joan Petersilia and Susan Turner, "Guideline-Based Justice: Prediction and Racial Minorities," in D. Gottfredson and M. Tonry, eds., *Prediction and Classification* (Chicago: University of Chicago Press, 1987), pp. 151–181.

27. Kevin Krajick, "Abolishing Parole: An Idea Whose Time Has Come," *Corrections Magazine,* June 1983.

28. James L. Beck, *Offender Perceptions of Parole Decision Making,* unpublished monograph, 1981.

29. Author's files.

30. 84 *Yale L.J.* 810, at 842.

31. *Id.*

32. French v. Ciccone, 308 F.Supp. 256, 257 (W.D.Mo. 1969).

33. Anderson v. Corall, 263 U.S. 193, 44 S.Ct. 43, 68 L.Ed. 247 (1923).

34. Charles Newman, *Sourcebook in Probation, Parole, and Pardons,* 3rd ed. (Springfield, Illinois: Charles C. Thomas, 1968), pp. 206–207; 84 *Yale L.J.* 810, 843; and 45 *Minn.L.Rev.* 803, 827 (1961).

35. Scarpa v. United States Board of Parole, 477 F.2d 278, 281 (5th Cir.1972), *vacated as moot,* 414 U.S. 809, 94 S.Ct. 79, 38 L.Ed.2d 44 (1973); and Menechino v. Oswald, 430 F.2d 403, 407 (2d Cir.1970), *cert. denied,* 400 U.S. 1023, 91 S.Ct. 588, 27 L.Ed.2d 635 (1971).

36. *Id.* at 281.

37. 84 *Yale L.J.* 810, 843.

38. 430 F.2d 403 (2d Cir.1970), *cert. denied,* 400 U.S. 1023, 91 S.Ct. 588, 27 L.Ed.2d 635 (1971).

39. *Id.*

40. See United States *ex rel.* Campbell v. Pate, 401 F.2d 55 (7th Cir.1968); *Palermo v. Rockefeller,* 323 F.Supp. 478 (S.D.N.Y. 1971); and *Monks v. New Jersey State Parole Board,* 55 N.J. 238, 277 A.2d 193 (1971).

41. 442 U.S. 1, 60 L.Ed.2d 668, 99 S.Ct. 2100 (1979).

42. Greenholtz v. Inmates of the Nebraska Penal and Correctional Complex, 442 U.S. 1, 14, 99 S.Ct. 2100, 2107, 60 L.Ed.2d 668, (1919).
43. *Id.*
44. *Id.*
45. *Id.* at 16.
46. *Id.* at 9–10.
47. *Id.* at 12.
48. American Correctional Association, *Standards for Adult Parole Authorities,* 2nd ed. (College Park, Md.: ACA, June 1980), at 242–248.
49. Greenholtz v. Inmates, *supra* note 42, at 18.
50. Morrissey v. Brewer, 408 U.S. 471, 92 S.Ct. 2593, 33 L.Ed.2d 484 (1972).
51. *Id.* at 19.
52. *Id.* at 22.
53. Rhine et al., *supra* note 1, at 32–33.
54. American Correctional Association, *Manual of Correctional Standards* (College Park, Md., June 1980), p. 500. See also Justice Douglas's separate opinion in Morrissey v. Brewer, 408 U.S. 471, 92 S.Ct. 2593, 33 L.Ed.2d 484 (1972).

Discussion Questions

1. Compare and contrast the autonomous, institutional, and consolidation models of parole organization. What is the pattern in your state?
2. What are the three major functions of a parole board?
3. Why is flexibility important in sentencing and in parole laws?
4. What are the primary qualifications of a "good" parole board member; of a parole officer? Why are these qualities important?
5. What methods are used to select parole board members? Which method do you believe is best? Why?
6. What are the three major duties of a parole officer?
7. What is a halfway house, and what purpose does it serve in parole release?
8. Define and discuss "graduated release" and its role in parole.
9. Why is good public relations necessary to parole's effectiveness?
10. In the final analysis, what is the most important characteristic of a parole system?
11. How is parole eligibility typically determined?
12. What is "good time" and what is its relationship to eligibility for parole consideration?
13. Explain the two primary methods of parole decision making.
14. Distinguish between the matrix guidelines method and the "guiding principles" guidelines method.
15. Why is unstructured discretion unfair to the inmate? Give some examples.
16. What three criteria do statutes typically establish for parole-release decisions?
17. What was the ruling in *Menechino v. Oswald?* How did it affect parole decision making?
18. What issues arise when "seriousness of the offense" is considered in parole decisions? What do you think about this issue?
19. In developing parole guidelines, what were the variables that were identified as explaining a large number of the board's decisions?

20. If you were a parole board member, what factors would you consider in attempting to arrive at a fair and just decision? Why?

21. What did James Beck find in his study on prisoners' perceptions of parole-release decision making? If you were a prisoner, what method would you prefer?

22. What were the issues, and what was the decision in *Greenholtz v. Inmates of the Nebraska Penal and Correctional Complex*? In light of the conservative composition of the present Supreme Court, what do you think will be the result of future decisions on this issue?

23. Where does the American Correctional Association stand on this issue?

American Correctional Association Standards for Parole Authority Organization, Administration, and Membership

ORGANIZATION AND LEGAL BASIS

2-1001 The jurisdiction has a single authority provided by statute which has parole decision-making power with respect to all offenders convicted of a felony who are sentenced to a term of imprisonment and are eligible for discretionary parole. (Important)

DISCUSSION: Jurisdiction refers to a governmental-level parole authority which handles convicted felony offenders. In order to ensure uniformity of procedures and to lessen the probability of disparate decisions, it is important that there exist a centralized source of parole decision-making in a given jurisdiction. Decision-making is defined here to mean release, revocation, and the establishment of the conditions of release. This does not exclude certain juveniles or misdemeanants under the authority's jurisdiction.

2-1002 When the parole authority is administratively part of a federal, state, or local overall correctional agency, it is independent from the control of any of the units in the agency in its decision-making functions. (Essential)

DISCUSSION: A central principle of parole decision-making is that a parole authority should base its decisions on an objective assessment of the needs of the offender and the community. Thus, while a parole authority needs to be sensitive to the views of many persons, particularly those who have responsibility for operating correctional programs, the authority must retain its autonomy if it is to serve its purposes. A wide variety of factors may be properly weighed in reaching its conclusions. However, the authority must resist outside efforts to unduly attempt to influence its decisions, such as those of the affected institution. (See related standard 2-1007.)

2-1003 While parole investigation and supervisory staff may be administratively independent from the parole authority, they are responsive to the authority in all areas determined by statute, policy, or procedures. (Important)

DISCUSSION: There must be cooperative effort between the parole authority and the parole investigation and supervisory staff in order to provide the offender with the best possible supervision. Feedback on the status of parolees is important to the parole authority's decision-making process. Likewise, changes in parole authority policy and procedure or conditions of parole can affect the work of parole supervisory staff.

2-1004 The parole authority has the power to require that general and specific conditions of parole be enforced during the supervision of parolees. (Essential)

DISCUSSION: Since a parole authority frequently bases its decisions on the assumption that certain specific procedures will be followed by parole supervisory staff, the authority should have the power to specify general and specific conditions regarding the supervision of parolees. This power should be indicated no matter where the administrative responsibility for field staff is located.

2-1005 All staff, including any hearing examiners employed by the parole authority, are directly responsible to the authority with respect to carrying out the policies of the authority. (Essential)

DISCUSSION: Hearing examiners should be considered staff of the parole authority and directly responsible to the authority both administratively and operationally. The decision to grant, deny, or revoke parole may be assigned to the hearing examiners. (See related standards 2-1047 and 2-1115.)

2-1006 The parole authority has the legal power to secure prompt and full information which it deems necessary from courts, probation, institutions, parole, halfway houses, and other agencies or staff which would be applicable. (Essential)

DISCUSSION: A parole authority cannot operate without the kinds of information necessary for its task. It is crucial that timely and accurate information be made available from the required sources in a form useful to parole decision-makers. Though the parole authority has legal authority to require the submission of such information, it should collaborate with the agencies involved in developing the means through which it is to be delivered and the format in which it is to be presented.

2-1007 The parole authority has power to grant or deny parole and does not serve merely as an advisory body to another official or agency (Essential)

DISCUSSION: In order to achieve competent and impartial parole decision-making, with sound policies and their consistent application, the parole authority should have the power to act with finality. Serving simply as an advisory board to an elected or appointed state official does not meet this test. Such arrangements negate the required autonomous character of parole decision-making. (See related standard 2-1002.)

2-1008 The parole authority has the statutory power to cause the arrest of parolees and the power to revoke parole. (Essential)

DISCUSSION: Basic to the functioning of the parole authority is the capacity to revoke as well as to grant parole. As with the power to grant parole, the authority's power to arrest and to revoke should be indicated by statute. Parole field staff may arrest parolees on the issuance of detention warrants.

2-1009 While the existence of a statutory limit may prevent discharge prior to two years of parole, the parole authority has the statutory power to dis-charge from parole in all cases subsequent to this limitation. (Essential)

DISCUSSION: It is sometimes costly to the resources of the jurisdiction, frequently an unnecessary impediment to a parolee, and always unfair to require a person to remain under parole supervision when it has been demonstrated that neither the jurisdiction nor he or she will benefit from continued parole supervision. The power to discharge from parole in some jurisdictions may apply only after statutory minimums of not more than two years have been met. Even if this is the case, the authority should have the ultimate power to discharge from parole. (See related standards 2-1124 and 2-1125.)

AUTHORITY MEMBERS

2-1034 Members of the parole authority are chosen through a system defined by statutes or administrative policy, and with explicitly defined criteria. (Essential)

DISCUSSION: Partisan political considerations have too frequently entered into the selection of parole authority members. Though, from time to time, qualified persons are appointed under a system dominated by political considerations, often the result has been the appointment of unqualified persons as parole authority members. It is imperative that explicitly established criteria be employed in the appointment of parole authority members.

2-1035 At least two thirds of the members of the parole authority have at least a baccalaureate degree. (Essential)

DISCUSSION: A variety of educational backgrounds may qualify a person to sit on a parole authority, and individuals who do not have baccalaureate degrees may be uniquely qualified by other training or experience to serve on a parole authority. However, a parole authority must have a capacity for policy formation and articulation, an awareness of contemporary research findings and correctional techniques, and skills in system planning and management. These tasks require that an authority include in its membership some members with the minimum of a baccalaureate degree.

2-1036 At least two thirds of the members of the parole authority have at least three years' experience in a criminal justice or juvenile justice position, or equivalent experience in a relevant profession. (Essential)

DISCUSSION: While a variety of experience can be appropriate, it is expected that the parole authority membership will include persons who have had substantial experience in professions, such as law and clinical practice, which are directly relevant to parole decision-making and policy development.

2-1037 Parole authority members represent a diversity of the significant population under the jurisdiction of the agency. (Essential)

DISCUSSION: It is vital for effective decision-making and public support that a parole authority be representative of the entire community, and that offenders are dealt with by persons who represent both sexes and the racial and ethnic groups in the jurisdiction.

2-1038 Members of the parole authority do not seek or hold public office which would represent a conflict of interest while a member of the authority. (Essential)

DISCUSSION: Members of the parole authority should not disenfranchise themselves during their term on the authority. During their term, however, political considerations should never enter the decision-making process. The avoidance of conflict of interest is essential to the objective role of the authority. (See related standard 2-1080.)

2-1039 Positions of members of the parole authority are full-time. In jurisdictions where the parole authority has a minimum of cases to be heard, the chairperson must be full-time but other members may be part-time. A full justification for such action is necessary. (Important)

DISCUSSION: The task and scope of the work of the parole authority is such that full-time members should be appointed. In small jurisdictions, or those where there are few cases to be heard by the authority, justification of an alternative to a full-time authority will be considered.

2-1040 Tenure on the parole authority is no less than five years. Legal provision allows for the removal of parole authority members for good and demonstrated cause only after a full and open hearing when one has been requested by the member. (Important)

DISCUSSION: While even longer terms are desirable, it is important that parole authority members have at least five-year terms on an authority to provide stability of membership and freedom from undue concern about reappointment. It should be understood that a term of five years does not mean that the expectation exists that a parole authority member will not be reappointed. Conversely, reappointment should not be considered automatic.

2-1041 If a fixed term of office is used in the appointment of parole authority members, the terms of the members are staggered. (Essential)

DISCUSSION: Continuity of policy is an important goal for a correctional system which seeks equity and efficiency. Static policy is not the general goal. Change will be an ongoing need; however, if it is to occur, it should be orderly with due regard for previous organizational history. Abrupt alterations of program which fail to consider prior efforts almost inevitably produce unwarranted disparities in decisions and make stable program development very difficult. In a key correctional unit, such as the parole authority, continuity of policy is a necessity, and staggered terms of appointment are one important means of achieving it.

2-1042 Salaries of parole authority members are within twenty percent of the salary paid to judges of courts having trial jurisdiction over felony cases. (Essential)

DISCUSSION: The decision-making responsibility of parole authority members is comparable to that of judges of courts having trial jurisdiction. This level of compensation can help attract persons with the required skills and experience to serve on parole boards.

SOURCE: Reprinted from the American Correctional Association Manual of Correctional Standards with permission of the American Correctional Association.

PAROLE CONDITIONS AND REVOCATION

11

CONDITIONS OF PAROLE

For most purposes, there are no differences between the conditions of probation and those of parole, and the discussion of probation conditions in Chapter 4 can be said to apply generally. Statutes may require that certain conditions be imposed upon parolees, and typically they give the paroling authority the right to impose such other conditions "as it may deem proper." Typical **parole conditions** direct that upon release, parolees will

- report to their parole supervisor,
- not change their county of residence without approval,
- work at gainful employment and support their dependents,
- make regular reports,
- refrain from the use of alcohol and narcotics,
- avoid association with former inmates of penal institutions and other individuals of bad character,
- obey all municipal, county, state, and federal laws and ordinances,
- conduct themselves as good citizens, and
- cooperate with their parole supervisor and the parole board.[1]

Special conditions may prohibit the possession of firearms or the use of a motor vehicle, payment of a fine or restitution, a community service order, residence in a community corrections center, or a period of "house arrest." Table 11–1 illustrates various parole conditions and the extent to which they are imposed in selected jurisdictions. A typical parole agreement that specifies conditions is shown in Figure 11–1.

As in the case of probation conditions, the courts will uphold reasonable conditions but will strike down illegal conditions or those considered impossible to fulfill. The courts also frown upon the imposition of unusual or "exotic" conditions. Generally, however, courts will uphold more stringent conditions for a parolee than for a probationer.

The tests applied to probation conditions in *People v. Dominguez*[2] are often cited as a proper measure of the reasonableness of parole conditions as well. The court ruled in that case that a probation condition that

- has no relationship to the crime of which the offender was convicted,
- relates to conduct that is not in itself criminal, and
- requires or forbids conduct not reasonably related to future criminality

does not serve the statutory ends of probation is invalid.

Rights of Parolees during Parole Period

Parolees have a right to personal liberty so long as they comply with the conditions of parole. Courts have ruled that parole conditions must be constitutional, clear, and reasonable and must contribute to the offender's rehabilitation and/or to the protection of society.[3] The American Correctional Association (ACA), in its *Standards for Adult Parole Authorities,* recommends that general conditions, which apply to all parolees, should require simply that a parolee observe the law, maintain appropriate contact with the parole system, and notify the parole officer of any change of

T A B L E 11–1

Selected Conditions of Parole in Effect in 51 Jurisdictions

CONDITION OF PAROLE	NUMBER OF JURISDICTIONS	PERCENTAGE
Obey all federal, state, and local laws	50	98.0
Report to the parole officer as directed and answer all reasonable inquiries by the parole officer	49	96.1
Refrain from possessing a firearm or other dangerous weapon unless granted written permission	47	92.2
Remain within the jurisdiction of the court and notify the parole officer of any change in residence	46	90.2
Permit the parole officer to visit the parolee at home or elsewhere	42	82.4
Obey all rules and regulations of the parole supervision agency	40	78.4
Maintain gainful employment	40	78.4
Abstain from association with persons with criminal records	31	60.8
Pay all court-ordered fines, restitution, or other financial penalties	27	52.9
Meet family responsibilities and support dependents	24	47.1
Undergo medical or psychiatric treatment and/or enter and remain in a specified institution, if so ordered by the court	23	45.1
Pay supervision fees	19	37.3
Attend a prescribed secular course of study or vocational training	9	17.6
Perform community service	7	13.7

SOURCE: Edward E. Rhine, William R. Smith, and Ronald W. Jackson, *Paroling Authorities: Recent History and Current Practice* (Laurel, Md.: American Correctional Association, 1991). Used with permission of the American Correctional Association.

residence. Special conditions, it states, should be added "only when they are clearly relevant to the parolee's compliance with the requirements of the criminal law. Conditions should not concern . . . the lifestyle of the offender, as such, but should be tested directly against the probability of serious criminal behavior by the individual parolee."[4] The ACA also recommends that as much as possible, the parolee should be encouraged to make known to the paroling authority his/her views about the conditions that will be imposed, and should have the opportunity to appeal any request of a parole officer to fix a new condition of parole.

Arrest, Search, and Seizure

It has been held that the premises of a parolee may be searched by his or her parole supervisor without a search warrant and without the parolee's consent.

FIGURE 11–1

Typical Parole Agreement

STATE OF CONNECTICUT
BOARD OF PAROLE

PAROLE AGREEMENT

You have been granted a parole by the Board of Parole. It will be effective on the date indicated or as soon thereafter as your parole program is approved by the Division of Parole.

Parole gives you the opportunity to serve the remainder of your sentence outside of the institution. The Board of Parole may grant you a certificate of early discharge from your sentence at the recommendation of your parole officer after you have shown satisfactory progress wile you are on parole. Until that time, or until the maximum expiration date of your sentence, you will remain in the legal custody of the Board of Parole and under the supervision of the Division of Parole of the Department of Correction.

A parole officer will be assigned to work with you and help you adjust to life in the community. The parole officer will attempt to help you and will be available for counseling should any problems arise. You are urged to talk over any difficulties with the parole officer. The parole officer will also submit reports on your progress to the Commissioner of Correction, and, if requested, to the Board of Parole.

It is also the parole officer's duty to make sure that you abide by the conditions of parole found *on the other side of this page.* Those conditions have been carefully designed as guidelines for acceptable behavior while you are on parole. If you should violate any of those conditions of parole, the officer has the authority from the Chairman of the Board of Parole and the Commissioner of Correction to return you to custody so that your parole status may be reviewed by the Board of Parole. By signing your name to *the other side of this page* you indicate your consent to abide by the standard and individual conditions of your parole listed *there,* as well as your awareness that failure to abide by those conditions will constitute a violation of parole and may result in your return to custody.

It is the hope of the Board of Parole in granting you this parole that you will accept it and its conditions as an opportunity to prove to yourself and to others that you are capable of living as a responsible, lawabiding citizen of society and of your community.

Parolee _____ No. _____ Release on or after _____

CONDITIONS OF PAROLE

1. Upon my release I will report to my parole officer as directed and follow the parole officer's instructions.
2. I will report to may parole officer in person and in writing whenever and wherever the parole officer directs.
3. I agree that the parole officer has the right to visit my residence or place of employment at any reasonable time.
4. I will notify my parole officer within 48 hours of any changes in my place of residence, in my place of employment, or of any change in my marital status.
6. I will notify my parole officer within 48 hours if at nay time I am arrested for any offense.
7. I will not at any time have firearms, ammunition, or any other weapon in my possession or under my control.
8. I will not leave the State of Connecticut without prior permission of my parole officer.
9. I will obey all laws and, to the best of my ability, fulfill all my legal obligations.
10. I will not at any time use, or have in my possession or control, any illegal drug or narcotic.
11. Your release on parole is based upon the conclusion of the Parole panel that there is a reasonable probability that you will live and remain at liberty without violating the law and that your release is not incompatible with the welfare of society. In the event that you engage in conduct in the future that renders this conclusion no longer valid, then your parole will be revoked or modified accordingly.
12. I also agree to abide by *the following* INDIVIDUAL CONDITIONS:

Signed _____

Witness _____ Date _____

For the Board of Parole _____
(*Chairman   Secretary*)

Home Confinement and Electronic Monitoring for Federal Parolees

Home confinement is a sentencing alternative available to eligible offenders who would ordinarily be incarcerated in an institution or placed in a halfway house. There are many types of home confinement programs, ranging from imposition of Late-night curfew conditions to 24-hours-per-day continuous detention. Enforcement techniques vary as well, from random contacts by a supervising officer to continuous electronic monitoring.

The use of electronic monitoring for federal offenders emerged out of an initial effort with an experimental "curfew" home-confinement program. On March 3, 1986, the United States Parole Commission implemented this experimental program (termed the *curfew parole program*) to provide a substitute for community correction-center residence for the 60-day period preceding the parole release date. The experimental program was designed for prisoners who would otherwise qualify for community treatment-center residence, but who had acceptable release plans and did not require the support services provided by the community treatment center. Under this program, qualified and approved prisoners had their release dates advanced for up to 60 days on the condition that they remain at their place of residence between the hours of 9 P.M. and 6 A.M. every night unless they were given permission in advance by their supervising U.S. probation officer.

By January 1991 approximately 4,000 offenders had participated in the program. At any one time approximately 150 offenders were on curfew parole. The U.S. Parole Commission reported that the violation rate had been very low.

SOURCE: Adapted from James L. Beck, Jody Klein-Saffran, and Harold B. Wooten, "Home Confinement and the Use of Electronic Monitoring with Federal Parolees," *Federal Probation*, December 1990.

Some states require that the parolee, as a condition of parole, give this permission. The condition has generally been upheld, although special problems arise when evidence of a new crime is obtained as a result of the search. In a New York case, a parole officer obtained a warrant charging a parolee with a violation and then went to the parolee's apartment. The officer charged the parolee with a parole-rule violation and conducted a two-and-a-half hour search, which yielded narcotics. The parolee was convicted on the new charge, and the conviction was upheld. The court said:

> Defendant appellant, as a parolee, was deprived of no constitutional rights by the search and seizure which was made under the circumstances of this case.[5]

In another New York case, the court noted that the **reasonableness standard** for a search and seizure is not necessarily the same when applied to a parolee as when applied to a person whose rights are not similarly circumscribed.[6] In a 1987 case involving a probationer *(Griffin v. Wisconsin)*, the United States Supreme Court held that the search of a probationer's residence without a warrant was "reasonable" within the meaning of the Fourth Amendment if it was conducted pursuant to a valid regulation regarding probationers. Although this case involves a probationer rather than a parolee, the ruling appears to apply to both, as the Court referred to fact that "probationers do not enjoy the absolute liberty to which every citizen is entitled, but only a conditional liberty dependent upon observance of special restrictions." This, of course, would apply (perhaps even more so) to parolees. A box near here summarizes the *Griffin* decision.

Griffin v. Wisconsin 483 U.S. 868, 107 S.Ct. 3164, 97 L.Ed.2d 709 (1987)

In this case a probation supervisor received a call from a police officer indicating that there were or might be guns in the home of a probationer. Unable to secure the assistance of the probationer's supervising officer, the probation supervisor, Michael Lew, accompanied by another probation officer, proceeded to the home of the probationer and conducted a search. Pursuant to their search they found a handgun. The probationer was subsequently charged with possession of a firearm by a convicted felon, and he moved to suppress the evidence seized during the search. This motion was denied, however, and he was ultimately convicted. He sought review, claiming that the search of his residence was unreasonable and that the fruits of the search should have been suppressed. The Wisconsin Supreme Court affirmed the conviction. It held that the "reasonable grounds" standard of Wisconsin's probation search regulation satisfied the condition of "reasonableness" under the United States Constitution. It further found that, because the information came from someone who had no reason to supply inaccurate information, it was sufficiently reliable. See *State v. Griffin,* 131 Wis.2d 41, 388 N.W.2d 535 (1986); 9 PPLR 76 (June, 1987).

On review by the United States Supreme Court, a five to four majority of the court found that the evidence seized pursuant to the search was properly admitted against the probationer. Justice Scalia's majority opinion noted firstly that Wisconsin law puts probationers in the legal custody of the State Department of Health and Social Services and renders them subject to certain conditions set by the court and the rules and regulations established by the Department. One of the regulations imposed by the Department permits a probation officer to search a probationer's home without a warrant as long as the officer's supervisor approves and so long as there are "reasonable grounds" to believe the presence of contraband—including any item that the probationer cannot possess under the probation conditions. The rule further provides that an officer is to consider a variety of factors in determining whether "reasonable grounds" exist. Among those factors are information provided by an informant, the reliability and specificity of that information, the reliability of the informant, the officer's own experience with the probationer, and the need to verify compliance with the rules of supervision and state and federal law. Citing these provisions, the majority then went on to find that the search of the probationer's home satisfied the demands of the Fourth Amendment because the search was carried out pursuant to a regulation that itself satisfied the Fourth Amendment's reasonableness requirement.

Citing a variety of situations where governmental investigators could properly conduct searches without adhering to the usual warrant or probable-cause requirements, the majority went on to note that a State's operation of a probation system presented "special needs," beyond normal law enforcement, that justified departures from the usual warrant and probable-cause requirements. The majority opinion noted that probation was simply one point on a continuum of possible punishments, ranging from solitary confinement in a maximum-security facility to a few hours of mandatory community service. Thus, to a greater or lesser degree, probationers do not enjoy the absolute liberty to which every citizen is entitled, but only a conditional liberty dependent upon observance of special restrictions. The majority found that the goals of supervision were intended to ensure that the restrictions imposed are in fact observed. Thus, the state's interest in supervision was a "special need" that permitted a degree of impingement upon privacy that would not be constitutional if applied to the public at large.

The majority then went on to find that a warrant requirement would interfere to an appreciable degree with the probation supervision system by setting up a magistrate rather than the probation officer as the judge of what type of supervision the probationer required. Thus, the majority held that a warrant was not required as a condition precedent to a probation search.

Turning to the issue of probable cause, the majority found that the probation regime would be unduly disrupted by such a requirement. Even more than the requirement of a warrant, a probable cause requirement would reduce the deterrent effect of the supervisory arrangement. Furthermore, the majority noted that the supervisory relationship was not entirely adversarial and that the imposition of a probable cause requirement on such a relationship might well be destructive. Stated the court [footnotes omitted]:

> In such circumstances it is both unrealistic and destructive of the whole object of the continuing probation relationship to insist upon the same degree of demonstrable reliability of particular items of supporting data, and upon the same degree of certainty of violation, as is required in other contexts. In some cases—especially those involving drugs or illegal weapons—the probation agency must be able to act based upon a lesser degree of certainty than the Fourth Amendment would otherwise require in order to intervene before a probationer does damage to himself or society. The agency, moreover, must be able to proceed on the basis of its entire experience with the probationer, and to assess probabilities in the light of its knowledge of his life, character, and circumstances.
>
> To allow adequate play for such factors, we think it reasonable to permit information provided by a police officer, whether or not on the basis of first-hand knowledge, to support a probationer search. The same conclusion is suggested by the fact that the police may be unwilling to disclose their confidential sources to probation personnel. For the same reason, and also because it is the very assumption of the institution of probation that the probationer is in need of rehabilitation and is more likely than the ordinary citizen to violate the law, we think it enough if the information provided indicates, as it did here, only the likelihood ("had or might have guns") of facts justifying the search.

Concluding that the search of the probationer's residence was "reasonable" within the meaning of the Fourth Amendment because it was conducted pursuant to a valid regulation governing probationers, the majority found it unnecessary to consider whether "any" search of a probationer's home by a probation officer was lawful when there were "reasonable grounds" to believe contraband was present.

The judgment of the Wisconsin Supreme Court was affirmed.

SOURCE: *Probation and Parole Law Reports*, Knehans–Miller Publications. Used with permission.

POWER TO ARREST A PAROLEE.   Many states give a parole officer the right to arrest a parolee without a warrant. Other states require that an **arrest warrant** be issued by the parole board.[7] In New York and Pennsylvania parole officers may arrest a parole violator without a warrant and receive authorization—a **temporary detainer**—by telephone immediately afterward. These temporary detainers must be replaced by an arrest warrant within 24 hours in Pennsylvania, and 48 hours in New York. Federal probation officers, who also supervise federal parolees, may arrest a parolee (or probationer) without a warrant if there is probable cause to believe that the person being supervised has violated a condition of his probation or release. Upon arrest, the probationer or releasee must be taken before the court having jurisdiction over him/her (or the last court that had jurisdiction over him/her) "without unnecessary delay."[8] Justification for these practices are found in the occasional need to take immediate action. Howard Abadinsky reported:

> When I was a parole officer in New York, it was not unusual to encounter parolees, unexpectedly, who were in serious violation of the conditions of their release. For example, heavily involved in abusing heroin (and obviously engaging in criminal acts to support the habit); prohibited from the use of alcohol (because of the dangerous nature of their behavior while under the influence) and intoxicated; child molesters found in the company of children. I could take such persons into custody immediately and use the telephone for detainer-warrant authorization.[9]

In other jurisdictions, such as Texas, the parole officer must request, in writing, a warrant from the parole board, although **emergency warrants** may be obtained by telephone in certain, very limited circumstances.[10] Other jurisdictions allow *citations* to be issued that require the parolee to appear for a hearing (Oregon), that order the parolee to appear before the parole-agency supervisor for a **case review** (Wisconsin), or that allow the parole officer to arrest the alleged violator and take him or her before a magistrate to determine if probable cause exists that the parole conditions have been violated, and if so, to issue a warrant for his or her arrest (Iowa).

The ACA *Standards* regards the arrest and detention of a parolee on violation charges as a serious act with profound implications for the parolee. Th ACA recommends that arrest should be made only with a warrant issued by "the affirmative approval of a parole authority member or the statewide or regional director of parole supervision services."[11] Standard 2-1107 requires:

> Warrants for the arrest and detention of parolees are issued only upon adequate evidence which indicates a probable serious or repeated pattern of violation of parole conditions and a compelling need for detention pending the parole authority's initial revocation decision.

REVOCATION OF PAROLE

The term **revocation** refers to the formal termination of conditional freedom and the reinstatement of imprisonment. For many years, the issue of revocation of parole has been controversial in the criminal justice field. The public tends to view the rate of parole violation as the criterion of parole success or failure. Criminal justice practitioners, in contrast, recognize that what may appear to be good parole results statistically can, in light of the quality and extent of supervision, indicate just the opposite.

One state may report a violation rate of 8 percent, but the only thing the state counts as a "violation" is the conviction for a new crime. This violation rate does not mean very much. Another state may report a much greater rate of violation, but it practices very close, intensive supervision and has a policy of enforcing *all* the rules of parole. In neither instance does the reported violation rate accurately appraise the jurisdiction's parole system.

Three Theories of Parole

What constitutes a violation of parole? Parole revocation practices in the past were often related to the "theory" of parole prevailing in a particular jurisdiction. Parole has variously been viewed as a form of grace, a contract, and as a different type of custody.

Advocates of the **grace theory** view parole as a privilege that is granted by the grace (or mercy) of the parole board. Under this theory, parole confers no particular rights to the recipient and is subject to withdrawal at any time. The **contract theory** holds that parole is a contract between the state and the parolee. Under the contract, a prisoner agrees to abide by certain conditions and terms and waives his/her rights to a hearing in case of violation. A violation of the conditions thus represents a breach of contract, and parole can be revoked. According to the **continuing custody theory,** the parolee remains in the custody of either the parole authorities or the prison warden and therefore his/her constitutional rights are limited. Revocation is merely a change in the *degree* of custody and requires little if any due process.[12]

Grace theory

The view that parole is a privilege and a matter of grace (mercy) by the executive. Parole confers no particular rights on the recipient and is subject to withdrawal at any time.

Contract theory

The view that parole represents a contract between the state and the parolee by which a prisoner agrees to abide by certain conditions and terms in return for his/her release. Violation of the conditions represents a breach of contract that allows parole to be revoked.

Continuing custody theory

The view that a parolee remains in custody of either the parole authorities or the prison and that his/her constitutional rights are limited. Revocation is merely a change in the degree of custody.

The Revocation Hearing

Regardless of the theory under which parole proceeds or the nature of the violation, the central issue of the parole revocation process is the right to a fair hearing. Until the 1970s, many jurisdictions' procedures for the return of parole violators were so informal that the term *hearing* was a misnomer. In many instances, revocation involved no more than the parole board's *pro forma* approval of the parole officer's request. In many areas, the revocation decision represented almost unfettered discretion of paroling authorities. In addition to minimal procedural formality, the grounds for revocation were also nonspecific, including such grounds as "poor attitude," "poor adjustment," and "failure to cooperate."[13]

Such procedures for the casual, quick return of parole violators rested primarily upon the grace theory of the parole grant. Parole officials operating under the grace doctrine did not view the revocation process as warranting such matters as due process, procedural regularity, matters of proof, hearing, or review.

A 1964 study of parole board revocations showed that there was no hearing at all in at least seven states. In jurisdictions where a hearing was provided, the alleged violator was rarely allowed counsel. Any witnesses to the alleged violation were almost always seen outside the hearing at the parole board offices; few were subject to confrontation or cross-examination. Although some states allowed parolees to have the assistance of lawyers at the time of the survey, no jurisdiction assigned counsel to indigent parolees.[14]

Pro forma

(Latin) As a matter of form. Done in a perfunctory manner. Done as a matter of course.

Court Decisions regarding Revocation

The appellate courts have intervened considerably in the parole process generally and in revocation procedures specifically. Until 1972, there was disagreement among the various jurisdictions as to whether a parolee had a constitutional right to a parole revocation hearing. Some jurisdictions provided for such a hearing by statute; in others, parole revocation could occur without either notice or hearing. Courts disagreed, as well.

One of the leading cases in the federal jurisdiction was *Hyser v. Reed*, decided in the District of Columbia circuit court in 1963.[15] The appellate court generally supported the common position that revocation was strictly a withdrawal of a privilege not requiring procedural due process, such as confrontation and cross-examination of witnesses or assistance of counsel. *Hyser* did, however, address the issue of *venue*—where the revocation hearing should take place. The court supported the U.S. Board of Parole practice of conducting a fact-finding hearing on the site of the alleged offense violation of conditions (referred to as an *on-site hearing*), with review at the institution only if the first hearing determined the offender should be returned.

Subsequent to *Hyser*, however, courts in some states and federal jurisdictions departed from the first part of the *Hyser* decision, namely, the lack of any right, constitutional or otherwise, for due process to be applied at revocation proceedings. Most courts that departed from *Hyser* did so on the basis of a United States Supreme Court decision involving deferred sentencing or probation revocation. In *Mempa v. Rhay,* the court held in 1967 that a state probationer

Consequences of parole revocation.

had a right to a hearing and to counsel upon allegations of violation of probation.[16] A number of courts interpreted the principle of *Mempa* to apply to parole as well. Since that decision, a great deal of discussion and controversy has occurred with regard to parole revocation and due process.

In 1972 the United States Supreme Court dealt with several crucial issues relating to parole revocation in the case of *Morrissey v. Brewer.*[17] Two parolees appealed an appellate court's decision on the ground that their paroles were revoked without a hearing and that they were thereby deprived of due process. The appellate court, in affirming the district court's denial of relief, had reasoned that parole is only "a correctional device authorizing service of sentence outside a penitentiary" and concluded that a parolee who is still "in custody" is not entitled to a full adversary hearing.[18]

In reversing the court of appeals's decision, the Supreme Court held that:

> . . . the liberty of a parolee, although indeterminate, includes many of the core values of unqualified liberty and its termination inflicts a "grievous loss" on the parolee and often on others. It is hardly useful any longer to try to deal with this problem in terms of whether the parolee's liberty is a "right" or a "privilege." By whatever name the liberty is valuable and must be seen as within the protection of the Fourteenth Amendment. Its termination calls for some orderly process, however, informal.[19]

The question is not merely the weight of the individual's interest, but whether the nature of the interest is within contemplation of the "liberty or property" language of the Fourteenth Amendment. The court stated that the state properly subjects a parolee to many restrictions not applicable to other citizens, and the parolee is not entitled to the full panoply of rights due a defendant in a criminal proceeding. However, due process requires that a parolee be given a **preliminary hearing** (often called an **on-site hearing**) to determine whether there is probable cause to believe that he or she committed a parole violation. At this preliminary hearing, usually held in jail, the parolee may appear and speak in his or her own behalf and may bring letters, documents, or individuals who can give relevant information to an independent, neutral, and detached hearing officer. The hearing officer need not be a lawyer or a judge.[20] The parolee should receive prior notice of the inquiry, its purpose, and the alleged violation, and the hearing officer should digest the evidence on probable cause and state the reasons for holding the parolee for the parole board's decision.

At the **revocation hearing,** which must be conducted reasonably soon after the parolee's arrest, these minimum **due-process requirements** must be met:

1. written notice of the claimed violation of parole,
2. disclosure to the parolee of the evidence against him or her,
3. opportunity to be heard in person and to present witnesses and documentary evidence,
4. the right to confront and cross-examine adverse witnesses (unless the hearing officer specifically finds good cause for not allowing confrontation),
5. a "neutral and detached" hearing body such as a traditional parole board, the members of which need not be judicial officers or lawyers, and
6. a written statement by the fact finders as to the evidence relied on and the reasons for revoking parole.

RIGHT TO COUNSEL AT REVOCATION HEARING.   In the *Morrissey* case the Court did not reach the question of the parolee's right to the assistance of retained or appointed counsel at each hearing. In one of the first cases decided after *Morrissey,* however, the California Supreme Court *en banc* held that "as a judicially declared rule of criminal procedure," a probationer was entitled to representation by retained or appointed counsel at formal proceedings for the revocation of probation. The court pointed out that a violation of a probation condition is often a matter of degree or quality of conduct, and that the point where a violation occurs is often a matter of technical judgment. It then quoted from *Goldberg v. Kelly* that "trained counsel in such circumstances can help delineate the issues, present the factual contentions in an orderly manner, and generally safeguard the interests of [the] client."[21]

In *Gagnon v. Scarpelli* the Supreme Court used similar reasoning to mandate a case-by-case determination of the need for counsel at probation and parole revocation hearings. The determination of the need for counsel is to be left to the discretion of the state authority responsible for administering the probation and parole system. The Court stated that in cases where a probationer's or parolee's version of a disputed issue can be fairly presented only by trained counsel, appointment of counsel for the indigent probationer or parolee should be made, "[a]lthough the presence and participation of counsel will probably be both undesirable and constitutionally unnecessary in most revocation hearings. . . ."[22] Both the Supreme Court and the California court refused to make the rule in *Morrissey* retroactive to a parole revocation that occurred before that decision.[23]

EN BANC:

(French) Designates a session of court in which all judges participate.

Resentencing after Parole Revocation

In some jurisdictions the parolee whose parole is revoked receives no credit on his/her sentence for the time spent on parole. In other jurisdictions, he/she receives credit on the sentence as **straight time;** that is, without the benefit of good-time credits. In a few states, the parolee receives credit on his or her sentence equal to the time spent on parole and also obtains reductions for good behavior earned while on parole. Generally, a parolee whose parole has been revoked may be reparoled. In some cases, he or she must remain in prison for a specified time before becoming eligible to be considered for reparole.

SUMMARY

There are no essential differences between probation and parole conditions. As with probation conditions, the conditions of parole are required to be constitutional, clear, and reasonable and to contribute to the rehabilitation of the offender and/or the protection of society. Generally speaking, however, courts will uphold the imposition of more stringent conditions on a parolee than on a probationer.

A revocation of parole is the formal termination of conditional freedom and the reinstatement of imprisonment. The central issue of revocation is the right to a fair hearing. Until the 1970s procedures in most jurisdictions were so informal that the word *hearing* was a misnomer. One study revealed that seven states allowed no hearing at all. In most cases the paroling authorities exercised almost unfettered discretion in revocation decisions. However, a revolution in due process for parolees and probationers with regard to revocation has occurred since the 70s. Federal courts have intervened considerably in the parole process and in revocation procedures. A series of appellate and U.S. Supreme Court decisions resulted in due-process requirements that compel the paroling authority to conduct a (1) preliminary hearing to determine if probable cause exists to believe that the parolee has committed a parole violation and (2) a revocation hearing by a "neutral and detached" hearing body such as a parole board. At the revocation hearing the parolee has the rights to notice and to disclosure of the evidence against him/her, to the opportunities to be heard and present witnesses and to confront and cross-examine adverse witnesses, and to receive a written statement by the fact finders of the evidence relied on and the reasons for revoking parole. The parolee (or probationer) also has the right to be represented by an attorney in cases where his/her version of a disputed issue can be fairly presented only by trained counsel.

In some states a parolee whose parole is revoked receives no credit on his/her sentence for time spent on parole. In other jurisdictions the parolee receives full credit for time on parole.

ENDNOTES

1. Model Penal Code, § 305.13. See also N.Y. Correct.Law § 215 (McKinney).
2. 236 Cal. App.2d 623, 64 Cal. Rptr. 290 (1967).

3. U.S. v. Consuelo-Gonzales, 521 F. 2d 259 (9th Cir. 1975); Porth v. Templar, 453 F.2d 330 (10th Cir., 1971).

4. American Correctional Association, *Standards for Adult Parole Authorities,* 2nd ed. (College Park, Md.: ACA, 1980), p. 28.

5. People v. Randazzo, 15 N.Y.2d 526, 254 N.Y.S.2d 99, 202 N.E.2d 549 (1964). A California case reached the same result; People v. Denne, 141 Cal.App.2d 499, 297 P.2d 451 (1956).

6. People v. Langella, 41 Misc.2d 65, 244 N.Y.S.2d 802 (1963); DiMarco v. Greene, 385 F.2d 556 (6th Cir.1967).

7. A former provision in the Texas law that permitted arrest without a warrant was ruled unconstitutional by the attorney general. Attorney General's Opinion no. 22 (March 11, 1958). The present Texas provisions read as follows: "Upon order by the Governor, the Board is authorized to issue warrant for the return of any paroled prisoner to the institution from which he was paroled."

8. 18 U.S.C.A. § 3606. (Added Pub.L.98-473, Title II, § 212(a)(2), Oct. 12, 1984, 98 Stat. 2003).

9. Howard Abadinsky, *Probation and Parole: Theory and Practice,* 4th ed. (Englewood Cliffs, N.J.: Prentice Hall, 1991), p. 224.

10. Although an emergency warrant may be issued on telephoned request from a parole officer, the board has traditionally limited the issuance of such warrants to situations that absolutely require immediate arrest and detention.

11. ACA, *supra* note 4, Standard 2-1106.

12. Henry Burns, *Corrections: Organization and Administration* (St. Paul; West), p. 308.

13. National Advisory Commission, *Report on Corrections* (Washington, 1973), p. 404.

14. *Id.* at 405.

15. 115 U.S.App.D.C. 254, 318 F.2d 225 (1963).

16. Mempa v. Rhay, 389 U.S. 128, 88 S.Ct. 254, 19 L.Ed.2d 336 (1967). Among due-process requirements, the *Mempa* court held that in order for probation to be revoked and a new sentence imposed, an offender must be provided counsel.

17. 408 U.S. 471, 92 S.Ct. 2593, 33 L.Ed.2d 484 (1972).

18. 408 U.S. at 474, 92 S.Ct. at 2596, 33 L.Ed.2d at 487 (1972).

19. 408 U.S. at 482, 92 S.Ct. at 2602, 33 L.Ed.2d at 493 (1972).

20. In most jurisdictions the hearing officer is a probation or parole officer who is not involved in the case; that is, not the officer who supervised the releasee, or who requested the revocation warrant. Some jurisdictions especially train and assign certain officers to perform this task; others rotate the job or assign it to whomever is available at the time.

21. People v. Vickers, 8 Cal.3d 451, 105 Cal.Rptr. 305, 503 P.2d 1313 (1972), *quoting* Goldberg v. Kelly, 397 U.S. 254, 90 S.Ct. 1011, 25 L.Ed.2d 287 (1970).

22. Gagnon v. Scarpelli, 411 U.S. 778, 93 S.Ct. 1756, 36 L.Ed.2d 656 (1973).

23. In re Prewitt, 8 Cal.3d 470, 105 Cal.Rptr. 318, 503 P.2d 1326 (1972).

DISCUSSION QUESTIONS

1. What "test" do courts use to determine whether to uphold or strike down a particular condition of parole? Give an example of a condition that would be held invalid.

2. What general conditions of parole are recommended by the ABA *Standards* for *all* parolees. What "test" is suggested by the ABA for a parole condition?

3. Different states have different rules regarding arrest warrants for parolees. What are three approaches discussed in the chapter? What is the law (or procedure) in your state?

4. Why is a jurisdiction's reported parole violation rate in itself not an accurate indicator of its parole system?

5. Explain the three "theories" of parole. How does each relate to the revocation process? What "theory" prevails in your state?

6. What parole revocation due-process requirements were established in *Morrissey v. Brewer?*

7. How was the "right to counsel" question answered in *Morrissey* and subsequent cases?

SUPPLEMENTAL READING

American Correctional Association Standards for Arrest and Revocation of Parole

DETERMINATION

2-1106 Warrants for the arrest and detention of parolees, pending a determination by the parole authority as to whether parole should be revoked, or provisionally revoked, are issued only upon the affirmative approval of a parole authority member or the statewide or regional director of parole supervision services. (Essential)

DISCUSSION: The arrest and detention of a parolee on violation charges is a serious act with profound implications for the parolee. In view of the loss of liberty which results from the issuance of a detention warrant, the need for such a warrant should be reviewed by a parole authority member or the statewide or regional director of parole services. The power to issue detention warrants should be exercised by such administrative personnel, not by the parole officer involved directly in the supervision process.

2-1107 Warrants for the arrest and detention of parolees are issued only upon adequate evidence which indicates a probable serious or repeated pattern of violation of parole conditions and a compelling need for detention pending the parole authority's initial revocation decision. (Essential)

DISCUSSION: The standard for the issuance of detention warrants may not rise to the standard of probable cause required for arrest on criminal charges. However, to justify issuance of a detention warrant, sufficient evidence should be produced to indicate that parole conditions have been seriously breached and that detention is required. Detention may be required in order to prevent injury to an individual or the public, to interrupt a serious continuing violation of parole, or to assure the presence of a parolee at a preliminary hearing when it is determined that the parolee would not attend voluntarily.

2-1108 When parole violation charges are based on the alleged commission of a new crime, a detention warrant is not issued unless the parolee's presence in the community would present an unreasonable risk to public or individual safety. (Essential)

DISCUSSION: The issuance of a detention warrant often precludes a parolee who is charged with committing a new crime from the possibility of bail or other forms of pretrial release. As a general rule, parolees should be able to seek the forms of pretrial release which are available to other criminal defendants. However, the presence of other serious parole violation charges or a danger to public or individual safety may justify the issuance of a detention warrant when a parolee is charged with committing a new crime.

PRELIMINARY HEARING

2-1109 When a parolee is arrested on a detention warrant, or when a detention warrant is lodged as a back-up to bail in conjunction with pending criminal charges, a preliminary hearing is held within fourteen calendar days after the arrest and detention of the parolee or the lodging of the detention warrant; however, when there has been a conviction or a finding of probable cause on new criminal charges, the preliminary hearing is not required. (Essential)

DISCUSSION: The United States Supreme Court case of *Morrissey v. Brewer* 408 U.S. 471, 92 S.Ct. 2593, 33 L.Ed.2d 484 (1972) requires, as a matter of due process, that a preliminary hearing be conducted as soon as possible after a parolee is taken into custody,

261

while evidence and sources are readily available. The purpose of the hearing is to determine whether probable cause exists to believe that parole conditions have been violated. Later cases in various jurisdictions have held that a conviction or a finding of probable cause on new criminal charges takes the place, for due process purposes, of the preliminary parole hearing.

2-1110 The preliminary hearing is held in or near the community where the violation is alleged to have occurred or where the parolee has been taken into custody. (Essential)

DISCUSSION: (See related standard 2-1109.)

2-1111 The preliminary hearing may be delayed or postponed for good cause, and the parolee may waive the hearing if first informed of rights pertaining to the hearing and of the consequences of waiving the hearing. (Essential)

DISCUSSION: Due process requires that any waiver of rights by the parolee be done knowingly and voluntarily. Therefore, the parole authority should assure that no form of coercion is used to induce a waiver of the preliminary hearing, and that the parolee understands the nature and consequences of the hearing before waiving it.

2-1112 The authority may delegate to a member of the parole administrative staff or to field officers the authority to conduct a preliminary hearing and make findings as to grounds for revocation. (Essential)

DISCUSSION: The *Morrissey* case provides that the hearing officer need not be a judicial official, but may be a parole staff member, so long as that staff member is impartial.

2-1113 The preliminary hearing is conducted by an administrative staff member or officer who has not previously been involved in the case. (Essential)

DISCUSSION: In view of the requirement that the hearing officer be impartial, it is inappropriate for the officer who supervised the parolee, or an individual who authorized the parolee's detention to conduct the preliminary hearing.

2-1114 At least three days prior to the preliminary hearing, the parolee is notified in writing of the time and place of the hearing, and of the specific parole violation(s) charged. The parolee is also advised in writing of the right to:

Present evidence and favorable witnesses
Disclosure of evidence
Confront adverse witness(es), unless the witness(es) would be subjected thereby to a risk of harm Have counsel of choice present, or, in case of indigent parolees who request assistance to adequately present their case, have counsel appointed Request postponement of the hearing for good cause (Essential)

DISCUSSION: Due process requires that the parolee receive notice of the hearing, of the specific acts alleged to constitute parole violations, and of all rights with respect to the hearing. Consistent with the United States Supreme Court case of *Gagnon v. Scarpelli*, 411 U.S. 778, 93 S.Ct. 1756, 36 L.Ed.2d 656 (1973), a parole authority should decide, on a case-by-case basis, whether to appoint counsel for an indigent parolee who requests such assistance. Among the factors to be considered in making this decision are: whether the parolee denies committing the alleged violation(s); whether there are mitigating factors which are complex or otherwise difficult to develop or present; and whether the parolee appears to be capable of speaking effectively for himself. (See related standards 2-1084 and 2-1118.)

2-1115 The person who conducts the preliminary hearing determines whether there is probable cause to revoke parole and hold the parolee for a revocation hearing before the parole authority. The parole authority may empower the hearing officer to make the provisional revocation decision, or merely to report his/her findings and recommendation to the parole authority for a decision as to revocation. The hearing officer issues a verbal decision or a recommendation immediately after the hearing and provides a written decision to the parolee within 21 calendar days of the hearing. (Essential)

DISCUSSION: The hearing officer should make a summary of the documents presented and responses made at the preliminary hearing in order to make a determination as to probable cause for revocation. Although the findings need not be formal, the officer should state the reasons for the determination and indicate the evidence relied upon.

2-1116 The parolee is returned to prison only when probable cause is found at the preliminary hearing and when it is determined, after considering the appropriateness of less severe sanctions, that the clear interest of the public requires reincarceration. (Essential)

DISCUSSION: The preliminary hearing has a usefulness that goes beyond the narrow fact-finding process. The hearing may provide an occasion to identify and reverse potentially harmful patterns of conduct, or to identify gaps in the program of supervision and recommend alternatives. The parole authority should consider not only whether a violation of parole has been committed, but also whether a less severe sanction is appropriate. (See related standard 2-1120.)

REVOCATION HEARING

2-1117 The revocation hearing is conducted within 60 calendar days after the parolee's return to prison as a parole violator; a delay or postponement for good cause may be approved by the authority chairperson or designate. (Essential)

DISCUSSION: The *Morrissey* case requires that the revocation hearing, as well as the preliminary hearing, be timely. Subsequent cases have held that a revocation of parole will be invalidated if, without justifiable cause, a revocation hearing is not provided within a reasonable time after the return of the parolee to prison. Delays or postponements should be granted only sparingly.

2-1118 The same procedural and substantive rights which are afforded to a parolee at a preliminary hearing are afforded at a revocation hearing. In addition, a parolee is provided an opportunity at the revocation hearing to demonstrate that, even if

parole has been violated, mitigating circumstances exist which suggest that the violation does not warrant revocation. (Essential)

DISCUSSION: The *Morrissey* case mandates essentially the same procedural guarantees for both hearings in the two-state revocation process, and also provides for an opportunity to present mitigating factors at the revocation hearing. This hearing also should go beyond the narrow fact-finding process, and the parole authority should weigh the best interests of the parolee and the public in making its final decision. (See related standard 2-1114.)

2-1119 Within 21 calendar days of the revocation hearing, the parolee is provided a written statement of the reasons for the determination made and the evidence relied upon. (Essential)

DISCUSSION: The parolee should be informed as soon as possible about the decision to revoke parole. A written statement of reasons and evidence relied upon is required under the *Morrissey* case and also promotes thoughtful decision-making.

2-1120 Alternatives other than further imprisonment are used in decision-making on parole violations. (Essential)

DISCUSSION: Although further imprisonment may be required, parole authorities should use warnings, short-term local confinement, special conditions, varieties of intensive supervision, referral to other community resources, and other alternatives to confinement. (See related standard 2-1116.)

2-1121 In jurisdictions where the parole authority has discretion to award or forfeit good-conduct deductions for time served on parole in the community, there are written guidelines for the award or forfeiture of such deductions. (Essential)

DISCUSSION: Careful review of individual cases is required in making a determination on provision of credit to the parolee for time served in the community. Written policy should state specific criteria for allowing or disallowing credit for time served in the community when a parolee is imprisoned for a parole violation.

2-1122 If it is decided that the offender is to be reincarcerated, there is no statutory or administrative prohibition against reparole on the original charge for which paroled. (Important)

DISCUSSION: Neither in law nor in practice should any predisposition operate to deny further parole consideration to a parole violator. The fact of parole violation should be considered in the context of an offender's total history in deciding the next appropriate action(s) after revocation of parole.

2-1123 After a revocation hearing, the parole authority immediately informs the offender of the next tentative release date. When circumstances, such as pending criminal charges or outstanding sentences to be served, prevent the setting of a tentative release date, or when the tentative release date is greater than one year after the revocation hearing, the parole authority sets a date for a review hearing within one year, and advises the offender of this date. (Essential)

DISCUSSION: In revocation decisions, no less than in release decisions, it is of paramount importance for the parole authority to minimize uncertainty in the mind of the offender. Tentative release dates should be set unless circumstances make it impossible to predict the offender's future eligibility status. The certainty of even a distant tentative release date is preferable to no date at all. When an obstacle to the setting of a date, such as pending criminal charges, is removed, the parole authority should advance the date of the review hearing to the earliest convenient time. (See related standard 2-1086.)

SOURCE: Reprinted from the American Correctional Association Manual of Correctional Standards with permission of the American Correctional Association.

III

INTERMEDIATE SANCTIONS

BURGEONING PRISON POPULATIONS AND high recidivism rates among felony probationers since the early 1980s have prompted the search for alternative sanctions for certain offenders. These are the offenders for whom a sentence of imprisonment is unduly severe and regular probation is too lenient. One study of felony probation in California sounded a clarion call for the development of "intermediate sanctions." In its 1985 report *Granting Felons Probation*, the RAND Corporation stated that:

> ... the current troubles are self-perpetuating. Without alternative sanctions for serious offenders, prison populations will continue to grow and the courts will be forced to consider probation for more and more serious offenders. Probation caseloads will increase, petty offenders will be increasingly "ignored" by the system (possibly creating more career criminals), and recidivism rates will rise. In short, probation appears to be heading toward an impasse, if not a total breakdown, if substantially more funds are not made available to create more prison space. Since that is highly unlikely (and also, we believe, undesirable), alternative "intermediate" punishments must be developed and implemented.

The growth in prison populations is forcing the use of court-ordered releases, population caps, and early parole to control populations. There have even been some experiments with housing prisoners aboard decommissioned ships, reminiscent of the prison "hulks" of 18th-century England. Probation has fared no better. Recidivism rates as high as 80 percent are regularly reported, and probation-officer caseloads of 200 are not unusual. Clearly, alternative solutions are needed.

Part III discusses some of these alternatives for bridging the gap between probation and parole. Here we examine house arrest, electronic monitoring, intensive supervision probation, restitution, community service, boot camps, intermittent imprisonment, and fines.

INTERMEDIATE SANCTIONS: BETWEEN PROBATION AND PRISON

Intermediate sanctions

Alternative punishments that fall
between probation and incarceration,
including house arrest, electronic
monitoring, community service,
restitution, fines, shock probation, and
intensive probation supervision.

Recent years have witnessed the evolution of a range of **intermediate sanctions** to fill the gap between regular probation and prison. All of these new sanctions are attempts to provide increased control over offenders within the community. Until the advent of these intermediate punishments, the courts were faced with the polarized choice of either probation or prison. Criminologists Norval Morris and Michael Tonry have written:

> Effective and principled punishment of convicted offenders requires the development and application of a range of punishments between prison and probation. Imprisonment is used excessively; probation is used even more excessively; between the two is a near-vacuum of purposive and enforced punishments.[1]

Morris and Tonry argue that we have been both too lenient and too severe. We have been too lenient with those probationers who need tighter controls and too severe with those prisoners who would present no serious threat to public safety if under supervision in the community.[2] They advocate the use of "intermediate punishments" such as intensive supervision probation (ISP), house arrest, electronic monitoring, restitution, community service orders, and fines. These punishments, they point out, to not exist in isolation. The fine is frequently combined with probation and incarceration. Electronic monitoring enforces house arrest and curfews, not being a sentence in itself. Community service orders are combined with probation or parole. All are sometimes combined with brief jail or prison terms.[3] Morris and Tonry maintain:

> For some offenders, a substantial fine may well be combined with an order that the offender make restitution to the victim, pay court costs, and be subject to a protracted period of house arrest, monitored electronically, for which the offender pays the costs. For others, intensive probation involving regular and close supervision by a supervising officer playing a police role and also by a caseworker may be combined with a defined period of residence in a drug treatment facility, followed by regular urinalyses to ensure the offender remains drug-free, and also an obligation to fulfill a set number of hours of community service—all strictly enforced.[4]

THE RAND STUDY

A 1976 report by the U.S. Comptroller General concluded that probation systems were "in crisis" and served neither the public interest nor the offender's.[5] Other studies of the period arrived at the same conclusion.[6] Perhaps the most important of these (that is, the most heeded) and the one that precipitated serious interest in "intermediate sanctions" was the one conducted by the RAND Corporation for the National Institute of Justice.[7] The **RAND study** used data from more than 16,000 California felony offenders and recidivism data from a subsample of 1,672 felony probationers in Los Angeles and Alameda counties (California) in its attempt to determine:

1. upon what criteria do courts determine which convicted offenders will be imprisoned and which will be granted probation,
2. what percentage of probationers are rearrested, reconvicted, and reimprisoned, and
3. how accurately can we predict recidivism?

The data revealed that a prior criminal record, drug addiction, being under community supervision at the time of arrest, being armed, using a weapon, and seriously injuring the victim were correlated with sentences to imprisonment, rather than to probation. Offenders represented by private attorneys, those who pleaded guilty, and those who had obtained pretrial release were less likely to be imprisoned.

The study found that within 40 months after receiving sentences to probation; 65 percent of the offenders were rearrested; 51 percent were reconvicted; 18 percent were reconvicted of serious, violent crimes; and 34 percent were reincarcerated. Moreover, 75 percent of the official charges filed against the sample involved burglary, theft, robbery, and other violent crimes—the crimes most threatening to community safety.[8] Probationers who were alike those imprisoned, in terms of criminal history and seriousness of their crime, were 50 percent more likely to be rearrested than the other probationers.

The RAND researchers found that the crimes and criminal records of about 25 percent of the offenders who were granted probation were indistinguishable from those of offenders who were sentenced to prison terms. They concluded that the courts have very limited ability to identify offenders who are likely to succeed on probation, and that "given the information now routinely provided to the court," the ability to predict which felon will succeed on probation "probably cannot be vastly improved."[9] The report concluded that granting felons probation poses a serious threat to public safety.

The researchers contended that the criminal justice system needs an "intermediate form of punishment for those offenders who are too antisocial for the relative freedom that probation now offers, but not so seriously criminal as to require imprisonment."[10] They recommended:

> A sanction . . . that would impose intensive surveillance, coupled with substantial community service and restitution . . . structured to satisfy public demands that the punishment fit the crime, to show criminals that crime really does not pay, and to control potential recidivists.[11]

Citing the **intensive supervision probation** programs (ISPs) that were then being developed in several states as models for programs nationwide, they stated:

> Several states have experimental programs in place which indicate that an intensive surveillance program (ISP) should have intensive monitoring and supervision; real constraints on movement and action; employment; added requirements of community service, education, counseling, and therapy programs; and mechanisms for immediately punishing probationers who commit infractions.[12]

The researchers predicted that intensive supervision programs would be the most significant criminal justice experiments of the next decade.

Intensive Supervision Probation (ISP)

A probation program of intensive surveillance and supervision in the community as an alternative to imprisonment.

INTENSIVE SUPERVISION PROBATION

Intensive supervision probation programs have developed rapidly around the country since the early 1980s.[13] Although ISP was originally designed to enhance rehabilitation and public safety by affording greater contact between the probation officer and the probationer, the purpose of more recent programs has been expanded to include reducing economic costs and alleviating prison overcrowding. ISPs are also seen as "socially cost-effective," because they are less likely than incarceration to contribute to the breakup of offenders' families, they allow offenders to remain employed, and they are less stigmatizing than prison. The programs vary from jurisdiction to jurisdiction, but most of them require multiple weekly contacts with probation officers, random night and weekend visits, unscheduled drug testing, and strict enforcement of probation conditions. Many require community-service restitution and some form of electronic surveillance.[14]

ISP Caseloads

Probation officers who supervise ISP clients generally have smaller caseloads than do those with regular probation caseloads. Probation and parole officers have long advocated smaller caseloads, contending that they allow the officers to give more assistance to the probationer in his or her rehabilitation efforts and provide greater protection to the community through increased surveillance and control. Whereas the average probation caseload is near one hundred offenders, ISP officers generally supervise twenty-five or fewer offenders.

A small, but persuasive body of research indicates that reducing caseload size does *not* increase the effectiveness of adult probation or parole supervision, when effectiveness is defined as the rate of recidivism.[15] In ISP programs, however, the reduced caseload size is (ideally) accompanied by more focused, extensive, and ubiquitous supervision than in regular probation.[16] Most ISP programs mandate specified levels of contact between probationer and probation officer and reduced caseload size. McCarthy and McCarthy explain:

> Each week, multiple personal contacts and collateral contacts with family and friends are employed to regulate the offender's travel, employment, curfews, drug use, and other relevant behaviors.[17]

The intensive supervision probation program in Georgia is one of the earliest and one of the most stringent. Georgia ISP officers supervise 25 probationers and are required to make at least five face-to-face contacts with each probationer each week. Weekly unannounced alcohol and drug testing and weekly check of local arrest records are also mandated.[18] Caseloads in Florida's intensive supervision program, called the Community Control Program (FCCP) are statutorily established at twenty or less. Supervision guidelines specify twenty-eight contacts—twenty-four personal and four collateral—per month.[19]

Evaluations of ISP

Early evaluations of ISP programs in Georgia, New York, and Texas found evidence that ISP was effective in reducing rearrests of probationers.[20] However, because of their closer contact with probationers, ISP officers discovered more rule violations than the regular probation officers. Therefore, the intensive supervision programs had higher failure rates than regular probation, even though their rearrest rates were lower.[21]

More recent evaluations question whether ISP programs were responsible for the reported successful outcomes. A 1990 study by the RAND Corporation found that judges used extra caution in sentencing offenders to the ISP programs in the early years because the programs were untested. Many programs limited participation to property offenders with minor criminal records, which undoubtedly helps to explain the lower rearrest rate.[22] When such biasing factors were controlled statistically, the researchers found no significant difference in the rearrest rates of ISP and regular probationers. Furthermore, in two of the three sites studied, there was no significant difference in the technical violation rates of regular-probation and ISP participants. The findings suggest that ISP programs are not effective for high-risk offenders *if effectiveness is judged solely by offender recidivism rates.*[23] However, ISP programs are designed to serve three primary goals: (1) to relieve prison overcrowding and the costs of incarceration, (2) to keep offenders from committing crimes in the community while they are involved in the program, and (3) to impose an "intermediate" punishment that is less severe than imprisonment but more severe than routine probation. The programs appear to be successful at imposing an intermediate punishment, for which court-ordered conditions are more credibly monitored and enforced than is possible with routine probation.[24] Other studies suggest that although the costs of ISP programs are substantially greater than those of regular probation, ISP is much more cost-effective than imprisonment.[25] Georgia, for example, estimates that it has saved $9,400 for each offender sentenced to ISP rather than prison. The Georgia program has also reported reduced recidivism, which would be expected to result in reduced police, court, and incarceration costs. Some observers doubt that ISP reduces prison populations, however. Norval Morris and Michael Tonry suggest that research evidence and experience show that "intermediate punishments" free up many fewer prison beds and save much less money than their proponents claim. They contend that judges often hesitate to impose a new intermediate punishment on offenders who would otherwise be sentenced to prison, because they doubt its (ISP) ability to deliver appropriate punishment and to prevent crime. Instead, they claim, judges impose new intermediate punishments on *probation bound* offenders.[26] Supporting this, in a study of Florida's Community Control Program, Florida State University criminologist Thomas Blomberg found that 28 percent of those placed in this prison-alternative ISP program would have received probation if "community control" had not been available as a sentencing alternative.[27]

Obviously, much more research and evaluation are required in order to adequately assess the effectiveness of ISP as a correctional alternative. Unless it can be shown that ISP is more effective than regular probation in deterring criminal behavior, its greater costs may not be justifiable.

SHOCK INCARCERATION

Shock incarceration refers to a brief period of imprisonment that precedes a term of supervised probation, in hope that the harsh reality of prison will serve

Shock probation

A brief period of incarceration—typically 30–120 days—followed by resentencing to a term of probation supervision.

to deter future criminal activity. A variety of shock incarceration formats are used, and they go by a number of names—*shock probation, shock parole, intermittent incarceration, split sentence,* and *boot camps.* The programs vary somewhat in design and organization, but all feature a short prison term, followed by release under supervision. The target population is young offenders with no previous incarcerations in adult prisons.

In **shock probation** (also called *shock parole* and *intermittent incarceration*), an offender is sentenced to imprisonment for a short time (the shock) and then released and resentenced to probation. The original shock probation program was established in Ohio in 1965. It was praised for limiting prison time, assisting in reintegration into the community, helping the offender to maintain family ties, and reducing prison populations and the costs of corrections.[28] The program's stated purposes were

1. To impress offenders with the seriousness of their actions without a long prison sentence.
2. To release offenders found by the institutions to be more amenable to community-based treatment than was realized by the courts at the time of sentencing.
3. To serve as a just compromise between punishment and leniency in appropriate cases.
4. To provide community-based treatment for rehabilitable offenders while still observing their responsibilities for imposing deterrent sentences where public policy demands it.
5. To afford the briefly incarcerated offender a protection against absorption into the inmate culture.[29]

Shock probation programs have been evaluated by a number of researchers. Success rates are reported to vary between 78 and 91 percent.[30] Programs are praised for limiting prison time, providing a chance for offenders to be reintegrated back into the community quickly, and for making offenders more receptive to probation supervision by illustrating the problems they will encounter if they violate the terms of their probation.[31]

Some authorities, including the members of the National Advisory Commission on Criminal Justice Standards and Goals, have criticized shock probation because of the perceived incompatibility of prison and probation. Critics claim that it defeats the purpose of probation by subjecting offenders to the destructive effects of imprisonment and disrupts their lives in the community and stigmatizes them for having been incarcerated.[32] Nicolette Parisi, in a study of federal probationers, found that a third of those who had received split sentences had previously been incarcerated on other charges, which negated the value of the "shock." Furthermore, Parisi was unable to find evidence that probationers who had first served a short period of incarceration were more successful than those who had not.[33]

Some jurisdictions also provide for a **split sentence** in which a short jail or prison term is actually a condition of probation. In the federal system, about 15 percent of all offenders receive some form of split sentence that includes jail as a condition of probation.[34] This is not to be confused with parole, as it is ordered by the court at sentencing and is a part of the sentencing procedure.

Recent studies show that the use of shock probation and split sentencing is increasing nationwide.[35] McCarthy and McCarthy report that nearly a third of those placed on probation in some jurisdictions, receive some sentence to confinement as well.[36]

Recent innovations such as **boot camps,** provide that the convicted offender reside in a correctional facility and participate in a program designed to instill a "healthy dose" of discipline and responsibility. Most boot camp programs are designed to provide an experience much like that of military basic training with intensive physical training, hard work, and little or no free time. After a specified period, typically 90–120 days, the probationer is released to regular probation supervision. These programs are very similar to "shock probation" but are administered by the probation agency, not by the state corrections department. They provide the court with an alternative disposition, stricter and more structured than regular probation, yet less severe than a prison sentence.

Boot camps have strong public appeal, and their use appears to be increasing. By 1992, approximately 23 states were operating boot camp programs—up from 11 states in 1989. Supporters of the concept contend that there is "some evidence" that the boot camp experience may be more positive than incarceration in traditional prisons. Moreover, they state, those who have completed such programs describe the experience as "difficult, but constructive." There is evidence, they assert, that recidivism rates for those who complete boot camp programs are approximately the same as for those who serve longer periods in traditional prisons or on probation.[37]

After a study of existing programs, however, Merry Morash and Lila Rucker warned in 1990 that boot camps hold potential for negative outcomes. Many boot camp environments are characterized by inconsistent standards, contrived stress, and leadership styles that are likely to reduce self-esteem, increase the potential for violence, and encourage the abuse of power.[38]

Boot camp

A residential correctional program designed to instill discipline and responsibility that resembles military basic training.

The boot camp experience.

HOUSE ARREST AND ELECTRONIC MONITORING

House arrest is not a form of probation, but rather, a condition of probation.[39] Electronic monitoring is a means of assuring that certain conditions of probation are met. Both have found acceptance in many jurisdictions because of their potential to satisfy the goals of imprisonment without the social and financial costs associated with incarceration.[40]

House Arrest

House arrest

Confinement of an offender in his/her residence instead of a correctional institution. Most house arrest programs require offenders to remain within their home during specified hours up to 24 hours per day.

House arrest, or **home confinement,** is neither a new concept nor a U.S. innovation. Galileo (1564–1642) was placed under house arrest by Church authorities for his heretical assertion that the earth revolved around the sun. More recently, Soviet physicist, Andrey Sakharov (1921–1989) was confined to an apartment in Gorky for "antistate" activities.

In contemporary America, house arrest is viewed as an alternative to incarceration and a means of easing prison overcrowding. Programs vary, but most require that offenders remain within the confines of their home during specified hours—ranging from 24-hour-per-day confinement to imposition of late-night curfews only.

Most states and the federal system now operate some form of house-arrest program. Florida, Georgia, Oklahoma, Oregon, Kentucky, and California all make extensive use of this option. By March 1991, Florida had 3,554 individuals under supervision in its house-arrest program, the Florida Community Control Program (FCCP). Of those, 340 were subject to electronic monitoring.[41]

Florida's "community controlees" (those under house arrest) are required to maintain employment and to participate in self-improvement programs, such as a GED program to obtain a high school diploma, drug and alcohol counseling, or other "life skills" programs. Many are required to perform community service as well. When they are not participating in work, self-help programs, or community service, they must be at their residence.

Community Control Officers' caseloads are limited by statute to twenty offenders and they work Saturdays, Sundays, and holidays. They are required to make a minimum of 28 contacts per month with each offender. Officers' schedules vary from day to day, resulting in regular, but random visits with the offenders. If an offender is not where he or she should be at any particular time, a violation of community control is reported to the court.

Some contend that the intrusiveness of house arrest violates a probationer's constitutional right to privacy in his or her own home. Others argue that the program is voluntary and that the offender has given up much of this right as a result of a felony conviction. Some critics suggest that surveillance by the use of electronic monitoring may constitute unreasonable search and seizure, and that because to be eligible for electronic monitoring programs, an offender must have a telephone and pay a fee for electronic surveillance, the program discriminates against those who cannot pay the fee or afford

On August 21, 1992, as Hurricane Andrew approached the South Florida coast and residential areas near the ocean were being evacuated, a Miami television station aired an announcement from the Florida Department of Corrections, advising persons under house arrest in the evacuation zone that they could leave their homes and seek shelter from the approaching storm—"but," the announcer admonished, "you should behave."

telephone service.[42] Joan Petersilia reports that some jurisdictions have avoided this criticism by basing the fees on a sliding scale and/or providing telephones for those who do not have them.[43]

Petersilia warns that house arrest/electronic surveillance programs are often inaugurated with unrealistic goals and expectations of success. She points out that since considerable self-discipline is required to comply with house arrest and many offenders are impulsive by nature, many offenders are likely to be unable to sustain the required behavior for long periods of time.[44] Several community control officers in Florida report that it is not unusual for the spouse of an individual on house arrest to complain that he or she "cannot stand another day" with the husband or wife at home all day. And, according to the officers, several house arrestees have requested that they be sent to prison, rather than continue on house arrest. One told his supervising officer, "If I have to spend any more time with my old lady, I'll probably kill her. Send me on down to Raiford [the state prison]."

Probationer with electronic monitoring device on ankle.

FIGURE 12–1

Key Decision Points where Electronic Monitoring Programs Are Used

SOURCE: James Byrne, Arthur Lurigio, and Christopher Baird, *The Effectiveness of the New Intensive Supervision Programs,* Research in Corrections Series, vol. 2, no. 2 (preliminary unpublished draft; Washington: National Institute of Corrections, 1989).

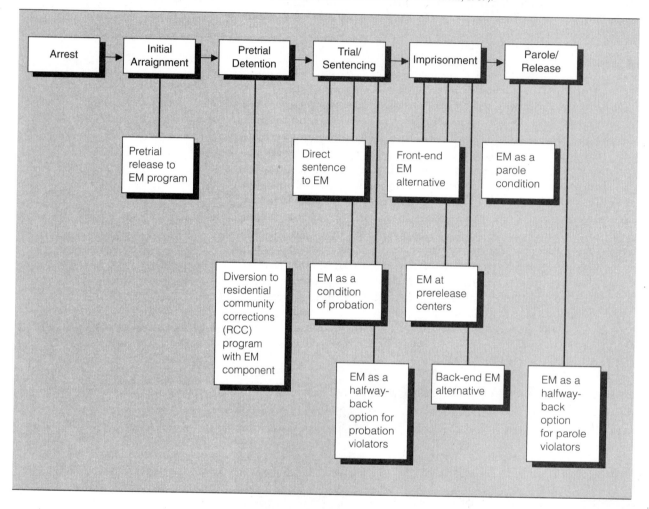

Electronic Monitoring

Electronic monitoring—a correctional technology, rather than a correctional program—provides verification of an offender's whereabouts. *EM,* as it is often referred to, is useful at many points on the correctional continuum, from pretrial release to parole, as shown in Figure 12–1.

By 1991 nearly 7,000 probationers were under electronic monitoring in the United States—about 13 percent of all those in intensive supervision programs. An additional 1,300 parolees were under electronic monitoring—about 8 percent of the 17,000 parolees under intensive supervision. Florida, Indiana, Michigan, and North Carolina make the greatest use of electronic monitoring for probationers. Texas, with 306 parolees under electronic monitoring, and Pennsylvania, with 223 parolees monitored electronically, make the greatest use of electronic monitoring for parolees. In 1991, these two states accounted for 38 percent of all parolees subject to electronic monitoring.

Two types of electronic monitoring devices are currently in use. Continuous-signaling devices constantly monitor the presence of an offender at a particular location. Approximately 60 percent of electronic monitoring devices are of this variety. Programmed-contact devices, representing 40 percent of electronic monitoring devices currently in use, contact the offender periodically to verify his or her presence.

Several manufacturers have introduced a "hybrid" device. It functions like a continuous-signaling device, but when the central computer notes that the offender may have left home at an unauthorized time, it telephones the offender and verifies that the person responding is the offender. If verification is not made, the violation is reported to correctional authorities.

CONTINUOUS-SIGNALING DEVICES. **Continuously signaling devices** have three components. A miniaturized *transmitter* that is strapped to the offender broadcasts an encoded signal at regular intervals to a *receiver–dialer* located in the offender's home. The receiver–dialer detects signals from the transmitter and reports to a central *computer* (or *receiver*) over the telephone lines. The central computer compares reports from the transmitter with the offender's curfew schedule and alerts correctional authorities to any unauthorized absences. The computer also stores information about each offender's routine entries and exits so that a report can be made.

PROGRAMMED-CONTACT DEVICES. **Programmed-contact devices** use a computer that is programmed to telephone the offender during the monitored hours, either randomly or at specified times. Most programs attempt to verify that the offender is indeed the person responding to the computer's call. Several methods are used. One uses voice-verification technology. Another requires the offender to wear a device that looks like a wristwatch. The device is programmed to transmit a unique number when a button on it is pressed into a touch-tone telephone in response to the computer's "call." A third system utilizes a plastic device that is strapped to the offender's arm. When the computer "calls," the module is inserted into a verifier box connected to the telephone. A fourth system uses visual verification at the telephone site.[45]

He's on the Run

A high school running back in Victoria, Texas, scored a touchdown Friday night while wearing a court-ordered tracking device on his wrist. Raydon Alexander must wear the device—which was wrapped in tape and gauze—because he was arrested on assault charges last month while on probation. Alexander was granted a one-night curfew exemption that allowed him to play.

Miami Herald, September 22, 1992.

Criticisms and Problems

Numerous criticisms have been leveled at electronic monitoring and house arrest, and various problems of implementation have been noted. Annesley Schmitt directed a major study of house arrest and electronic monitoring and observed that offenders must learn to handle the equipment properly and that their families must adapt to using the telephone sparingly so that computer "calls" can be completed. Poor telephone service, bad wiring, and "call-waiting" and "call-forwarding" features on the telephone have caused technical problems. Offenders who live close to FM radio stations or transmitters have had difficulty receiving and sending the required information via the electronic devices. Correctional authorities reported unanticipated costs—for extra telephone lines, special interconnections, underestimated long-distance charges, and supplies.[46] A Texas probation agency reported that its programmed-contact computer malfunctioned and called one probationer more than 300 times in one night.[47] Charles Friel and Joseph Vaughn[48] reported such other problems as:

- Large metal objects, such as furnaces and refrigerators, between the transmitter and receiver have interrupted transmissions and caused false alarms.
- False alarms have occurred when offenders curled up while sleeping, positioning their body between the receiver and transmitter and blocking the signal.
- Probationers living in mobile homes, constructed largely of metal, have experienced transmission problems.
- Power outages have caused the systems to "crash."
- Batteries in the devices worn by probationers sometimes fail.

Other critics are concerned that the widespread use of house arrest with electronic monitoring may result in "net-widening." Although the program was developed as an alternative to imprisonment, it is sometimes inappropriately used with offenders who would otherwise have been placed under regular probation supervision. Friel and Vaughn caution:

> Using the technology with individuals who would be granted probation anyway is potentially abusive. It has already been pointed out that this application is likely to raise costs without necessarily increasing benefits. In addition, it widens the correctional net needlessly and is an undue invasion of privacy.[49]

RESTITUTION AND COMMUNITY SERVICE

Restitution

Restitution is another popular intermediate sanction. It may require an offender to repay the victim(s) of his or her crime for financial losses resulting from the crime—**monetary restitution**—or to serve the community in some way as symbolic restitution—**community-service restitution.** Both are commonly ordered as conditions of probation or parole and may also be used as diversionary devices, providing offenders the opportunity to avoid having a criminal record altogether.[50] In **diversion** situations, a first-offender (usually) is ordered to perform community service or to pay monetary restitution during a period when his or her case is "continued" by the court. After the required restitution is satisfied, the court dismisses the charges.

RESTITUTION IN HISTORY.   Like house arrest, restitution has a long history. The Old Testament specifies fivefold restitution for stealing and then killing an ox and fourfold restitution for stealing and killing a sheep. Double-restitution is mandated for stealing (Exodus 21). Leviticus commands that restitution plus an additional fifth be made by robbers (Leviticus 6). The Code of Hammurabi, developed 1792–1750 B.C., mandates thirtyfold restitution if the victim is a "god" or a "palace" and tenfold restitution if the victim is a "villein" (a low-status laborer).[51]

British philosopher, Jeremy Bentham (1748–1833) prescribed restitution as an essential means of making the punishment fit the crime. In the mid 1800s, Quaker prison reformer, Elizabeth Fry saw restitution as a mechanism of offender rehabilitation, stating that "repayment is the first step toward reformation."[52]

During the 1960s and 1970s, the various national commissions on criminal justice and the model codes of the era emphasized the value of restitution both as punishment and rehabilitation. The Model Penal Code proposed that an offender placed on probation may be required to "make restitution of the fruits of his crime or to make reparation in an amount he can afford to pay, for the loss or damage caused...."[53] The National Advisory Commission on Criminal Justice Standards and Goals (1973) considered restitution as a factor that might mitigate the imposition of a prison sentence.[54] Both the American Bar Association and the National Council on Crime and Delinquency support the use of restitution as a condition of probation.

PURPOSES OF RESTITUTION.   Burt Galaway, an early proponent of restitution as a correctional tool, delineated five purposes of restitution:

1. Restitution provides a less severe and more humane sanction for the offender. This purpose is particularly important in diversionary programs for minor offenders and juveniles.
2. Restitution aids the rehabilitation of the offender and it integrates the punitive and rehabilitative purposes of the criminal law. Because the rationale incorporates the notion that punishment is related to the extent of damages done, it is perceived as just by offenders and allows them a sense of accomplishment as they complete the requirements. Restitution also provides offenders a socially appropriate, concrete way of expressing their guilt and atoning for their offenses.
3. Restitution benefits the criminal justice system by providing an easily administered sanction that reduces demands on the system.
4. Restitution may reduce the need for vengeance in the administration of criminal law, as offenders are perceived as responsible persons taking active steps to make amends for their wrongdoing.
5. Restitution provides redress for crime victims. Galaway suggests, however, that helping crime victims should not be the primary aim of a restitution program. Too many crimes go unsolved, and in many, the arrest does not result in a conviction. Even when a conviction is secured, restitution might

not be the appropriate sanction. Thus, restitution will help only a small number of crime victims. He suggests, instead, a publicly funded victim-compensation program.[55]

Community Service

As we have said, community service is a form of symbolic restitution. It is defined as "unpaid service to the public to compensate society for some harm done by the crime." It might consist of working for a tax-supported or nonprofit agency, such as the YMCA, Girl Scouts, a public park or library, a poverty program, or a public works program. It may involve picking up roadside litter or removing graffiti. In community-service restitution, the offender repays the community he or she offended by performing some service for it, rather than by making monetary reparation.

Like monetary restitution, community-service restitution is both punitive and rehabilitative. It is punitive in that the offender's time and freedom are restricted until the work is completed. It is rehabilitative in the same way as monetary restitution; it allows offenders to do something constructive, to increase their self-esteem, to reduce their isolation from society, and to benefit society through their efforts.

Community service is distinct from monetary restitution programs. As one scholar observed:

> Community service orders are generally more applicable than restrictive programs, since they may be employed even when the victim is indemnified against loss, where no victim can be identified, and where an identified victim will not cooperate.[56]

Performing community service.

Further, community service provides an alternative form of restitution for offenders who are unable to make meaningful financial restitution and for those whose financial resources are so great that monetary restitution has no punitive or rehabilitative effect. As the search continues for less costly and more effective methods of dealing with offenders, community service is a major trend in U.S. corrections.

Contemporary Uses of Restitution and Community Service

THE MINNESOTA RESTITUTION CENTER.   Minnesota provided the prototype for contemporary restitution centers. Established in 1972, the Minnesota Restitution Center (MRC) accepted adult males who had been sentenced to the Minnesota State Prison for two years or less and had served at least four months of their sentence. Recidivists, violent offenders, and professional criminals were not eligible for the program, nor were middle-class persons who could make restitution without the assistance of the Center. While in prison, the inmate, with the assistance of a Restitution Center staff member, met with the victim face-to-face to establish a restitution plan. After the parole board approved the restitution plan, the offender was released on parole to the Restitution Center, where he lived, secured employment, and fulfilled the terms of the agreement. The offender could also receive additional services there, including group therapy, supervision in the community corrections center, and assistance in obtaining employment. Although the MRC was considered a success, it was closed in 1976 because the number of property offenders being sent to prison was reduced by the implementation of the state's Community Corrections Act.

Michael Milkin must complete 2,400 hours of community service as a condition of his release from prison.

THE GEORGIA RESTITUTION PROGRAM.   Georgia based its restitution program on the Minnesota model. Unlike the Minnesota model, however, Georgia residential programs—known as *community diversion centers*—serve both probationers and parolees. Residential centers located throughout the state house twenty to forty offenders each for up to five months. During their stay, center residents develop restitution plans, receive individual and group counseling, and are referred for a variety of other services as needed. They may also be required to work at community service projects on weekends and during evening hours. The offenders normally remain at the center until their restitution is completed.

One evaluation of the program revealed that about 85 percent of the participants were rearrested within 18 months after release. Although this does not suggest a great reduction in recidivism, the program's economic benefits are considerable. McCarthy and McCarthy state:

> During a one-year period, the residents earned a total of $128,437 in restitution payments; [and] 8,372 hours of community service were provided. Over $150,000 was paid in state and federal taxes, and over $200,000 was spent in the local communities for clothing, transportation, recreation, and personal items. In addition, the total cost of care per individual has been much less for restitution center residents than prison inmates.[57]

THE TEXAS EXPERIENCE.   Based on the earlier models of Minnesota and Georgia, Texas established "rehabilitation centers" (formerly "restitution centers") where nonviolent offenders, as a condition of probation, live for up to one year. While there, the residents work at their regular job. Their pay is submitted directly to the center director, who deducts the amounts for room and board, support for dependents, supervision fees, and restitution to the victim(s). The remainder is returned to the resident after release from the center. During off-work hours, the residents are required to perform community service. According to a 1986 report by the Texas Adult Probation Commission, 88.4 percent of rehabilitation center residents successfully completed their term of residence without violating their probation.[58]

FINES AS INTERMEDIATE SANCTIONS

Fines are routinely imposed for offenses ranging from traffic violations to drug trafficking. University of Connecticut criminologist George Cole, who has conducted an extensive study of the use of fines in U.S. criminal justice, estimates that well over $1 billion in fines is collected annually by courts across the country.[59] Cole found that judges in lower courts (fines in 86% of cases) were more positively disposed to using fines than were those in higher courts (fines in 42% of cases). In recent years, however, fines have been used more often in conjunction with other penalties, such as probation or imprisonment. In 1988, Ivan Boesky was fined more than $100 million and sentenced to 18 months in prison for violating Securities Exchange Commission regulations regarding insider trading. The federal Comprehensive Crime Control Act of 1984, effective November 1, 1987, specifies that for every sentence to probation, the court must also order the defendant to "pay a fine, make restitution, and/or work in community service."[60]

Some judges, however, are reluctant to use fines because of the difficulty of collecting and enforcing them. As Cole points out, other branches of government enforce other penalties imposed by judges, but fines must be enforced directly by the courts, and judges have little incentive to expend their own resources to administer the collection of fines. In addition, many judges point out that offenders tend to be poor and may have no means other than additional criminal activity to obtain the funds to pay their fines. Affluent offenders, on the other hand, can "buy their way out of jail" when fines are an integral part of the sentence.[61]

Despite the problems associated with using fines in criminal sentencing, prison and jail overcrowding and large probation caseloads have served to direct many judges' attention to the use of fines.[62] In 1988, a court in New York initiated a program to make fines a more meaningful sentencing option. Basing their program on European precedents, judges in the New York court adjust fines to offenders' financial means. Such fines, referred to as **day fines,** are figured as multiples of the offender's daily income.[63] Thus, a truck driver and a stock broker might be fined the same multiple of a day's pay, which might make the driver's fine $500 and the stock broker's $10,000.

In their book *Between Prison and Probation,* Morris and Tonry note that the use of fines as punishment for crime "holds promise of a much wider swath."[64] They specify some characteristics of fines that make them the "punishment of choice for most crimes":

1. Although in current practice fines are generally set in amounts too modest to be calibrated meaningfully in relation to serious crime, in principle, fines can vary from small change to economic capital punishment.
2. Although in current practice fines are too often haphazardly administered and collected, in principle, fines can be collected with the same vigor and ruthlessness that characterize our friendly neighborhood finance companies.
3. Although in current practice fines seem unfair to the poor and unduly lenient to the rich, in principle, fine amounts can be tailored to the offender's assets and income so as to constitute roughly comparable financial burdens.[65]

Presently, patterns in the use of fines vary widely. Observers predict greater emphasis on fines in the future, however, both as a sentence in itself and in conjunction with other sentences.

Summary

With more than 1.25 million persons in jails and prisons and 2.5 million on probation, the criminal justice system must acknowledge the need for intermediate sanctions—alternatives to traditional sentencing options. In this chapter, intensive supervision programs (ISP), electronic monitoring and house arrest, restitution, community service, and fines have been suggested as means of achieving a rational system of corrections and alleviating some of the problems associated with incarceration and probation.

ENDNOTES

1. Norval Morris and Michael Tonry, *Between Prison and Probation: Intermediate Punishments in a Rational Sentencing System* (New York: Oxford University Press, 1990), p. 3.

2. *Id.*

3. *Id.* at 7.

4. *Id.* at 8.

5. U.S. Comptroller General, *State and County Probation: Systems in Crisis* (Washington: Government Printing Office, 1976).

6. See J. Banks, A. L. Porter, R. L. Rardin, T. R. Silver, and V. E. Unger, *Phase I Evaluation of Intensive Special Probation Projects* (Washington: U.S. Department of Justice, 1981); Robert M. Carter and Leslie T. Wilkins, "Caseloads: Some Conceptual Models," in Robert M. Carter and Leslie T. Wilkins, eds., *Probation, Parole, and Community Corrections,* 2nd ed. (New York: Wiley); M. Neithercutt and D. M. Gottfredson, *Caseload Size Variation and Difference in Probation/Parole Performance* (Washington: National Institute of Juvenile Justice, 1973); Robert Martinson, "California Research at the Crossroads," *Crime and Delinquency* 23, no. 2 (Spring 1976).

7. Joan Petersilia, Susan Turner, James Kahan, and Joyce Peterson, *Granting Felons Probation: Public Risks and Alternatives* (Santa Monica, Calif.: RAND Corporation, 1985).

8. *Id.* at vi–vii.

9. *Id.* at viii.

10. *Id.* at ix.

11. *Id.*

12. *Id.*

13. *Id.* at iv.

14. Joan Petersilia, *Expanding Options for Criminal Sentencing,* (Santa Monica, Calif.: RAND Corporation, November 1987).

15. See Roger J. Lauen, *Community-Managed Corrections* (Laurel, Md.: American Correctional Association, 1988); Neithercutt and Gottfredson, *supra* note 6; Stuart Adams, *Evaluation Research in Corrections* (Washington: Government Printing Office, 1975); Carter and Wilkins *supra* note 6; and Edward E. Rhine, William R. Smith, Ronald W. Jackson, *Paroling Authorities: Recent History and Current Practice* (Laurel, Md.: American Correctional Association, 1991). Also see Chapter 6, Supervision in Probation and Parole, *supra,* for a discussion of the SIPU and San Francisco Project.

16. Belinda Rogers McCarthy and Bernard J. McCarthy, Jr. *Community-Based Corrections,* 2nd ed. (Pacific Grove, Calif.: Brooks/Cole, 1991), p. 122.

17. *Id.*

18. Billie S. Erwin and Lawrence A. Bennett, "New Dimensions in Probation: Georgia's Experience with Intensive Probation Supervision (IPS)," *Research in Brief* (Washington: National Institute of Justice, January 1987), p. 2.

19. Florida Department of Corrections, *An Implementation Manual for Community Control* (1983), p. 22.

20. Todd R. Clear and George F. Cole, *American Corrections,* 2nd ed. (Belmont, Calif.: Brooks/Cole Publishing Company, 1990), p. 268.

21. *Id.*

22. Joan Petersilia and Susan Turner, *Intensive Supervision for High-Risk Probationers: Findings from Three California Studies* (Santa Monica, Calif.: RAND Corporation, November 1990).

23. *Id.* at 5.

24. *Id.* at 9. See also Petersilia et al., *Felons, supra* note 7, at 66.

25. Howard Abadinsky, *Probation and Parole: Theory and Practice,* 4th ed. (Englewood Cliffs, N.J.: Prentice Hall, 1991), p. 344.

26. Norval Morris and Michael Tonry, "Between Prison and Probation: Intermediate Punishments in a Rational Sentencing System," *NIJ Reports,* January–February, 1990, p. 9.

27. Personal communication, August 1992.

28. Larry Siegel, *Criminology,* 4th ed. (St. Paul: West, 1992), p. 561.

29. Harry Allen, Chris Eskridge, Edward Latessa, and Gennaro Vito, *Probation and Parole in America* (New York: Free Press, 1985), p. 88.

30. *Id.*

31. Joseph J. Senna and Larry J. Siegel *Introduction to Criminal Justice,* 5th ed. (St. Paul: West, 1990).

32. National Advisory Commission, *Report on Corrections,* (Washington, 1973), p. 321.

33. Nicolette Parisi, "A Taste of the Bars," *Journal of Criminal Law and Criminology* 72 (1981), pp. 1109–1123. Cited in Senna and Siegel, *supra* note 31, p. 510.

34. Senna and Siegel, *supra* note 31, at 509.

35. Belinda R. McCarthy and Bernard J. McCarthy, Jr., *Community-Based Corrections,* 2nd ed. (Pacific Grove, Calif.: Brooks/Cole, 1991), pp. 127–128.

36. *Id.*

37. Doris Layton MacKenzie, "Boot Camp Programs Grow in Number and Scope," *NIJ Reports,* November/December 1990.

38. Merry Morash and Lila Rucker, "A Critical Look at the Idea of Boot Camp as a Correctional Reform," *Crime and Delinquency,* April 1990, pp. 204–222.

39. Also called *home detention* and *home incarceration.*

40. Abadinsky *supra* note 25, at 347.

41. Joseph E. Papy and Richard Nimer, "Electronic Monitoring in Florida," *Federal Probation,* March 1991.

42. Elise Kalfayan, ed., *RAND Checklist* (Santa Monica, Calif.: RAND Corporation, January 1989), p. 2.

43. Petersilia, *supra* note 14.

44. *Id.*

45. Annesley K. Schmidt, "Electronic Monitoring of Offenders Increases," *National Institute of Justice Reports,* Jan.–Feb. 1989, p. 4.

46. *Id.*

47. Personal communication.

48. Charles M. Friel and Joseph B. Vaughn, "A Consumer's Guide to Electronic Monitoring," *Federal Probation* 50, no. 3 (September 1986), pp. 3–14.

49. *Id.* at 12.

50. Siegel, *supra* note 28, at 561.

51. McCarthy and McCarthy, *supra* note 35, at 137.

52. *Id.* at 140.

53. American Bar Association Commission on Correctional Facilities and Services and Council of State Governments, *Compendium of Model Correctional Legislation and Standards,* 2nd ed. (Washington: ABA, 1975), p. III-48.

54. *Id.* at III-58.

55. Burt Galaway, The Use of Restitution. *Crime and Delinquency* 23(1), 1977.

56. Ken Pease, "Community Service Orders," in Michael Tonry and Norval Morris, eds., *Crime and Justice: An Annual Review of Research,* vol. 6 (Chicago: University of Chicago Press, 1985), p. 52.

57. McCarthy and McCarthy, *supra* note 35, at 154.

58. Rolando del Carmen, Betsy Witt, Thomas Caywood, and Sally Layland, *Probation Law and Practice in Texas* (Huntsville, Texas: Criminal Justice Center, Sam Houston State University, 1989), p. 4.

59. George Cole, *The American System of Criminal Justice,* 6th ed. (Pacific Grove, Calif.: Brooks/Cole, 1992).

60. 18 U.S.C. 3563 (a) (2).

61. *Id.*

62. *Id.*

63. James A. Inciardi, *Criminal Justice,* 4th ed. (Fort Worth, Texas: Harcourt Brace Jovanovich, 1993), p. 445.

64. Morris and Tonry, *supra* note 1, at 114.

65. *Id.* p. 114.

DISCUSSION QUESTIONS

1. What factor(s) brought about the development of intermediate sanctions?

2. What do Norval Morris and Michael Tonry mean when they say that criminal justice and corrections are both too lenient and yet too severe?

3. What were the conclusions of the RAND study of probation? What did the RAND researchers recommend?

4. How does intensive supervision probation (ISP) differ from regular probation?

5. Discuss the relationship between caseload size and recidivism.

6. What are the purposes of shock incarceration? How successful has it been? What are some of the problems associated with these programs?

7. Discuss the evolution and use of "boot camps." What are some of the issues surrounding them?

8. What are the advantages and disadvantages of house arrest?

9. How does electronic monitoring support house arrest? What ethical and social criticisms are associated with EM?

10. How do electronic monitoring devices work? What are some of the technical problems associated with them?

11. How are restitution and community service used as a correctional tool? What are their purposes? How do monetary restitution and community service differ? How are they alike?

12. Why don't more judges use fines as intermediate sanctions? What is a "day fine," and how does it overcome one of the major problems associated with fines?

When Probation Becomes More Dreaded than Prison

As prisons have become more and more crowded, pressure has increased to divert some serious offenders to community-based sanctions. In response, most jurisdictions have established, or are experimenting with, various kinds of intensive supervision programs (ISPs). However, these alternatives to prison are themselves still on trial. It remains to be seen whether ISPs can punish and control serious offenders effectively enough to meet the dominant objectives of imprisonment: imposing "just desserts" and "incapacitating" criminals.

A major obstacle in testing their effectiveness is getting sufficient numbers of truly "prison-bound" offenders into these programs. Judges seem hesitant to impose community-based sanctions because of their concern for public safety and their belief that ISPs are not punitive enough for such offenders.

This article focuses on the second concern: Are community sanctions punitive enough to convince the public that the "punishment fits the crime"? Having studied the development of these intermediate sanctions, I have discovered that some serious offenders feel that ISPs are at least as punitive as imprisonment—if not more so. If this is true, then offenders' perceptions should be considered in structuring sanctions and in making sentencing decisions.

Why is this issue worth studying? The most pragmatic reason is that ISPs offer some hope of relieving prison overcrowding—without draining the public purse. If it can be shown that other—less expensive—sanctions also have punitive qualities, then perhaps the public might accept that community-based sanctions are appropriate and quite consistent with their demand to "get tough" and hold criminals accountable for their crimes. If this link were made, the criminal justice system could save money and operate a system with more rehabilitation potential.

More theoretical, but possibly more compelling, these hypotheses question some basic assumptions that underlie sentencing decisions, the structure of sanctions, and resource allocation in the criminal justice system. Consequently, those assumptions may be partly responsible for today's "crisis in corrections." It would probably have been salutary to question these assumptions long ago, but under present circumstances it is imperative to do so.

PUNISHMENT FOR WHOM?

This country bases assumptions about "what punishes" on the norms and living standards of society at large. This practice overlooks two salient facts: First, most serious offenders neither accept nor abide by those norms—otherwise they wouldn't be offenders. Second, most of the people who even "qualify" for imprisonment today come from communities where conditions fall far below the living standards most Americans would recognize. If their values and standards differ, why should their perceptions of punishment be the same? Nevertheless, criminal sanctions reflect society's values—negatively. The demand that serious criminals go to prison implies that prison imposes conditions that are intolerable and frightening to the law-abiding citizen. The belief that community sanctions are too lenient implies that no matter what conditions probation or parole impose, remaining in the community is categorically preferable to imprisonment.

When crime rates were lower and minor crimes could land a person in prison, many offenders might have shared these perceptions. Apparently, feelings are different among offenders who face prison sentences today. In several states, *given the option of serving prison terms or participating in ISPs, many offenders have chosen prison.*

Pearson (1988) reports that about 15 percent of offenders who apply to New Jersey's ISP program retract their applications once they understand the conditions and requirements. Under the New Jersey structure, this means that they will remain in prison on their original sentences.

One of the more striking examples comes from Marion County, Oregon, which has been cooperating with researchers from the RAND Corporation in a randomized field experiment. Selected nonviolent offenders were given the choice of serving a prison term or returning to the community to participate in ISP. These offenders have been convicted, and the judge has formally imposed a prison term. After conviction, they were asked if they would agree to return to the community and participate in ISP, rather than go to prison. During the 1-year study period, about a third of those eligible for the experiment have chosen prison instead of ISP.

What accounts for this seeming aberration? Why should anyone prefer imprisonment to remaining in the community—no matter what the conditions? Can we infer from this that prison conditions seem less "punishing" than ISP requirements to these offenders? To consider this possibility, we first need to understand why imprisonment may have lost some of its punitive sting.

HAS THE PUNITIVE POWER OF IMPRISONMENT DIMINISHED?

Zimring and Hawkins (1973:190) note that sanctions are most likely to deter if they meet two conditions: "the social standing is injured by the punishment," and "the individual feels a danger of being excluded from the group." It is hard to imagine that prison terms have either of these attributes for repeat criminals.

Possessing a prison record is not as stigmatizing as in the past, because so many of the offender's peers (and other family members) also have "done time." A recent survey shows that 40 percent of youths in state training schools have parents who have also been incarcerated (Beck et al., 1988). Further, about a quarter of all U.S. black males will be incarcerated during their lives, so the stigma attached to having a prison record is not as great as it was when it was relatively uncommon (Bureau of Justice Statistics, 1985).

In fact, far from stigmatizing, imprisonment evidently confers status in some neighborhoods. Particu-

larly for gang-affiliated and career criminals, a prison sentence enhances status when the offender returns to his neighborhood, especially in the inner cities. California's Task Force on Gangs and Drugs (1989) reported that during public testimony, gang members themselves "repeatedly stated that incarceration was not a threat because they knew their sentences would be minimal. Further, some gang members considered the short period of detention as a "badge of courage, something to brag about when they return to the streets." (1989:29). And according to the California Youth Authority, inmates steal state-issued prison clothing for the same reason. Wearing it when they return to the community lets everyone know that they have "done hard time."

As for employment opportunities, imprisonment has had increasingly less effect for the people in question. As William Julius Wilson (1987) makes painfully clear in *The Truly Disadvantaged,* employment opportunities have been shrinking for people of lower economic status, especially in urban areas, so the effect of a prison record may not be as dramatic as it was when jobs were more plentiful.

Some have argued that for poor people, prison may be preferred, but few scholars take such discussions seriously. It is undoubtedly true, however, that the quality of a person's lifestyle when free certainly has some bearing on the extent to which imprisonment is considered undesirable. The grim fact—and national shame—is that for most people who go to prison, the conditions inside are not all that different from the conditions outside. The prison environment may be far below the ordinary standards of society, but so is the environment they come from. As the quality of life that people can expect when [they are] free declines, the relative deprivation suffered while in prison declines.

Social isolation is another presumably punitive aspect of imprisonment. Again, the values of society surface in the belief that when a person goes to prison he is "among aliens." In prison, he is isolated from the kinds of people he would customarily (and by preference) be among. For today's inmates, that is less likely to be true. The newly admitted inmate will probably find friends, if not family, already there.

The warden of Pontiac Penitentiary described it thus:

When a new guy comes up here it's almost a homecoming—undoubtedly there are people from his neighborhood and people who know him . . . (as quoted in Jacobs, 1984:33).

He goes on to recall how a ranking gang member, upon entry to prison, received a "letter from the ranking chief welcoming him into the family." As for real family, the warden in a Washington, D.C., jail recently noted that his facility currently contained three generations of a particular family at once. He remarked that, "It was like a family reunion for these guys."

Some even suggest that prison serves as a buffer for offenders who find the outside world particularly difficult. One man, just released from a Massachusetts prison, said:

I have literally seen guys who have been released walk out the door and stand on the corner and not know which direction to go. And they eventually go back to prison. As horrible as it is, prison provides some sort of community.

And, finally, the length of time an offender can be expected to actually serve in prison has decreased—from 18 months in 1984 to 12 months in 1987. But more to the point, for marginal offenders (those targeted for prison alternatives), the expected time served can be much less. In California, Texas, and Illinois, 2- to 3-year prison sentences often translate into less than 6 months actually served. In Oregon, prison crowding has created a situation in which a 5-year sentence can translate into 3 to 4 months of actual time served (Clear and Hardyman, 1990). Particularly when the prison system is the subject of a court order and offenders are released because of a "cap," prison terms can be quite short. Offenders on the street seem to be aware of this, even more so with the extensive media coverage such issues are receiving.

For the above reasons, then, it seems at least plausible that prison terms (on average) are not perceived as being as severe as they were historically. No one has ever surveyed prisoners or ex-convicts to find out how punitive they think imprisonment is. However, one could say their actions answer that question implicitly: More than 50 percent of today's prison inmates have served a prior prison term. Add prior jail sentences, and the percentage rises to 80 percent (Innes, 1988). Knowing what it's like, 80 percent of them evidently still think that the "benefits" of committing a new crime outweigh the "costs" of being in prison.

This implies a lot about how punitive prison is for these offenders. However, it does not explain why they would choose imprisonment over intensive probation.

Why Would Offenders Choose Prison Over ISPs?

For many offenders, it may seem preferable to get that short stay in prison over, rather than spend five times as long in an ISP. But what about the relative conditions? If the speculations above have any validity, better a short time in conditions that differ little from your accustomed life than a long time in conditions that are very different from the "ordinary standards" of your community.

Taking Marion County, Oregon, as an example, consider the alternatives facing convicted offenders:

ISP. The offender will serve 2 years under this sanction. During that time, the offender will be visited by a probation officer two or three times per week, who will phone on the other days. The offender will be subject to unannounced searches of his home for drugs and have his urine tested regularly for alcohol and drugs. He must strictly abide by other conditions set by the court—not carrying a weapon, not socializing with certain persons— and he will have to perform community service and be employed or participate in training or education. In addition, he will be strongly encouraged to attend counseling and/or other treatment, particularly if he is a drug offender.

Or

Prison. A sentence of 2 to 4 years will require that the offender serve about 3 to 6 months. During his term, he is not required to work, nor will he be required to participate in any training or treatment, but may do so if he wishes. Once released, he will be placed on 2 years' routine parole supervision, where he sees his parole officer about once a month.

For these offenders, as for any of us, freedom is probably preferable to imprisonment. However, the ISP does not represent freedom. In fact, it may stress and isolate repeat offenders more than imprisonment does. It seems reasonable that when offenders return to their communities, they expect to return to their old lives. The ISP transforms those lives radically.

Their homes can be searched, and they must submit regularly to urine testing. Offenders may well consider such invasions of their homes and lives more intrusive and unbearable than the lack of privacy in prisons— where it is an expected condition of life. The same is true of discipline and social isolation. By definition, imprisonment limits freedom of movement and activity, but once a person is in his own community, curfew and other restrictions may seem harder to take. Ironically, he may be less socially isolated from his peers in prison than in ISP.

WHY DO OFFENDERS' PERCEPTIONS MATTER?

Having established the counter-intuitive fact that some serious offenders prefer imprisonment to ISPs, what are we to make of it? Whatever else, it does argue for reconsidering the range of sanctions this country has and the assumptions they reflect. The point is not to insist that on any absolute scale ISP is "worse" than prison. Rather, it is to suggest that the scale we currently use needs reexamining.

For the people who are likely to come under either sanction, how society at large views those sanctions is largely irrelevant. How offenders view punishment ought at least to be considered. This is implied in Jack Gibbs statement: *"No legal action can deter if it is not perceived as punitive by those who are subject to it, and whether or not sanctions deter depends in part on the extent to which they are perceived as severe"* (1975:119).

If, as this article has argued, today's serious offenders have different views from most of us about what punishes, those views should at least be identified and considered in structuring sanctions.

In fact, it is our perspective, and not necessarily theirs, that must bear much of the blame for the current "crisis in corrections." From the public's perspective, imprisonment is horrible and should, thus, punish and deter. Even a cursory look at crime rates and time served shows that this has become a dangerous illusion.

Because the public wants the courts to "get tough on crime," the prison population has doubled over the past 10 years. Yet, the rate at which violent crime is committed is also substantially higher. The United States continues to have not only the highest rate of incarceration for street crimes in the world, but also the highest level of violent crime (Kalish, 1988).

It is clear that prison is not effectively deterring offenders. But what other sanctions might? ISPs pro- vide a potentially feasible means to this end. However, they need to be tested more effectively. This requires putting more truly "prison-bound" offenders in these programs and analyzing the outcomes. As noted earlier, one obstacle to such testing has been judges' apparent belief that the ISPs do not impose sufficient punishment for inveterate repeaters. If that perception can be changed, the ISPs could get thorough, systematic testing. One way to change that perception is to document what the early results mentioned above indicate—that some offenders see ISPs as more punitive than short prison terms.

STUDYING OFFENDERS' PERCEPTIONS OF SANCTIONS

How completely we have based our sanctions on the perceptions of the law-abiding is borne out by a review of the literature. Very few studies have attempted to rank sentence severity, and *those studies have not included offender populations in their samples.* If we want sanctions to be punitive for today's offenders, we need to sample offenders and analyze their responses. Outlined below is a tentative strategy for beginning such research.

To test these ideas, one would begin by having different populations (including offenders and nonoffenders) rate the perceived severity of a wide range of currently administered sanctions, including jail, regular probation, intensive probation, house arrest, electronic monitoring, etc.

The exact details of the rating task would need to be worked out, but one would begin by presenting pairs of sanctions and asking each respondent to select the more severe of the alternatives. In addition to collecting information on sanctions, one would also collect respondent characteristics such as status (e.g., free or incarcerated), age, race, and sex, prior record, and whether the offender had experienced the specific sanction types being measured.

Once the perceptions of severity were obtained, one would compute scale scores for the various sanctions using paired-comparison scaling techniques. From this stage, one could build multiple regression equations containing the desired sanctions as independent variables and the scale values as the dependent variables. In this way, the coefficients would represent the sanction severity for each component sanction. Additional analyses could also be performed to take into account the influence of demographic characteristics and other variables (such as experience with a sanction) on perceived severity of sanctions. These would be incorporated in additional regression models. It seems that such a research effort would be policy relevant, particularly as the move toward sentencing guidelines gains momentum.

If prison is losing its "punitiveness," it is interesting from a number of research and policy perspectives. For example, if researchers scale sanctions to reflect seriousness—which they do in every sentencing and deterrence study—they may not be correct. Probation is always weighed as "out" and prison as "in." But there are now different levels of "out" that need to be taken into account. Sentencing commissions (e.g., the United States Sentencing Commission) have attempted to recommend sentences commensurate with the seriousness of the crime, but have been unsure how to weight these new "intermediate sanctions." A number of states (e.g., Delaware) have wrestled with how to move past the in/out line of the Minnesota guidelines to include a more graduated approach, but have made little progress.

If community-based punishments can be designed so that they are seen as punitive by offenders, then perhaps policymakers—who say they are imprisoning such a large number of offenders because of the public's desire to get tough with crime—might be convinced that there are other means besides prison to extract punishment. As the report by Fogel (1975) said, "One reason for preferring incarceration is simply that we have not found another satisfactory severe punishment." Perhaps, if we can show that other sanctions can be equally severe, then the United States will begin to get over its preoccupation with imprisonment as the only suitable sanction for serious offenses. If this occurs, corrections costs could be reduced. But more importantly, since these programs require the offender to work and participate in treatment, rehabilitation is more likely.

SOURCE: Joan Petersilia, "When Probation Becomes More Dreaded than Prison," *Federal Probation*, March 1990. Notes deleted.

Boot Camp Programs

Boot camp prison programs are being used increasingly as a sentencing option for young drug offenders and others convicted of nonviolent offenses.

The number of such state programs for adults now operating throughout the country has grown to 21, up from 14 a year ago. Seventeen states now use boot camps—also known as shock incarceration—compared to 11 states in May 1989. Three states have begun programs in 1990: New Hampshire, Maryland, and Arkansas. Another three are planning to begin programs before the year is out: Connecticut, Pennsylvania, and Wyoming. County and juvenile jurisdictions are also considering shock programs. Figure 1 and Table 1 give the latest statistics, contrasted with those published a year ago.

Most shock incarceration programs are designed for young, nonviolent offenders serving time on their first felony convictions, although the programs are not limited to these individuals. Some criminal justice officials view shock incarceration as a promising approach for controlling offenders who would otherwise be sentenced to probation.

The overall picture that emerges from a review of existing programs is that of a common core based on the military atmosphere, discipline, youth of the offenders, and a common goal of providing punishment without long-term incarceration.

However, programs differ as to who is responsible for placing offenders in the program—the judge or corrections department—whether offenders may enter the program or drop out of it voluntarily, the location of the program, and the supervision of offenders upon release. Programs also differ greatly in the number of hours devoted to physical training, drill, work, education, and counseling. But frequently offenders in these programs spend more time in rehabilitative-type activities such as education or counseling than they would in a regular prison.

FIGURE 1

Shock Incarceration Programs in the United States, July 1990

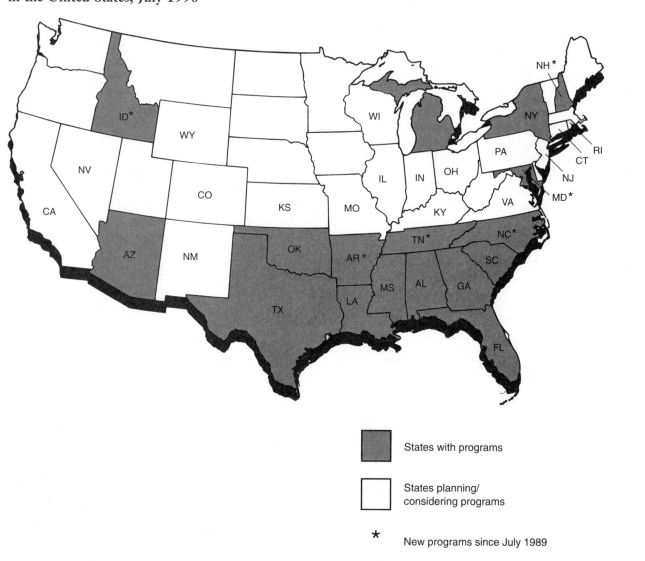

States with programs

States planning/
considering programs

* New programs since July 1989

GROWING KNOWLEDGE

Some conclusions are emerging from research:

■ Programs vary greatly, and any evaluation must begin with a description of the program and its objectives.

■ There is some evidence that the boot camp experience may be more positive than incarceration in traditional prison.
■ There is no evidence that those who complete boot camp programs are angrier or negatively affected by the program.

TABLE 1

Characteristics of Shock Incarceration Programs, 1990

STATE	YEAR PROGRAMS BEGAN	NUMBER OF PROGRAMS	NUMBER OF PARTICIPANTS (MALE/FEMALE)	NUMBER OF DAYS SERVED	MAXIMUM AGE LIMIT	FIRST FELONY?	NONVIOLENT ONLY?
Alabama	1988	1	127 male	90	none	no	no
Arizona	1988	1	150 male	120	25	yes	no
Florida	1987	1	100 male	90	25	yes	no
Georgia	1983	2	250 male	90	25	yes	no
Idaho	1989	1	154 male	120	none	no	no
Louisiana	1987	1	87 male / 1 female	120	39	no	yes
Michigan	1988	1	120 male	120	25	no	no
Mississippi	1985	2	225 male / 15 female	110	none	yes	yes
New York	1987	5	1,500 male / 102 female	180	30	yes	yes
North Carolina	1989	1	54 male	93	24	yes	yes
Oklahoma	1984	1	150 male	90	25	yes	yes
South Carolina	1987	2	98 male / 13 female	90	24	yes	yes
Tennessee	1989	1	42 male	120	30	yes	yes
Texas	1989	1	200 male	90	25	yes	no

■ Those who complete shock programs report having a difficult but constructive experience. Similar offenders who serve their sentences in a traditional prison do not view their experiences as constructive.

■ Boot camp recidivism rates are approximately the same as those of comparison groups who serve a longer period of time in a traditional prison or who serve time on probation.

■ Programs differ substantially in the amount of time offenders spend in rehabilitative activities.

■ Success may be contingent on the emphasis on rehabilitation—giving offenders the training, treatment, and education needed to support new behavior—during incarceration and an aftercare during community supervision.

On the basis of early research results, visits to programs, interviews with staff and inmates, and reviews of related research, several observations can be made.

Some evidence suggests that offenders change in a positive way during their brief incarceration. Parolees who complete the programs are generally much more positive about their experiences than those released from regular prison. However, those who are not ready to change may drop out of the program.

Research also suggests that returning to the home environment may present such overwhelming difficulties for offenders that positive changes during incarceration cannot be sustained. New York, with the largest shock incarceration program of any state, has identified maintaining positive change as a possible problem and has developed an "after shock" program to help offenders while they are under supervision in the community.

Most of these programs are not merely a time of punishment through hard labor and exercise. In almost all shock programs, offenders receive more treatment (through counseling or education) than they would in the general prison population. One question raised by research is whether the boot camp atmosphere enhances the effect of treatment or whether an intensive treatment program alone would have the same effect.

However, physical training, drill, hard labor, and the boot camp regime may be important in several ways.

Offenders who are near the end of their time in shock incarceration report that these activities result in their "getting free" of drugs and becoming physically fit. They also mention the advantage of learning to get up in the morning and being active all day.

The radical changes these activities produce in everyday living patterns may have other effects. They shake up the offenders, creating stress at a time when offenders may be particularly susceptible to outside influences. This is an excellent time for them to reevaluate their lives and change their thinking and behavior.

SOURCE: Doris Layton MacKenzie, "Boot Camp Programs Grow in Number and Scope," *Research in Action* (Washington, D.C.: National Institute of Justice), November/December 1990. Notes deleted.

Community Service: A Review of the Basic Issues

INTRODUCTION

It is clear that the use of community service as a sentencing alternative is a major judicial and correctional trend in the United States. In part driven by tax-limiting initiatives such as Propositions 13 in California and 2.5 in Massachusetts, community service seemingly has high potential in the continued search for more effective and less costly methods of dealing with offenders. The trend toward community service also is driven by economic considerations brought about by the efforts to balance the federal budget. These efforts forecast that there will be a reduction in federal funds available to states, counties, and municipalities that will impact the criminal justice systems generally and correctional systems specifically.

In addition to these economic influences, the prospects for community service were significantly bolstered by enactment of the Federal Comprehensive Crime Control Act of 1984, effective November 1, 1987, which states:

If sentenced to probation, the defendant must also be ordered to pay a fine, make restitution, and/or work in community service.

Changes and directions in the federal correctional system—probation, parole, and institutions—have often established trends for corrections at state and local levels.

The definition of community service varies in the professional literature, but for purposes of this commentary, it is a court order that an offender perform a specified number of hours of uncompensated work or service within a given time period for a nonprofit community organization or tax-supported agency. It clearly is distinguished from monetary *restitution* to the victim or payment of a *fine* to a political jurisdiction: restitution and fine, as in the federal legislation noted above, also may be part of a court order. In a generic sense, community service has been labeled as "restitution"—a sanction imposed by an official of the criminal justice system requiring an offender to make a payment of money or service to either the direct or a substitute crime victim. Community service has had other labels, among them court referral, reparation, volunteer work, symbolic restitution, service restitution, and, for those individuals who perform community service without an adjudication of guilt, pretrial diversion and pretrial intervention.

More pragmatically, however, the specific use of community sanctions is of recent origin, emerging conceptually in England in the late 1960s and operationally in 1972 with Parliament granting the courts authority to order convicted offenders to perform community service. Within just a few years, the program was expanded in England and introduced into the United States and Canada.

Considerable literature on this sentencing and correctional alternative has been generated since that time, and at least two major bibliographies are now available which reflect that growing interest.

There are several issues which should be carefully reviewed prior to the decision to begin community service as a sentencing alternative or enhancement. The purpose of this article is to review the more significant issues and the options available to the judicial and correctional decision makers as each issue is examined. The issues include, but are not limited to, judicial and correctional philosophy, offender eligibility, criteria for selection, organizational models for community service, community service investigations, sentencing considerations, assignments to community service programs, supervision, and evaluation.

JUDICIAL AND CORRECTIONAL PHILOSOPHY

Community service, as with any other sanction, should support the overall philosophical orientation of the criminal justice system and its judicial and correctional decision makers specifically. That philosophical orientation—whether it be rehabilitation, restitution, deterrence, retribution, punishment, or something else, singly or in combination—should be translated into community service program goals, objectives and orientation. Simply stated, operational decisions should be developed from some shared understandings about community service as a sentencing alternative—an alternative to confinement, to fines, to restitution, and/or to other traditional penalties, with special attention focused upon the offender and the community. Operationally, a community service program developed to increase the penalty to an appropriate level of deterrence or just desert may be significantly different from one established to repay the community for damages that the offenders have done or to help the community meet its needs for unpaid workers.

It is not our purpose to argue here what the purposes for community service should be, but it is important to emphasize the need for decision makers to specify why community service would be a useful sentencing alternative for them. If they state the goals that they seek with community service, they can design programs to achieve these goals.

OFFENDER ELIGIBILITY

Community service has been utilized mostly by the lower courts for individuals convicted of offenses considered less serious, especially misdemeanors, including traffic violations. An option to be considered is the use of community service for more serious offenders. Within the federal system, even apart from the Comprehensive Crime Control Act requirements, community service has been ordered for whitecollar and corporate offenders, and even for corporations. The inclusion of felons, in addition to misdemeanants, appears a rational expansion of community service, providing that the threat to community safety is always considered and minimized. The issue of dangerousness clearly is a critical correctional issue.

Concerns about dangerousness may be reflected in mandated exceptions to the utilization of community service for persons (1) committing certain types of offenses, (2) exhibiting particular traits or characteristics in their background, such as drug addiction, or (3) committing offenses with weapons or violence. Indeed, as the question of offender eligibility is considered, it may be appropriate to consider whether there is any reason why individuals entering into or being processed through the criminal justice system, who otherwise are deemed appropriate for a judicial or correctional release to the community, should be barred from community service. This would include adults and juveniles, felons, and misdemeanants, probationers and parolees, individuals and corporations, and those convicted of offenses as well as those diverted from the justice system.

SELECTION FOR COMMUNITY SERVICE

Selection for community service requires a dual focus: on the offender and on the community. In considering individuals, explicit and objective criteria are necessary to prevent in community service the sentencing disparities which have been so well documented nationwide in other sentencing options. It has been noted that

(t)he lack of standards or guidelines means that similar offenders can receive very different community service sentences for the same offense from a given judge, from two judges in the same jurisdiction, or from judges in different jurisdictions.

Allegations that community service sentences are applied in an unfair or discriminatory fashion also flow from a lack of criteria. The question of equity assuredly will surface if the community service sanction is applied only to the poor and the minorities or, contrastingly, only to middle- or upper-income offenders.

In determining selection criteria, the assignment of an offender to community service requires attention to community safety, to the offender's attitude and special skills or talents, to the seriousness of the offense, the availability of a suitable community service placement, and the wisdom of selecting other sentencing alternatives. As the community is examined, several other important issues emerge, including the public's attitude toward specific offenses and offenders, as well as the impact of community service on perceptions of the justice system by the citizenry. It is important that the public see community service as both a benefit to the community and a reasonable judicial disposition of the offender.

The process by which the criteria are established may be as important as the criteria themselves. It has been suggested that a "core group of advocates"—consisting perhaps of members of the judiciary, corrections, and the community—join together to establish the standards for selection to community service.

ORGANIZATIONAL ISSUE

A community service program of any size requires some administrative structure. The two most common administrative entities are the probation agency and a volunteer bureau. There may also be a combined effort in which the probation agency has some oversight of those functions which are uniquely offender-connected within the volunteer bureau. In this case, the probation office and the private organization have mutually supportive and compatible roles. A third type of administrative entity is the private organization created solely for the purpose of overseeing community service activities. An example of this third type is the Foundation for People, a nonprofit corporation established in Los Angeles under the aegis of the Probation Office of the U.S. District Court for the Central District of California. One of its several activities is to work with federal courts to arrange as community service for white-collar offenders their assistance in the vocational training, counseling, and job-placement of blue-collar offenders.

There are several important distinctions which enter into the issue of the probation agency, volunteer bureau, or other entity providing the organizational structure for community service. The probation agency and the volunteer bureau are established in the community and have important connections with other organizations that already play a role in community-based corrections which could serve as the foundation for the community service function. Probation, as an established part of the criminal justice system, can provide a legitimacy and stability to a community service program and affect both judicial and community acceptance. Volunteer bureaus long have been involved in identifying and matching community needs with individuals able to offer a variety of services.

Regardless of the agency charged with the community service function, it is assumed in this writing that the order to community service is usually a condition of probation. However, it may be appropriate for community service to be ordered by the court without probation, particularly for less serious offenses, and in those smaller jurisdictions in which the court has continuous firsthand contact with the agency providing the community service function. The organization with the administrative responsibility must be able to provide some form of community service investigation, discussed below, as well as to supervise community service. Therefore, it must have the authority to insure compliance with the court order.

In making an organizational decision, there is a need to focus upon two basic functions—the development of some type of plan for joining offenders with community service and for supervision of these offenders in that service obligation. These functions parallel the traditional investigation and supervision functions of probation, but this similarity is not to be interpreted as a preference for the probation agency option. Let us examine these functions separately.

THE COMMUNITY SERVICE INVESTIGATION

A number of important issues surface in a community service investigation and report, especially in the development of a plan for community service. Some of the issues are

■ What constitutes an appropriate community service investigation?

■ What is an appropriate format for a community service report?

■ Should there be an investigation and report on all individuals eligible to receive a community service sentence or only on specific individuals? If the latter, is it at the direction of the court, the discretion of the probation agency or volunteer bureau, or upon request by the prosecutor or the defendant or the defense attorney?

■ Should a community service investigation and report be separate from, an adjunct to, or part of the formal presentence investigation and report? Indeed, for some minor offenses, would a community service investigation and report be an appropriate substitute for a presentence investigation and report?

■ How much (additional) time should be allowed for the investigation, the preparation of a report, and the development of an appropriate plan?

■ Does the community service investigation and report require a "specialist" familiar with the community and its needs and able to connect offender and community?

■ Should the community service investigation and report be conducted before or after the imposition of a community service requirement?

■ Should the agency responsible for the investigation and report also be charged with supervision of the community service?

■ From an administrative perspective, how many community service investigations and reports are the equivalent of a presentence investigation and report?

Some Sentencing Considerations

The addition of community service as a sentencing alternative creates several unique issues for the court. Obviously, traditional considerations relating to the imposition of sentence remain, such as the concern for justice, equity, protection of the community, and rehabilitation. If there is an order of community service in lieu of confinement in a local custodial facility, a question of equivalence arises. At bottom, and as a question—how many hours of community service are the equivalent of a day in custody? Is it a day for a day, two for one, three for one, or some other ratio? If it is a day for a day, then is the equivalent of a 30-day jail sentence 30 8-hour days of community service, or 90 8-hour days? In the interests of fairness and equity, these ratios need to be established.

If on the other hand, the court wishes to impose community service instead of a fine—perhaps because the offender simply will be unable to pay a fine—what is the dollar equivalent of an hour of community service work? Is it the minimum wage, the prevailing wage in the community, or is it equal to the offender's normal hourly rate—perhaps $4 an hour for one offender and $25 an hour for another? Is it more equitable to have a uniform "equivalency" or to have equivalence individualized? If the latter, one of these offenders could work off a $1,000 community service obligation with 250 hours of service; the other could accomplish the same in 100 hours.

Community service can be thought of as providing some of the equity that is credited to the day-fine principle pioneered in Scandinavia and now found in several other nations, including Austria and West Germany. Under this principle, an offender is sentenced to a fine of his or her earnings for a given number of days, so that the amount of money involved varies with the size of the earnings. As administered in Sweden, the fine is collected by that country's equivalent of our Internal Revenue Service, which collects all taxes or other money owed to the government. This agency determines the amount of the fine from its records of the offender's past taxable earnings, deducts an amount for necessities and dependents, but imposes some fine per day of the penalty even on those whose only income is from welfare. They collect almost every fine without jailing by allowing installment payments with interest for those who cannot pay immediately, but attaching salaries and even seizing possessions if there is a persistent failure to pay. Our courts, by imposing a penalty of a specified number of days of community service, are getting the same amount of service from each offender punished in this way, regardless of contrasts in the price that the services of different persons command per day when compensated in the free market.

It seems essential that the court fix both the precise number of hours of community service to be performed and the period of time during which the obligation is to be completed. Regardless of whether the number of hours was determined by the nature of the offense or the background of the offender, some other "arithmetic" needs to be completed. That arithmetic focuses on the balance between the number of hours to be performed and the length of time given for completion of community service. An order for 400 hours of community service approximately equals 1 day or perhaps two evenings of service per week for a year. Is that a reasonable assessment when examining all of the factors—the offense, the offender, the offender's family and employment obligations, the community's needs for the service to be performed, and the feeling that "justice was done"? Or would 400 hours of community service over *2 years* be more appropriate, considering all of the variables?

One last numeric item—there seemingly should be both a minimum and maximum number of hours which can be ordered. It is assumed that there is some number of hours below which the administrative burden to the agencies involved in the delivery of community services would be inefficient and ineffective, and a number above which the offender could not hope to comply with the order. While we do not intend to be prescriptive here, the courts need to establish a meaningful range; perhaps from a 30-hour minimum, equivalent to 1 day a week for 1 month for a minor offense or offender, to as much as perhaps 400 hours per year for 5 years, a total of 2,000 hours of service, for the most serious offense or offender that still would permit imposition of a community-based correctional alternative.

COMMUNITY SERVICE ASSIGNMENTS

Following an investigation and report, and an order by the court for community service, there is a requirement to assign the offender to a specific community activity. As noted, this assignment may be made through a probation agency, volunteer bureau, or other organization designated to administer the community service effort. There are two basic perspectives about the assignment issue. The first argues for a matching of offender and community service on the basis of the skills or talents of the offender and the documented needs within the community. An often cited example is the assignment of a physician ordered to perform community service to a program in which medical skills may be utilized, such as a public health or "free" medical clinic of some sort. This kind of matching of abilities and needs may or may not seem as appropriate as a second type of matching: attempts to connect the community service assignment to the offense committed. For example, the assignment of an offender without medical service skills convicted of driving under the influence to a hospital emergency room—where there is considerable opportunity to see the harm done by drinking drivers—may not provide much relevant service.

An alternative to either of these two types of matching is the more-or-less random assignment of offenders to community activities as offenders become available through the system and community needs are identified. Simply put, if two or three projects are identified as valid community needs requiring the services of 25 individuals, one assigns to these projects the next 25 offenders ordered to community service by the court, regardless of the number of hours ordered or the special abilities of the offender. The offender may be allowed to request participation in one or the other of the community services identified. This method has the advantage of simplicity, and perhaps some basic equity, although it is clear that the hypothetical physician mentioned above is not providing the most meaningful service to the community, particularly if the community service project at that time is clearing trash from the side of the road.

All approaches require basic data about the offense, offender, and the community service requirements, but the matching approach—in contrast to randomness—requires considerably more data about these matters. Personal data about skills and abilities are needed, as is related information about employment schedules, indicating hours of the day and days of the week which are available for service, and special clothing or other needed equipment. Indeed, systems involved in matching also require considerable specificity about the nature of the tasks to be accomplished and the skills required of the offender for their accomplishment. A large matching system most likely would be computer-based, whereas a smaller system might simply use 3- by 5-inch index cards.

A number of other related issues surface about the assignment phenomena: what agencies are eligible to receive community service? Agencies with a religious orientation or involvement might be ineligible because of perceived violations of the doctrine of separation of church and state, while assignments to political organizations, public interest or pressure groups, or controversial collectivities of citizens create other problems. Then, too, there are special problems associated with organized labor and with some citizen perceptions that community service deprives "honest citizens" of employment opportunities. Even apart from the issue of legitimacy of organizations to receive services, there are questions as to whether such community services should be provided to *individuals* as opposed to *organizations* . . . for example, to individual victims of crime.

SUPERVISION OF COMMUNITY SERVICE

The supervision function, whether performed by a probation agency, volunteer bureau, or other organization, also raises some significant issues. Among them are questions which focus upon *disclosure* about the offender, the offense, and personal background to the community organization receiving the offender's service. Is there a reverse side of that coin which assures the offender at least a minimum right to *privacy*? And during the time that the offender is performing community service, does the community service sponsoring agency—the volunteer bureau, for example—have some degree of *liability* for the offender's behavior? Or if the offender is injured while performing community service, are there *disability* rights vested in that service? And should individuals sponsoring community service activities have *personal insurance* to protect them against a variety of potential legal actions which may grow from the connection to community service? While the *charging of fees* to offenders for probation services has been emerging nationwide, would it be appropriate for similar charges to be extended for community service investigations and supervision? Finally, would it be appropriate for the tax-supported agencies or the nonprofit community organizations receiving community services to pay the court for the services received?

Apart from these issues, there are more traditional questions about community service supervision, ranging from the identification of those who provide it, frequency of contact with the offender and the community service supervisor or agency, the nature and schedule of reports, reassignment determinations, and the overall relationship between probation supervision and community service supervision, particularly if two separate agencies are involved.

Under some circumstances, there may be important questions raised about compliance with the community service court order. What constitutes a violation: would it be a failure to complete all of the assigned hours in the prescribed time or, in the shorter timeframe, a failure to appear to perform service on one or more occasions? Would a belligerent or disruptive attitude warrant cessation of a community service order? Probation and parole supervision long have had explicit conditions or standards of behavior. Is there a need for a parallel series of community service guidelines for those involved in both the supervision and performance of community service?

EVALUATION OF COMMUNITY SERVICE

At a minimum, two areas of community service need assessment. The first centers upon measures of offender success and failure; the second upon some determination of cost–benefits. The cost–benefit analyses must consider both the criminal justice system *and* the community. In short, effectiveness and efficiency are required targets for analysis.

Definitions of success and failure for offenders involved in the many varieties of community corrections long have been troublesome. Although we do not address that conflicted arena here, we note that community service does not make those assessments simpler, but rather more complex. An overall evaluation should go beyond that which could be generated by data as to whether or not the offender completed the required number of hours of community service within the court-ordered period of time.

Several examples may illustrate the complexity. The first focuses upon the definition of success and failure by asking about how the two are related in probation *and* community service. As an example, consider an offender who successfully completes a court-ordered community service obligation but is declared in violation of probation for behavior that is not related to the community service. How is that overall offender performance to be assessed?

If costs are the focus of evaluation, two quite different sets of cost data may be examined. The first may be the value of services provided the community—these calculated at some arbitrary hourly or daily rate such as the national minimum wage or an average local wage. The overall dollar value of the services provided are the number of hours of service multiplied by the value of those hours for a given period of time.

A second set of data may be derived from the "savings" obtained by having offenders provide community service instead of being in local custody. This may be calculated as the daily custodial rate multiplied by the number of confinement days not served. It is quite probable that estimates of monies saved by the justice system from non-incarceration of offenders who are performing community service may be markedly different from estimates of the value of the community service developed from hourly or daily wage comparisons, and that the two might be added. This difference would grow if calculated to include welfare assistance given to families of confined offenders. If community service serves as an alternative to the capital costs of constructing a custodial facility, the savings—even when prorated in some fashion—become enormous. And if these community services generate activities and projects which otherwise might not have been accomplished—that is, things which the community could not have done without these court-ordered services—perhaps some other dollar equivalents would be justified.

Finally, improvements in community feelings about "justice" generally and the criminal justice system specifically on one hand or the improvement of the offender's personal feelings of self-worth which may be generated from performing a service to the community on the other, cannot be measured readily, but nevertheless need assessment.

SUMMARY

Community service as a sentencing option has an operational history of about 15 years. There is every reason to believe that its utilization in America and elsewhere will expand significantly during the next decade. Because it has evolved and grown so rapidly, there has not yet been adequate time or attention given to identification of the issues that surround its usage or to develop standards for that usage. Indeed, there is some evidence of a failure to understand that the many issues which have been or yet may be identified are completely interrelated, one with the other.

The authors have not been prescriptive, but would argue that there is a mandate to examine carefully a number of issues about community service. Some of these have been identified—judicial and correctional philosophies, offender eligibility and selection criteria, organizational arrangements, community service investigations and supervision, sentencing considerations, community service assignments, and evaluation. If community service is to become a truly viable sentencing option, these areas need thoughtful consideration by those academicians, administrators, practitioners, and researchers concerned with criminal justice.

SOURCE: Excerpted from Robert M. Carter, Jack Cocks, and Daniel Glaser, "Community Service: A Review of the Basic Issues," *Federal Probation*, March 1987, pp. 4–10. Notes deleted.

Fines as Criminal Sanctions

The fine is one of the oldest forms of punishment, its history predating Hammurabi. In 1973 the Task Force on Corrections of the National Advisory Commission on Criminal Justice Standards and Goals found that "properly employed, the fine is less drastic, far less costly to the public, and perhaps more effective than imprisonment or community service." Until very recently, this recommendation has gone largely unheeded because too little was known of what constitutes proper administration of fines. Today, however, with record jail and prison populations and probation caseloads steadily rising, the fine is gaining renewed attention—especially since Western Europe increasingly uses fines even in nontrivial cases.

In the United States, fines are more widely used than many recognize: Well over a billion dollars in fines are collected in criminal courts each year. This form of punishment is used in some form by virtually all American courts, ranging from its rare use as the sole sanction for a felony in general jurisdiction courts to its regular use either alone or combined with other, often non-custodial sanctions in courts of limited jurisdiction.

How can fines be used more effectively in criminal cases? In the studies summarized here researchers describe and analyze court experience with imposition and enforcement of fines, concluding that judges and prosecutors need to consider more innovative uses of fines, particularly when offenders pose no serious threat to community safety. An effective fine program requires that judges have adequate information about offenders' economic circumstances and use it in setting fine amounts. It also requires improved collection methods. The result can relieve pressure on probation services and jails while promoting confidence that sentences are fair and punishment is certain.

PROS AND CONS

Proponents of the wider use of fines argue that:

■ It can be an effective punishment and deterrent for crimes of varying levels of severity. It can deprive offenders of their ill-gotten gains and, for some, contribute to rehabilitation.
■ It can combine with other noncustodial sanctions to meet multiple sentencing goals.
■ It can be adjusted to a level appropriate to an offender's individual circumstances and the seriousness of the offense.
■ It is relatively inexpensive to administer, usually relying on existing agencies and procedures.
■ It is financially self-sustaining; unlike incarceration and probation, fines produce revenue.

However, critics argue that:

■ Because fines cannot achieve the sentencing goal of incapacitation, they are inappropriate for offenders who pose a risk to the community.
■ Even when incapacitation is not the goal, fines tend to be low, thus limiting their degree of punishment.
■ Fines are easier for more affluent offenders to pay than for poorer offenders.
■ If a fine is high enough to avoid those problems, it is difficult to collect and adds to the administrative burdens of the court.
■ It is impossible to fine indigent offenders, because the fine cannot be collected and may result in imprisonment for default.

These conflicting views reflect different perceptions of how fines actually work and their potential utility. Recent research on the use of fines, here and abroad, provides a base for improving policy and practice in this area.

CURRENT USES OF FINES

A survey of 126 different types of courts around the country shows fines being used extensively (see Table 1), including use for a broad range of criminal offenses, some of which are not trivial (see Table 2). Judges in courts of limited jurisdiction report they impose fines, either alone (36 percent) or in combination with another penalty, in an average of 86 percent of their sentences. General-jurisdiction judges report imposing fines about half as often (42 percent); fines as a sole penalty in less than 10 percent on average.

TABLE 1

Frequency of Fine Utilization for Cases Other than Parking and Routine Traffic Matters, by Type of Court

TYPE OF COURT	ALL OR VIRTUALLY ALL CASES	MOST CASES	ABOUT HALF OF CASES	SELDOM	NEVER	TOTAL
Limited jurisdiction	19	38	10	7	0	74
General jurisdiction (felony, misdemeanor, ordinance violation)	1	15	7	5	0	28
General jurisdiction (felony only)	0	5	4	13	2	24
TOTAL	20	58	21	25	2	126

SOURCE: Hillsman, Sichel, and Mahoney; telephone survey.

TABLE 2

Types of Offenses for Which Fines Are Commonly Imposed, by Type of Court

	LIMITED JURIS. N = 74	GEN. JURIS. (FELONY, MISD., AND ORDINANCE) N = 28	GEN. JURIS. (FELONY ONLY) N = 24	TOTAL N = 126
N = 126				
Driving while intoxicated/DUI	54	22	2	78
Reckless driving	30	9	0	39
Violation of fish and game laws and other regulatory ordinances	24	3	0	27
Disturbing the peace/breach of the peace/disorderly conduct	32	8	1	41
Loitering/soliciting prostitution	15	4	0	19
Drinking in public/public drunkenness/carrying an open container	14	5	0	19
Criminal trespass	10	2	1	13
Vandalism/criminal mischief/malicious mischief/property damage	9	3	3	15
Drug-related offenses (including sale and possession)	23	10	11	44
Weapons (illegal possession, carrying concealed, etc.)	6	2	1	9
Shoplifting	17	3	0	20
Bad checks	14	2	0	16
Other theft	19	9	8	36
Forgery/embezzlement	2	3	2	7
Fraud	1	4	1	6
Assault	29	14	5	48
Burglary/breaking and entering	2	6	6	14
Robbery	0	1	3	4

Fines are most often imposed on first-offenders with known ability to pay. A third or more judges overall report imposing a fine in more than half the cases in which an adult first offender is sentenced for offenses such as these:

- sale of an ounce of cocaine
- fraud in a land deal
- embezzlement of $10,000
- assault with minor injury
- auto theft of $5,000 value
- harassment
- bad check

However, fines are not now being used in American courts as an alternative to incarceration or probation. If fines are used at all in cases at risk of imprisonment or community supervision, they tend to be add-ons to other sanctions. Few judges seem to use the fine alone if the offender has a prior record and the offense is moderately serious. This contrasts sharply with practices in some Western European criminal courts, where the fine is often a sole penalty and is widely used for repeat offenders.

As a policy matter, fines are viewed as an alternative to short-term imprisonment. In West Germany, when new legislation encouraged judges to avoid sentences to imprisonment of 6 months or less, such sentences dropped from 113,000 a year (20 percent of the total) to under 11,000 (1.8 percent) without any increase in longer-term imprisonment. Instead, fine-alone sentences increased from 63 percent of the total to more than 80 percent.

AMOUNTS OF FINES

Most state penal codes set maximum amounts of fines for particular classes of offenses. Within that maximum, judges have wide discretion in setting the amounts of fines. Maximums tend to be low, although legislatures in many states are increasing them in anticipation that judges will need higher amounts to fine better-off offenders. Fines actually imposed by judges tend to be well below statutory limits, partially reflecting the frequent judicial practice of imposing other monetary penalties as part of the sentence. These include restitution, victim compensation, court costs, directed contributions to governmental or private social agencies, probation supervision fees, and payment for alcohol or drug treatment.

At least 31 states authorize imposition of court costs; 11 states authorize surcharges on fines; 7 states permit "penalty assessments" on offenders. One Texas judge explained why he used fines infrequently: "After paying $56 court costs, $10 fee to the Crime Victim Compensation Fund, $200 public defender fee, and $100 to $500 in probation supervision fee, the defendant will be sufficiently punished."

"Tariff systems," however, appear to account more than other factors both for the low amounts imposed as fines in the United States and the limited use of fines as sanctions. Tariff systems are informal understandings that fixed fine amounts will be imposed on all defendants convicted of a particular offense. These amounts are generally based on what can be paid by the poorest offenders. But the retributive trend in sentencing tends to focus judges' attention on the severity of a crime.

Lacking models of other ways to set fine amounts and also often lacking adequate financial information on defendants, judges apparently limit their use of the fine because tariff systems restrict their ability to reflect the seriousness of a crime.

INFORMATION FOR SENTENCING

Judges were asked to indicate how often they were provided information on an offender's background and economic status and how useful they found this information. In all courts, judges were more likely to have information about criminal records and the in-

TABLE 3

Judges' Information on Offenders' Economic Status, by Jurisdiction

	GENERAL (%)	LIMITED (%)
Employment	88	64
Income	74	41
Assets	57	25

SOURCE: Cole, Mahoney, Thornton, and Hanson; mail survey.

stant offense than about the offender's family and economic status. In fact, although courts of limited jurisdiction are more likely to assess fines, general-jurisdiction judges have more economic information (Table 3). In both kinds of courts, judges said the criminal record and circumstance of the offense are the most helpful information in determining the sentence and that the assets and income of the offender are the *least useful* information.

In view of the tariff system, this opinion is less anomalous than it might seem. If the variation in amounts of fines is limited and is related primarily to the seriousness of offenses, judges would have relatively little use at sentencing for information on offenders' economic status. This in turn may explain the lack of consideration judges give to fines as sole sanctions for repeat offenders convicted of nontrivial crimes. If we are to explore policies emphasizing fines as a primary sanction and as an alternative to incarceration and probation, we must help judges routinely obtain information on offenders' economic circumstances and to increase the weight such information is given.

Obtaining financial information is relatively simple. Many European courts have been accomplishing these tasks smoothly for years, often in order to use a system of fine-setting known as "day fines." Under day-fine systems, the number of fine *units* (or severity of punishment) is determined by the seriousness of the offense but *without regard to the offender's means*. The *monetary* value of each unit is then set explicitly in relation to what the offender can afford. In Europe, this second stage relies primarily on self-reported information. These courts, which use fines extensively and in high amounts, find that reliance on defendants to provide information on their economic status is not a barrier to the wider imposition of fines.

JUDGES' ATTITUDES ON FINES

Judges across this country acknowledge many of the supposed advantages of fines as sentences. Furthermore, they disagree with many of the arguments against them. However, there seems to be little relationship between judges' attitudes toward fines and their use of them.

Judges tend to agree that fines are relatively easy to administer, that they help prevent crowding in correctional facilities, that they can be adjusted to fit the severity of the offense and the offender's income, and that fines help reimburse the costs of maintaining the criminal justice system. The majority of judges also *disagreed* that statutes prevented them from imposing high fines, that decisions of the U.S. Supreme Court prevented their fining poor people, and that fines have no rehabilitative effect.

The survey revealed, however, that two views about fines commonly held among judges are a major impediment to the wider use of fines: That fines allow more affluent offenders to "buy their way out," and that poor offenders cannot pay fines. Over half the judges agreed that "fines ordinarily have little impact on the affluent offender"—61 percent in courts of general jurisdiction and 53 percent in limited jurisdiction. While 61 percent of general-jurisdiction judges agreed that "there is no effective way to enforce fines against poor people," half the limited-jurisdiction judges—who do most of the fining in American courts—disagreed.

Upper-court judges are charged with sentencing offenders who are convicted of the more serious range of offenses. They would tend to hold the traditional assumption that high fine amounts are required to reflect offense severity and to regard it as unreasonable to assess such amounts on the poor. Equity considerations would also suggest to these judges that they cannot sentence more affluent offenders to significantly higher fine amounts. While these same issues arise in the lower courts, they are probably less of an impediment because of the more limited range of

seriousness of offenses dealt with in these jurisdictions. The low fine amounts in these courts reflect less serious offenses; they are viewed as collectible from poorer offenders and, as tariffs, may be applied to the more affluent as well.

The survey revealed, finally, that judges' attitudes about fines, whether positive or negative, are not held very intensely. Until very recently, there has been little systematic examination of fine use and administration and virtually no attention to the potential advantages, disadvantages, or operational implications of expanded use of fines.

COLLECTION AND ENFORCEMENT

Among criminal sanctions, monetary penalties are typically the only ones implemented primarily by the court. For most other sanctions, the sentencing judge relies on another agency of government, usually in the executive branch, to see that the sentence is carried out. The effectiveness of fine administration has important implications for the fine as a penal sanction and for the court as an institution. A fine is a court order. If it is not paid, the integrity and credibility of the court is called into question.

If fines *are* collected and enforcement regarded seriously, on the other hand, the resulting punishment may have rehabilitative value and deterrent consequences. If fines are known to be collected, judges and prosecutors may be more likely to see them as a useful alternative to incarceration or probation. Finally, the payment of fines may be seen by the community as an important means of rendering deserved punishment while reimbursing the public treasury.

Many judges perceive problems in fine collection and enforcement procedures, but they are generally unaware what practices are effective. Research in the United States and in England emphasizes, for example, that aspects of the sentencing process itself are associated with the subsequent effectiveness of fine collection. These include setting the amount at a level the offender is able to pay, making only limited use of installment payment plans, and allowing relatively short periods of time for payment. However, such practices are not commonly followed by American courts.

EFFECTIVE ENFORCEMENT

What can be done if the offender fails to pay a fine? Research in England and West Germany indicates that simple procedures, such as prompt notification to an offender that payments are in arrears, have positive results. Full payment occurs in many cases without further, more coercive and costly action. In American courts, however, routine notification letters are not common. Instead, courts tend to move immediately to issuance of an arrest warrant for the offender who has not paid. Sixty-eight percent of upper-court judges and 85 percent of lower-court judges said this was their procedure.

Reliance on warrants raises several important policy issues, including relationships within the justice system. Although enforcement of a warrant is important to the court, evidence abounds that serving a warrant for non-payment of a fine has low priority for law enforcement agencies. And American courts generally give little professional administrative attention to enforcing fines. A major reason for this is that many professional court administrators dislike taking the role of bill collector when the administrative costs may be greater than the amount of the fine. As a result, courts rarely designate one person or position as having ultimate responsibility for overseeing the outcome of a sentence to a fine and for seeing to it that the process is properly carried out. Thus, no one is responsible or accountable if enforcement breaks down. There are few incentives to make fining a success, but rather incentives to pass the enforcement task on to someone else—to the police via an arrest warrant, for example.

Judges tend to view the actions of offenders as the major fine-collection problem, rather than inadequacies in the court's administrative mechanisms. Sentencing judges tend not to be familiar with the administrative tasks involved in enforcing fines except when defendants in default are brought before their bench. However, research both in England and in the United States indicates that sound administrative procedures must be set for fines to be collected routinely. It should be possible to do this without overly burdensome costs or undesirable levels of coercion. Assuming fines are set properly in the first place with respect to the offense and to the offender's means, the court must make plain at sentencing that it views the fine as a serious obligation for which it unequivocally expects payment. Otherwise, specific coercive means will be employed.

The offender's payments must be closely monitored by people who take the collection responsibility seriously and who are held accountable for it. When an offender does not meet the terms set by the court, enforcement actions would be immediate and personal, with a steady progression of responses creating mounting pressure and increased threats of greater coercion. Careful tracking of payments, swift notification by letter and telephone that payments are due, and credible threats of greater coercion (including the seizure of property) are effective. Research suggests that most nonpayment cases result from improperly set fines, administrative ineptitude, and failure to credibly threaten at the proper time.

FINES AND FAIRNESS

Many persons convicted of criminal offenses are poor. To what extent is it feasible to impose a fine and enforce it as a punishment for criminal behavior by such persons? Being poor does not necessarily mean being entirely without financial resources. There are varying degrees of poverty, somewhat obscured by uniform application of the label "indigent." Some poor people have income for comforts as well as necessities. Others have few comforts, but manage on small budgets. Still others are destitute, people who have no home and receive no social services. At the low end of the poverty spectrum—where we find a group of offenders who are in extreme need—fines are probably inappropriate, unless the offense is trivial and a nominal fee can be suspended.

Fines are meaningful elsewhere along the spectrum, however, even for persons with income well below the poverty line—including welfare recipients, the working poor, the temporarily or seasonally unemployed. A fine imposed on a member of these groups may require substantial economy—and it should do so if it is to be truly a punishment. But paying a fine need not require grave hardship if it is tailored not only to the offense but also to the offender's resources.

At the other end of the spectrum are those offenders who are not by any conventional definition poor.

Significant amounts of fines may be required to ensure an appropriate sanction in these cases, even if the offense is not major.

Many judges recognize these realities and tend to focus on a defendant's ability to pay a particular fine rather than whether he or she is too poor to be fined at all. Indeed, poor people *are* being fined both in this country and in Europe, although both practices and views vary considerably. Most judges surveyed indicated that they would be less likely to impose a fine if the defendant was unemployed or on public assistance—but 38 percent of the limited-jurisdiction court judges said that this would make no difference in their sentencing decision. Another 6 percent said it would increase the likelihood they would impose a fine.

In order to develop an effective fine policy, we must think of offenders as ranging along a spectrum of economic circumstances as well as along a spectrum of offense severity and culpability. Only thus can prosecutors and judges think of fines not as a penalty for less

serious crimes or an addition to other penalties, but as an integral part of their sentencing repertoire. Table 4 shows how judges tend to think now. However, there would seem to be some potential for reducing the use of incarceration in cases such as this in which the criminal behavior carries a low risk of danger, yet the offense seems to require punishment and not merely an admonition.

Experiences of courts in several Western European countries provide tested sentencing methods—particularly the use of the day fine—that could enable American judges to tailor fine amounts more precisely to variations in both severity of offenses and means of offenders.

THE DAY FINE

The day-fine system is a Scandinavian sentencing practice that has been adapted for use in West Germany. It enables sentencing judges to impose monetary punish-

TABLE 4

Judges' Choice of Sanctions in Hypothetical Larceny Case, by Type of Court

The hypothetical case: A 24-year-old male defendant is charged with larceny and criminal possession of stolen property. He is alleged to have removed a $40 pair of slacks from a department store, concealing them in a box that had a forged store receipt and leaving without paying. He was arrested outside the store. The defendant pleaded guilty to the criminal possession charge, and the larceny charge was dropped.

Custody status: On $1,000 bail.

Family status: Single with no dependents.

Employment status: Janitor earning $160 per week.

Offender's record: 1979 Bad check Convicted—restitution.
1980 Bad check Dismissed.
1981 Larceny Convicted—6 months' probation.
1982 Larceny Convicted—1 year probation.

The instruction: On the basis of this information, we would like your estimate of the sanction you would likely impose.

SANCTION	GENERAL JURIS. N = 631 JUDGES		LIMITED JURIS. N = 478 JUDGES	
	%	N	%	N
Jail/prison only	40	252	27	130
Jail/prison plus fine	15	92	27	130
Jail/prison plus fine plus other	18	112	23	111
Jail/prison plus sanctions other than fine	17	109	11	54
Fine only	2	15	4	20
Fine plus sanctions other than jail	5	34	6	28
Other sanctions, alone or in combination, not including jail, prison, or fine	3	17	1	5
TOTAL	100	631	100	478

ments commensurate with the seriousness of the offenses and the culpability of the offender, while at the same time taking account of offenders' differing economic circumstances. The basic notion is that the punishment should be proportionate to the severity of the offense but equal across individuals with differing financial resources.

Consider two offenders with similar criminal histories convicted of similar offenses but with different incomes and assets. Both would be "fined" the same number of units of punishment; however, the one who is more affluent would be fined a total dollar amount that is greater than the poorer offender is fined. In the event of default, however, the sanctions imposed (e.g., jail time) would be the same for both, because they would be based on the number of units of punishment, not the dollar amount.

Could European day-fine systems be adapted to American courts? About four out of five judges agreed that one of the advantages to fines is that they can be adjusted to fit the income of offenders as well as the severity of offenses. We can observe individual judges around the country attempting to do just this by modifying tariff systems to approximate the more formal day-fine systems of Europe. U.S. judges cannot always accomplish this in a systematic fashion, partly because of the lack of routine information on offenders' means. But many judges (and prosecutors) around the country appear to be open to the idea; over half the judges felt a day-fine could work in their own courts, and many said they were willing to try it.

The day-fine concept is attracting increased attention among American criminal justice planners and practitioners as they struggle with the problems of crowding in jails and prisons and as they become more dissatisfied with present sentencing alternatives. A first effort to test the concept scientifically in American courts is underway in Staten Island, New York, with support from the National Institute of Justice, where a day-fine experiment is being planned by the Vera Institute of Justice in collaboration with the Richmond County District Attorney and the Richmond County Criminal Court.

RECOMMENDATIONS FOR JUDGES

■ Fines and other monetary sanctions are punishments and should be imposed high enough to reflect the seriousness of the offense and the prior record of the offender. At the same time, the amount must be within the offender's ability to pay.

■ In setting the fine, accurate information on the offender's economic status should be sought and the total of all monetary sanctions taken into account.

■ The defendant should be informed that prompt payment is expected, be told where to pay it, and advised of the consequences of nonpayment. The time allowed for payment should be relatively short, although unusual circumstances may suggest some flexibility.

■ Incentives should be used to encourage prompt payment. They may include reductions for early payment, penalties for lateness, and imposition of a suspended sentence to jail or community service.

■ Judges should use data on sentencing practices to periodically reexamine the ways they use fines, both alone and combined with other sentences.

RECOMMENDATIONS FOR COURT ADMINISTRATORS AND CLERKS

■ Courts should ascertain what offender-related information is regularly provided to sentencing judges. Where there are gaps such as lack of information on offender income and assets, procedures should be devised to ensure that such information is consistently provided. For example, a probation department, pretrial services agency, or defense counsel could provide the information on a simple one-page form.

■ Judges should be regularly given data on the types of sanctions imposed on offenders convicted of specific types of crimes.

■ Using individual case records, fines-management information systems should be developed, containing six basic types of data: sentence imposed, inventory information, input–output information, effectiveness in collecting fines, processing times and procedures, and identification of problem cases. Courts should improve collection methods, and sentencing judges should be aware of the methods used.

■ Administrative responsibility for enforcing monetary sanctions should be clearly fixed, with a senior member of administrative staff held accountable for the court's performance.

■ Goals for effective fine administration (e.g., percentage of cases in which fines are fully collected within 30 or 60 days) should be set, and the court's enforced performance monitored against these goals.

■ Procedures should be established to identify defaulters promptly and institute action against them.

■ Courts should make direct contact with offenders who fail to pay within the time period set. Prompt, noncoercive reminder letters and phone calls should be tried before a warrant is issued. Judges should be fully aware of the procedures and their effectiveness.

RECOMMENDATIONS FOR LEGISLATION

■ Where statutory ceilings on fine amounts are low, these should be raised.

■ Judges should be required to take account of offenders' economic circumstances in imposing fines and other monetary sanctions.

■ Statutory restrictions on the use of the fine as a sole sanction for specific offenses should be removed.

■ Statutes that provide for flat "dollars-to-days" equivalencies when fine balances are unpaid should be revised to ensure that offenders convicted of similar offenses and with similar prior records should serve essentially similar jail terms in the event of default.

■ Courts should undergo a periodic outside audit at least every 2 years to ensure that records are adequately maintained and that appropriate procedures are followed in enforcing fines and handling the money paid.

■ State court administrators should be explicitly authorized to establish basic minimum standards or requirements for recordkeeping and statistical reporting.

SOURCE: Sally T. Hillsman, Barry Mahoney, George Cole, and Bernard Auchter, "Fines as Criminal Sanctions," *Research in Brief* (Washington: National Institute of Justice, 1987). Notes deleted.

IV

COLLATERAL ISSUES IN PROBATION, PAROLE, AND COMMUNITY CORRECTIONS

BECAUSE SUCH OVERWHELMING IMPORTANCE is attributed to the direct consequences of criminal conviction—imprisonment, parole, probation, and execution—the routine loss of civil rights that accompanies a criminal conviction is often overlooked. This is understandable but unfortunate. It is unfortunate because the civil disabilities that follow a conviction have long-term detrimental effects on the offender's ability to reintegrate into society.

The routine loss of civil rights—also referred to as the *imposition of civil disabilities*—upon conviction of a felony, a "crime of moral turpitude," or "an infamous crime" carries serious effects that may last a lifetime. It is impossible for probation and parole officers to serve probationers or parolees adequately unless the officers know about the legal restrictions that follow a declaration of guilt for a criminal offense. Officers may also function inadequately if they are unfamiliar with the means available for minimizing these harmful effects.

For probationers, minimizing the detrimental effects of conviction be-

gins at the time of adjudication, since the type of adjudication may determine whether any significant collateral consequences will follow. Thus, if an offender is placed on probation after a suspension of imposition of sentence—as opposed to suspension of execution of sentence—that person may not be regarded as "convicted" and may be spared the collateral consequences of conviction. This depends on a number of factors, primarily whether the law of the state where conviction occurs defines *conviction* broadly or narrowly. The probationer who has not been convicted can normally expect his or her full civil rights to be automatically restored upon successful completion of probation.

For the parolee who has been sent to prison as a direct consequence of a criminal offense, there is normally no question of whether conviction has occurred. Civil disabilities will be imposed both during and after the period of confinement. The only hope for this person to regain any such forfeited civil rights is through some legal restoration process. Probationers who are convicted for the purposes of the law of the state in which they were placed on probation also must seek such legal restoration of forfeited rights if they are not to be permanently affected by their losses.

Probation and parole officers need to be aware of the collateral consequences of conviction in order to help the probationer or parolee to regain lost rights upon discharge. Obviously, every probation and parole officer needs to understand the realities of probation or parole status as they daily confront the releasee.

Chapter 13 examines the initial forfeiture of civil rights, the circumstances of such a forfeiture, and the specific rights that are affected. The chapter also discusses the indirect collateral consequences of conviction: the so-called social stigmatization of ex-offenders and the often irreparable damage to one's "good moral character" by virtue of a criminal conviction. The various methods of restoring forfeited civil rights are discussed in Chapter 14.

DIRECT AND COLLATERAL CONSEQUENCES OF CONVICTION

Have you been convicted of a crime in the past ten years other than misdemeanors and summary offenses?

Yes ☐   No ☐

If yes, explain circumstances and disposition of matter below.

KEY TERMS

Direct sanctions
Collateral consequences of
   conviction
Civil rights
Political rights
Outlawry
Attainder
Civil death
Good moral character
Moral turpitude
Public office
Public employment
Surety bond
Fidelity bond
Social stigmatization

Collateral consequences of conviction

Disabilities that follow a conviction that are not directly imposed by a sentencing court—such as loss of the right to vote, serve on a jury, practice certain occupations, or own a firearm.

Civil rights

Rights that belong to a person by virtue of citizenship.

INTRODUCTION

The distinction between the direct and collateral consequences of conviction deserves our consideration. Conviction is usually followed by the imposition of sanctions, both criminal penalties and civil disabilities. We normally think of these sanctions as only the **direct sanctions**—a fine, commitment to a penal or correctional institution, commitment to an institution or program for specialized treatment, probation, or some combination of these—but they also include collateral consequences.

Collateral consequences are disabilities that accompany conviction that are not directly imposed by the sentencing authority. They stem from the *fact of conviction* and are imposed by operation of law, the decisions of licensing or other administrative bodies, and by private individuals, such as when an employer refuses to hire an ex-convict. Most such adverse decisions of licensing bodies and private individuals result from the perception that a convicted offender lacks "good moral character." Since benefits under licensing laws are customarily restricted to persons of "good moral character," this is one of the most damaging effects of conviction.

Collateral consequences also include certain incidental criminal and quasi-criminal sanctions that may follow a conviction. Examples of these are restrictions on the ownership, control, or possession of firearms; suspension or revocation of a driver's license; dishonorable discharge from the armed forces; certain criminal registration requirements; impeachment as a witness; and special requirements relating to application for pardon or other forms of executive clemency.

Thus, although collateral consequences are normally considered as the loss of *civil* rights or the imposition of civil disabilities, they may actually involve effects that have a criminal nature or that are very closely related to the criminal, rather than the civil, realm. Law professor Richard Singer has observed that, ". . . for many criminals—particularly for the 50 percent of convicted persons who are never imprisoned—[these consequences] are anything but collateral; they are, in fact, the most persistent punishments that are inflicted for crime."[1] Moreover, the number of convicted persons suffering from collateral consequences is substantial, about 14 million.[2]

The overall effects of a conviction on an offender—direct *and* collateral consequences—are the criminal and civil disabilities or penalties that the person actually suffers. This "real" sentence results from fixed legislative penalties, the sentence imposed by the sentencing authority, the operation of good-time statutes and of suspended-sentence and probation and parole laws, and the disabilities that result from decisions of licensing bodies and the actions of private individuals, including the disabilities that result from loss of "good moral character."

Civil and Political Rights Defined

A **civil right** is a right that belongs to a person by virtue of citizenship. **Political rights** are those that relate to the establishment, support, or management of government. Civil rights usually include political rights, but sometimes the two kinds of rights are distinguished. For example, a resident alien may not exercise political rights, such as the right to vote or to hold political office, but has full enjoyment of civil rights.

In common usage, and in some statutes, the word *citizenship* is sometimes used to mean "civil rights." It is sometimes stated that conviction deprives the offender of citizenship, or that a pardon restores the convicted person to citizenship. This is an unfortunate use of words, for a conviction does not deprive a natural-born citizen of citizenship.

In the 1958 case *Trop v. Dulles,* the accused, convicted of desertion in time of war, was deprived of his United States citizenship. The Supreme Court declared that to deprive a man of his citizenship and thus condemn him to "statelessness" is "a penalty more cruel and punitive than torture, for it involves a total destruction of the individual's status in organized society."[3] In a later case, a statute that attempted to deprive citizenship from persons who leave the United States to avoid the draft was likewise declared unconstitutional.[4]

Although a person cannot be deprived of citizenship as a result of conviction, that person can and does lose civil and political rights and suffers from certain civil disabilities. The civil penalties and disabilities are seldom mentioned in a court's sentence, but the offender experiences them as a collateral consequence of conviction.

History of Civil Disabilities

Civil disabilities as a consequence of crime have been traced back to ancient Greece.[5] The Greeks called the disability *infamy,* a word that found its way into Anglo-American criminal law in the term *infamous crimes.* Infamous crimes carried severe penalties, as well as the additional sanctions of outlawry and attainder. **Outlawry** deemed a person outside the protection and aid of the law. In effect, it established a kind of "open season" on the offender, who could be hunted down and killed by any citizen. This person, who was "attaint," lost all civil rights and forfeited all property to the Crown through **attainder.** The individual's entire family was declared corrupt, which made them unworthy to inherit his or her property. The theory behind both outlawry and attainder was that since the offender had declared war on the community by committing an infamous crime, the community had the right to retaliation and retribution against the offender.

The Constitution of the United States forbids "bills of attainder,"[6] and similar provisions against attainder or its effects are found in the constitutions and statutes of various states. Although the outlaw was a familiar figure in pioneer society, particularly in Western pioneer society, outlawry as a form of punishment was expressly forbidden.

Outlawry

In old Anglo-Saxon law, the process by which a criminal was declared an *outlaw* and placed outside the protection and aid of the law.

Attainder

At common law, the extinction of civil rights and capacities that occurred when a person received a sentence of death or outlawry for treason or another felony. The person's estate was forfeited to the Crown.

Civil Disabilities Today[7]

In spite of constitutional and statutory provisions against outlawry and certain aspects of attainder, every state has enacted civil disability laws that affect the convicted offender. The loss of rights and the civil disabilities that result from such laws vary from state to state and crime to crime.[8] They range from **civil death,** which deprives the criminal of all or almost all civil rights while he or she is serving a prison sentence,[9] to loss of political rights, revocation of occupational licenses, and denial of employment opportunities. Such things as pension rights, rights under workers' compensation acts, and benefits under insurance policies may be lost, and marital status and the right to prevent the adoption of one's children may be affected.

Some rights are automatically lost upon conviction; others can be lost according to judicial or administrative discretion. Still others are denied by the decisions and actions of private individuals. In some cases, conviction results in the loss of rights only within the particular state; in other cases, the loss extends to other states, as is true for a federal offense. According to some statutes, a conviction must be followed by incarceration for a specified period before rights are lost; in such cases, the right is not lost if conviction is followed by probation or where the sentence to probation is not considered a conviction. Other statutes provide that conviction alone leads to forfeiture. Some rights are permanently lost and cannot be restored; others are automatically restored upon completion of the sentence or may be restored by action of the executive or a court. To determine the status of a particular convicted offender's rights, one must examine the statutory provisions, judicial decisions, administrative rulings and practices, and actions of individuals in both the state of conviction and the state in which a particular right is sought to be enforced.[10]

Extent of Loss of Rights

The civil penalty may amount to a complete denial of a right, or it may merely impose restrictions and conditions upon its exercise. In some jurisdictions, for example, the right to vote and the right to hold public office are denied for life unless they are restored by pardon or special proceeding. On the other hand, a conviction (except a conviction for perjury) generally does not completely disqualify the offender from serving as a witness—the effect is to permit the proof of the conviction to be shown in impeachment of the individual's testimony. Statutes concerning marital status may automatically give the spouse grounds for divorce, or give the spouse grounds for divorce only if the conviction is accompanied by imprisonment for a specified length of time. Generally in the matter of civil disabilities, the particular right must be considered in order to determine the extent of the loss.

Loss of Rights during Probation Period

The rights of the probationer during the probation period are determined basically by whether the probationer has been convicted. If the probated offender is deemed to have been "convicted," he or she loses those rights that any convicted person in that jurisdiction loses. As we shall see, however, special statutory provisions for expunging the conviction and restoring those rights may exist. On the other hand, if probation has been ordered before the imposition of sentence, application of the narrow definition of *conviction* in particular situations may serve to protect the probationer from the loss of civil rights. In a state where the court may exercise its power to grant probation in either of two ways—by suspending imposition of sentence, or by imposing a sentence and thereafter suspending its execution—some probationers lose their civil rights and others do not.

Justification for Imposing Civil Disabilities

Many deprivations during imprisonment can be justified in that they are appropriate to the punitive aims of imprisonment. For example, to hold public office, to serve as a juror, and to carry on one's business are obviously incompatible with the nature of imprisonment. In addition, certain deprivations are useful as independent sanctions for criminal behavior. For example, suspending or revoking a driver's license for a conviction involving driving while intoxicated or under the influence of drugs is appropriate; it is likely to be a highly effective deterrent, and it proposes to protect society from the particular kind of danger that person poses. Few of the present laws regarding loss of civil rights upon conviction can be so justified. The laws have not been rationally designed to accommodate the varied interests of society and the individual convicted person.[11]

Such consideration prompted the American Bar Association to suggest in its *Standards relating to Probation* that most civil rights be retained by the probationer:

> Every jurisdiction should have a method by which the collateral effects of a criminal record can be avoided or mitigated following the successful completion of a term of probation and during its service.[12]

The commentary accompanying this standard—Standard 4.3—points out that at the very least, the statutes that authorize a sentence of probation should also address the problem of collateral disabilities and provide a method by which their effect can be individualized to the particular case.[13]

Let us now consider some specific civil and political rights that may be lost or restricted upon conviction.

CIVIL AND POLITICAL RIGHTS AFFECTED BY CONVICTION

In this section we discuss in detail some of the most important civil and political rights that may be forfeited, restricted, or otherwise affected by virtue of conviction or imprisonment in a state penitentiary in one or more states. They are

- all civil rights (civil death)
- the right to claim good moral character
- the right to hold public office
- the right to vote
- the right to serve on a jury
- the right to be a witness

■ employment-related rights, such as the right to an occupational license, to public employment, to private-sector employment, and to be bonded
■ the right to own a firearm

Civil Death

By far the most severe civil penalties are suffered by the offender who is declared "civilly dead."[14] Civil death statutes are gradually being repealed or their more drastic provisions eliminated. At one time, the laws of seventeen states provided that a person convicted of a felony and sentenced for life (or in some instances, sentenced to death) is to suffer civil death. Today only four states have civil death statutes. In Idaho, New York, and Rhode Island, civil death statutes apply to all persons sentenced to life imprisonment. In Mississippi, persons sentenced to imprisonment for a wide range of felony offenses suffer civil death.[15] Persons placed on probation do not suffer the penalties of civil death unless their probation is revoked and they become subject to the penalties imposed on persons committed for a term of years in a civil death state.

Loss of Good Character

Good (moral) character

The totality of virtues that forms the basis of one's reputation in the community.

One of the most inclusive and damaging consequences of a conviction is loss of **good character,** or as it is sometimes phrased, *good moral character.* Because good character is not a civil or political right, loss of good character is not customarily included in a list of rights lost upon conviction. In practical effect, however, this loss constitutes the basis for statutes and practices that deny the offender licenses and other employment benefits. The loss is serious, because there is considerable doubt that pardon or other proceedings to expunge a conviction restore the person's good character.

Right to Hold Public Office

The laws of the federal government and of many states and municipalities disqualify all convicted persons or persons convicted of certain crimes from holding public office. A public office has been defined as an "agency for the state, the duties of which involve in their performance the exercise of some portion of the sovereign power, great or small."[16]

State prohibitions take two forms:

1. Most states' statutes expressly bar persons convicted of felonies, infamous offenses, or specified offenses from holding public office.
2. Some states indirectly bar convicted felons from holding public office by requiring that a holder of public office be a qualified voter. Most states disqualify convicted felons as voters, however, which precludes them from holding public office.[17]

Federal statutes and the United States Constitution also contain provisions that exclude certain offenders from holding certain positions in the government of the United States. With the limited exception of Section 3 of the Fourteenth Amendment,[18] the Constitution does not bar offenders from holding any position in the federal government. Congress, however, may bar ex-felons from holding any nonconstitutional public office.[19] Rudenstine notes that Congress has passed statutes that exclude persons convicted of specified offenses from holding any nonconstitutionally created federal office. These offenses include falsifying, destroying, or removing public records or documents; receiving compensation in matters affecting the government; rebellion; and treason.[20]

Burton, Cullen, and Travis report that 19 states permanently restrict the right to hold public office after a felony conviction unless the convicted person receives a pardon or is otherwise restored to full franchisement. Twenty-one states return the right to hold public office after discharge from probation, parole, or prison. A few states permit probationers to hold public office while still on probation.[21]

The thrust of the *National Advisory Commission Standards* would seem to prohibit holding public office only during a period of actual confinement, and presumably would permit the holding of a public office during a period of probation that did not involve confinement.[22]

Right to Vote

Although the right to vote is considered a fundamental right of citizenship, it is generally held that it can be denied to convicted felons. The provisions of the constitutions and laws of fifty states and the District of Columbia that remove or limit the convicted offender's right to vote vary widely.[23] Disfranchisement may follow convictions of a felony, an infamous crime, a crime involving moral turpitude, and specified other offenses.

The California Supreme Court, in a case decided in 1973, declared that the provisions of the California constitution and statutes that deprived the convicted felon of the right to vote violated the "equal protection" clause of the U.S. Constitution.[24] The case was overruled by the United States Supreme Court, in the case of *Richardson v. Ramirez*, which held that a state may strip ex-felons who have fully paid their debt to society of their fundamental right to vote without running afoul of the Fourteenth Amendment.[25]

Nothing in *Richardson v. Ramirez* requires a state to deny the vote to the person on probation or parole or to the convicted felon, however. Thus, some states disqualify persons only during a period of imprisonment, which may result in preserving the right of a person on probation to vote. Currently, 11 states permanently deny convicted felons the right to vote unless pardoned (or restored to citizenship through some other method). The other jurisdictions vary widely in their handling of convicted persons' voting rights. About half of the remaining jurisdictions deny the vote only while the felon is under correctional supervision (prison, probation, or parole).[26] California and Illinois restrict prisoners and parolees but allow probationers to vote. In 12 jurisdictions the right is suspended only until the convicted person is released from prison.[27] Delaware and Texas suspend the right for a period of years (10 and 2, respectively) after completion of sentence. Four states[28] do not restrict

A cherished freedom which can be lost by a conviction.

the right to vote by convicted felons unless they have been convicted of treason, bribery, or some other specified offenses.[29]

Right to Serve on a Jury

The exclusion of convicted persons from jury service has its origin in the common law. Most states have enacted the common law rule and exclude persons from jury duty if they have been convicted of felonies, infamous crimes, crimes involving moral turpitude, or of certain specified crimes.[30] The right to serve on a jury is permanently deprived in 31 jurisdictions. Eleven states, however, permit felons to serve on juries after they have fully completed their sentences.[31] Colorado, North Dakota, and Oregon suspend the right only until the offender is released from incarceration. Connecticut and Mississippi require an additional delay after the sentence is completed. The federal rule is that citizens are not competent to serve on a federal grand or petit (trial) jury if they have been convicted of a crime punishable by imprisonment for more than one year.[32] A statute that provides that only citizens having "good character" can serve on a jury also serves to disqualify

A conviction may exclude a person from jury duty.

the person with a criminal record. If the law requires that only persons who are qualified electors can serve on the jury, loss of the right to vote following a conviction carries with it the right to serve on a jury.

Right to Be a Witness

The common law disqualified as a witness any citizen convicted of treason, felony, or crimes involving fraud or deceit. This absolute disqualification extends today in a few states to persons convicted of perjury or subornation of perjury.[33] The usual situation today, however, is that a person who has been convicted of a crime is permitted to testify, but the fact of the conviction may be shown to impeach (discredit) his or her testimony. The theory behind both absolute disqualification and impeachment is that a person who has been convicted of a crime cannot be trusted to give truthful testimony; thus, the court and the jury are entitled to take the conviction into account. The witness can be asked if he or she has been convicted of a felony or other crime and must answer truthfully. Opposing counsel is then at liberty to argue that because the witness is a convicted offender the testimony should not be believed. This does not mean, of course, that the jury (or the court) will disbelieve the witness. The jury or the judge may decide that the convicted offender is indeed telling the truth and give the individual's testimony the weight accorded to the testimony of any other witness.

The Supreme Court, in *Davis v. Alaska,* placed the constitutional right of confrontation by a defendant in a criminal case above any considerations that might protect the offender on probation against impeachment.[34] At issue in the case was whether an adjudication of delinquency could be shown against a prosecution witness, although the statutes of Alaska, as the statutes of many states, provide that an adjudication of delinquency is not a conviction. The

The right to be a witness can be affected by conviction.

Court held that the right of the defendant to confront the witness and to inquire into all circumstances that might affect the witness's credibility was paramount over the statutory policy against permitting the use of an adjudication of delinquency for impeachment purposes.[35]

Right to an Occupational License

Federal, state, and local governments throughout the United States restrict entry into more than 350 occupations and professions through licensing requirements.[36] These restrictions—of which there are in excess of 2,000—affect more than ten million people.[37] For example, the state of California has passed legislation requiring the licensing of automobile mechanics.[38]

In all of the states and in the federal government, the right to obtain or hold an occupational license is affected by a criminal record, and similar provisions restrict the convicted offender's right to hold jobs covered by the licensing regulations of cities and towns. Disqualification may result from the express words in general statutes—as for example, in the business or professional code—or from the licensing acts governing the particular trade or profession. Both the renewal and initial granting of a license are affected by a criminal record, and power to revoke an existing license is granted to the licensing agency as well as to the courts. Even without express words, statutory or even administrative requirements that a license may be issued only to "persons of good moral character" effectively exclude the convicted person.[39]

The exact provision of licensing statutes vary from state to state, from occupation to occupation, and even within occupations. The criminal record that disqualifies may be a felony, a misdemeanor, a felony with moral turpitude, a crime with moral turpitude, or an infamous crime. The conviction that disqualifies may be interpreted according to the narrow or the broad definition of *conviction*.

Occupations that Require a License in Many Jurisdictions

embalmer
junk dealer
midwife
liquor dealer
taxicab operator
solicitor and canvasser
vocational nurse
watchmaker
guide-dog trainer
tourist camp operator
inhalation therapist
dental hygienist
massage parlor operator
water well contractor
operator of a "public cart"
psychiatric technician

trading stamp dealer
night clerk
practical nurse
seller of horse meat
minnow dealer
fur dealer
sewage work operator
florist
photographer
seller of lightning rods
weigh master
fish and game guide
surveyor
manicurist
milk dealer
operator of hotel, lodge, or home for the aged
anthracite coal mine inspector
mine foreman
police/officer
oil and officer gas inspector
forester

money lender
motor car dealer
manufacturer of narcotics
seller of hearing aids
operator of driver training school
hospital administrator
threshing machine operator and dealer
tile layer
yacht salesperson
tree surgeon
pest controller
well digger
potato grower
hypertrichologist (hair remover)
dealer in scrap tobacco
landscape architect
billiard hall owner and operator

Source: D. Rudenstine. *The Rights of Ex-Offenders*, New York, Avon. 1979.

Unfortunately, rehabilitation—whether evidenced by a pardon, successful completion of probation, certificate of good conduct, expungement proceedings, "sealing" of the record of conviction, or otherwise—does not effectively open the door to professional and occupational licenses. This is true not only with the imprisoning state; it is also inevitable if the offender moves to a different state. The lack of uniformity in the laws and practices of the various states and localities makes it almost impossible for persons with criminal records to determine where they might be allowed to apply their training and skills, whether they acquired them in or out of prison.

The Requirement of Good Character

The most serious obstacle to the offender who seeks to enter a licensed occupation arises from two facts:

■ Many, if not most, licensing statutes require that the licensee possess "good character."

■ It is almost-universally assumed that a person who has been convicted of a criminal offense is *not* of "good character."

The obstacles created by the provisions and assumptions about good character are all the more serious because there is considerable doubt that there is any way for a convicted person to restore his or her good character. Although pardon and other forms of wiping out convictions may remove particular civil disabilities and, for example, permit the convicted person to vote or serve on a jury, such a pardon or expungement proceeding does not necessarily, or even by implication, restore good character.[40]

Most, if not all, professions require that the applicant for licensing prove good character. This requirement is usually statutory, but even when the provision is not expressed, courts have found that the licensing authority has the implied power to bar persons who are "morally unfit" from being licensed.[41] Conviction of a crime is generally held to be evidence that the offender lacks the requisite character for the professional license.[42] In some instances, however, the rule is that the fact of conviction is evidence only of *loss of* good character, and additional inquiry is made to determine if the offense involved **moral turpitude**—conduct that is offensive to society.

Because the public's moral standards vary with place and time, it is impossible to know which crimes do and which do not involve moral turpitude. The terms *good moral character* and *good character* are also susceptible to changing meanings. Thus, as a practical matter, licenses are refused or revoked according to the meanings licensing agencies place on such terms. In general, however, a licensing agency regards a conviction as conclusive evidence of bad character, and such decisions are seldom overruled by the courts.[43]

Moral turpitude

An act of baseness, vileness, or depravity in the private and social duties a person owes to other humans or to society in general that is contrary to the accepted, customary rule of right and duty between persons. A grave infringement of the moral sentiment of the community. A felony or a misdemeanor that is contrary to the public's moral standards.

Right to Public Employment

The term *public employment* is often used interchangeably with the term *public office*, although there are certain technical distinctions between the two. Elective positions in federal, state, and municipal governments as well as some appointive positions are generally regarded as **public offices.** A public office may not be compensated, as for example, positions on a school board or even positions on a municipal council. **Public employment,** on the other hand, is paid employment with some type of governmental agency. The vast majority of government jobs are considered "public employment."

Most state statutes permit public employment for persons convicted of a felony. Only six states (Alabama, Delaware, Iowa, Mississippi, Rhode Island, and South Carolina) permanently deny public employment to convicted felons. Some statutes allow employment after completion of sentence (Indiana and Texas). Eight states (Arkansas, California, Massachusetts, Nevada, Ohio, Tennessee, Virginia, and West Virginia) allow convicted felons public employment, but they give the hiring agency or the civil service commissioner the right to deny public employment to a convicted offender on the sole basis of his or her felony conviction. In four states (Arizona, Florida, Pennsylvania, and Wisconsin) a felony conviction may not be the sole grounds for denial of public employment unless the offense bears a direct relationship to the position sought. Additionally, eight states (Colorado, Connecticut, Kentucky,

Loss of "good character" may affect employment.

Minnesota, New Jersey, New Mexico, New York, and Washington) require a "direct relationship" test *and* consideration of other factors such as rehabilitation, the time lapse since offense, the offender's age at the time of conviction, and the nature and seriousness of the offense. Seventeen states (Alaska, Hawaii, Idaho, Illinois, Kansas, Louisiana, Maryland, Missouri, Montana, Nebraska, New Hampshire, North Carolina, North Dakota, Oklahoma, Oregon, South Dakota, and Wyoming) permit public employment after final completion of sentence, since civil rights are restored at this time.

There are no statutory restrictions on public employment by convicted persons in the District of Columbia, Maine, Utah, or Vermont.[44]

Private Employment

A job applicant with a criminal record faces almost insurmountable barriers to private employment. It is difficult to identify the nature and extent of these barriers because of the complexity and diversity of private employment and because of the reluctance of some private employers to admit that they discriminate against ex-convicts. Discrimination based on age, sex, or race is unlawful, and it has been held that a private employer's refusal to hire a job applicant because of his or her arrest record violates the applicant's civil rights.[45] This protection does not extend to persons who have been convicted of a criminal offense, however. The distinction between "conviction" and "criminal offense" is left almost completely to the private employer's discretion. The probationer, regardless of his or her technical legal status, is a convicted person as far as the general public is concerned.

Some business and trade organizations and private employers make a point of providing jobs to convicted offenders. The Solution to Employment Problems (STEP) program of the National Association of Manufacturers is one such effort.[46] In this and similar programs, employers provide equipment and instructors to train offenders while they are in prison and then guarantee them jobs upon their release.

Right to Be Bonded

A bond is a certificate or evidence of an obligation. A simple bond is signed only by the person who is "bonded," the *principal.* A **surety bond** is signed by the principal and by other persons, known as *sureties,* who promise to pay money in the event that the *assured,* the party in whose favor the bond is written, suffers damage because the principal fails to perform as agreed. A bail bond, for example, guarantees the appearance of the accused (the principal) for trial. If the accused fails to appear, the bail bondsman (the surety) must either locate the principal and return him or her for trial or forfeit the amount of the bond to the state (the assured).

Almost any kind of job where the employee handles money or merchandise may require the employee to be bonded. Thus, a person who cannot be bonded cannot work in a bank, a store, or a warehouse. That person cannot become a truck driver, responsible for valuable shipments of goods, if the job specifications require the posting of a bond. Similarly, collection agents, bookkeepers, door-to-door canvassers, ticket-takers, ice cream vendors, and holders of milk routes each may need a surety bond before they will be allowed to assume their duties.

Private individuals are sometimes sureties on bonds for friends or relatives, but most surety bonds are written by insurance and bonding companies that are in the business of writing bonds. In the typical situation, the employee (or sometimes the employer) pays a fee for the bond, and in return, the insurance company agrees to pay any losses to the employer occasioned by the dishonesty or unlawful acts of the employee.

No bonding company is required by law to furnish a bond to all applicants. The decision to write or deny a bond is with the surety. The company makes a careful investigation of all persons who request bonds and refuses to bond persons they consider to be poor risks. Since they refuse to bond poor risks, the saying goes that "bonding companies bond only those who don't need it." The loss of the right to be bonded that follows a criminal conviction is not so much a loss of the *right* to be bonded as it is the loss of the *ability* to get a bond. This is because almost without exception, a person with a criminal record is considered a poor risk. Irrespective of any other obstacle, this inability to be bonded may constitute the final barrier to employment.

The U.S. Department of Labor, through the Employment and Training Administration, offers fidelity bonding coverage for job applicants. The coverage is available to persons who cannot obtain suitable employment because they have police, credit, or other records that prevent their being covered by the usual commercial bonds. Ex-offenders are eligible for the bonds if (a) they are qualified and suitable for the particular position, and (b) they are not commercially bondable under ordinary circumstances. The applicant applies for the bond through a state employment office, and the bond becomes effective when the applicant has begun work and the manager of the local employment service office or other authorized representative of the state agency has certified the bond.[47]

Unfortunately, few ex-offenders seek to take advantage of this program. Both employers and prospective employees seem to lack information about the bonding that is available through the state employment agencies. It is a sad fact that ex-offenders generally refrain from applying for jobs that require bonding.

Right to Own a Firearm

The right to own a firearm is possibly the most restrictive of all civil disabilities lost by conviction. Federal law restricts convicted felons from owning firearms, yet every state except Idaho and Vermont (which rely on federal law) has statutory restrictions equal to or more stringent than the federal statutes.[48] As Burton, Cullen, and Travis point out, "The rationale behind this restriction, of course, is to keep weapons out of the hands of dangerous individuals and to protect an unsuspecting public."[49] Thirty-one states restrict firearm ownership to persons convicted of "any felony." In eighteen states, only a conviction of a serious crime or a crime of violence prohibits the offender from owning a firearm.[50]

SOCIAL STIGMATIZATION OF EX-OFFENDERS

Stigmatization and loss of social status are probably the most severe of the collateral consequences of a felony conviction. The status degradation that follows a person with a court record extends beyond the offender's discharge from the correctional process. This is particularly true when the person is committed to a state or federal correctional institution after conviction.

A kind of circular effect can be observed in the assignment of such a status. Ex-offenders suffer from civil disabilities that bar them from jobs and entry into professions. Society thus limits their occupational choices to jobs considered menial. The public then views all ex-offenders as holding menial jobs and characterizes them as members of a lower stratum of society. Membership in the lower strata of society forecloses opportunities for more prestigious jobs, and the possibility of movement into the upper levels of society is restricted. The result is the creation of a permanent class of outcasts who can never be assimilated into the mainstream of community life.[51]

It is, of course, an open question whether the removal of continuing civil disabilities would change community attitudes toward the offender. Attention must also be paid to the proposition that the public has a right to know of the previous criminal record in order to protect itself against the recidivist offender. It is probable that removal of civil disabilities will not in itself change the public attitude toward the offender, but distinctions must be made. The imposition of civil disabilities should bear some rational relationship to the offense committed and to the function to be performed. Different treatment must be accorded the hard-core recidivist offender and the rehabilitated offender, and a way must be found to distinguish one from the other. Procedures for removing disabilities must be simplified and provide for a restoration of "good character" when circumstances warrant. Most important of all, affirmative education efforts must involve the public in corrections and in the welfare of the ex-offender. Professionals in law enforcement and corrections and the leaders of the bench and bar must concern themselves with the removal of the inconsistencies and inequities that characterize the consequences of conviction today.

SUMMARY

Conviction is followed by both direct and collateral consequences. Direct consequences include fines, probation, imprisonment, and other sanctions imposed by the court. Collateral consequences are those disabilities that follow a conviction that are not directly imposed by a court, such as loss of civil and political rights and loss of "good moral character." The overall effects of a conviction are thus direct and collateral *sanctions.*

The particular rights lost by conviction depend on the crime for which the offender was convicted and the jurisdiction in which the conviction occurred. There is little agreement among states as to which rights are lost by conviction or the manner by which the rights may be restored, if they may be restored at all.

Apart from the loss of rights by operation of law or from interpretations by administrative bodies and licensing agencies, the convicted individual also loses social status and suffers from social stigmatization. He or she is usually thought to have lost their "good moral character," a loss that often results in further collateral sanctions—such as the loss of employment opportunities.

Procedures for removing disabilities should be simplified and should provide for restoration of "good moral character" when circumstances warrant.

ENDNOTES

1. Richard Singer, "Conviction: Civil Disabilities," in Stanford Kadish, ed., *Encyclopedia of Crime and Justice* (New York: Free Press, 1983) pp. 243–248.
2. Velmer S. Burton, Jr., Francis T. Cullen, and Lawrence F. Travis III, "The Collateral Consequences of a Felony Conviction: A National Study of State Statutes," *Federal Probation,* September 1987, p. 52.
3. Trop v. Dulles, 356 U.S. 86, 78 S.Ct. 590, 2 L.Ed.2d 630 (1958).
4. Kennedy v. Mendoza-Martinez, 372 U.S. 144, 83 S.Ct. 554, 9 L.Ed.2d 644 (1963).
5. Damaska, "Adverse Legal Consequences of Conviction and Their Removal: A Comparative Study," 59 *J. Crim. L.C. & P.S.* 347 (1968).
6. U.S. Const. art. 1, § 9, cl. 3.
7. Much of the material on the current status of civil disabilities of convicted persons for this chapter was obtained from the excellent study by Burton, Cullen, and Travis, *supra* note 2.

8. For the definitive study on collateral consequences of a conviction, see "The Collateral Consequences of a Criminal Conviction," *Vanderbilt Law Review* 23, no. 5 (Oct. 1970). The authors acknowledge their substantial obligation to that publication for much of the material set out in this chapter. More recent publications relied on include Joseph G. Cook, *Constitutional Rights of the Accused*, 2nd ed. (San Francisco: Bancroft–Whitney, 1986); Burton, Cullen, and Travis, *supra* note 2; and Velmer S. Burton, Jr., Lawrence F. Travis III, and Francis T. Cullen, "Reducing the Legal Consequences of a Felony Conviction: A National Survey of State Statutes," *International Journal of Comparative and Applied Criminal Justice* 12, no. 1 (Spring 1988), pp. 101–109.

9. These statutes often apply only to persons serving a life sentence or sentenced to death, though some civil death statutes affect persons serving a term of years in a state penitentiary. Burton et al. *supra* note 2, report that only four states practice civil death. Three (Idaho, New York, and Rhode Island) enact civil death only when the offender has been sentenced to life imprisonment. Mississippi attaches civil death for a conviction for bribery, theft, arson, obtaining money or goods under false pretenses, perjury, forgery, embezzlement, or bigamy.

10. The most complete and current listing with which we are familiar is in Burton, Cullen, and Travis, *supra* note 2. This study covers state law only.

11. *Id.*

12. ABA, *Standards, Probation,* Standard 4.3.

13. *Id.* at 54–65.

14. Harry David Saunders, in "Civil Death: A New Look at an Ancient Doctrine," 2 *Wm. & Mary L. Rev.* 988 (1970), wrote: "Since conviction of a felony at early common law resulted in the death penalty, the effect of civil death was normally unnecessary. Although the convicted felon was considered dead by law, it mattered little which rights were lost and which were retained, for his natural state was soon to coincide with that of his legal state by means of execution. Thus, civil death was a practical way of settling the earthly affairs of a convicted felon soon to be executed."

15. Burton et al., *supra* note 2, at 57–58.

16. Yaselli v. Goff, 12 F.2d 396 (2d Cir. 1926).

17. D. Rudenstine, *The Rights of Ex-offenders.* New York, Avon 1974.

18. No person shall be a Senator or Representative in Congress, or elector of President or Vice-President, or hold any office, civil or military, under the United States, or under any state, who, after having previously taken an oath of a member of Congress, or as any officer of the United States, or as a member of any state legislature, or as an executive or judicial officer of any state, to support the Constitution of the United States, shall have engaged in insurrection or rebellion against the same, or given aid or comfort to the enemies thereof. But Congress may by a vote of two-thirds of each house, remove such disability." U.S. Const. Amendment XIV, § 3.

19. It is ironic that the Constitution would not disqualify a convicted felon from serving as President, Vice-President, or in either house of Congress.

20. Rudenstine, *supra* note 17, at 36–37.

21. Kansas, North Dakota, Oklahoma, and Oregon. California, the District of Columbia, Maine, and Massachusetts generally permit all convicted offenders to hold public office except those convicted of bribery, perjury, embezzlement, election offenses, and treason. Burton et al., *supra* note 2, at 57.

22. *National Advisory Commission Standards,* Standard 16.17.

23. Rudenstine, *supra* note 17, at 161–170.

24. Ramirez v. Brown, 9 Cal. 3d 199, 107 Cal.Rptr. 137, 507 P.2d 1345 (1973).

25. Richardson v. Ramirez, 418 U.S. 24, 94 S.Ct. 2655, 41 L.Ed.2d 551 (1974).

26. Alaska, Arizona, Connecticut, Georgia, Kansas, Louisiana, Maryland, Minnesota, Nebraska, New Hampshire, New Jersey, New York, North Carolina, Oklahoma, South Carolina, South Dakota, Washington, West Virginia, Wisconsin, and Wyoming.

27. Colorado, District of Columbia, Hawaii, Idaho, Indiana, Michigan, Missouri, Montana, North Dakota, Ohio, Oregon, and Pennsylvania.
28. Maine, Massachusetts, Utah, and Vermont.
29. The current status of voting rights lost by conviction was obtained from Burton et al., *supra,* note 2 at 54.
30. Rudenstine, *supra* note 17, at 120, 121.
31. Arizona, Illinois, Kansas, Louisiana, Michigan, Minnesota, North Carolina, South Dakota, Washington, West Virginia, and Wisconsin.
32. 28 U.S.C.A. § 1865 (b) (5).
33. *Subornation of perjury* means to procure or induce another to commit perjury.
34. Davis v. Alaska, 415 U.S. 308, 94 S.Ct. 1105, 39 L.Ed.2d 347 (1974).
35. *Id.*
36. Rudenstine, *supra* note 17, at 82–83.
37. *Id.*
38. Florida has recently enacted a similar statute (1993).
39. Rudenstine, *supra,* at 83–85.
40. New York issues a Certificate of Good Conduct to convicted persons after five years of good conduct. A few New York licensing statutes require recognition of the certificate. For example, N.Y.Gen.Bus.Law § 74 (McKinney), covering private investigators.
41. *Dorf v. Fielding,* 20 Misc.2d 18, 197 N.Y.S.2d 280 (1948). A person convicted for running a house of prostitution was denied a license to sell second-hand goods.
42. *Application of Brooks,* 57 Wash.2d 66, 355 P.2d 840 (1960), *cert. den.* 365 U.S. 813, 81 S.Ct. 694, 5 L.Ed.2d 692 (1961).
43. Some decisions require a hearing before denial of license, particularly if the criminal record is remote. *Peterson v. State Liquor Authority,* 42 A.D.2d 195, 345 N.Y.S.2d 780 (1973).
44. The current status of restrictions on public employment was obtained from Burton et al., *supra* note 2, at 56.
45. *Gregory v. Litton Systems, Inc.,* 316 F.Supp. 401 (C.D.Cal.1970). An employer was enjoined from denying a job to a black applicant because of his arrest record on the ground that blacks are arrested more frequently than whites.
46. The National Association of Manufacturers operates its S.T.E.P. (Solutions to Employment Problems) in correctional institutions as part of work-release programs in certain federal institutions.
47. U.S. Department of Labor, *Guidebook for Operation of the Federal Bonding Program,* November 1990.
48. Burton et al., *supra* note 2, at 57.
49. *Id.* at 58.
50. Current status on restrictions on the right to own a firearm was obtained from Burton et al., *supra,* at 57.
51. E. Sutherland and D. Cressey, *Principles of Criminology* (Philadelphia; J. B. Lippincott, 1966).

DISCUSSION QUESTIONS

1. Discuss the distinction between direct and collateral consequences of conviction.
2. Distinguish between civil and political rights.
3. What were the facts and the holding in *Trop v. Dulles*? How is this case related to question 2 above?
4. Compare and contrast the concepts of *outlawry* and *attainder.*

5. What is the general trend with regard to loss of civil rights upon conviction? Why do you think this is so?

6. What is civil death? What is the status of civil death in the 1990s?

7. Discuss the loss of rights during probation. What are the issues?

8. What are the justifications for imposing civil disabilities on convicted persons?

9. What is the current status of loss of the right to vote as a civil disability upon conviction? How have the courts ruled on this issue?

10. Assuming that obtaining honest work is desired by ex-offenders, how do laws that restrict employment and licensing affect recidivism?

11. In what respects is social stigma a civil disability?

Pardon and Restoration of Rights

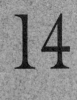

KEY TERMS

Pardon
Absolute (full) pardon
Conditional pardon
Commutation
Automatic restoration of rights
Certificate of discharge
Expungement
Certificate of rehabilitation
Sealing
Certificate of relief from
   disabilities
Good moral character
Direct relationship test

THE PROBLEM

We have seen that a conviction for a criminal offense or an adjudication of delinquency is followed by direct consequences in the form of criminal sanctions and collateral consequences in the form of loss of civil rights. The rights affected by a conviction include voting rights, the right to hold public office, employment opportunities, and judicial rights such as the rights to sue, execute legal instruments, serve on a jury, and testify without impeachment. Certain marital and parental rights also may be lost, and some rights relating to property—including insurance, workers' compensation, and pension benefits—may be impaired.

The direct consequences of conviction—the criminal sanctions—end with the completion of the sentence. Generally, a sentence is completed on the day the offender is released from an institution or discharged from probation or parole supervision. In contrast, the collateral effects of a conviction or adjudication—the loss of civil rights, employment opportunities, and so on—generally continue for the offender's lifetime or until some affirmative act occurs that by law prevents the continuance of the civil disabilities or serves to "wipe out" or reduce them. As we will see, these affirmative acts are of limited value; some because they are not intended to completely reduce or wipe out the conviction, others because they cannot reach occupational licensing practices or the private employer. Almost all procedures for restoring civil rights have the additional weakness of not wiping out a criminal conviction or adjudication of delinquency; they do not restore "good character." In this chapter, we examine some of the methods used to minimize the effects of a conviction or adjudication of delinquency.

The methods of removing the collateral consequences of a conviction or adjudication include pardon, automatic restoration of rights upon application, expungement, sealing, court decisions, governors' executive orders, and legislative acts. Unfortunately, the methods in use do not seal, expunge, nullify, or restore in any practical, effective way.

PARDON

Pardon

An executive act that mitigates or sets aside punishment for a crime. The power to pardon is generally vested in state governors, but the President has the power to pardon for federal offenses. Pardons are either conditional or absolute (full).

Operating as a distinct subsystem of the criminal justice process, **pardon** fulfills a necessary function. Yet, despite its importance to a well-balanced system of justice, it has received little scholarly attention. This lack of study has led to its misapplication and to confusion about its nature and function.

Even the courts have been misled into ambiguous and insupportable holdings. Some jurisdictions have held that a pardon wipes out the crime as though it had never happened. Other jurisdictions have held that for some purposes, a pardon does not wipe out the fact of a conviction. Thus the recipient of a pardon is regarded not as a "new person," but as a convicted criminal. This is true, for example, when the pardoned criminal takes the stand as a witness in a trial his or her testimony may be impeached by the fact of the previous conviction, though a pardon had been granted.

Ideally, the pardon's effect should reflect the grounds for which it is granted. A pardon that is granted because later evidence showed the convicted person to be innocent should wipe out the crime for all purposes, whereas, a pardon granted because a prisoner helped stop a prison riot probably should not.

The Power to Pardon

Historically, the power to pardon belonged to the king or sovereign. Since a crime was considered to be an offense against the king, he was deemed to have the power to forgive it. In early American law, however, the power to pardon was generally given to the legislature. When it was granted to the executive, it was severely restricted. By the time the Constitution was written, the older rule was again followed. The President was given the power of pardon except in cases of impeachment.[1] In most states today, the power to pardon is placed in the governor, either acting alone or in conjunction with some official or board.[2]

When granted to the governor, the power may be without limitation, or it may be restricted. In a number of states, the governor's power to pardon does not extend to treason and impeachment. When the governor's power is restricted in this manner, these excepted crimes may usually be pardoned by the legislature. Normally, the power to pardon does not extend to violations of municipal ordinances; it extends only to offenses against the state. In some states, the power to pardon permits a pardon at any time after charge or indictment; in others, the power can be exercised only after "conviction." Other states forbid pardon until the minimum sentence or a certain length of sentence has been served, or until after a stated number of years of successful parole. Where the state law so provides, both absolute and conditional pardons may be issued.

Objectives of Pardon

The pardoning power was originally seen as a method of righting legal wrongs and of freeing the innocent. Later, a commutation of sentence, or a pardon, became an acceptable way to correct unduly severe sentences or to recognize mitigating circumstances that were not taken into consideration at the trial. The divergent views concerning the infliction of the death penalty have often been expressed in the use of the power of executive clemency to reduce the sentence to life imprisonment. Prisoners who are old, infirm, or have a fatal illness are often pardoned for humanitarian reasons, and escaped prisoners who have rehabilitated themselves after their escape are occasionally pardoned in recognition of their exemplary lives during the period of freedom. The pardoning power is sometimes used to prevent deportation of an alien and sometimes—in the form of amnesties or general pardons—to achieve political purposes.[3] President Carter, for instance, granted amnesty to Vietnam-era draft evaders who fled to Canada.

The pardoning power, used either alone or in connection with special statutory proceedings, is now frequently used to remove the civil disabilities that are a collateral consequence of a conviction. It is its use for this purpose of restoring civil rights that is our chief concern in this chapter.

Kinds of Pardons

Full pardon

A pardon that frees the criminal without any condition whatever. It reaches both the punishment prescribed for the offense and the guilt of the offender.

Pardons, generally, are either full (absolute) or conditional. A **full pardon** freely and unconditionally absolves an individual from the legal consequences of his or her crime and conviction. A **conditional pardon** does not become operative until certain conditions are met or after the occurrence of a specified event. A conditional pardon generally does not restore the full civil rights of the offender unless there is express language to that effect in its proclamation.

Connecticut has used the pardon process—and the related clemency action of commutation—routinely to accelerate parole eligibility for certain inmates serving life sentences. The U.S. Supreme Court noted that as many as 75 percent of all "lifers" in Connecticut benefited from such relief.[4]

Conditional pardon

A pardon that becomes operative when the grantee has performed some specific act(s) or that becomes void when some specific act(s) transpires.

Delivery and Acceptance of Pardons

A pardon is not effective until it is delivered, and until delivered, it may be revoked. An absolute pardon need not be accepted by the prisoner.[5] A conditional pardon, however, must be accepted, since a prisoner may prefer to serve out his or her sentence rather than accept the conditions attached to the pardon.

Commutation

Changing a punishment to one which is less severe; as from execution to life imprisonment.

Revocation

A full pardon, once delivered, cannot be revoked. A conditional pardon may be revoked for violation of the conditions imposed. Some courts have attempted to restrict the right of the governor to revoke a conditional pardon by prohibiting revocation without some sort of determination that the person pardoned has violated the conditions.

Procedure for Obtaining a Pardon

The procedure for obtaining a pardon is fixed by statute or by regulations of the pardoning authority. Generally, the convicted person must apply for a pardon, and some time must elapse after release from confinement or discharge on parole before the offender may apply.[6] When the offender makes application he or she is required to notify certain persons, typically the prosecuting attorney, the sheriff, and the court of conviction. Posting, publication of a public notice, may be required. There may be limitations on repeated applications for pardon, as for example, a minimum time interval between applications. In most cases, the pardoning authority conducts an investigation. A hearing on the application may be held, which is open to the public in some states.[7]

Legal Effects of a Pardon

The most important question the offender asks about a pardon is What rights are restored by a pardon? The general answer to this is that a pardon restores certain civil rights that were lost upon conviction. To determine the precise legal effects of a pardon, one must examine both statutory and case law in the jurisdiction where the pardon is granted. This subsection discusses the general rules with respect to the question.

There are two points of view as to whether a pardon wipes out guilt. The classic view, which represents the minority position today, was expressed by the U.S. Supreme Court over a century ago:

> A pardon reaches both the punishment prescribed for the offense and the guilt of the offender; and when the pardon is full, it releases the punishment and blots out the existence of the guilt, so that in the eyes of the law the offender is as innocent as if he had never committed the offense. If granted before conviction, it prevents any of the penalties and disabilities consequent upon conviction from attaching; if granted after conviction, it removes the penalties and disabilities and restores him to all his civil rights; it makes him, as it were, a new man, and gives him new credit and capacity.[8]

The opposite and majority view, stated in *Burdick v. United States*, is that a pardon is an implied expression of guilt and that the conviction is not obliterated.[9]

Depending on which view prevails in a given state, the relevant statutory or constitutional provisions, and the reasons for the granting of a pardon in a particular case, a number of consequences follow.

ENHANCEMENT OF PUNISHMENT. Depending on the statutory provisions and court interpretations, an offense for which the offender has been pardoned may or may not be "counted" in enhancement-of-punishment procedures for declaring the offender a "habitual offender." The minority position is that if the pardon is held to have wiped out the offender's guilt, or if it was issued on the basis of a finding or belief that the offender was in fact innocent of the offense, then it will probably not be used for enhancement. The majority position, however, is that inasmuch as the pardon does not wipe out guilt for the underlying offense *but, indeed, implies guilt,* the conviction remains and may serve to enhance punishment at the trial of a subsequent offense.[10]

RIGHTS TO VOTE, SERVE ON A JURY, HOLD PUBLIC OFFICE, AND BE A WITNESS. A full pardon generally restores the ordinary rights of citizenship, such as the rights to vote and hold public office. The effect of the pardon may be set out in the state constitution or statutes or in the regulations of the pardoning authority. Pardon restores eligibility for public office, but it will not restore a person to any public office he or she held at the time of conviction. A commutation or a conditional pardon, however, does not have the effect or restoring rights or of removing disqualifications for office.[11] Generally, a conviction for which a witness has been conditionally pardoned, can also be used to impeach him or her. Some states bar the showing of a conviction that has been pardoned, however, and even those that do not will allow the fact of the pardon to be offered in rebuttal.

LICENSING LAWS.   Generally, where an occupational licensing law disqualifies persons convicted of crime, a pardon does not remove the disqualification, nor does it automatically restore a license that has been revoked on the ground of a criminal conviction. Some decisions have indicated that although loss of a professional license is a "penalty," the proceedings to revoke a license are not penal.[12] The revocation of professional license is thus not a conviction for which the executive has the power to pardon. The California statute that provides generally that a pardon shall

> operate to restore to the convicted person all the rights, privileges, and franchises of which he has been deprived in consequence of said conviction or by reason of any matter involved therein,

adds significantly that

> nothing in this article shall affect any of the provisions of the Medical Practices Act, or the power or authority conferred by law on the Board of Medical Examiners therein, or the power or authority conferred by law upon *any* board which permits any person or person to apply his or their art or profession on the person of another [bemphasis added].[13]

AUTOMATIC RESTORATION OF RIGHTS

Burton, Travis, and Cullen reported in 1988 that all but eight states (Alabama, Arkansas, Iowa, Mississippi, Nevada, New Mexico, Rhode Island, and Virginia) have laws for **automatic restoration of rights** upon completion of sentence. Twenty states[14] provide automatic restoration of all civil rights upon completion of sentence. The remaining 22 states restore one or more of the rights lost by conviction after the sentence is completed.[15]

The New Hampshire statute, which provides automatic restoration by virtue of a **certificate of discharge,** reads, in part:

> . . . the order, certificate, or other instrument of discharge, given to a person sentenced for a felony upon his discharge after completion of service of his sentence or after service under probation or parole, shall state that the defendant's rights to vote and to hold any future public office of which he was deprived by this chapter are thereby restored and that he suffers no other disability by virtue of his conviction and sentence except as otherwise provided by this chapter.[16]

The laws of the other nineteen states that grant automatic restoration of rights are basically similar, but the provisions differ somewhat. The Illinois Unified Code of Corrections, for example, contains this language:

> On completion of sentence of imprisonment or on a petition of a person not sentenced to imprisonment, all license rights and privileges granted under the authority of this State which have been revoked or suspended because of conviction of an offense shall be restored unless the authority having jurisdiction of such

license rights finds after investigation and hearing that restoration is not in the public interest.[17]

The Wisconsin statute is one of the oldest and most comprehensive statutes providing that every person who has been convicted of a crime obtains a restoration of his or her civil rights by serving out the term of imprisonment or otherwise satisfying the sentence. The statute reads, in part:

> *Civil rights restored to convicted persons satisfying sentence.* Every person who is convicted of crime obtains a restoration of his civil rights by serving out his term of imprisonment or otherwise satisfying his sentence.[18]

Most courts consider the effect of automatic restoration of rights to be equivalent to that of a pardon. Typically, the conviction can be considered in any subsequent criminal action and under the enhancement statutes. The ex-offender is not restored to eligibility to receive an occupational or professional license and must report the conviction on job application forms.

EXPUNGEMENT

Purpose of Expungement Statutes

The word *expunge* means "erase." Thus the purpose of **expungement** statutes is to allow the record of a crime to be "erased," destroyed, as if it never happened. Says one author:

Expungement

("An erasure") Process by which the record of a criminal conviction (or juvenile adjudication) is destroyed or sealed after expiration of time.

> It is not simply a lifting of disabilities attendant upon conviction and a restoration of civil rights. . . . It is rather a redefinition of status, a process of erasing the legal event of a conviction or adjudication, and thereby restoring to the regenerate offender his status quo ante.[19]

The typical expungement statute does not specify automatic restoration of rights, because it requires affirmative action by the offender. Expungement differs from the issuance of "certificates of relief of good conduct" (as in New York), in that the issuance of the certificates restores rights without attempting to wipe out the criminal record.

A study of expungement statutes reported in 1988 that twenty-eight states have some method of judicial restoration of civil rights.[20] Eligibility for expungement, however, varies widely. In eight states (Arkansas, Idaho, Illinois, Massachusetts, North Dakota, Oklahoma, South Dakota, and Texas), expungement statutes apply only to probationers. Four states (Maryland, New Jersey, Oregon, and Rhode Island) expunge records only for nonviolent offenses or low-grade felonies. Five jurisdictions (Ohio, Oklahoma, Oregon, Rhode Island, and Utah) allow expungement of felony offenses only for first-offenders. Alaska allows expungement for crimes other than firearms convictions. Minnesota and Michigan require that the offender be 21 years of age before expungement. California permits the conviction for a felony to be set aside along with a **certificate of rehabilitation.**[21] The remaining eleven states (Arizona, Delaware, Florida, Iowa, Kansas, Louisiana, Maryland, Nevada, New Hampshire, Washington, and Wyoming) have expungement or some related judicial process in varying degrees to restore civil rights for convicted offenders.[22]

Expungement after Successful Completion of Probation

Adult probation laws of many states contain procedures that permit the probationer, either after completion of probation or after a specified period on probation, to apply for an order that terminates the probation and wipes out the conviction. Texas statutes, for instance, provide that at any time after the defendant has satisfactorily completed one third of the original probationary period or two years of probation, whichever is less, the court may reduce or terminate the period of probation.[23]

The American Bar Association *Standards relating to Probation* recommend that:

> Every jurisdiction should have a method by which the collateral effects of a criminal record can be avoided or mitigated following the successful completion of a term on probation and during its service.[24]

Two approaches are taken by present statutes on the subject:

1. deferring the formal adjudication of guilt through the period of probation and discharging the defendant following successful service without ever declaring the defendant guilty, and
2. permitting the withdrawal of a guilty plea and a dismissal of the charges following the successful service of all or part of the probation term.

The ABA advisory committee cites with approval the Maryland procedures, which permit placing a consenting defendant on probation after the determination of guilt but before a formal entry of judgment. The purpose of such a provision is to offer the offender the possibility—upon successful completion of probation—of avoiding the disabilities that attach to a felony conviction.[25]

All of the statutes and model codes and standards discussed in this section serve at least a limited purpose of mitigating the effects of a conviction but they apply only to probationers. Some states, such as California, have enacted statutes that extend opportunities for expungement to offenders who have not been placed on probation as well.

SEALING

Sealing

The legal concealment of a person's criminal (or juvenile) record such that it cannot be opened except by order of the court.

Sealing statutes have the same objective as expungement statutes in that they seek to erase the record of a conviction. However, they go further; they attempt to actually **conceal** the fact of conviction. Typically, these statutes relate to juveniles or to persons who were under the age of twenty-one when they committed the crime. Sealing statutes are defended on the basis of public policy, which demands that certain documents and records be treated as confidential, and therefore not be open to indiscriminate inspection, even though they are in custody of a public officer or board and are of a public nature. Examples of such documents include those kept on file in public institutions concerning the condition, care, and treatment of inmates and those in offices charged with the execution of laws relating to the apprehension, prosecution, and punishment of crimes. Nevertheless, only a few states have sealing statutes, and the statutes that do exist tend to be limited in scope, and the procedures for sealing, cumbersome.

Sealing provisions in juvenile court statutes must be read with reference to other provisions in those statutes that restrict access to juvenile records to persons with a legitimate interest in the protection, welfare, or treatment of the child and that provide for the destruction of fingerprints. The provisions in the juvenile codes that specifically state that neither an adjudication of delinquency nor a commitment is a "conviction" and the statutes that give the juvenile court the authority to dismiss a petition and set aside findings are also related. The sealing statutes operate to provide additional protection.

RESTORATION OF RIGHTS UPON APPLICATION
Removal of Disabilities

Some states provide by statute for procedures to be initiated by the offender to remove the disabilities that follow a conviction. These procedures differ from expungement procedures in that they do not attempt to wipe out the conviction. They are more or less straightforward attempts to remove the disabilities that are collateral consequences of conviction. Typically, the certificate or other document that is furnished upon completion of the proceedings specifies the rights that are restored.

New York provides for two main ways of regaining some of the rights lost upon conviction. A first-offender, or a former offender who has been convicted of more than one misdemeanor in addition to one felony, can apply for a **Certificate of Relief from Disabilities.**[26] The Certificate of Good Conduct, available to all offenders, is granted five years after release from custody, subject to certain conditions.[27] An ex-offender must possess one of these certificates in order to apply for a job or license barred by virtue of a criminal conviction. As we have said, California provides a Certificate of Rehabilitation to all offenders who complete their sentence. The purpose of the certificate is to facilitate employment opportunities and to assist in occupational or professional licensing.

These certificates and the order of the court usually serve to restore the ex-offender to such political rights as the right to vote and provide him or her with a document that is some evidence of his or her good conduct since release from custody. Nonetheless, they do not prevent a prospective employer or a licensing agency from taking the fact of his or her conviction into account in deciding whether to give the offender a job or a license.

National Advisory Commission Standards

The National Advisory Commission on Criminal Justice Standards and Goals makes proposals that address the needs for legislative action for eliminating the loss of rights that accompanies conviction and limiting the restrictions imposed during confinement, the procedures for expungement, and restoration of rights upon application. The commission recommends repeal of statutes that impose civil disabilities on the convicted offender except those that restrict the rights to hold public office and serve on a jury during confinement. The commission recommends adoption of a procedure that would deny a license or governmental privilege to selected criminal offenders only when there is a direct relationship between either the offense committed or the characteristics of the offender and the license or privilege sought. It recommends procedures that will allow an ex-offender to have his or her conviction expunged from the record and supports the restoration of civil rights upon the expiration of sentence.

Court Decisions

Elsewhere in this book we have discussed the broad and narrow definitions of *conviction*. It is clear that in many cases in which the broad definition was adopted (i.e., where sentencing constitutes a conviction), the purpose and the effect of the decision were to protect the defendant's right to practice his or her profession or engage in other licensed occupation.[28] As one author has noted, the difference between two burglars on probation in California can be dramatic. Whereas the sentenced burglar (broad definition) has lost all civil rights, the unsentenced burglar (narrow definition) is a provisional or conditional felon and, as such, retains his or her civil rights and is subject to no disabilities except those prescribed in the terms of probation.[29]

Similar attempts to minimize the effects of a conviction can be seen in cases that narrow the definition of *moral turpitude* or *infamous crime*.[30] Some of these cases are forerunners of the "reasonable relationship" statutes, which require that a reasonable relationship exist between conviction and the rights or privileges the convicted person is deprived of. In the *Otsuka* case,[31] where the issue was the right to vote, the court limited the meaning of *infamous crime* to those offense where the elements of the crime are such that the person who committed it may reasonably be deemed to pose a threat to the integrity of the elective process.

An important Supreme Court decision reached the issue of whether an ex-convict can possess "good moral character" as generally required in licensing statutes. In the case of *Schware v. Board of Bar Examiners*,[32] the evidence showed that the applicant for the New Mexico bar examination had used several aliases in the twenty years prior to his application, had been arrested but never tried or convicted, and had been a member of the Communist Party seventeen years earlier. The State Board of Bar Examiners refused to permit him to take the bar exam on the ground that he had not shown "good moral character." The Court reversed the decision of the board, stating that a state cannot exclude a person from the practice of law or from any other occupation in a manner or for reasons that contravene the due-process or equal-protection clause of the Fourteenth Amendment. The Court emphasized that the applicant had done nothing in the fifteen years preceding the application to reflect adversely on his character.[33]

A significant decision was handed down by the District of Columbia Court of Appeals in the case of *Miller v. District of Columbia*.[34] The agency involved had denied a vendor's license to an applicant, a former offender, because it found that he was not rehabilitated. Reversing the agency and finding that the applicant was rehabilitated, the court not only ordered the agency to grant the applicant a license, but also went on to express "serious concern" about the agency's lack of standards. The court said, in part:

Unless there are some standards relating the prior conduct of an applicant to the *particular* business activity for which he seeks a license, the power to deny a license inevitably becomes an arbitrary, and therefore, unlawful, exercise of judgment by one official, a graphic example of which is so clearly revealed by the record in this case.

Restoring Good Moral Character

None of the methods and procedures we have examined in this chapter for removing or reducing the collateral consequences of a criminal conviction restores **good moral character** to the ex-offender. They all suffer from this overriding deficiency. Since licensing statutes almost universally require that the holders of a professional or occupational license be of "good character" and many private employers of nonlicensed workers impose the same requirement, the effect is, to quote one author, "to close the door of hope to a person once sentenced for a crime, frustrating his chances for rehabilitation in a useful occupation for which he is trained."[35]

One of the problems in applying the standard of "good moral character" is, of course, the vagueness of the term. The Supreme Court in *Konigsberg v. State Bar* noted that:

> the term [*good moral character*], by itself is unusually ambiguous. It can be defined in an almost unlimited number of ways, for any definition will necessarily reflect the attitudes, experiences, and prejudices of the definer. Such a vague qualification, which is easily adapted to fit personal views and predilections, can be a dangerous instrument for arbitrary and discriminatory denial of the right to practice law.[36]

Yet the rule remains as it was when announced by the Supreme Court in 1898:

> [The state] may require both qualifications of learning and of good character, and if it deems that one who has violated the criminal laws of the state is not possessed of sufficient good character, it can deny to such a one a right to practice medicine, and further, it may make the record of a conviction conclusive evidence of the fact of the violation of the criminal law and of the absence of the requisite good character.[37]

This rule has been generally observed in subsequent legislation and court decisions.[38]

Bad Character

The early law on restoring good moral character developed in the law of pardons. The general rule there seemed to be that all disqualifications that are imposed solely because of bad character—which may be incidentally evidenced by a conviction for a crime—are unaffected by a pardon. According to this rule, a pardoned felon was thus restored the rights to vote, serve on a jury, receive a pension, and testify in court, since these are rights the individual had not lost simply because of bad moral character. When the exercise of a right is associated with a character requirement, however, the result is different. In that case, the conviction may be evidence, even conclusive evidence, of bad

Good (moral) character
The totality of virtues that forms the basis of one's reputation in the community.

character, unaffected by the pardon, and by extension of the same reasoning, unaffected by certificates of rehabilitation and similar procedures.[39]

Thus, when a qualification of good moral character is written into a licensing statute or into a statute prescribing qualifications for public office, it has been held to be within the power of the legislature to require that weight be given to the fact of a criminal conviction as evidence of bad character. An Ohio court stated:

> Whatever the theory of the law may be with regard to a pardon, it cannot work such moral changes as to warrant the assertion that a pardoned convict is just as reliable as one who has constantly maintained the character of a good citizen.[40]

The Direct Relationship Test

Although the authority of legislatures to impose civil disabilities on offenders and of licensing authorities to consider convictions in determining good character has not been seriously eroded, the trend is to impose what is becoming known as the **direct relationship test.** In a case in which the California Supreme Court declared that several convictions for participating in civil rights demonstrations did not determine an applicant unfit to admission to the bar, the court stated the fundamentals of this test:

> The nature of these acts, moreover, does not bear a *direct relationship* to petitioner's fitness to practice law. Virtually all of the admission and disciplinary cases in which we have upheld decisions of the State Bar to refuse to admit applicants or to disbar, suspend, or otherwise censure members of the bar, have involved acts which bear upon the individual's manifest dishonesty and thereby provide a *reasonable basis* for the conclusion that the applicant or attorney cannot be relied upon to fulfill the moral obligations incumbent upon members of the legal profession.[41]

THE STATUS OF CIVIL DISABILITIES TODAY

Civil disability statutes in general, and licensing statutes in particular, are being attacked in the courts on several grounds. The authors of "The Collateral Consequences of a Criminal Conviction"[42] effectively summarized the problems and proposed solutions. They argued that:

1. Civil disability laws are overbroad, in that the laws of most jurisdictions provide for the blanket imposition of disabilities upon a criminal conviction.
2. The laws are inconsistent.
3. Although most jurisdictions provide for the eventual restoration of convicted criminals' rights, these procedures are of limited effectiveness and, as a result, many ex-convicts suffer disabilities long after deprivation is justifiable.
4. Among the disabilities suffered, the loss of employment opportunity is one of the most onerous. This is increasingly true as the number of licensed occupations continues to increase. Under existing laws, discrimination against convicted criminals by private employers is perfectly legal.
5. Although regulations of many public and licensed occupations are necessary, many of the regulations are unreasonable, and procedures with respect to denial and revocation of licenses are not fair.

344

Attacks on the constitutionality of civil disability laws are being made on the following grounds:

1. Civil disability laws are bills of attainder.
2. Imposition of civil disabilities is cruel and unusual punishment.
3. Procedures with reference to the imposition and application of civil disability laws violate due process.
4. Civil disability laws deny equal protection.

In addition, these laws achieve none of the objectives of modern correctional theory and actually impede offenders' rehabilitation, both within the correctional institution and in the community. Recommendations to ameliorate these situations include:

1. elimination of unnecessary restrictions,
2. reasonable application of necessary restrictions,
3. adoption of the direct relationship test,
4. greater participation by the sentencing court in determining the civil disabilities to be imposed on the individual defendant, and
5. automatic restoration of rights and privileges five years after the convict's release into the community.

Summary

Although the direct consequences of a conviction end with the completion of the sentence, most of the collateral consequences continue for the lifetime of the offender—unless some affirmative act takes place to prevent the civil disabilities from attaching or serves to "wipe out" or reduce them. The methods used to restore rights include pardons, automatic restoration of rights, expungement, sealing, and restoration of rights upon application. None of these, however, has the effect of restoring "good moral character," a requirement of all professional and occupational licensing boards and many private employers. This has the effect of denying employment to many ex-offenders and thereby frustrates their chances for rehabilitation in a meaningful occupation.

Civil disability laws achieve none of the goals of modern corrections. Although reasonable restrictions on some ex-offenders are justified—where there is a direct relationship between the crime committed and the functions and responsibilities of the licensed business or profession—the arbitrary barring of convicted persons from most licensed occupations serves no realistic public purpose and may, in fact, have negative consequences for society.

Endnotes

1. U.S. Const. art. II, § 2, cl. 1. ". . . and he (the President) shall have the power to grant reprieves and pardons for offenses against the United States except in cases of impeachment."
The President has no power to pardon a state offender. *In re* Bocchiaro, 49 F.Supp. 37 (W.D.N.Y. 1943).

2. In California, by virtue of its constitution, the general authority to grant reprieves, pardons, and commutations of sentence is with the governor. Calif. Const. art. V, § 8, Cal.Penal Code § 4800, *et seq.* The Board of Prison Terms has replaced the Advisory Pardon Board as the investigative/advising agency. Cal.Penal.Code § 4801.

In New York, the power to pardon lies with the governor by consitutional provision. N.Y. Const. art. IV, § 4.

In Texas, the application for pardon is directed to the Board of Pardons and Paroles, and the governor may not grant a pardon unless it has been recommended by the board. However, the governor may refuse to grant a recommended pardon. Tex. Const. Art. IV, § 11. Texas Admin. Code, Title 37, § 143.1.

3. Other forms of executive clemency that are utilized to carry out these pruposes include commutation of sentence, reprieve of execution, emergency medical reprieve, and remissions of fines and forfeitures. Rudenstine, at 141–2 (1979).

4. Conn. Board of Pardons v. Dumschat, 452 U.S. 458, 101 S.Ct. 2460, 69 L.Ed.2d 158 (1981).

5. In Biddle v. Perovich, 274 U.S. 480, 47 S.Ct. 664, 71 L.Ed. 1161 (1927), the Supreme Court, in a case where the President had commuted a death sentence to life imprisonment, held that an acceptance of the pardon was not necessary. The Court held that a pardon is not an act of grace, but is a tool for the public good. Justice Holmes wrote that a pardon is not an act of grace, but a "determination of the ultimate authority that the public welfare will be better served" by a pardon.

6. In Texas for example, an applicant must show a minimum of one year of good behavior after release from prison and completion of his or her sentence before an application can be made. A pardon will not be considered for an inmate still in prison unless his or her innocence has been established beyond a reasonable doubt, nor will a pardon be issued to a dead person.

7. The hearings are open in New York, closed in California. No hearings are provided for in Texas.

8. *Ex parte* Garland, 71 U.S. 333, 18 L.Ed. 366 (1867).

9. Burdick v. United States, 236 U.S. 79, 59 L.Ed. 476 (1915).

10. State v. Walker, 432 So.2d 1057 (La.Ct.App.1983); Durham v. Wyrick, 665 F.2d 185 (8th Cir.1981).

11. *Ex parte* Lefors, 303 S.W.2d 394 (Tex.Crim.App.1957).

12. Marlo v. State Board of Medical Examiners, 112 Cal. App. 2d 276, 246 P.2d 69 (1952). Murrill v. State Board of Accountancy, 97 Cal. App. 2d 709, 218 P.2d 569 (1950).

13. Cal.Penal Code § 4853 (West).

14. Arizona, Colorado, Florida, Hawaii, Illinois, Kansas, Louisiana, Michigan, Minnesota, Missouri, Montana, Nebraska, New Hampshire, Ohio, Oregon, South Dakota, Tennessee, Washington, Wisconsin, and Wyoming.

15. Velmer S. Burton, Jr., Lawrence F. Travis III, and Francis T. Cullen, "Reducing the Legal Consequences of a Felony Conviction: A National Survey of State Statutes," *International Journal of Comparative and Applied Criminal Justice* 12, no. 1 (Spring 1988), p. 106.

16. N.H.Rev.Stat.Ann. § 607-A:5.

17. Illinois Unified Code of Corrections, § 1005-5-5(d).

18. Wis. Stat. Ann. § 57.078.

19. Gouth, "The Expungement of Adjudication Records of Juvenile and Adult Offenders: A Problem of Status," *Wash.L.O.* 149 (1966).

20. Burton et al., *supra,* note 15, at 105–106.

21. Burton et al. *supra* note 15) report that the certificates are generally granted after completion of the sentence in order to facilitate employment or licensing. New York has a similar procedure.

22. The current status of expungement statutes is obtained from study by Burton et al., *supra,* at 105–106.

23. Tex.Code Crim.Proc.Ann. art. 42.12, § 7 (Vernon).

24. American Bar Association, *Standards relating to Probation,* § 4.3.

25. American Bar Association, *Standards relating to Sentencing Alternative and Procedures,* pp. 68–69.

26. McKinney's Consol.Laws on N.Y., Correction Law §§ 701–03.

27. N.Y.Exec.Law § 242(3) (McKinney).

28. State Medical Board v. Rodgers, 190 Ark. 266, 79 S.W.2d 83 (9135).

29. "The Effect of Expungement on a Criminal Conviction," 40 *S.Calif.L.Rev.* 127–47 (1967).

30. Otsuka v. Hite, 51 Cal.Rptr. 284, 414 P.2d 412 (1966). The court held that a burglar no longer would be considered as convicted of an "infamous crime" for purposes of disfranchisement.

31. *Id.*

32. Schware v. Board of Bar Examiners, 353 U.S. 232, 77 S.Ct. 752, 1 L.Ed.2d 796 (1957).

33. *Id.* See also Mindel v. United States Civil Service Commission, 312 F.Supp. 485 (N.D.Cal. 1970); and Morrison v. State Board of Education, 82 Cal.Rptr. 175, 461 P.2d 375 (1969).

34. Miller v. District of Columbia, 294 A.2d 365 (D.C.App.1972).

35. Entrance and Disciplinary Requirements for Occupational License in California," 18 *Stan.L.Rev.* 533–50 (1962).

36. Konigsberg v. State Bar, 353 U.S. 252, 77 S.Ct. 722, 1 L.Ed.2d 810 (1957).

37. Hawker v. New York, 170 U.S. 189, 18 S.Ct. 573, 42 L.Ed. 1002 (1898).

38. In 1960, the Supreme Court itself refused to overturn a civil disability law. De Veau v. Braisted, 363 U.S. 144, 80 S.Ct. 1146, 4 L.Ed.2d 1109 (1960).

39. See, generally, "Note, Constitutional Law—Power of Legislature to Exclude a Pardoned Felon from a Civil Service Position," 27 *Iowa L.Rev.* 305–09 (1942).

40. State *ex rel.* Attorney General v. Hawkins, 44 Ohio St. 98, 5 N.E. 228 (1886).

41. Hallinan v. Committee of Bar Examiners, 65 Cal.2d 447, 55 Cal.Rptr. 228, 421 P.2d 76 (1966).

42. This summary relied heavily on the definitive study of loss and restoration of civil rights by convicted offenders, "The Collateral Consequences of a Criminal Conviction," 23 *Vanderbilt Law Review* 929, 1970.

Discussion Questions

1. Compare and contrast the two types of pardon.

2. Who has the power to pardon, and under what circumstances may a pardon be granted?

3. What are the legal effects of a full pardon? Does a pardon wipe out guilt? What are the two major positions on this issue?

4. How does a pardon affect the right to vote; the right to serve on a jury; the right to hold public office; the right to serve as a witness?

5. Does a pardon restore a person's license to practice a profession? Explain.

6. How do various states deal with the issue of automatic restoration of rights upon completion of sentence? What is the trend?

7. What is expungement, and how do the various states handle this issue? What is the American Bar Association position?

8. How are sealing and expungement alike and different?

9. Discuss sealing in juvenile court. What does the Uniform Juvenile Court Act recommend?

10. How do various jurisdictions address the issue of restoration of rights following a conviction?

THE EFFECTIVENESS OF PROBATION AND PAROLE

15

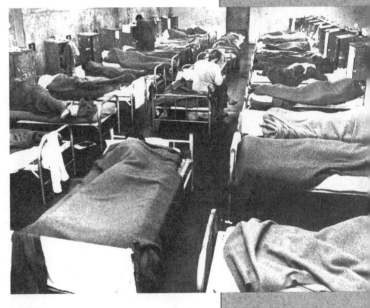

PAROLE

Since the early 1970s public disillusionment with traditional probation and parole as mechanisms for controlling crime has grown. Parole, in particular, has been widely criticized as a "revolving door" to prison that reduces the impact of criminal sentences and threatens public safety. Critics claim that studies have failed to provide any assurance that paroled inmates will not continue their criminal activities while under supervision. Media attacks on parole have focused attention on highly controversial releases such as that of Lawrence Singleton in 1988. Singleton had been convicted of raping a 15-year-old girl, cutting off both her arms and leaving her to die on a hillside in California, and he was paroled after eight years. The public responded with outrage. The community to which Singleton was paroled refused to accept him. Alternative parole plans were thwarted by other communities. Finally, Singleton was paroled to live on the grounds of San Quentin Prison.

The Singleton case is not an isolated one. More than 500,000 felons are on parole, and the media report violent crimes committed by parolees daily. Moreover, parole has been attacked by critics from across the political spectrum—from Senator Edward Kennedy to former U.S. Bureau of Prisons Director Norman Carlson, by prisoner advocate groups, and by prisoners themselves. By 1990, in response to the widespread perception that parole was not serving the public interest, more than a dozen states had abolished parole or severely restricted their paroling authorities' discretionary power.

PROBATION

Probation also has been criticized. Before the "get tough on crime" era of the 1970s and 1980s, the public generally assumed that probation was reserved for less serious, nonviolent offenders, and unless some probationer committed a particularly shocking or violent crime, little attention was paid to it.[1] However, as Joan Petersilia and her associates observed in 1985:

> The flood of convicted felons has overwhelmed the prisons of most states. Many states have taken stopgap measures, such as double- or triple-celling in established facilities, putting up "tent cities," and converting other correctional facilities into secure prisons. All these measures take time and money, and in an era of severe budget difficulties, money may be more of a problem than time. *Consequently, sentencing of criminals to probation is increasing, as the courts look to alternative forms of community sentencing to ease prison overcrowding.*[2] [Emphasis added.]

As prisons became crowded, courts began to rely on probation as a disposition for greater numbers of individuals who had committed serious offenses. As probation utilization increased and more serious offenders were assigned to their caseloads, probation officers faced a crisis of quantity and quality. There were too many probationers and too few probation officers for the supervision to be effective.

| HOW EFFECTIVE ARE PROBATION AND PAROLE?

The efficacy and viability of probation and parole as community-based sanctions have been the subject of much debate and research since the 1970s: Do they indeed protect the public from further harm by the offender; do they indeed have any rehabilitative value? So far, there is no consensus. Much of the problem lies in the inability of researchers to agree on how to define and measure "effectiveness." The most commonly used **measure of effectiveness** is **recidivism,** but it has no universally accepted definition. One observer writes:

> Different studies have defined it variously as a new arrest, a new conviction, or a new sentence of imprisonment, depending on the kinds of data they had available or their project goals. As a result, it is exceedingly difficult and complex to make comparisons about their results.[3]

Indeed, studies of probation and parole outcomes demonstrate that the rate of "success" depends on the definitions used by the researchers. Ralph England's early study found that about 18 percent of federal probationers received new *convictions* after they were placed on probation.[4] More recently, Joan Petersilia reported that 65 percent of a sample of California probationers were *arrested* within a 40-month follow-up period after their conviction, and that 51 percent were *convicted* in the period.[5] A Bureau of Justice Statistics study of 79,000 felons placed on probation in 17 states in 1986 illustrates the problems associated with reporting "success" or "failure" on probation.[6] The researchers, Langan and Cunniff, found that 43 percent were *rearrested* for a felony within three years while still on probation. However, they also found that 46 percent of the probationers had been sent to prison or jail or had absconded within the three years. Further, 71 percent had either completed their probation term or were still on probation three years later. Each of these figures is correct in context. The dilemma is to determine which statistic represents the rate of recidivism. As they stand, these figures could represent either success or failure of probation.

Another study, of 3,995 young parolees in 22 states, found that within six years of their release from prison, 69 percent of the group were *rearrested,* 53 percent were *convicted* for a new offense, and 49 percent were *reimprisoned.*[7] Although these findings indicate a high rate of recidivism—whether it is defined as arrest, conviction, or return to prison—they are misleading. A closer reading reveals that only 37 percent of the sample were rearrested *while still on parole.* Consequently, it is difficult to compare these findings with those of studies that measure recidivism during the parole period only. Moreover, there was no comparison group (control group) in this study. In evaluating parole as a release mechanism, parolees' recidivism rates should be compared with the rates for persons released to mandatory supervision and those for persons released at expiration of sentence.

We are left with the question we began with: Are probation and parole effective? The answer appears to be "It depends." It depends on

- how recidivism is defined,
- whether recidivism is measured only during the periods of supervision,

■ whether recidivism rates are compared to rates of offenders of similar age and criminal history or simply reported with no comparison group, and
■ importantly, which findings in a single study are cited and for what purpose.

Langan and Cunniff's study for the Bureau of Justice Statistics, for instance, could be used to support contentions that probation is effective (71 percent were still on probation or had completed probation three years later) *or* that probation is ineffective (46 percent had been sent to prison or had absconded within three years).

The preponderance of evidence suggests that a majority of probationers and parolees complete the supervision period successfully. This conclusion does not, however, answer the question, Are probation and parole effective? Completion of a probation or parole term without revocation may represent the probation/parole officer's failure to adequately supervise the offender. Violations, particularly technical violations, might not come to the attention of an officer who cannot or refuses to supervise closely. On the other hand, closer supervision would probably reveal a larger number of technical violations, which could be reflected in higher recidivism statistics, yet many of the particular offenders may not be considered failures by their supervising officers or the respective courts.

To illustrate this point, consider these examples, which would sound familiar to any experienced probation or parole officer. Which probationer/parolees are successful, and which are not?

1. The probationer/parolee has not been arrested for any offense during the term of supervision but was cited several times for technical violations, such as failure to report, failure to maintain employment, and excessive use of alcohol.
2. The parolee has no known technical violations but was arrested on two occasions for failure to pay court-ordered child support. A review of the records indicates that he got very far behind while incarcerated, but has been paying regularly since being placed under supervision. He has not been able to "catch up" the delinquent balance, however, and his ex-wife regularly files charges of delinquent child support against him.
3. The probationer/parolee has no known technical violations, yet was arrested for driving under the influence of alcohol two months after being placed under supervision. She agreed to enter an alcohol treatment program, and there have been no further reported violations. Her alcohol-treatment counselor reports that her progress is favorable.
4. The parolee has no new crimes and no technical violations. However, he has a "bad attitude" and refuses to cooperate with the parole officer beyond the bare minimum required by his parole agreement.
5. The probationer is arrested and convicted for a felony committed *before* being placed on probation. He receives a new prison term. He has no arrests for offenses committed while on his current probation term.
6. The probationer/parolee successfully completes five years' supervision with no arrests or technical violations. One year before he is scheduled to be terminated from supervision, he is arrested for a new offense. This is the first time in his adult life that he has gone more than six months without being arrested.
7. The probationer/parolee is not arrested for any new offenses, and there are no reported technical violations. The supervising officer has been advised

repeatedly by law-enforcement authorities that the probationer/parolee is heavily involved in narcotics trafficking.

8. The parolee was released from prison a year ago. He is working regularly and has no reported violations. One evening when returning from a movie with his wife he is involved in a minor traffic accident. In the ensuing events, he and the other driver exchange blows, and both are arrested. He is charged with simple assault and fined $200.

It is apparent that the question of which of these probationer/parolees are "successful" cannot be answered by arrest and conviction statistics only. A strict accounting might conclude that only #4 and #7 are successful. A subjective analysis might suggest that #4 and #7 are failures.

So, What Does the Future Hold?

Probation, parole, and other community-based correctional measures have always been faced with such dilemmas. Because the meaning of *recidivism* is not self-evident, there can be no definitive conclusion on these correctional practices' effectiveness. We believe that when probation and parole are granted appropriately and probationers and parolees are supervised adequately, the human and economic benefits outweigh the risks to public safety. However, using probation and parole merely to regulate prison populations is *not appropriate utilization*.

Joan Petersilia and her associates argue that the problem may be self-perpetuating. As prisons continue to fill up, increasing numbers of more "serious" offenders will be placed on probation and released on parole in order to make room for newly arriving inmates.[8] They reason that this situation will

> . . . cause more petty offenders to be "ignored" by the system (potentially creating more career criminals) and increase recidivism rates. In short, we are marching toward an impasse, if not a breakdown, in the system. . . .[9]

Unless unlimited funds for new prisons are provided (an unlikely occurrence), existing probation and parole programs and practices must be reevaluated and restructured. We believe that this requires the development and application of an array of intermediate punishments for those whose crimes and criminal histories mitigate against traditional community-based practices and yet who, under appropriate conditions, can be maintained in the community for punishment.

Intermediate Sanctions

Intermediate sanctions, such as intensive-supervision probation, house arrest, "boot camps," and other programs that emphasize surveillance, control, and risk management appear to us to represent the immediate future of community corrections. Intermediate punishments have great intuitive appeal. They afford community-based corrections a "tougher image," they appear to provide a greater deterrent to crime, and because of their more strict supervision and surveillance, they offer a higher level of community protection than do traditional probation and parole. Between 1980 and 1985, forty states implemented intensive-supervision probation programs. The early research into these programs' effectiveness is encouraging.

SUMMARY

Probation and parole have come under attack for failing to provide any assurance that released offenders will not continue their criminal activity while under supervision. However, research has not provided conclusive evidence that these community-based correctional programs have either failed or succeeded. Determining success or failure is difficult, since recidivism, the conventional measure of effectiveness, is defined differently by different researchers. Moreover, strict reliance on arrests, convictions, or reimprisonment may not provide a valid measure of success or failure.

A review of the research indicates that when probation or parole is inappropriately granted—in order to relieve prison overcrowding, for example—neither the offenders' needs nor society's are met. When granted and supervised appropriately, probation and parole can be effective.

The public demands correctional programs that satisfy both punishment and public-safety objectives. For a majority of the more serious offenders—those who cannot be maintained safely under regular probation or parole supervision, yet for whom prison is too severe a sanction—a range of intermediate punishments may be safe and effective. These intermediate punishments—intensive supervision probation, house arrest with electronic monitoring, intermittent incarceration, and restitution programs—represent the future of community corrections.

ENDNOTES

1. See Joan Petersilia, Susan Turner, James Kahan, and Joyce Peterson, *Granting Felons Probation: Public Risks and Alternatives* (Santa Monica, Calif.: RAND Corporation, 1985), p. 1.
2. *Id.*
3. Petersilia et al., *supra*, at 20.
4. Ralph W. England, "A Study of Postprobation Recidivism among Five Hundred Federal Offenders," *Federal Probation* 19 (1955), pp. 10–16.
5. Petersilia et al., *supra*.
6. Patrick A. Langan and Mark A. Cuniff, "Recidivism of Felons on Probation, 1986–1989," Bureau of Justice Statistics, Special Report, February 1992.
7. James J. Beck and Bernard J. Shipley, "Recidivism of Young Parolees," *Bureau of Justice Statistics Special Report,* 1987.
8. Petersilia et al., *supra*, at 78.
9. *Id.*

DISCUSSION QUESTIONS

1. Discuss the issue of recidivism. How is recidivism conventionally measured? What problems are related to these measures?

2. Can you suggest any other methods for determining the effectiveness of probation and parole?

3. Imagine that you are the probation or parole officer supervising the eight probationers/parolees described in the chapter. In two or three sentences, evaluate each case as a success or as a failure.

4. For what kind of offender is probation an appropriate disposition? Why?

5. How might you justify parole for a violent offender who has served eight years of a ten-year sentence?

6. How do intermediate sanctions differ from regular probation and parole? What kinds of offenders would you expect to benefit most from such programs? What is the benefit to society?

7. What do you believe is the future of community-based correctional programs?

SUPPLEMENTAL READING

Alternative Sentencing: Selling It to the Public

MICHAEL N. CASTLE
GOVERNOR OF DELAWARE

Intermediate sanctions and the problem of obtaining community acceptance for them are subjects that have come to the fore in today's policy discussions concerning prison crowding, crime, and justice. Any governor, mayor, or county executive can tell you that these remain politically and publicly sensitive issues. People expect government to protect them. They do not want government proposing programs that put unrehabilitated criminals back into their communities. The pressure they can bring to bear against these programs is difficult to overcome.

People too often assume that public protection means prison, and that anything less than complete incarceration for all criminals will endanger public safety. Such an attitude is understandable, and that, perhaps, is why we have been so slow to challenge and to abandon the delusion that "out of sight, out of mind" will make our world safer.

Successful intermediate sanctions programs have been adopted in many communities, despite the burden of public resistance. But accomplishing change means putting an end to the old-fashioned and inaccurate concept that criminal justice means prisons and *only* prisons.

Delaware has managed this. And because prison crowding is a problem that every state must muster its resources to overcome, I urge you to look from a new point of view as we consider what can be done to help any state solve it. Public officials have been known to blame their predecessors for the difficult situations they inherit. I am fortunate that *my* predecessor left me the groundwork for managing our state's prison population. Governor du Pont led the effort to reform sentencing practices and attitudes in Delaware. Serving as Lieutenant Governor and now as Governor , I have learned critical lessons about the need for intermediate sanctions, and how to gain public support for them.

Before examining some of the benefits to be derived from implementing a program of intermediate sanctions, let's look at some facts.

■ Nationwide, about 1 in 50 persons is under the control of correctional authorities.
■ In the last decade, national per capita expenditures grew 21 percent, but corrections expenditures grew 65 percent.
■ The nation's prison population essentially doubled during the 1980s to more than 600,000 people. If you include the jail population, that's a million people behind bars.
■ The growth of America's prison population is over 10 times that of the general population.

The average person may be quite alarmed by these statistics and will wonder how government is handling these large increases in prison population. It may appear that our prisons are bursting at the seams, and that this could cause dangerous criminals to be allowed back on the streets. What's more, prison construction costs nationwide in 1987 averaged $42,000 per bed, according to a report by the National Conference of State Legislators; costs in some states were as high as $110,000 per bed.

This is enough to give any governor, judge, warden, or police officer pause. But consider this issue as a typical consumer, someone who is struggling to balance a checkbook and make ends meet. Think about how your dentist, your auto mechanic, or your child's teacher would react if you told them how much money is being taken out of their pockets to build prison beds and take care of criminals.

The average person in Delaware annually pays $1,000 in state personal income tax. It would take the total state tax collected from 15 Delaware residents to pay for just 1 prisoner for only 1 year. Tell people that and you not only get their attention and anger, but you get their interest in perhaps doing things differently.

Many taxpayers do not know that they pay a substantial price for the very prisons they demand, while policymakers do but have taken this knowledge for granted. We cannot afford this attitude any longer. We must look at things from the public's point of view so we can understand its concerns and address them effectively. It is our obligation to help stem the demand for prisons and long sentences for every convicted offender, by educating the public about the alternatives. Skeptics may doubt that we can change public opinion dramatically in this area. Fortunately, facts and experience prove the skeptic wrong.

I believe the public will not only permit but will support intermediate sanctions. A case in point: When the Edna McConnell Clark Foundation asked hundreds of Alabama residents how they would sentence 20 convicted offenders, virtually all thought prison appropriate. After some explanation of costs and alternatives, the same people "resentenced" most of these cases to intermediate sanctions. This demonstrates that an educated public will support alternative sanctions.

CONVINCING PEOPLE ALTERNATIVES EXIST

Once you open people's minds to the "prison-only" problem, you must convince them that viable alternatives do exist that still protect their personal safety. Never lose sight of the fact that this is a very personal and human issue. Show people that there are programs nationwide where violent or habitual felons are assured prison beds only because many of the nuisance shoplifters, technical probation violators, or petty thieves are being punished in other meaningful ways.

Make the public understand that dangerous criminals will still be put in prison; that intermediate sanctions are necessary to reintegrate offenders so they have a better chance of becoming successful citizens and not continuing lives of crime. Communities should not be allowed to place the entire burden of reform on the correctional system. If we can provide useful and effective alternatives without costly incarceration, we all benefit.

Several states have helped pave the path for public acceptance of intermediate sanctions by successfully implementing and developing alternative programs that have convinced people to abandon the "prisons-only" concept. But in order to convince people, you must show them that there are programs that do, in fact, work. Here are a few programs that you are probably already aware of, which may even be replicated in your own state. Consider them as an average person would.

■ In New York, there are several community residences that provide housing and life services for women released early from prison so they can reestablish their families and begin their reintegration into society.
■ A county in Arizona uses the day-fine sanction for nonviolent felons, a program modeled after one in New York and linked to the offender's ability to pay.
■ There are various Intensive Probation Supervision Sanctions around the Nation. Many are modeled on the first such program, which was established in Georgia. Figures from New Jersey's program show that while 30 percent of those undergoing intensive supervision have been returned to prison for violations, only 2 percent of those who successfully completed probation have been convicted of new indictable offenses.

To the average person who has taken the first step and realized there is a problem both with overcrowding and cost, these examples can be very comforting. But you cannot sell intermediate sanctions based on cost savings alone, or on a few programs that work. It is your responsibility to go even further in gaining public acceptance.

CREATING A CONSENSUS FOR CHANGE

Prisons will always play a role in the criminal justice system, but they cannot continue to play the central role that they have in the past. In Delaware, we are working to expand one of our current men's facilities by 460 beds, and to build a replacement for our women's facility. We are, in fact, under federal court order to ease crowding at our present women's prison. And while I am displeased at having to put additional beds into our system, the situation would be much worse if we did not have an alternative sentencing program in place.

Several years ago, Delaware embarked on a program designed to ensure punishment commensurate with the severity of the offense, and with due regard for resource availability and cost. The effort we made was twofold: to change our correctional system, and to change public opinion and attitudes. But before you can implement an awareness campaign, you must join with key groups to determine exactly what your philosophy will be. In Delaware we began with a broad survey of the situation in order to reach agreement that the status quo was not working, and we were able to use this information to build a consensus for change.

Our breakthrough came when we concluded that the solution was not putting more offenders in larger prisons, but that the structure of our system was inadequate. We wanted to sentence smarter, not just tougher. And it did not make sense to have such a gross dichotomy—offenders either in prison or out on the street under general probation. Instead, we envisioned a five-level continuum of punishment.

Having accepted that a restructuring was necessary, we turned to the issue of philosophy of sentencing. Although we agreed that a new structure for sentencing was in order, one which included a continuum of punishments, we had not yet agreed on a philosophy to determine what kinds of offenders would qualify for what levels. With general agreement regarding the severity of punishment, we advocated, in priority order:

■ removing the violent offender from the community
■ restoring the victim to his preoffense status
■ rehabilitating the offender.

By providing programs of supervision to nonviolent property offenders, we would reserve more of our limited and costly prison facilities for robbers, drug dealers, and others who assault or prey on our population.

To accomplish these goals, we began our work by establishing, by legislative act, a Sentencing Accountability Commission (SENTAC). It served as a forum for our target publics to study intermediate sanctions, debate them, and search for specific programs to create. But its express purpose was to devise a workable program to gain control of prison population problems, and not simply to *reduce* the prison population.

With representation from all facets of criminal justice, the commission developed a defined continuum of sanctions, based on the degree of supervision and control that needed to be exercised over each offender. We then went directly to our public opinion leaders—

legislators on criminal justice committees, prominent judges, and others—and educated them, answered their questions, and made them a part of the process. During this process we were able to hear concerns in a controlled environment and prepare the case for the general public. And by making the leaders part of the process, we gained some of our strongest and most effective advocates.

The result was a continuum comprising five levels of increasingly restrictive sanctions as well as cost-control mechanisms. As a dynamic and fluid system, it allows offenders either to earn their way out of prison by good behavior and conformity with the rules, or to work their way further into the system by repeated nonconformity or additional offenses.

■ *Level V* is full incarceration with complete institutional control.
■ *Level IV* is quasi-incarceration where a person is supervised for 9 to 23 hours per day in programs such as halfway houses, electronically monitored house arrest, and residential drug treatment.
■ *Level III* is intensive supervision involving 1 to 8 hours a day of direct supervision, in which criminals are subject to curfew checks, employment checks, and close monitoring for attendance in treatment programs.
■ *Level II* is "normal" field supervision with 0 to 1 hour of contact per day.
■ *Level I* is the lowest level of supervision.

This structure allows us to view existing or future programs, punishments, or combinations of the two, in a broad and logical framework. Now let's look at these levels on a human scale to see how they work.

Joe has been convicted of unlawful sexual intercourse, has a prior history of violence and burglary, and is obviously a threat to public safety. Under our system he was sentenced to 6 years of full incarceration followed by 1 year at Level III and 2 years at Level II. Not only is Joe kept out of the community for a long period of time, he is gradually integrated back into society under careful supervision.

On the other hand, Jill was convicted of shoplifting and has one prior offense for misdemeanor theft. Obviously she does not pose the same threat to society that Joe did, so she was sentenced to 1 year of intensive supervision under Level III, with the additional conditions of paying court costs and fines, getting a job, and not entering the store where the crime occurred.

These stories illustrate how the continuum works to put Joe behind bars for a long time, but then ease him back into society, and how it works to punish Jill commensurate with the degree and nature of her less serious crime, while not requiring that she needlessly sit in prison and waste taxpayer money.

I should note at this point that while some administrative leeway is allowed by the Department of Corrections in the three lower levels of supervision, the offender is primarily under the control of the sentencing judge. This allows the judge latitude in structuring punishment that truly fits both the crime and the criminal. Compliance with the standards by judges is not subject to appeal. Our experience during the first 2 years has been that the sentences fall within the presumptive range over 90 percent of the time and that the majority of noncompliant sentences are lower than standard levels.

Implicit in the use of alternatives is the need to create programs and offender slots. Before our five-level system became law, we invested time, energy, and funds to develop an intensive supervision unit. We now have over 700 Level III slots and over 500 Level IV slots for offenders.

One other aspect that we found to be of utmost importance was an intense effort to meet with and train everyone in the state judicial and correctional system on the definitions and use of the five-level system. It was essential to have a single contact point to which questions and problems could be directed. Herein lies another human aspect of this issue. The people creating and implementing these programs must be the best in their fields and must possess the determination to see hurdles as opportunities and not unsolvable problems. In Delaware, we had dedicated professionals who made intermediate sanctions their highest priority; we had community groups willing to work hard; and we had state employees, including judges, who made the commitment we needed to see our efforts through good times and bad.

A key element of this accountability system is the cooperation between the executive, the legislative, and the judicial branches of state government. The administration must budget for the creation and continuation of the alternative programs as well as for corrections itself. The cooperation of the legislature was

necessary in Delaware to codify the five-level system and to make changes in the statutory punishment limits for individual offenses. The judiciary joined, cautiously at first and then enthusiastically, in the effort by establishing sentencing standards under administrative court order, in large part because the SENTAC legislation reserved to the judiciary the responsibility for establishing the sentencing standards.

People made the difference as we worked toward reaching a consensus for change. Through creation of mutually agreed-upon philosophies that were both politically and publicly acceptable, we were able to develop this five-level continuum as Delaware's solution to the "prison-only" problem.

With a program supported by the three branches of government and key community groups, we were able to implement a public awareness strategy designed to mobilize public support for our new initiatives. The strategy's key components included use of the following:

- reasonable expectations
- pilot programs
- program evaluations
- ongoing communications.

First we established reasonable expectations. To attain any degree of success you must initially establish realistic goals and avoid speculation about results. Creating false hopes will all but ensure failure. By spelling out goals that you ultimately achieve, you develop credibility for your efforts.

Second, we developed pilot programs or contracted with already established programs. Using an incremental approach that built on one small success after another, we generated a growing wave of public momentum that, for the first time, had the average person considering alternatives to prison.

Third, we evaluated programs not only to determine their effectiveness but to demonstrate careful planning and forethought, with complete consideration for the public's safety.

Fourth, and perhaps most important, is communicating results on an ongoing basis. It has been almost 3 years since our five-level continuum was enacted, yet I continue to look for opportunities to discuss our successes with the general public. SENTAC has been tremendously successful. But it would not have been feasible, let alone successful, if not for a carefully planned and executed public acceptance campaign, such as the one I have described.

Have we succeeded in any of the goals we set for ourselves? Has it made a difference to Delaware? And has the public accepted it? You probably know that for years our state has been close to the top of the list of states in the number of persons incarcerated per 100,000. In 1989, our number was 349 per 100,000. None of our neighbors has reached that level yet, but they are all getting closer.

What is important for our discussion today is that our *growth* rate appears to be slowing, even though we are subject to the same crime rate trends as our neighbors. Considering only the last 2 years, the incarceration rate in Delaware increased by only 5.8 percent. By comparison, Maryland's rate increased by 15.8 percent, Virginia's increased 22.4 percent, New Jersey's 22.3, New York's 25.8, and Pennsylvania's 31.6 percent. Over the last 5 years, Delaware is the only state I have named that can exhibit a consistent slowing in the growth rate. We attribute this trend to the manner in which our judges and other members of the criminal justice community have embraced the five-level system and the way they have chosen to replace a historic predilection for imprisonment with a graduated use of sanctions. I believe this behavior is a direct result of mobilizing public input and support.

Can we put a price on our progress? The costs of our system in 1989 were studied by Kay Pranis of the Minnesota Citizens Council on Crime and Justice under a grant from the Edna McConnell Clark Foundation. We currently have over 700 persons in our intensive supervision program at an annual cost of approximately $2,300 per offender. If only half of them are true diversions from jail, we still have a program savings of $5.4 million per year. In this program and our home confinement and halfway house programs alone we can demonstrate a total savings of almost $8 million annually.

Evaluating public acceptance is obviously much more subjective than measuring cost savings. But I can tell you that none of our statistical successes would have been possible without a degree of public support and acceptance that we must continually nurture and cultivate.

We have not solved all the problems of crime in Delaware. But we do believe that with continued use

of SENTAC to combine a system of sentencing standards with a graduated continuum of sanctions and supervisory programs, Delaware is well on the way to achieving an affordable means of planning for and managing a correctional system that is effective, acceptable, and accountable to the citizens of our state.

CONCLUSION

We cannot *build* our way out of our current prison crisis, but we *can* manage and control our prison growth and maintain the integrity of the criminal justice system. By carefully developing sensible sentencing policies and a wide range of sanctions, and implementing an aggressive public education initiative, we have held offenders accountable to the public and the legal system and have held ourselves accountable to the public. SENTAC was given a clear charge to develop a plan for reform that included sentencing guidelines and a time deadline. Through long discussions and compromise, a workable system was developed and is now in place, proving that intermediate sanctions can work when interested parties and the general public are both a part of the process.

There is nothing magical about our five-level continuum. What is essential is to make available an array of sanctions that is effective for *your* particular offender population, flexible enough to be responsive to the needs of specialized offender populations, and sensitive to the resource limitations and public concerns in your jurisdiction.

Always remember that while this is an issue of public concern, it is within your power to make it an issue of public interest and support as well.

Remember that this is a human issue and not an institutional one.

Remember that it is people's perception of their personal safety as well as allocation of their hard-earned money that you must address.

Remember that change is not easy but is certainly achievable through consensus building.

And finally, remember that it is people, your community members, whom you must make your partners in solving and preventing future correction problems.

SOURCE: Michael N. Castle, "Alternative Sentencing: Selling It to the Public," *Research in Action* (National Institute of Justice, September 1991). The author is governor of Delaware.

Table of Cases

Glossary

Abjuration An oath to forsake the realm forever taken by an accused person who claimed sanctuary.

Advisory board Panel of citizens, judges, or other public officials who act as advisors to the judiciary in setting broad general policy or in determining other aspects of probation services and administration.

Amercement A monetary penalty imposed on a person for some offense, he being "in mercy" for his conduct. It was imposed arbitrarily at the discretion of the court or the person's lord. *Black's Law Dictionary* distinguishes between amercements and fines in that fines are certain, are created by some statute, and can only be assessed by courts of record; amercements are arbitrarily imposed.

American Correctional Association The ACA was founded in 1870 with the stated primary purpose of "exert[ing] a positive influence on the shaping of national correctional policy and . . . promote[ing] the professional development of persons working within all aspects of corrections." It also develops standards for correctional practice, accredits agencies, and provides technical assistance.

American Probation and Parole Association (APPA) The professional association for probation, parole, and community corrections workers. The APPA disseminates information about probation, parole, and community corrections to its members; provides technical assistance to community corrections agencies and governing bodies; conducts training; establishes and monitors professional standards; and provides a forum for a broad range of correctional issues and controversies.

Annulment To nullify, make void, abolish. An act that deprives a criminal conviction of all force and operation.

Attainder At common law, the extinction of civil rights and capacities that occurred when a person who had committed treason or a felony received a sentence of death or outlawry for his crimes. The effect was that all his estate was forfeited to the Crown.

Autonomous model of parole organization An organizational pattern in which parole decisions are made within an autonomous body not affiliated with other agencies of the criminal justice system. Most common pattern for adult paroling authorities.

Benefit of clergy An exemption for members of the clergy that allowed them to avoid being subject to the jurisdiction of secular courts.

Boot camp A residential correctional program designed to instill discipline and responsibility that resembles military basic training.

Civil rights Rights that belong to a person by virtue of citizenship.

Classification Determination of the level of needed supervision (usually in terms of minimum, medium, maximum, etc.) based on the probationer/parolee's risk of recidivism and need for services.

Collateral consequences of conviction Disabilities that follow a conviction that are not directly imposed by a sentencing court—such as loss of the right to vote, serve on a jury, practice certain occupations, or own a firearm.

Community service A special condition of probation that requires offenders to perform unpaid work for civic or non-profit organizations. Community service may be regarded as a substitute for financial compensation to victims or as symbolic restitution.

Consolidation model of parole organization An organizational pattern in which parole decisions are made by a central authority that has independent powers but that is organizationally situated in the overall department of corrections.

Continuing custody theory The view that the parolee remains in custody of either the parole authorities or the prison and that his/her constitutional rights are limited. Release on parole is merely a change in the *degree* of custody.

Contract theory The view that parole represents a contract between the state and the parolee by which a prisoner agrees to abide by certain conditions and terms in return for his/her release. Violation of the conditions represents a breech of contract that allows parole to be revoked.

Deferred adjudication   A form of probation which, after a plea of guilty or *nolo contendere,* defers further proceedings without an adjudication of guilt.

Determinate sentence   A sentence to imprisonment for a fixed period of time as specified by statute; also known as *flat, fixed,* or *straight* sentence.

Electronic monitoring   The use of small electronic transmitters attached to offenders' bodies to monitor their movement and thus enhance probation officers' surveillance capabilities.

En banc   (French) Designates a session of court in which all judges participate.

Expungement   ("An erasure") Process by which the record of a criminal conviction (or juvenile adjudication) is destroyed or sealed after expiration of time.

Filing   A procedure by which an indictment was "laid on file," or held in abeyance without either dismissal or final judgement, in cases where justice did not require an immediate sentence.

Good (moral) character   The totality of virtues that forms the basis of one's reputation in the community.

Good time   Reduction in sentence for institutional good conduct.

Grace theory   The view that parole is a privilege and a matter of grace (mercy) by the executive. Parole confers no particular rights on the recipient and is subject to withdrawal at any time.

House arrest   Confinement of an offender in his/her residence instead of a correctional institution.

Indeterminate sentence   A sentence to imprisonment in which the duration is not fixed by the court but is left to be determined by some other authority (usually a parole board or other agency) after some minimum period is served. The basis of parole.

Institutional model of parole organization   An organizational pattern in which parole release decisions are made primarily within the institution. Advocates of the institutional model believe that because institutional staff are most familiar with the offender and his/her response to institutional pro-

grams, they are most sensitive to the optimal time for release. Most commonly used in the juvenile field.

Intensive supervision probation (ISP)   A probation program of intensive surveillance and supervision in the community as an alternative to imprisonment.

Intermediate sanction   Alternative punishments that fall between probation and incarceration, including house arrest, electronic monitoring, community service, restitution, fines, shock probation, and intensive probation supervision.

Interstate Compact for the Supervision of Parolees and Probationers   An agreement among the states to supervise probationers and parolees for each other.

Jail time   Credit allowed on a sentence for time spent in jail awaiting trial or mandate on appeal.

Judicial reprieve   Withdrawal of a sentence for an interval of time during which the offender was at liberty and imposition of other sanctions was postponed.

Just deserts   The concept that the goal of corrections should be to punish offenders because they *deserve* to be punished, and that punishment should be commensurate with the seriousness of the offense.

Justice model   The correctional practice based on the concept of "just deserts." The justice model calls for fairness in criminal sentencing, in that all persons convicted of a like offense will receive a like sentence. Prisons are viewed as a place of even-handed punishment, not rehabilitation. This model of corrections relies on determinate sentencing and abolition of parole.

Mandatory release   Conditional release to the community that is automatic at the expiration of the maximum term of sentence *minus* any credited time off for good behavior.

Mark system   Credits for good behavior and hard work. In Alexander Maconochie's mark system on Norfolk Island, convicts could use the credits or *marks* to purchase either goods or time (reduction in sentence). In this system, the prisoner progressed through stages from strict imprisonment, through conditional release, to final and complete restoration of liberty, with promotion being based on the marks accredited. One of the historical foundations of parole.

Medical model   The concept that given the proper care and treatment, criminals can be changed into productive, law-abiding citizens. This approach suggests that people commit crimes due to influences beyond their control, such as poverty, injustice, and racism. Also called the *rehabilitation model.*

Model Penal Code   A criminal code developed by the American Law Institute as a simpler, more consistent statement of the law that states could use as a model, if they wished, whenever they undertook to revise or modernize their criminal codes.

Net-widening   The tendency for social-control mechanisms to encompass a larger (or a different) population than originally planned.

Offender-based presentence investigation report   A presentence investigation report that seeks to understand the offender and the circumstances leading to and surrounding the offense and to evaluate the potential of the offender as a law-abiding, productive citizen.

Offense-based presentence investigation report   A presentence investigation report that focuses primarily on the offense that was committed, the offender's culpability, and the offender's criminal history.

Outlawry   In old Anglo-Saxon law, the process by which a criminal was declared an *outlaw* and placed outside the protection and aid of the law.

Pardon   An executive act that mitigates or sets aside punishment for a crime. The power to pardon is generally invested in state governors, but the President has the power to pardon for federal offenses. Pardons are either conditional or absolute (full).

Conditional Pardon: A pardon that becomes operative when the grantee has performed some specific act(s) or that becomes void when some specific act(s) transpires.

Full Pardon: A pardon that frees the criminal without any condition whatever. It reaches both the punishment prescribed for the offense and the guilt of the offender.

Parole   The conditional release, by an administrative act, of a convicted offender from a penal or correctional institution, under the continued custody of the state, to serve the remainder of his or her sentence in the community under supervision.

Parole d'honneur   French for "word of honor," from which the English word *parole* is derived.

Parole guidelines   Guidelines to be followed in making parole release decisions. Most guidelines prescribe a "presumptive term" for each class of convicted inmate depending on both offense and offender characteristics.

Paroling authority   An administrative body (usually 3–19 members) empowered to decide whether inmates shall be conditionally released from prison before the completion of their sentence, to revoke parole, and to discharge from parole those who have satisfactorily completed their terms.

Presumptive sentence   A statutorily determined sentence convicted offenders will *presumably* receive if convicted. Offenders convicted in a jurisdiction with presumptive sentences are assessed this sentence unless mitigating or aggravating circumstances are found to exist.

Pretrial diversion   A form of probation imposed before a plea of guilt that can result in dismissal of the charges; used primarily with offenders who need treatment or supervision and for whom criminal sanctions would be excessive.

Probation, regular   The release of a convicted offender by a court under court-imposed conditions for a specified period during which the imposition or execution of sentence is suspended.

Probation, term of   The length of probation.

Probation conditions   The rules or terms under which a court releases an offender to community supervision. Conditions of release fall into two categories, standard and special. *Standard* conditions are imposed on all probationers in a jurisdiction. *Special* conditions are tailored to fit the particular needs of a individual offender.

Recognizance   Originally a device of preventive justice that obliged persons suspected of future misbehavior to stipulate with and give full assurance to the court and the public that the apprehended offense would not occur. Recognizance was later used with convicted or arraigned offenders with conditions of release set. Recognizance was usually entered into for a specified period.

Restitution   A condition of probation that requires offenders to compensate their victims for damages or monetary losses incurred as a result of their crimes.

Revocation   The withdrawal of either probation or parole because the behavior of the offender was in violation of the conditions agreed upon. Revocation requires the offender to begin or continue serving his or her sentence.

Risk assessment   Determination of an offender's risk of recidivism and appropriate classification and case management strategies. This is most often accomplished by using actuarial prediction scales based on variables shown to be empirically correlated with success or failure on probation or parole.

Salient Factor Score   The parole guidelines developed and used by the United States Parole Commission for making parole release decisions; served as the model for parole guidelines developed in many other jurisdictions.

Sealing   The legal concealment of a person's criminal (or juvenile) record such that it cannot be opened except by order of the court.

Security for good behavior   A recognizance or bond given the court by a defendant before or after conviction conditioned on his being "on good behavior" or keeping the peace for a prescribed period.

Sentencing guidelines   Standardized instruments designed to provide clear and explicit direction to the court in determining the appropriate sentence. Guidelines typically consider offense severity and the offender's prior record. A matrix that relates these factors may be used.

Shock probation   A brief period of incarceration—typically 30–120 days—followed by resentencing to a term of probation supervision.

Supervision The oversight that a probation and/or probation officer exercises over those who are placed in his/her charge during a term of probation or parole. There are several "models" or approaches to supervision, including:

Casework model—the probation/parole officer serves primarily as a counselor, dispensing "treatment" to "clients" in a one-on-one therapeutic relationship.

Brokerage model—the probation/parole officer attempts to determine the needs of the probationer/parolee and refers him/her to the appropriate community agency for services. Also called the *community resource management model.*

Community Resource Management Team (CRMT) model—a form of "brokerage" model in which caseloads of probationers/parolees are "pooled" and served by more than one officer, each specializing in one or more areas, such as drug/alcohol services or employment. The officer specializing in a particular area develops linkages to the community agencies that provide those services. Thus, a drug/alcohol specialist would assess the probationer's needs in the area of substance abuse, refer him/her to community agencies that provide substance abuse services, and monitor the probationer's progress in this area.

Justice model—supervision is geared to helping offenders comply with the conditions of their release. The traditional rehabilitative function is voluntary and is brokered through the appropriate community agencies.

Suspended sentence An order of the court after a verdict, finding, or plea of guilty that suspends or postpones the imposition or execution of sentence during a period of good behavior.

Technical violation Infractions of a probation or parole condition not involving violation of a law.

Ticket-of-leave* A license or permit given to a convict as a reward for good conduct, originally in the penal settlements, which allowed him to go at large and labor for himself before his sentence expired, subject to certain restrictions and revocable upon subsequent misconduct. A forerunner of parole.

Ticket-of-leave man A convict who has obtained a ticket-of-leave.

Transportation The forced exile of convicted criminals. England "transported" convicted criminals to the American colonies until the Revolution and afterward, to Australia. The foundations of the transportation system are found in the law of 1597, 39 Eliz. c.4, "An Acte for Punyshment of Rogues, Vagabonds, and Sturdy Beggars." The act declared that obdurate idlers "shall . . . be banished out of this Realm . . . and shall be conveyed to such parts beyond the seas as shall be . . . assigned by the Privy Council."

Victim impact statement Information in a presentence investigation report about the impact of the offense on identifiable victims or the community.

Black's Law Dictionary, 6th ed.

Name Index

Index

A

Abearance, good, 6
Abel v. State, 100
Abjuration, 5
Adamson v. State, 99
Adjudication, deferred, 28
Advisory boards, 108
Alcohol abusers
  alternative sentencing for, 35
  supervision of, 127–28, 146–48
Allocution, right of, 36
Almond v. State, 98
Amercement, 4
  distinguishing between fines and, 4
American Bar Association Minimum Standards for Criminal Justice
  on advisory boards, 108
  on civil disabilities, 317
  on expungement, 340
  on probation, 31–32, 33
  on proceedings following revocation, 167
  on state administered probation, 105
  on suspended sentences, 10
  on term of probation, 87
American Bar Association Standards Relating to Sentencing Alternatives and Procedures
  on disclosure of presentence investigation report, 53, 55
  on discretionary conditions, 80
  on dispositional alternatives, 80
  on presentence conferences, 36
American colonies, transportation of convicted criminals to, 195–96
American Corrections Association Standards
  on arrest and detention of parolee, 254
  on arrest and revocation of parole, 261–64
  on determinacy, 212
  on parole authority organization, administration, and membership, 243–45
  on parole hearings, 237, 238

  on rights of parolees, 248–49
American law, early, 6–7
American Probation and Parole Association (APPA), 76
Anderson v. Coral, 235*n*
Appel v. People, 98–99
Armstrong v. Manzo, 173*n*
Arrest, house, 274–75
Ash v. U.S., 160
Attainder, 315
Attorney General's Survey of Release procedures, 207
Australia, transportation of convicted criminals to, 196–97
Automatic restoration of rights, 338–39
Autonomous model of parole organization, 225–26

B

Bacchiaro, In re, 335*n*
Bail, 6–7
Bail bond, 326
Baker v. State, 162*n*
Beardon v. Georgia, 82
Bench parole, 192
*Benefit of clergy, 4–5
Berrigan v. Sigler, 85
Bey v. Connecticut Board of Parole, 17*n*
Biddle v. Perovich, 336*n*
Bills of attainder, 315
Blunt v. U.S., 163*n*
Bond, right to, 326–27
Boot camp programs, 34, 273, 291–94
Braum v. People, 95
Brodus v. State, 98
Brokerage model of supervision, 121–22
Brown v. State, 95
Burchell v. State, 100
Burdick v. U.S., 337
Burkett v. State, 166*n*
Burns v. U.S., 30*n*

C

Cambers v. State, 94
Capital punishment, in early criminal law, 4
Caseloads and work load computation, 135–36
  San Francisco Project, 136–37
  Special Intensive Parole Unit (SIPU) study, 136
  specialized caseloads, 137
Case record, 137–38
  chronological, 152
Case review, 254
Casework model of supervision, 120
  development of, 134–35
Certificate of discharge, 338
Certificate of rehabilitation, 339
Certificate of Relief from Disabilities, 341
Character
  bad, 343–44
  loss of good, 318
  requirement of good, 323–24
  restoring good moral, 343–44
Chase v. Page, 177*n*
Chestnut v. State, 95
Civil death, 316, 318
Civil disabilities
  history of, 315
  justification for imposing, 317
  present status of, 315–16, 344–45
Civil rights, 314–15
  automatic restoration of, 338–39
  extent of loss of, 316
  impact of conviction on, 317–27
  impact of pardon on, 337–38
  loss of, during probation period, 316–17
  restoration of on application, 341–42
Classification in supervision, 129–30
Clergy, benefit of, 4–5
Client-management classification, 135
Collateral consequences, 314
Collett v. State, 95

O

Occupational license
  and requirement of good character, 323–24
  right to, 322–23
Offender-based presentence investigation
    reports
  contents of, 48–49
  sample, 69–74
Offense-based presentence investigation
    report
  contents of, 49–51
  sample, 60–68
Olivas v. *State*, 162*n*
On-site hearing, 11, 164, 255, 257
Ordonez v. *State*, 99–100
Otsuka v. *Hite*, 342
Outlawry, 315
Overcrowding, 34, 44–45
Owens v. *Kelley*, 85*n*, 93–94

P

Palermo v. *Rockefeller*, 235*n*
Pannell v. *Jones*, 166*n*
Pardon, 334–35
  conditional, 193, 336, 337–38
  court decisions on, 342–43
  definition of, 334
  delivery and acceptance of, 336
  distinction between parole and, 192–93
  full, 193, 336, 337
  kinds of, 336
  legal effects of, 337–38
  objectives of, 335–36
  power to, 335
  procedure for obtaining, 336–37
  and restoration of good moral character,
    343–44
  royal, 4
Parens patriae, 235
Parole, 350
  bench, 192
  concept of, 192
  conditions, 248–49
    recent court decisions on, 92–100
    special conditions, 248
    typical, 248
  criticisms of, 350
  and determinacy, 209–12
  development of, in United States, 199–
    200
  as distinguished from, 192–93
  and due process and, 234–38
  effectiveness of, 351–53
  elements of effective, 220
  eligibility for, 228–29
  flexibility in sentencing and parole laws in,
    220–22

freedom from political or improper influ-
    ences in, 225
future for, 353
good-time policies, 215–16
government administration of, 225–26
guidelines for, 227, 230–32
versus mandatory release, 192
medical model of, 206–9
origins of, 193–95, 202–3
postrelease supervision, 215
prerelease preparation within institution,
  227
prisoners' perception of, 232–34
proper procedures in, 226–27
public attitude toward, 227–28
public opinion on, 206–7
qualified staff in, 223, 225
reforms in, 43
release decision is, 229
reprieve, 213–14
research and statistics on effectiveness,
  228
resentencing after revocation of, 258
revocation of, 254–58
rights of parolees on, 248–49
theories of, 254
and traditional decision making, 229–30
Parole agreement, 250
Parole board, 220, 222
  characteristics of, 224
  qualified, 222–23
  selection and term of members, 222-23
Parole d'honneur, 193
Parolee
  arrest, search, and seizure of, 249, 251
  power to arrest, 253–54
  rights of, 248–49
  supervising alcohol- and drug-abusing,
    146–53
Parole officer
  functions of, 223, 225
  right of, to arrest parolee, 253–54
Parole plan, 227
Paroling authority, 220
Pastore v. *U.S.*, 97
Persall v. *State*, 92
Philadelphia Society for Alleviating the Mis-
    eries of Public Prisons, 199
Placing out, 14
Political rights, 314–15
  impact of conviction on, 317–27
Postrelease supervision, 215
Predispositional report, 35
Preliminary hearing, 11
Preponderance of the evidence, 163
Prerelease centers, 227
Presentence conferences, 36
Presentence investigation (PSI) report,
  35–36
  criticisms of, 56–57

legal problems concerning the, 53
  disclosure, 54–56
offender-based
  contents of, 48–49
  sample, 69–74
offense-based
  contents of, 49–51
  sample, 60–68
preparation of, 51–52
  evaluative summary, 53
  initial interview, 52
  investigation and verification, 52–53
  time of, 53–54
purposes of, 48
Presumptive sentencing, 43–44, 210
Pretrial diversion, 28
Prewitt, in re, 257*n*
Price, People v., 166*n*
Prisoner
  perceptions of parole selection, 232–34
  state and federal statistics on, 25
Prison Population Control, 214
Private employment, 325–26
Privilege theory, 30, 235
Probation, 350
  adults on, 26, 27
  advisory boards in, 108
  appropriateness of, 36–37
  availability of, 32–34
  criticisms of, 350
  effectiveness of, 351–53
  eligibility for, 30–31
  expungement after successful completion
    of, 340
  future for, 353
  history of, 10–14
  impact of changing concepts of probation
    on administration, 106–7
  intensive supervision, 24, 27, 28
  interstate compacts on, 109–10
  issues in administration of, 113
    classification, 113
    community resources, 114
    contracted services, 114–15
    management information systems, 113
    operations and procedures, 113
    scheduling, 113
    staff recruitment and retention, 115–16
    training, 116–17
  judicial versus executive, 105–6
  organization of, 102–3
  parole as distinguished from, 192
  probation as disposition, 102
  probation as process, 102
  as preferred disposition, 31–32
  pretrial diversion, 28
  quality of, 32–34
  recidivism of felons on, 180–83
  regular, 24
  revocation after expiration of term, 163–64

PHOTO CREDITS

KALAMAZOO VALLEY
COMMUNITY COLLEGE

Presented By

Jeff Shouldice